Meir B

MW00657072

THE MARKET WHISPERER

A New Approach to Stock Trading

The Guide to Success and
Economic Empowerment

Contento de Semrik

Meir Barak

THE MARKET WHISPERER

A New Approach to Stock Trading

Senior Editors & Producers: Contento de Semrik

Senior editor: Seree Cohen Zohar
Editor: Melanie Rosenberg
Design: Silvia Ludmer-Cohen
Photographer: Peleg Alkalai

ISBN: 978-965-550-310-4

International sole distributor:
Contento BestSellers Inc.
616 Corporate Way, Suite 2-4182
Valley Cottage, NY 10989
semrik10@gmail.com
www.semrik.com

Please Note: The information presented in this book is for learning purposes only. None of the
content is to be seen as recommendations to be followed precisely, but as general concepts intended
to expand your knowledge and personal abilities. The author is not responsible for any direct and/
or indirect damage that may be caused as a result of any topic detailed in this book. None of the
information in this book is to be seen as an investment recommendation or as an alternative to
individually adapted consultancy. Meir Barak does not offer investment or profile consultancy, and
may hold or activate stocks mentioned in this book. In any event, it is recommended you contact a
legal, financial, or professional qualified consultant. Stock trading is not suited to everyone, and is
considered a tough field.

Dedicated with love to my dear partner Carina and our gorgeous girls Sharon, Adi and Arielle, who are always supportive and have never doubted me, no matter what idea I came up with (and there were many) or how crazy it sounded.

And also dedicated –

To all of you who are willing to turn your lives around in order to succeed

CONTENTS

Foreword

The Crash

In my thirty-sixth year, I became a penniless father of three little girls, the youngest of whom was three months old. The business I'd nurtured for thirteen years had just slipped between my fingers. Identifying the brewing problems before I did, my business partner had embezzled the last few thousands of dollars left in our bank accounts. Our employees jumped ship. I was saddled with a debt of some half-million dollars to banks and suppliers. What did I have in abundance? Tears.

To fall so low is a situation I'd wish upon no one. Money pressures, I quickly discovered, cause psycho-emotional pressures: depression that manifests in loss of appetite, lack of motivation to work, and a growing inability to sleep. I had no clue how to cope with these problems. All the business management literature I'd been exposed to dealt with "how to succeed" and "how to earn millions." But when did you ever see a book of tips for those owing millions? No doubt this is because "losers" aren't expected to write books and are not assumed to have interesting life stories. And who would want to read a loser's story, anyhow...

Fascinatingly, all the business consultants who'd earned income from me over the years evaporated as soon as the fountains of money dried up. I'd hoped that at least the police would help in retrieving the funds my partner had stolen; I hoped in vain. With very apparent indifference, they completed the complaint forms, had me sign a declaration, and sent me away to fend for myself. Three years later, when I decided to lodge a complaint against the police department's handling of my file, an investigator called me in and threatened that if I didn't withdraw my objections, I'd be charged with submitting a false claim. Clearly, all the taxes I'd paid over the years were also of no avail in protecting me.

The downward spiral continued. Initially, banks sent me politely-worded payment demands. Next, lawyers sent somewhat less polite letters. They wanted their money, and they wanted it pronto. They, too, began to air threats while foreclosing my accounts and simultaneously adding fuel to the fire with more fines, commissions, and interest at gray market rates. In less than a year, a half-million dollars ballooned into one million. What does one do? How can the debt be covered? What about the house and mortgage? How can interest be repaid when it charges ahead at the speed of a red Ferrari Turbo?

Most people who find themselves in this situation declare bankruptcy, raise their hands in despair, and disappear from the market. Today, I understand them. Very few of them ever return to business activities. But I was never part of the majority crowd. Instead, I took the advice of a lawyer who deftly gave me one of the best, most effective pearls of wisdom I had ever heard: "Don't seek the protection of the courts of law. Don't deny the debts. Admit they exist, speak to the debtors, reach an arrangement, and pay them off!"

I did as he had suggested. The banks gave me some breathing space, reduced the debts and interest, and left me some room to maneuver, hoping that I'd repay the debts. That was all I needed. Instead of weeping over my bitter plight, their flexibility was a huge motivator to return to business activities and take my future in hand.

Upward Trend

It was 2000, the slowdown of the tempestuous hi-tech run-up to Y2K. A short while before the dot-com bubble burst, I held rich business experiences and numerous ideas for innovative Internet products that would conquer the world during the period when millions of dollars still flowed freely to Internet startups. Within just a few short months, I established a fantastic startup, recruited partners, and raised several million dollars. Money was flowing again.

The hi-tech life was good to me. But like so many others in hi-tech, especially after the bubble had burst, the market collapsed, and investor funds ran dry, I felt as though I was stuck in one place. I was bored with waking up early every morning, getting to work before traffic started, returning home late after the traffic jams, and catching up with my family pretty much only on weekends. I experienced a mini-crisis one day when my wife asked me to take our little girl to kindergarten, which I happily did. But when we arrived, my daughter turned to me and said, "Daddy, that was my kindergarten two years ago..."

I sought a way to leave the rat race, pay back my debts, and make that one big hit. I also wanted to move into a lower gear and be closer to my family. In short, I wanted to make millions without working too hard.

There are very few legal ways to earn large sums quickly. I reviewed the options, and chose an area I'd always loved: stock trading. From short-term trading, so I'd heard, you could get rich quick.

I did very well. Within five years I was able to leave hi-tech, repay all my debts, and become very comfortable. I went from a negative balance of millions of dollars to a surplus of several million. I live the American dream. The stock market made my dream come true. How did it happen?

It was harder than I imagined!

It's amazing how things are cyclical. Just thirteen years ago, I was still a diligent hi-tech employee with no clue about the markets. The only thing I did know was that loads of money shifted there, and I was determined to get my hands on some of it.

My first problem, which everyone wishing to succeed must face, was: should I give up my salary? Should I take the risk, leave my job, and try a new direction? Only very few are prepared to do that. Most of us are just too scared, and for good reason. I understood that if I were to realize my dream, I'd have to take that risk.

Back then, I thought stock trading would be child's play. I opened an account with a broker (I'll explain how and why later) and innocently believed I'd succeed to buy cheap and sell high. How did that first year end? With a loss, of course. Now, twelve years later, I know I was clueless, lacked experience, and was somewhat arrogant. In actuality, I was ripe prey for the pros. It took me a long time to discover that behind every stock market deal are two sides: the pro and the idiot. For the first year, I usually filled the role of the latter.

Score: 1-0 for the Market

There are moments in life that become etched in our memories until the day we die. Do you remember where you were when the Twin Towers came down? I certainly do. Similarly, I remember my very first transaction.

On the day I opened my first trading account, I rushed to buy 1000 stocks of TEVA Pharmaceuticals. My very first trade! I was so excited. I remember my pulse hammering away. The whole thing was a rush. I didn't see or hear anything else around me, I was so thrilled. The outside world just seemed to disappear. There was a cone of silence, inhabited only by me and my stocks.

| SMART MONEY | Behind every stock exchange transaction, there are two parties: the pro and the idiot. But sometimes, the idiot lucks out! |

I was glued to the computer screen, counting anxiously, watching every movement of every cent. Suddenly, when the stock went up ten cents, I got scared it would drop down again, and I pressed the sell button. Idiot! TEVA climbed $1.50 over several hours. A potential profit of $1500 ended up being a mere $100. Never mind. Not so terrible for a first transaction. I convinced myself that I was pleased as could be.

Then, suddenly, doubt rose in my mind: did the sell order really go through? I knew I'd hit the sell button, so why did the trading platform still show those 1000 stocks in my account? To be on the safe side, I hit the sell button a second time. Whew! Now it indeed seemed like I'd succeeded. My heart rate slowly returned to normal, and I took a drink of cool water. Three minutes of effort, and a profit of $100. What a financial genius I was! Not bad at all for my first effort as a trader. Or so I thought…

I celebrated my success and opened the trading platform again an hour later. To my horror, I discovered my account showing a loss of $400 caused by a "short trade" of 1000 shares. What on earth was a "short"? From the little I knew, a short was a method for profiting from a dropping stock. What I couldn't figure out was how the devil I got into this, and how to get out of it. Meantime, TEVA continued to move up like a rocket shooting for the moon, and for every cent it climbed, $10 was being wiped from my account! Not a happy moment.

I did know that being in a short with a stock running up is not a good idea at all. Pressure, sweat, a day's salary gone in an hour, TEVA not stopping to breathe for even a moment, and my trading account evaporating before my eyes! What should I do next?

I phoned the broker's client service center. After some nerve-wracking Muzak-filled minutes, my answer came through. Apparently, to exit a short of 1000 shares I needed to buy 1000 shares. I bought and closed the platform. What a relief. Later I understood the sequence of events: when I had sold the first time around, the trade platform had not updated immediately, making me think the sale hadn't gone through. But it had; so that when I pressed the sale button again, I was actually telling the system, "I've just sold 1000 shares I don't have." That put my account into a "short." But don't worry, we'll learn what that is later in the book.

My first day of trade ended in burning failure. Score: 1-0 for the market.

The Breakthrough

Call me persistent, call me stubborn, but I wouldn't give in. I continued buying, selling, and losing for almost an entire year. As time passed, more and more questions surfaced, yet remained unanswered. A year of losses taught me one certain thing: trading is a profession like any other, and like all professions, you need to learn to become successful. I set out looking for help.

To be a stock trader, you don't need a diploma. Everyone can open an account, trade, and make pointless moves, just like I did. That's also why most traders fail. I knew there were those who succeeded, however, and I believed I could find ways to become part of that group. I sought them. I found them.

Before the Internet, trading rooms could be found throughout the United States. This is where traders met, working together as professionals. In today's Internet age, most trading rooms have closed down, and activities have moved to chat rooms which any trader can join for a monthly fee. These rooms are where you can hear professional traders, whom we at Tradenet call "analysts," discuss trends, listen to their instructions, ask questions and basically trade with them in real time without ever leaving your home. I was so happy to join one of those trading rooms, and immediately felt like I'd come to the right place.

What an amazing world I'd discovered. The analysts bought and sold, in real time, successfully. Two analysts, Mark and Chris, are well known and have become my friends. They are the people to whom I owe most of my basic training. It seemed my path to success was paved. All I needed to do now was to listen to the analysts and copy their moves. So simple!So why was it so difficult?

What can be so difficult about copying a professional trader's actions? The answer is simple: because we all have our own level of comprehension about what is unfolding before us, and we decide to do things differently for our own reasons. Here's an example: Chris buys a stock that goes up 4% today, based on his feeling that it will continue to rise, whereas I think, "Is he crazy? He's going to lose. It's already gone up a lot!" Over time I saw that whenever I couldn't precisely understand Chris's decision, I couldn't accept it either. During that period, my trades looked more or less like this: Chris bought. I bought. I flee with my small profit, afraid to lose what I'd already profited. Chris waits, and makes a handsome profit. In other instances, when the stock was trending down, Chris would quickly get out, while I would stay, hoping that it would come back to my cost. Eventually, I'd be forced to exit with an unpleasant loss. In short, Chris would profit and I'd lose. Yes. It was definitely time to start learning.

Statistics famously tout the figure that 90% of active traders lose money. If you are among them, the solution is simple: do exactly the opposite of what you think. At first I had trouble figuring the upside down logic of the profession. I found that precisely those stock trades I considered risky, if not downright dangerous, revealed themselves as the biggest winners, whereas the ones I would choose and which appeared to be less scary and more reliable, were less successful. Of course, in my early trading history, I chose only those that failed.

But over time, I also discovered this tendency was not exclusive to me. It's very natural for an experienced trader to view the market completely different than a beginner. To succeed, the beginner needs to learn the basic principles, and slowly undergo a psychological revolution. Because I'd skipped the stage of learning fundamentals and jumped straight into the deep end, I concluded that I needed to understand the market. It was time to "go back to the drawing board" and learn the basics.

I knew what I had to do. I contacted Chris, the head analyst of the trading room, presented myself as a member, and asked him to be my personal mentor. I was very happy when he agreed, and we settled on a fee. I packed a bag and took the first flight out to his home in Phoenix, Arizona.

I remember our first meeting like it was yesterday. I was shocked to meet a "boy" in his early thirties, who already had many years of Wall Street experience under his belt serving as a "market maker" for a well-known trading company, and later as an independent, successful day trader. Two black cars, both Lexus models, were parked at his luxurious home in a wealthy suburb of Phoenix, making it perfectly clear with whom I was dealing. Chris came from an average family, and had made most of his money as a day trader. Like so many others I met over the years, Chris left an excellent job that brought him hundreds of thousands of dollars each year, in order to earn his own way as a day trader!

SMART MONEY | *The market operates according to known rules. There is no need to invent a new method in order to earn money. Just adopt the existing ones.*

In Phoenix, the market opens at 6:30 in the morning. We started our day of study at 6:00, and when trading was over at 1 PM, we were off to play golf. I was dumbfounded at Chris'sworkday structure; I was amazed at his self-control, and awed by his familiarity with the market. I was completely bowled over by the inherent potential for moneymaking through trading.

The stock market operates according to clear rules, I was surprised to learn, and these are known chiefly to the professionals who make their livelihood through trading. It would be too obvious to say that from that day on, my life changed beyond recognition.

Success!

Within just a few months of my return home, I went from losing to breaking even, and then from breaking even to profit. Some two years after I made my first transaction, I succeeded in generating a monthly income that allowed me to leave my job. Within just a few years, I moved from hi-tech employment to the freedom of a home on the sea, playing golf, swimming in my private pool--and no more than two to three hours a day of pleasant trading. I had just achieved the American dream.

I was proud of my achievements and loved trading, but more than all else, I enjoyed teaching new traders. At first I taught several friends at home, using the same method Chris had taught me. Friends I'd taught for free brought their friends, who became paying members. Some were from the hi-tech realm who wanted precisely what I had done: to change the course of their lives.

They studied, they traded, and they joined the trading room alongside Chris and Mark, until that remarkable moment when most of the trading room's members were... my students! At this stage I was awarded a position as an analyst, together with Chris and Mark.

Simultaneously, wishing to divert the stream of students away from my private home space, I established Tradenet, the school for day trading. Over the years, Tradenet has become one of the largest in the world, with branches in many states, trading rooms in diverse languages, and the training experience of tens of thousands of students. Throughout Tradenet's existence I've continued, with only rare exceptions, to trade daily from home. I'm not prepared to give up on the comfort of working from home. Life is short, and every moment should be enjoyed!

From an economic viewpoint, I've been"comfortable" for a long while now. I don't need to sell books, teach or even trade in order to earn my living. But I'm writing this book nonetheless because I love my profession, and I love to teach. Deep in my soul, I'm a true teacher. That's where my greatest satisfaction lies. Now that I've changed my life and that of so many others, I consider it my obligation to write this book, which can help change your life too.

I have reached the stage where I feel the time has come to share my secrets and my experience in the hope that you, too, will take a small step forward on the road to financial independence and live the good life you were meant to lead. I know how to teach you to join the pros and make big money, but I'm also offering this warning: if you're not determined and committed to success, you'll lose money. You have to want to become successful and be willing to learn and make mistakes along the way.

Who Is This Book For?

This book is for all those who want to change their lives, improve their incomes, and most importantly, enjoy the thrill and fun of trading stocks.

This book is for all those who have zero knowledge, background or experience in trading or in finance, which was my position just a little over a decade ago. Even if you do have some experience with the capital market, you'll find the rules of professional trading different from those with which you're familiar.

This book is for you, especially, if you have a degree in Economics. You're in an even worse position than others, so forget the degree. You'll find that the stock exchange's behavior is nothing like that described in your textbooks!

Introduction

The Stock Exchange Is for Pros

Always remember that when you buy a share of stock, someone is selling it to you. Some people seem to think that "the bank" or "the broker" is selling it.

That's not the case. The person selling the stock believes it is valuable at precisely the same time as you're thinking it's cheap. In other words, if you buy at a price that the seller feels is expensive, what, in your opinion, is the seller thinking about you?

Correct. The seller is probably thinking you're an idiot. When the seller is a pro and you're not, he's almost always right.

SMART MONEY	*A pro trader once told me that a pro's job is to find the idiots willing to buy from him…*

The stock exchange is my place of work. I am a pro. I make my income from people who think they can take my money. The only way the cash flow in my trading account will grow is if I make someone else's smaller. I profit from the money lost by investors, the public, or the herd that doesn't understand the rules of the game. Only a very few lucky folks along the way have used their courage and determination to profit and lead the rest of the herd.

Stock Exchange or Casino?

A dictionary entry defines the stock exchange as "an organized market in which businessmen meet in order to sell and buy stocks or commodities such as diamonds, cotton, coffee and sugar."

Such sweet talk! Such a lovely, respectable place to work that must be! Businesspersons meet and earn profits. Every mother's dream-come-true for a successful child!

Now I will offer my definition. A more correct and precise one cannot be found in any dictionary. "The stock exchange is a gambling club in which the house members (pros, institutional traders, the State) take advantage of the public's greed in order to profit from their mistakes."

Yes, I said "take advantage," no less! Words such as equities, stocks, bonds, options, and futures hide a far greater truth known to the professional players in the capital market: "Profit at the public's expense." Call it "commissions," or "management fees." Call it "capital gains tax" or whatever you will. Once the professionals and the country have stripped you of these, you're left with no money. Instead, they've scooped it up. To the professionals' amazement and sheer joy, this truth remains concealed from the biggest player of all in the stock exchange: the public. I have frequently said this, and will repeat it once more: if you're not a professional, do not go anywhere near the stock exchange. The more I say it, the more people think I'm just crazy. Conclusion: if the public's compulsion to gamble cannot be suppressed, there is only one thing left to do: profit from its money.

Who Knows How the Market Will Move?

The person able to constantly, correctly foresee how the market will develop, or how a particular stock will move, has yet to be born. Nonetheless, there exists a multitude of analysts and fund managers who claim otherwise, attempting to justify an investment with academic intellectualism, and thus preserve their source of income.

The well-oiled academic system and stock market requires self-nurturing, justifying its "raison d'etre." I have no reason to be angry with the system, because it's impossible to fight human nature. It is quite reasonable that those involved would want to justify their knowledge, and preserve their incomes. Most mature and smart folks in the stock market would privately agree with me that in actuality they know nothing at all of the future. But they would never admit as much in public, as a public admission is tantamount to announcing the failure of the entire enterprise. They are comfortable with cooperating with the system and continuing to assure the public by offering empty promises, which they hope will be realized with a good bit of luck.

Trying to predict the future can be compared to traveling in a fog. At a distance the fog looks thick, but seems to thin out as it gets closer. So it is with the capital market. The shorter we make the prediction framework, the clearer things become, even if there is still a degree of fog preventing us from seeing things perfectly. If I ask you where you will be in exactly six months, can you provide a precise answer? If, on the other hand, I ask where you will be tomorrow morning, it is more feasible that you will know and end up being correct.

Nor am I any different in this respect. I, too, lack any knowledge of how the market will play out. By contrast, sometimes when the fog clears a little, I can, within reasonable bounds, successfully predict the direction of the market or a specific stock for a span of several minutes, several hours or even several days ahead. In those rare instances when the fog entirely lifts, we can even see several weeks ahead.

For Success, Advantage is Vital

Making a living requires an advantage. What's your profession? Do you have some kind of advantage? Of course you do! If you had no advantage to offer, your client would go to your competitor. As with every profession, the same is true for stock traders. You need an advantage!

Trading is like managing your own business. As with any business, if you fail you'll need to close the business, fire the manager (that's yourself in this case), and find a new source of income.

Prior to investing in any business, you need to ask the following: Who are your competitors? How can you beat them?

The owner of a business needs to understand his or her advantage. Is the advantage in quality? In service? Location? Products? Without a clear advantage, your business will fail.

A stock is a commodity like any other commodity. Don't buy stocks if you have no clear advantage to offer. If you've decided to become a stock trader, you must be able to identify the advantage and make the best use of it, operating just as you would in any other business activity.

Most of the public is defined as long-term investors. They believe in their ability to identify companies which, over a long term of some months or even years, will rise in value. The media is full of calculations showing the millions you could have made had you bought 1000 Microsoft stocks in 1980. Warren Buffett is known for having made billions through long-term investments. Generations of investors were nurtured on these tales of good fortune and attempts to duplicate them.

Wake up! Just because a select few got lucky does not mean that most people make money investing in the long term!

History ignores the greatest majority of investors. That's the 90%

who lose their money. Many investors who made hundreds of percent profit in the 1980s and 1990s lost everything in the decade between 2000 and 2010.

Example

Let's examine what might have happened had you bought the ETF (Exchange Traded Fund) of the S&P 500 known as SPY in January 1999, and sold it in August 2011:

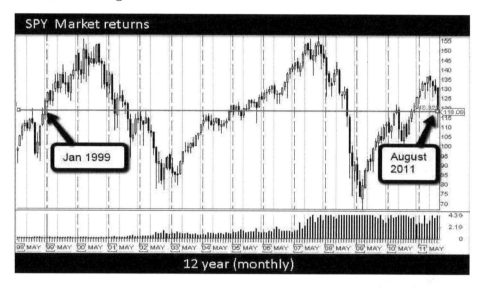

In January 1999, you would have paid the identical amount for this ETF as in August 2011, whereas in that same timeframe, you could have received a risk-free yield from any bank of at least 50% based on interest rates at the time.

The Long Term

Let's assume you're reading an article about a company with wonderful prospects. Let's assume that the analysts also like this company. Do you have any advantage? You and another half-million people have heard about this company and read the same article. Where is your advantage over other readers? The public company's typist, who for a minimum wage typed up the quarterly report before it was published, knows more than you. The typist has the advantage, not you.

- No one can predict price movement over the long term. I can't, you can't, nor can the best analyst in the world. Beware of anyone who claims otherwise.

- Always remember: there is someone who will profit and someone who will lose from every analyst recommendation.
- Remember that behind every stock transaction, there is a buyer or seller who feels he or she is smarter than you.
- Remember: the big money is not where information is clearly divulged to the public. If 90% of investors lose their money, then they're clearly doing something wrong!

The Mid-Term

A range of several weeks to months is the inherent advantage for hedge funds. They operate with large sums, making it difficult for them to maneuver in the short term, and they are justifiably fearful of the long term. Due to the capital they hold, they can support stock prices for periods of time, which increases their chance of profit. Their advantage is in shifting large amounts of money and being somewhat skilled at knowing where money is currently flowing. Although sometimes they also lose.

The Short Range

The very short term, measured in seconds or minutes, is the market makers' and specialists' advantage, which we will learn more about later. They, in contrast to the rest of the general public, pay no commissions. They receive the commissions! Because their role involves coordinating real-time buy and sell commands, they know far better than we do which direction the wind is blowing, and they take advantage of the very short term. You will never find them buying a stock because they believe in the company's product or management!

An Example of "Advantage"

When long-term investors want to protect their investment in a stock, they generally use a protective "stop order," which will automatically perform a sale if the stock price drops lower than a specific figure. The stock exchange's hours of activity overlap the working hours of the average investor, making it difficult for such a person to constantly follow the price movementin real time. The average investor relies on the broker to carry out the automated stop order.

How does that help us? Average investors, whom we will call "retail investors," review their investments at the end of each week and place protective stop orders into the system according to the price movement during the week that passed. These stop orders await automatic execution while the retail investors are at their day jobs. The automated stop orders will be executed when the preset conditions appear.

Our advantage:
- Looking at the stock's graph, it's easy to estimate the point where automated stop orders will be executed. Can this information be used to someone's advantage? Of course it can!
- Let's say that at a certain price, we see a strong chance for a heavy concentration of stop orders.
- In other words, if the stock price drops to this figure, a large number of stop orders will go live, which could likely push the stock price down further.
- Can we profit from the expected drop? Of course! We can sell "short" (which we'll learn more about later) and profit from the price drop. This is how making use of information can be an advantage.

I relate to stock trading just as any other business. I won't trade without an advantage. I know that competitors are operating against me and want my money no less than I want theirs. I know that to survive and profit, I must identify my advantage and maximize it. I recommend that you, too, relate to your money with due respect and conduct yourselves accordingly.

Precise Knowledge or Art?
Day trading stocks is an independent profession in which we buy cheap and sell at a high price, taking advantage of other players. As traders, our goal is to succeed in about 65% of the trades that we make over time. Day trading is a simple profession to view, but difficult to implement. It's simple, because the rules are simple. It's difficult because of the psychological inhibitors that express both our fear and greed.

SMART MONEY	*Day trading is an art integrated with precision knowledge. The rules for the precision knowledge can be learned, but the art needs to be developed.*

Day trading lies partway between relying on precise knowledge and being an art. Day trading will not be successful if based on technical analysis alone. If that's all that was needed, it would be accounting.

A winning trader succeeds in merging knowledge and artistry. This book sets out to provide you primarily with knowledge, and a touch of artistry. The artistry is up to you to garner as you work hard and accrue experience. You can teach someone to paint, but only a select few will go on to make works of art that others appreciate and place a value on. The same is true of trading.

The Difference between Trade and Investment

As you've surely realized, this book does not deal in stocks as an investment, but rather in stock trading, which is actually no different from any other field of business. An art dealer, for example, is very different from an art collector. The art dealer will not buy famous paintings and store them in the safe for decades, hoping their value will rise. The art dealer buys a painting only if he or she estimates there is a certain range of profit in a short-term sale. Like all of us, the art dealer needs to pay a mortgage and cover food and other living expenses.

The stock trader is just like the art dealer: both buy and sell in order to create the profit that provides for their livelihood. Professional traders buy stocks at a price they know is too low, with the intent of selling at a price they know is too high. Stock traders also make mistakes. But a stock trader who succeeds more often than errs can make a living from the profession.

In contrast to the trader, investors do not try to earn their living from the market. Investors turn their funds over to the management of others, or manage their funds by themselves in the hope of positive yields. Investors may improve or worsen their long-term financial status, but cannot assure payment of their credit card bill at the end of each month. A trader plans in advance how much money to risk with each transaction, whereas the investor might, during tough times, discover that most of his or her money has evaporated. Traders sleep peacefully knowing that most of their money is in cash, whereas the investor is exposed to market fluctuations.

Traders use "fast money." Investors use "slow money." Can $100 in the hands of a trader be the same as $100 in the hands of the investor? Not at all. When the stock exchange ends the year with increases at 6%, the investor's funds have followed all trends over the year, and therefore these funds are called "slow money." By contrast, traders enter and exit on each day of trade. An overall yearly change of 6% comprises hundreds of trade days and tens of weeks during which the market rises or drops several percentages. Traders follow these ups and downs, and unlike the investor, traders use that same $100 many times, sometimes thousands of times over. The trader's money is "fast," as it enters and exits the market incessantly. We could say that a trader's money works harder. The investor's money is "slow." The trader's "fast money" piggy backs on the "slow money."

Trading is my profession. Investment is not. I don't negate the validity of investment, especially if you're good at it. But I do know that investments will never lead to a monthly salary from the market. I do believe that most of your free money should be invested, if not in the stock exchange, perhaps in real estate. But that's not my field of expertise.

What Did I Know about the Stock Exchange When I Started Out?

Nothing. A little more than a decade ago, I started from scratch. I didn't know how to buy or sell stocks, and I knew nothing about the fundamental concepts. One important rule was clear to me, however: money in the stock exchange, as in any business, is earned by buying cheaply and selling for much more. In point of fact, there's not much difference between selling vegetables in an open air market and trading stocks on Wall Street, apart from the fact that you'll find more books have been written about Wall Street. Add to stock trading the comfort of working from your home, plus the potential for high profits, and you have the best recipe for self-employment.

Stock trading is a simple profession. People tend to make simple things complex. I believe that all any reasonable person needs for success is the absolute determination to win. Even if you are clueless and have no experience, don't be deterred. You're starting out at exactly the same point I did.

This book is meant for you. It will lead you, step by step, at your own pace, to a broader understanding. You need to make an uncompromising decision to succeed. Now, to be absolutely certain you'll let no obstacle stand in your way to success, close the door to your room, take a deep breath, and shout at the top of your lungs: I'm going to make it!

What Will You Learn from This Book?
• Fundamentals of trading
• Choosing the right broker and trading platform
• How to choose winning stocks

• How to profit from rising or falling markets
• Technical analysis
• Basic and advanced trading methods
• Financial and risk management
• Trading psychology
• Self-empowerment

Having trained thousands of traders, I know just what tools you'll need to conquer the market. I know where to direct your focus, and what to warn you about.

This is a practical and professional book written by an experienced trader who trades daily with his own money.

This is the first, and last, book you'll ever need in order to succeed in day trading.

Who's Afraid of Being Independent?

Stock trading is an independent business. When you trade in stocks, you're exposed to financial risk, as in any business. A salaried employee who fails will never return his salary to his employer, even if the employer incurred a loss. At the most, the salaried employee will be fired. A self-employed person will pay for every error with his or her own money. By contrast, a self-employed person who is successful will earn far more than the wildest dreams of the average salaried employee.

Do you have it in you to be self-employed? Are you prepared to work without a salary and risk your money? Are you psychologically ready for the risk? I encounter all kinds of students. Sometimes a new student will ask, "Meir, I understand I won't earn big money at the outset, but can I be sure that within the first few months I'll earn at least as much as an average salary?" Oops! An employee-based question. A self-employed person would never ask such a thing. Being salaried is not bad, but to be independent, you need to be made of something tougher. A self-employed trader can work less, enjoy more, and profit ten times higher than a salaried employee, but must be willing to take the risk. Be warned: without the willingness to risk your money, you'll get nowhere in trading.

Let's now assume you're ready to take the risk and are determined to become independent. You can still have alternative business interests other than stock trading. At this point, we need to draw up some comparisons:

Commitment. Most businesses require a brick and mortar office, usually rented. Rent is a long-term commitment: rent payments, management fees, municipal taxes, electricity, water, maintenance and more. By contrast, a stock trader works from home. Your current expenditure might grow slightly, but there are no long-term commitments.

Responsibility. A business requires employees, consultants, an accounting staff, legal counsel....a great big headache and heavy responsibility to provide for individuals who are dependent upon you. Knowing that in the good old days I needed to be responsible for paying my employees' salaries caused me many a sleepless night over the years. A stock trader doesn't employ anyone. It's the trader, the computer, and the Internet. A huge advantage!

Investment. Every business demands investment: vehicles, office machinery and supplies, advertising, printing, premise renovation and more. In addition to a significant minimum investment, you'll need working capital to ensure ongoing activities until a positive flow develops. The stock trader needs a good computer, several screens, and working capital that allows opening the trading account and having funds to trade. That's it!

The risks. It's rare to see a business close without causing sorrow and pain. Businesses close in hard times. Debts pile up, employees pressure for raises, and banks suddenly cut off their lines of credit, leaving the business without oxygen. Assets and stock, which under regular circumstances are worth their purchase value, are thrown out or sold for pennies. A stock trader can limit losses to a specific part of his or her investment. Show me any other business where you can limit your loss!

The possibilities. In most businesses, it's hard to be creative. The sorry fact is that most self-employed people make less than salaried employees. The professional stock trader does not operate within a competitive business reality that limits his or her possibilities. The sky's the limit!

Not everyone is suited to being a stock trader, just as not everyone's suited to being self-employed. Setting up a business requires commitment, responsibility, investment, and risk. If I had to choose a field to be self-employed in, undoubtedly my top choice would be one with the lowest risk and highest possibilities.

From my experience, I've learned that the chances of success for a beginning trader who must earn a livelihood from trading are far lower than for those who simultaneously maintain their original source of income. I want you to start out small and at the same time, maintain another source of income. I want you to succeed slowly and safely, knowing you have a secure amount of money coming in, reducing the pressures to generate immediate income. If you've left your job or are between jobs, don't rely on trading profits. If you don't place all your hopes on trading profits, you'll profit. If you feel pressured to profit, you'll end up losing.

What's Needed for Success?

A successful trader needs three basic components:
- Thorough knowledge and follow-up at the beginner stage
- The proper trading environment: that is, a quality computer and a hi-speed Internet connection
- An account with a professional broker who can provide fast, effective charts and executions.
  We will discuss all three elements throughout the book.
  The chain is only as strong as its weakest link. Each of the components below is important to your chain, which is your business. If you want your business to do well, invest in each of them, from the enrichment stage (learning) to the daily tools stage (trading system).

How Much Can I Earn?

After completing the training stage, you need to set income targets. A realistic target for successful day traders is to double their money each year, which means that a starting capital of $10,000 won't allow you to maintain a reasonable lifestyle unless you live in a Vietnamese village. At the other end of the scale, a trader seeking a reasonable quality of life will trade with $30,000 and more. As US citizens, the "day trading margin rules" will require you to deposit no less than $25,000.

If your annual income depends on the amount of money in the trading account, why not deposit more and profit more? Eventually that might be the right move, but initially it is not, for two reasons. First, not everyone has the required capital available, and secondly, there are psychological limitations until you become proficient. To trade with larger sums means being psychologically prepared for larger fluctuations in profit and loss. The mental ability to cope with these fluctuations is acquired only after years of trading. Do I display emotion over large profits or losses? Rarely. Any of my days of trading can end in large profits or large losses of thousands of dollars. I'm accustomed to these fluctuations, and because the majority of my trading ends in profits, I can psychologically cope with losses of a scope that just ten years ago would have caused me sleepless nights. Each of us has our own level of psychological limitation: therefore, trading too early with sums that are too large may lead to losses. Every trader must find the most suitable figure, based on the personality aspect rather than financial abilities. As time passes and you gain experience, your psychological resilience will strengthen, and you will hopefully trade a larger account.

How Many of You Will Make It?

Sadly, very few. How many businesses make it? Statistics show that only one in five businesses survives and become successful. Is that a good reason not to open a business? Of course not! It's a good reason to open five businesses in the hope that one of them will succeed! If you're a reasonable person with a high level of determination, persistence, self-control, willingness to learn, and reasonable capital, you'll succeed where most have failed. The ball is in your hands. Don't let statistics scare you. The human race would not have gotten far if no one had ever been willing to take a risk.

So Why Did I Write This Book?

I believe that this book can improve the quality of life for many of its readers, even if they aren't involved in professional trading. I believe that everyone should become familiar with, and take advantage of, the stock exchange to the best of his or her ability. I believe that even if you don't trade, you'll still be able to learn, and avoid the capital market's dangers that can easily ambush you. I believe that in our current economic reality, every person must hold a second profession, because you can never know when one of them will become useless. I also believe it is our obligation to make the best use of our advantage over the average investor attempting to profit from the stock exchange without any knowledge or experience.

I believe we all deserve to enjoy this short life we have on earth. I derive great pleasure from a successful day of trading and believe I can help you get that feeling, too. It brings me great joy to hear a graduate of my course tell me about his or her successes. That's where my realization and gratification lie, and that's my proud signature on the history of trading. My returns are the satisfaction and pleasure you get from your success. Once you've become successful, email me and make my day!

Welcome!

... to the fascinating world of stock trading. It's the most realistic virtual reality on earth, a reality in which every person with a computer and Internet access can earn a living from any location in the world. It's the fairest profession in the world, in which everyone has the chance to become a millionaire through his or her own personal capabilities, without regard to race, gender, age, nationality, or language. **Best of luck!**

1

Allow Me to

Introduce You...

to the Stock

Exchange

The Stock Exchange: My Place of Work

A Devoted Fan

We're such strange creatures. We identify with our city, root for our favorite football team, and even feel proud of our place of work, as long as our salary keeps rolling in. The stock exchange is my place of work, and it makes me feel proud. It's because of traders like me that it continues to exist and flourish. I contribute to its existence by increasing trading volume, and in return, I get the chance to earn my income. As future fans, here's the history of your future place of work.

Who Needs the Stock Exchange?

Companies need money in order to develop their business. They can recruit money from their stockholders or borrow from banks. The disadvantage in bank loans, as we all know, is that unfortunately the loan must be repaid. Not only must the initial sum be returned, but banks also have this annoying habit of adding interest. In short, a company requiring a bank loan burdens itself not only with the repayment of the initial figure, but also the added amount of interest, all of which slows down the company's progress. But a brilliant bypass action was invented: money that doesn't need to be returned! It's called **IPO** – Initial Public Offering.

What is a Stock?

The IPO is an event in which a company sells shares of stock to the public in return for the public's money. What is a stock? It's a document that gives its owner the right to a part of the company. When a company is formed, the company's owners decide the number of shares that comprise the company. If this is a new company, with no performance, we can presume the value of its shares is zero. Once the company begins operations, accumulating contracts, patents, income and profit, its value rises. The value of its shares rises accordingly. But the "value of a stock" is an abstract concept. A company's transactions fluctuate frequently, which makes it difficult to determine the true value of its stock.

When a company offers shares to the public, it is selling part of its stock. The sale is a recruitment of money by the company which the company does not need to return. Buyers believe they are purchasing cheaply, and hope that in the future they will sell for more. From this point on, the shares are traded between buyers and sellers who for the most part are not the company's original owners. To protect the interests of both buyers and sellers, and to improve reliability and create greater fluidity, it was decided that stock trading would be conducted within the controlled environment of the stock exchange.

Can any company offer shares to the public and become a "public company?" No. A company wishing to recruit money through the stock exchange must meet tough criteria related to sales turnover, profits, and financial stability. Not every company needing money is interested in going public, because after making the offering, it will need to continue upholding tough regulatory standards which might limit its progress; it will be required to become transparent, which exposes its secrets to the public including its competitors. This is a costly endeavor, and the company will also be required to include the public that holds its shares in its decision-making processes. In short, there are no free lunches.

The Stock Exchange's Early Days

Stock trading is documented in ancient writings as early as 400 BC, but the most significant, initial sale of stocks to the public occurred in Amsterdam in 1602 with the establishment of the Dutch East India Company as an international spice company.

The Netherlands

The essential difference in this case was the fact that from the outset, the company's stocks were meant to be sold to the public. In actuality the public had little impact on the company's management, which remained in the managers' control. The Dutch East India Company was highly successful and for decades, from its inception through 1650, paid its stockholders an average annual dividend of 16%. Over the years, additional public companies were established in Amsterdam, and stock trading took on an organizational nature. In 1688, the first book in history dealing with stock trading was published. Its author, Joseph de la Vega, was a successful Spanish-Jewish trader. He wrote the book using a dialogue format between a stock holder, a trader, and a philosopher. The book described in fine detail the relatively ingenious conduct of the Amsterdam Bourse, and even offered valuable tips to its readers.

London

Some few years later in London, 1693, the first bonds began to be traded. Immediately afterwards, several British public companies began trading. London's first stock traders operated in coffee shops on Change Street, adjacent to the Royal Exchange, the trading center they were not allowed to enter because of their known "bad habits." In 1698, one John Casting, whose preferred spot was in "Jonathan's Coffee House," began hanging a list of stocks and their prices outside the coffee house. This list is considered the first milestone in establishing London's stock exchange.

The First Bubble

Over the years to follow, several companies rose and fell, but the most widely-known case was that of the South Sea Company, established in 1711 for the purpose of trade with South America. The company's shares were snapped up, their price rocketing upwards. Within a few years, it became apparent that expectations of successful trading with "The New World" were exaggerated, and in 1720 prices fell in one sudden drop, creating the first bubble burst in history. In reaction, the British Parliament created the "Bubble Act." Enthusiasm for the stock exchange dissipated for several decades. In 1789, stocks and bonds began to be traded in the United States.More on that later.

Wall Street –
The Wall and the Money

Wall Street has taken on many different semblances since its first transaction. Most of the changes arose from the ongoing struggle between two immensely powerful parties: the investment houses and the government. The former has constantly sought to operate without supervision, taking advantage of any and every opportunity for stretching their long arms deep into the public's pocket. They have never been averse to any dirty trick: trading with insider knowledge, disseminating misinformation or incorrect data through media channels, or organizing raids on a specific stock are all examples of the commonly-known methods of manipulation that have made Wall Street professionals so loathsome to the public. More than two centuries after Wall Street's establishment, the 2008 financial crisis shows us that nothing has changed.

SMART MONEY	*Wall Street has never been averse to any dirty trick that deceives the public. The tricks get smarter, and then so does their regulation. It's a never-ending game.*

On the other side of the divide, the government has generally sought to set the rules and regulations that restrain the insatiable appetites of Wall Street traders for money. In short: government-set regulations. Often, legal prohibitions don't help at all, and prohibited actions spread anyway. For example, instead of recruiting a newspaper to publicize false information, companies were assisted by a **grading company** that rates performance of other companies. This sways public opinion because the public is told to view the grading companies as legitimate. But the grading company often receives its income from the reviewed company! The conflicts of interest apparently didn't bother anyone.

A turnaround in the relationship between Wall Street and the government occurred as a result of the 1929 Crash, which critically affected the entire United States financial system. The Crash led to a serious economic slump of epic proportions that lasted several years, known as "The Great Depression."

Despite all these permutations, Wall Street has basically remained the same. Jesse Livermore traded on Wall Street from the end of the 19th century to the early 20th century. His book *How to Trade in Stocks*, and Lefèvre's *Reminiscences of a Stock Trader*, a biography of Livermore, show that Livermore would have had no trouble trading successfully were he alive today.

Eighty years have passed since the 1929 Crash, and it seems that the lessons learned from that devastating event have been forgotten. Currently, at the time of this book's writing, a new chapter is being written in Wall Street's history. The credit crunch, known as "The Sub-Prime Crisis," hit Wall Street like a bolt of lightning. Despite a fairly quick recovery developing during the two years from the lowest point of the slump, its lessons are still unclear. The crisis hit with full force across the entire financial system of the US, and first and foremost on Wall Street, so much so that some feel Wall Street is losing its top billing in international finance markets. But before we mourn Wall Street, it's worth checking how it all began.

Wall Street is in New York's Lower Manhattan. It was so named because in 1653, a wall was built there by Peter Stuyvesant, the Dutch governor of the city then known as New Amsterdam, to protect the city's residents from the "Indians" as they were known at the time, and from a possible British invasion. The wall itself was never put to the test, but lent its existence to the name of the street running alongside it.

SMART MONEY	*Regulation, like the stock market, develops as a result of crises that lead to bubbles. But unlike a bubble, it never bursts. By nature, it always progresses and never regresses.*

In 1789, to cover debts of the government and its colonies, the first United States Congress, via its central bank, issued what were known as Treasury Bonds to the value of $80 million. These were sold to the general public. In those days, Manhattan's population numbered around 34,000 and Wall Street was still an unpaved dirt road. Along its sides, trading houses stood and transacted international commodity sales. Very quickly, Wall Street's trading houses also began selling lottery tickets, stocks, and bonds. The hottest items during that period, and in fact the item around which speculative trading began, were bonds. In those days, a person wishing to buy or sell stocks or bonds had to issue a public notice or sell to friends. As demand developed, two renowned trading houses of the time, Leonard Bleecker at 16 Wall Street, and Sutton & Harry at 20 Wall Street, began holding supplies of bonds and stocks.

Stock trading began to develop. Investors assisted in setting up and developing companies by investing their money in return for a Deed of Shares confirming their investment in writing and providing them with a holding in part of the company. These deeds served as security and proof of ownership, and assured the investor's stock in the company. This led to several synonyms that would come into use over time, among them Securities (signifying they were securely held by their owner) and Equities (indicating entitlement to part of the capital).

In March of 1792, a New York trader named William Duer, who also served as the US Assistant Secretary of the Treasury at the time, was investing in a scheme to buy up the US debt to France at a discount. The plan failed and Duer lost his entire wealth and more, but the ramifications of his failed investments contributed to the Panic of 1792, where he fell into bankruptcy. The term "crash" was applied to these events. It was one of many that would take their place in Wall Street's history. Following this crash, traders decided to institutionalize their activities and establish one place where it would be possible to control and document all transactions. In May of 1792, the traders and market makers signed the "Buttonwood Agreement," named such because it took place beneath the sycamore (buttonwood) tree that stood outside 68 Wall Street. The agreement saw the formal establishment of the New York Stock Exchange and the setting of standardized trade commissions.

The famous NYSE (New York Stock Exchange) edifice was built in 1827 on the corner of Wall Street and Hannover Street. In 1842, a competing stock exchange was established known as AMEX, the American Stock Exchange. Simultaneous to the worldwide economic prosperity, Wall Street developed its role as the most important international financial center.

In the late 1890s and early 1900s, a new phenomenon began to pick up steam. Throughout the United States, "stock shops," also known as "bucket shops," sprouted up. The term was imported from Britain, where it had clear connotations of illegal activities. Clients of these shops traded in stocks for speculative purposes without actually making a stock exchange transaction: in actuality, gambling. A trader "played" on the stock price without actually buying the stock. When the trader profited, the shop lost, and vice versa: a casino for all intents and purposes. The stock rates were continually telegraphed in from New York throughout the entire trading day. They were called out by one clerk and simultaneously written down by another on a large board facing the public. Because the shop's interests were diametrically opposed to those of the trader, swindling was endless, and these shops were perceived as unreliable. A detailed description of these activities is found in Edwin Lefèvre's *Reminiscences of a Stock Operator*, mentioned earlier as a biography of one of the biggest traders, Jesse Livermore. In 1930, during the Great Depression, these shops were made illegal, and the fun and games came to an end.

Establishing the SEC –
Securities and Exchange Commission

As part of the lessons learned from the Great Depression, and seeking to prevent a future repetition of the processes that contributed to the 1929 Crash, the Congress established the first regulatory body to supervise the United States capital markets. It was set up in 1934 and called the SEC, the Securities and Exchange Commission. The SEC determined standards geared to preventing the development of those factors that led to the Crash, particularly manipulation of prices and use of insider information. Over the years, the SEC instituted many regulatory changes which continue to contribute to enhancing trust in the capital market.

When the public shows greater trust in the capital market, the market's activities expand and crash risks such as those of 1929 decrease. Regulatory ordinances that seem obvious to us now were not in place in the past. Currently, for example, a public company is obligated to convey significant notifications to the public via conference calls, before conveying them to insiders. Sound natural? That's one of the regulations set by the SEC only a few years ago. The SEC's task has yet to be completed. In fact, it seems it will never be completed. Insider information is still the most normal way to make small capital gains in the market. It is Illegal and stinky, but whenever there's been a lot of money on the table, there are those looking for the get-rich-quick shortcuts. Even today, only a small percentage of those taking advantage of insider information are held accountable.

Meet the Stock Exchanges

The stock markets are comprised of several stock exchanges. A stock exchange is a business like any other. It makes a profit from commissions and services. The stock exchanges compete among themselves, appealing to different business niches. Each stock exchange has its own uniqueness, technology, advantages, and of course, its typical disadvantages.

The New York Stock Exchange (NYSE)

The NYSE (www.nyse.com) is located on the corner of Wall and Broad Streets. It is the largest in the world as far as the market value of the companies traded on it. The market value, known as market capitalization or "market cap," multiplies the number of shares of stocks held by the public by their stock exchange-traded price. If you calculate the market cap of stocks traded in the NYSE, you will reach a peak period combined value of more than ten trillion dollars! More than 3000 companies comprise the NYSE trading list.

Prior to the terror attacks of September 11, 2001, it used to be possible to stand at the stock exchange's gallery window and watch it in action. Now, to enter the gallery, you need to get a special entrance license, or become a photographer for CNBC, Bloomberg or others, or know someone with a key function who can request a permit for you. But once in the gallery, you'll see something amazing that is part of a disappearing world. Traders scurry among dozens of work stations, broadcasting commands with odd hand signals, and navigating their way through mountains of notes transferred from buyer to seller and carelessly let to fall on the trading floor.

Because I was acquainted with the well-known television commentator who goes by the name "Dr. J," I was lucky enough to receive the amazing chance to join a CNBC photo shoot of S&P 500 options traders in the Chicago Stock Exchange. I stood, fascinated, surrounded by dozens of traders shouting and pushing as though in a football game. Later I learned from Dr. J, a former pro-football player, that one of the conditions of acceptance for work on the trading floor known as "pit" is the height, weight, and physical ability to push aside competing traders!

The unavoidable is happening to the biggest stock exchange in the world, too. Computers are slowly taking over all processes, despite strong opposition by the traders. Computerized trading brings greater competition, fewer commissions, greater transparency for the public, and higher execution speed: exactly what the public wants, and precisely what the companies that employ floor traders don't want. It started small. NASDAQ, the United States' first computerized stock exchange, became the model. The NYSE was then forced to respond to public pressure and incorporate automatic systems which initially managed only a small part of the turnover of high-volume stock trading. Over the years, this was used to silence the public. Political pressures were handled on the quiet through phone calls between CEOs of the mega-corporations and the appropriate politician. Despite the opposition, the revolution was actually completed over the past few years, and currently most of the NYSE operations are computerized. Now, when I buy or sell a stock at the speed of a nanosecond, I remember a distant bad dream of just a few years ago, when I taught Tradenet students that the execution time of a NYSE transaction could take up to two minutes from the time the button is pressed!

The AMEX Stock Exchange

The American Stock Exchange (www.amex.com) was established in New York in 1842. AMEX is the third-largest stock exchange in the US, after the NYSE and NASDAQ. Trade there focuses mainly on stocks of small to mid-size companies and a range of ETFs, Exchange Traded Funds, about which we will learn more later. AMEX operates similarly to the NYSE, using the tender method of their market makers (we'll learn more about them later, too). AMEX belongs to NASDAQ and its volume of activities is relatively low. AMEX, like NYSE, has also moved most of its processes to quick, effective computerized execution.

Founding NASDAQ

1971 saw an important change take place. The NASDAQ stock exchange was established, and unlike the NYSE, NASDAQ computerized all its trade processes. The NASDAQ computers are in Connecticut and link to more than 500 market makers' computers, allowing electronic trade in one click. From that point on, market makers no longer needed to compete over each other's shouts on the trading floor. Everything was push-button. The result: commissions slowly dropped, the quality of service improved, competition grew, and companies of a new type issued stocks and raised trillions of dollars. Within two decades, and with the proliferation of the Internet, NASDAQ was accessible in the home of every trader. For the first time, the road to private trading was opened. We can, in fact, say that the profession of day trading as we know it now was born with NASDAQ's founding.

Crises

If you run a statistical check of the average period between each crisis throughout market history, you'll discover that during your own adult lifetime, at least three crises will occur. In other words, if you're a short-term investor, there's a reasonable chance that sooner or later you'll lose a sizeable portion of your capital. That's one of the risks of the market for investors. For someone with the good luck to experience a first crisis around the age of forty, there's a good chance of survival, but if it catches you when you're sixty-five, I'm not certain you'll manage to save your pension. An exception is the last decade, 2000-2010, during which two of biggest crises in market history occurred in close proximity: the Dot-Com Crash and the Sub-Prime Crash.

The Great Depression:
Black Monday and Tuesday, 1929

The crash of Black Monday, October 28, 1929, with its 12.8% drop, followed the next day by Black Tuesday with its 11.73% drop, are known as "The Great Crash," which led to a ten-year economic slump known worldwide as "The Great Depression." The crisis occurred on the heels of the era known as "The Roaring Twenties," a contrasting period of some ten years during which America wildly celebrated the victory of the First World War, living on endless credit, with real estate prices going through the roof.

Unlike other crashes, the Great Depression lasted several years, dipping to an all-time low in July 1932, which marked the lowest slump of the entire twentieth century's capital market. The market only recovered to its pre-slump level in November 1954. In actuality, young adults who held stocks prior to the slump spent the bulk of their adult lives waiting for the recovery.

Black Monday, 1987

As in other crashes, herd panic swayed the game on October 19, 1987. In 1929, the "herd" flooded the streets and swamped brokers' offices. In 1987, the "herd" blocked the brokers' telephone lines. Hysterical "sell at any price" and "get me out" orders arrived from the entire United States. At some point, the brokers and market makers stopped answering the calls, and the market collapsed, out of control. The crisis commenced in Hong Kong, spread to Europe, hit the United States and caused an index drop in just one day of 22.8%, marking the greatest ever single-day drop. Despite this event, and somewhat surprisingly, 1987 ended in net gains for the year!

As always following a bubble's burst, someone needs to earn a living from creating new regulations and setting new standards. Within the bubble's craziness, the SEC put forward new rules meant to protect the private investor and prevent a repeat of this event. The newly-instigated changes focused on the market makers' role. The SEC decided that in order to guard the market from panic crashes and prevent a "sellers only" situation, market makers would be obligated to buy a certain amount of shares from the public during rate drops. The new law was passed shortly after the crash, and calmed the regulators' consciences for another brief period.

The Dot-Com Crisis

The dot-com bubble burst on Monday, March 13, 2000, following five years of sharp rises. On that Monday, the start of the trading week, the market opened with a gap of 4% down on the NASDAQ index as a result of the miserable timing of several parties which simultaneously sold shares in Cisco, IBM and Dell at a value of billions of dollars. The drop ignited a wave of sellers, leading eventually to a loss of 9% over the next six trading days.

SMART MONEY	*Crises are good for traders! High fluctuation, public panic, and the ability to execute shorts are important tools in the hand of an experienced trader.*

The bubble was structured around the euphoria which peaked with the invention of new, unprecedented economic models based on "market penetration" instead of profits and on "unadvertised costs" and other innovations that matched the spirit of the times. For as long as money flowed into the hi-tech industry, especially in light of the low interest rates of 1998 and 1999, the boom kept growing. In 1999 and the start of 2000, when the government increased the interest rates six times in succession, money was made more expensive, and the new economic models began to collapse like a house of cards.

At the peak of the crisis, the NASDAQ index representing the technological stocks lost some 80% of its value, and the S&P 500 lost 46%. I personally experienced this crash as a hi-tech entrepreneur and beginning trader. I recruited millions of dollars from investors for startups I established, and rode the peaks and valleys of that period from every angle possible. These were also my initial years as a trainee trader. In fact, I owe the positive change in my life to the Dot-Com Crisis, which left me, as so many others like me, unemployed, and forced me to seek an alternative in the world of stock trading.

The Credit Crunch (Sub-Prime)

The credit crunch, more commonly known as the "Sub-Prime Crisis," burst onto the American market in the summer of 2007 and developed into an overall worldwide economic crisis. Its opening shot was in September 2008, with the collapse of Lehman Brothers Investment Bank and the nationalization of AIG Insurance Company. The panic peaked in October and November 2008, during which the market lost some 30% of its value (yes, October once again...). Prices continued dropping until they reached their low in March 2009. In the final run, in just eighteen months from the October 2007 peak, the market lost 57.4% of its value.

The source of the crisis, as with the 1929 Crash, is in the decade of almost unlimited credit at low interest rates given to anyone who asked for it, as well as in the real estate market which developed into a boom, then burst and dragged worldwide lending banks down with it.

Crises of the Past Decade (S&P 500 Index)

The Dot-Com Crash began in [1] March 2000, dropped until [2] September 2002, and lost a total of 46% value. From this point the market rose to a peak [3] in October 2007. The Sub-Prime Crash [4] began in October-November 2008, reaching its lowest point [5] in March 2009.

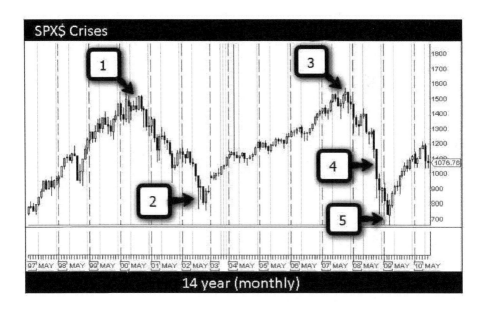

Crises and Traders

During crises, market fluctuation and trade volume increase, and therefore we, the traders, flourish at such times! Unlike the majority of the public, we also know how to profit from drops: further on we will study the principles of shorting. The first crisis I experienced as a trader was the Dot-Com Crash of 2000 to 2002. Unfortunately, as a novice trader, I was insufficiently experienced to benefit from the events, but I did benefit from the rises that followed. The Sub-Prime Crisis, by comparison, was a real celebration. In October 2008, I tripled my trading account in one month alone!

Who's Selling to You?

When you buy or sell a stock, someone is on the other side, selling to you or buying from you. Who is that person, what's his or her role, and what's guiding him or her?

"Market Makers"

When you want to buy or sell a stock, you need someone with whom to make that transaction. Have you ever thought about what might happen if you want to sell, but there's no buyer? At what price would the sale order be executed? Can you and several more sellers cause the crash of a stock because, for a short period, there was no buyer on the other side? Market makers are the people always willing to fulfill the role of "the other party," even if they don't buy and sell the way you do. The role of market makers is to constantly stand behind the stock. They set buy and sell orders in advance, with fixed spreads, and hence, they "make the market" for that stock.

How do market makers profit? Their profit derives from the spread (the difference) between the sale and purchase prices. For a company with a volume of millions of stocks per day, a profit of one cent can amount to $10,000 per day for every million shares traded. Not a bad income at all!

It's not always that simple in the market makers' world. They take no small amount of risks in that the stock moves in the opposite direction from the actions they execute. On the NASDAQ exchange, to ensure that the market will remain competitive and that the spreads set by the market makers will remain as limited as possible, the stock exchange encourages activity by a large number of market makers for the same stock. When a specific stock is being handled by dozens of market makers, the individual investor is assured of high volume and competitive spreads.

Specialists

Specialists are the NYSE's version of NASDAQ's market makers. In contrast to the NASDAQ, in the NYSE each stock is allocated to only one specialist. The specialist may be allocated several stocks to trade simultaneously, but each stock will be traded by only that single specialist.

Specialists hold a dual role. Firstly, they must provide reasonable liquidity when there are no buyers or sellers for the stock, by buying and selling to their own accounts. This prevents fluctuation during periods when there are no other buyers or sellers. Secondly, they serve as brokers for the brokers, by setting buy and sell orders and carrying them out at the best price possible, known as "best execution." For example: when a certain broker is interested in executing a sell order for a client for a stock priced at $50, but the client's order is to buy at $49 in the hope that the stock will drop to this level, the specialist keeps the order on his or her book, called "booking the order," and executes it when the price reaches the client's preference. The law requires that specialists must respect the client's interests over their own at all times. Until just a few years ago, prior to computerization, every buy and sell order went through a specialist. Currently, most NYSE executions take place via automated trading, similar to the NASDAQ format.

The ECN Revolution

The role of market makers and specialists is important, but it's not as though they work for free. The fact is that they make their profits from the spread between the bid and ask, which means that we pay their price.

An ECN (Electronic Communication Network) allows us to forego their intermediate services. The ECN is a network of computers that allows buyers and sellers to connect and set buy and sell orders without the "mediation" of market makers. ECNs began operations in 1969 with the very first system known as "Instinet," which initially was used only by the market makers for transactions between one another.

Due to the lack of liquidity that led to the 1987 collapse, laws were passed forcing market makers to respect electronic orders. These laws saw the first usage of ECN systems by the public. Currently, the majority of orders we execute are placed through ECNs.

Stock traders, in contrast to investors, use "Direct Access" trading programs, which we'll study later on. Through direct access programs, we can choose to send buy or sell orders directly to market makers, or to the range of ECN systems. Another popular option is to use the services of a broker who will automatically choose the most suitable direct access channel for you in terms of execution speed and cost.

So How is All This Connected to You?

At the basic level, none of this needs to interest you. You can open an account with a broker, deposit your money, and learn how to buy and sell stocks. As long as you're trading only in small quantities of several hundred shares per click, you can use your broker's auto-routing and ignore all the background activity. When you develop into a more serious trader and increase your quantities, known as positions, to thousands of shares per click, you'll come across instances where you'll receive only part of the quantities you require (partial executions) and often at prices higher than you wished. For large positions, it's worth routing your orders to different destinations in order to gain speed and liquidity. But it will take some time to get to that stage, and by then you will be more familiar with and better understand additional routing options and their significance.

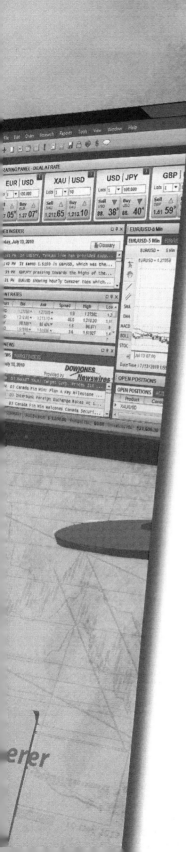

2

Day Trading and

How to Get Started

Stage by Stage on the Road to Fame

Are You Disciplined?

This is the stage where you need to maintain self-discipline. The rules of stock trading are simple, but because of our personality quirks, everyone still tends to behave differently. The average person's psychological behavior does not match the behavior of the market. Greed, on one hand, and fear on the other cause us to react in precisely the opposite manner than is required. From now on, you'll need to accept and respect these rules undisputedly.

Eight Stages on Your Path to Success

1. Don't read too much instructional material. This book will be all you need. Information-overload will take you out of focus and confuse you. After some months of trading, once you've gained experience and internalized the basic principles, then read more.
2. Find an experienced personal mentor who can walk you through your initial steps, or join a course. Self-study is not a sufficient solution. Just as driving can't be learned only by reading a textbook, so it is with trading.
3. Before trading with real money, ask your broker for a demo system that will let you practice. *Be diligent about using the demo for no more than a few days.* Using it for longer creates the dangerous illusion that you're immune to any kind of psychological effects resulting from the pressures of trading in real money. Believe me, you're far from immune!
4. Open an account with a broker and deposit a sum suited to your financial abilities. You should absolutely not deposit a sum of money that will endanger your financial status. A too-large amount will cause you tremendous psychological pressure and lead you to break discipline, with dreadful results.

5. Don't trade alone. You're still far from ready! Make sure you have ongoing, real time follow-up. Join an online trading room and listen to what experienced traders have to say. Then try to emulate their actions.

6. Trade in small quantities. You're not safe from errors. Your initial goal is to successfully conquer the market while trading in small quantities and creating minimal profits or losses, all for the sake of your learning curve and not for getting rich quick. Only when you have greater control and stable profitability should you increase the amount.

7. Keep a trading diary in which you list every action you take, with notes and conclusions (to be discussed further). When we don't write the details down, we forget them.

8. Read this book a second time once you have some experience. Only in the second reading and having traded with real money will you understand the significance of the assistance this book offers. Read the book a third time one year later.

Don't try to learn alone. It never ends happily...

What's your profession? Engineering? Law? Computer technician? No matter what it is, I'm sure you invested serious study time, whether it was a technical course for computer repair or long years in academic institutions. I'm sure you never thought you could be a successful professional without studying and then devoting more time to internship. It always amazes me that people think they can succeed in stock trading without investing in their studies!

It's amazing to discover that most of the independent traders never bothered to study in any formal framework. In one of the most complex professions around, most of the people active in the capital markets rely on their gut feeling and luck.

SMART MONEY	*When we manage other people's money, we feel obligated to study. When it comes to managing our own, we behave recklessly and even negligently.*

When we handle someone else's money, we feel the need to study, but when it comes to our own, we behave irrationally and rely on a "third sense" to get it right. How strange it is that we lose our faith in education when it comes to our own funds. This must be one of the oddest phenomena in human behavior. Stock trading is a profession like any other. It is also one of the few professions that can bring you sweet, swift financial success. But when it comes to your own money, you shouldn't be thinking about the opportunities, but rather the risks! Remember, every time you buy a stock, someone else is selling it to you. Sometimes I'm the seller. Are inexperienced buyers on the other side of the transaction so certain they can beat me and take my money and that of other pros like me? Professional traders like me have all paid seriously with our time and money for this education and experience. I have news for you: we have no intention of letting anyone beat us!

Have you heard the claim that ninety percent of traders lose? It's one hundred percent correct! In fact, I'm sure the number is even higher. The greater majority of those losing traders are people who think they can trade without learning the trade! There's no need for a license or diploma to become a day trader. The conditions for joining the profession are simple, and anyone without the slightest previous experience can learn to uphold them: open a trading account, deposit funds, buy, and sell. Anyone filling these criteria can be defined as a "day trader." Is it any wonder, then, that the probability of success is so low? I was there too, and made the same mistake. I faced failure any number of times. It would have placed me squarely in the sad statistic of losers. I survived, but no more than ten percent of new traders will be stubborn enough to survive. The ones that do, accruing experience and knowledge, are the ones that will profit from the funds of those who don't invest in knowledge. My job is to ensure that you learn, and that you join the winners. The more you learn, the greater your chances of success.

You can acquire theory from books, but you need more than that. You need to take a course. Courses cost money, but they save you more than you spend. Sometimes, a tip from an experienced instructor is worth far more than the cost of the course. Even if you feel that you already have that basic knowledge and fairly broad experience in the capital markets, the additional information you will learn in a course is worth the effort of joining one. Without an optimal education, you'll be forced to rely on your good luck. And if that's the case, you might as well forget trading and just take a joy ride to Las Vegas. There, at least, you'll lose with a smile as you sip drinks on the house.

Hardware, Software, and the Internet

Reliable hardware is an essential link. It is very worthwhile making a clear distinction between the old home-use computer containing tens of programs and possibly even dormant viruses, and your trading computer, though that's not a necessity at the outset.

SMART MONEY	*An effective computer and screens are the most important tools in trading.*

Initially, it's enough to use a home computer with a single screen. As you progress, it is recommended that you switch to a high-quality computer linked to four screens, each a minimum of 21 inches, but preferably a 23 inch size. Further on, I will show you my work station and detail the function of each screen.

Hi-speed Internet is vital for the execution speed of orders. Internet connection reliability is crucial. Remember, though, that communications breakdowns are part and parcel of day trading, but they can be greatly reduced if hi-speed, reliable connections are secured.

The Advantage of the Group: Using Trading Rooms

Stock trading is easier to perform when you're part of a group. A novice trader will find it difficult to go it alone in locating suitable stocks, making the best decisions, and maintaining high level self-discipline. In an online trading room in which many others are also active, the novice trader finds solutions for all these problems.

Trading rooms are not a new invention, even if the online versions are. Professional literature has been discussing them for at least the past 150 years. They were always the places where traders swapped views, got help or instruction, and tips on hot stocks. Joining a trading room helps overcome one of the biggest issues faced by the day trader: self-discipline. When a large group makes a joint decision, it will usually be far more correct than the decision of the lone novice trader.

I joined an online trading room in my first year of trading. I remember listening to the analyst, as the trading room's instructors are known, and thirstily absorbing every word he said. As the years passed, I too became an analyst of that very same trading room, and later the head analyst of the Tradenet room.

Have I already mentioned that you don't need to leave the house in order to join the trading room? In the distant past, trading rooms were crowded physical places: noisy, filled with the smoke of umpteen cigars and cigarettes. Over time, they became crowded computer rooms, just as noisy and just as smoke-filled. Now they exist on the Internet, where you can join a large group of traders in the comfort of your own home environment. You gain all the advantages of a real time trading room without the smoke and the noise. Actually, several years ago when I described the wonders of the Internet trading room to a group of traders, one turned to me and expressed his interest in joining, provided I could promise him "they don't smoke there!"

And what's the role of the novice trader in the online trader room? Very simple: to listen, learn, and copy the pros as much as possible. Clear and easy. The novice will encounter experienced traders, listen to their discussions as they trade, learn from their actions, and receive real time support as needed. Even experienced pros have trouble trading without a trading room. About half of the actions I take on any given day derive from ideas expressed by other traders in the room. Even if they're relatively new traders, they can still raise some effective ideas.

| **SMART MONEY** | *The online trading room is a chat room that links other stock traders' homes. In the online trading room, you will listen, learn, and execute transactions together with the pros.* |

Trading rooms also have their disadvantages. The diversity of trading methods and the professional jargon that dominates the discussions can set a novice's head spinning. When you join the trading room, you will first need to learn that jargon, and only then try to focus on the methods best suited to you. Over time, you should be able to adopt the most appropriate method and stick with it. If you try to imitate too many methods as used by various analysts, you'll get nowhere fast. Bottom line, you'll need to find the niche that matches your nature, focus on it, and ignore the "white noise"of traders and analysts that you feel are not a good match.

That's also exactly how you should relate to the diverse information you'll find in this book. If you try to utilize it all simultaneously, you'll end up using none of it. Focusing is an important trait. Expanding your knowledge can be done over the long term as you accumulate experience and confidence. Highlight that sentence and come back to it in a year's time. Right now, it means little. In a year, you'll understand.

Tradenet runs online trading rooms at various levels, suited to beginners and advanced traders, and in various languages. These serve traders in different countries. The trading rooms are a service, and carry a fee. For the professional trader earning his or her living from the market, the service is vital and its cost marginal, but for the beginner, the cost seems high. Think of it as part of your tuition.

Your Guide to Opening a Trading Account

When you buy a stock, for both technological and regulatory reasons, you need the services of an agent known as the **broker**. The broker mediates between you and the stock exchange. When you deposit your money with your chosen brokerage company, you receive (usually free of charge) trading software that connects your buy and sell orders to the various stock exchange computers.

The broker might be the bank that enables buying and selling stocks along with additional banking services, or it may be an independent company specializing solely in providing brokerage services. Usually a specialized broker will be cheaper and more effective than the bank.

In the not too distant past, people wishing to buy or sell stocks had to take themselves off to the broker's offices, wait in a queue, and pay a hefty commission. In short, a loss of no small amount of money even before the stock rose by just one cent. Active traders bought and sold stocks at cheaper prices through phone calls with the broker's transaction room, and highly active traders set up expensive communications systems connecting them directly with the various brokers. Those days are well over. The Internet revolution brought the stock exchange directly into the personal computer of every single person in the world who wishes to buy and sell stocks. In fact, the public now has access to the most advanced trading systems which, not so long ago, served only the professionals. Data that once could be accessed by only the privileged few is now open to public use.

As the Internet continued to develop, trading programs developed, procedures were totally computerized, and commissions dropped. The minimum commission when I started out as trader stood at $15, and it's now $1.50 with ample room for it to drop further. The more the commission fees dropped, the more useless brokers' phone-in transaction rooms became. Rooms that were populated by tens if not hundreds of employees turned into a desert of screens and computers, serving only a small number of traders who still have not internalized the Internet revolution, and are willing to pay exorbitant commissions for an unnecessary phone call. Commission markdowns and Internet penetration, together with new technological developments such as mobile phone applications that allow buying and selling, have led the trading world to the portals of additional population strata.

How to Open an Account with a Broker

Opening a stock trading account is a simple procedure. All you need is to complete several forms and add a color scan of your current valid passport, and a utility bill such as from the electricity company or a bank statement proving your current address. Every broker will be happy to help you complete the process in one brief phone call. When the forms are certified after the broker has checked the data, the broker will provide you with details of the bank account to which you transfer money. Usually 24 to 48 hours later, your account with the broker will be credited. The broker will then send you an email with installation instructions for the trading platform and an initial password which you can later change. When you first operate the trading platform through your dedicated password, you will be able to see your deposit in your account, awaiting your order. If you surf to the broker's site, you can then use the same password to view your execution history. The entire process should take between one to five days to complete.

Can Your Bank Be Your Broker?

Theoretically, yes. Practically, no. Yes, because every bank is a broker that also enables you to buy stocks in every stock exchange. Yes, because your money is already held by the bank, and you therefore have no need to transfer it to a separate broker's account. Nonetheless, several problems arise. Banks will generally collect commissions from you that are from five to fifty times higher than those collected by specialist brokers. Banks will generally provide a limited, cumbersome trading platform that does not display real time data and is usually suited only to long-term investors, and definitely not suited to day traders. Later we will review the requirements of trading platforms. Finally, I have yet to come upon a bank able to provide you with the necessary tools.

How to Choose a Broker

Many brokers would be happy to provide you with a trading platform, but not all of them are suited to a professional trader. You need to distinguish between brokers who designate their services to the public of long-term investors, the category where most brokers fall, and those who provide web-based platforms. They are known as **Online Brokers**. Professional brokers supplying direct access platforms allow fast navigation of direct orders to any target. Professional brokers provide trading platforms which are not web-based, but which usually require downloading and installing software and allow the trader to send orders directly to the stock exchange computer without using a slow, costly method. These are called **Direct Access Brokers**. To be a successful day trader, you must work only with **Direct Access Brokers**.

How to Choose a Trading Platform

The trading platform is the most important link in the system connecting trader and broker. I know traders whose trading volume is so large that they could significantly decrease the commissions they pay if they'd move to a competing broker, but may prefer to stay with a more expensive broker because of their satisfaction with the broker's trading platform.

The trading platform lets the trader route buy and sell orders directly to the stock exchange computer. The trading platform you will use must include charting which will help you follow stock rates in real time.

SMART MONEY	*Commissions aren't the main consideration when choosing a trading platform. Execution speed and reliability are far more important to the trader than the commission charged.*

Just as a skilled carpenter will not compromise on the quality of the saw, so a professional day trader will never compromise on the quality of the trading platform, as any such compromise will end up being very costly. Think for a moment about what might happen if a trader wanted to buy a stock at the breakout point, but the order is delayed and the transaction is missed because the stock has risen higher than the requested price. The trader's frustration will be immense.So will the long-term financial damage.

The **direct access system** lets the trader buy and sell stocks direct from any destination with liquidity at the moment of execution. If the trader wishes to do so, the order can be routed directly to an **ECN** which provides the stock exchange's liquidity. Alternately, the trader can direct the transaction directly to the market makers. There are advantages and disadvantages with direct routing to any destination according to the quantity of shares needed and the speed of execution, but the direct access system leaves that choice in the trader's domain, which is how it should be. For the most part, the trader will prefer executions of up to several thousand shares, considered a large amount, routing the orders via the broker's automated routing system. The system will automatically find the cheapest and most rapid route much faster than the trader can. For a professional trader, a delay of one or two seconds can in some cases mark the difference between profit and loss. In other instances where the quantities are large or the commission is more significant than the execution speed (a method we'll learn about later), the trader may want to route the order direct to the market makers.

It is very clear that a trading system supporting direct access is far better and more effective. If so, why is it that most brokers don't allow direct access? More on that later.

With Which Brokers Should You Never Work?

The online broker, unlike the direct access broker, is interested in delaying the execution of transactions. If a transaction is delayed, it could lodge even greater profit in the broker's pocket beyond the regular commission: for example, imagine a situation in which a client sells 1000 Microsoft stocks and simultaneously another client with the same broker wants to buy 1000 Microsoft stocks. The broker will prefer to execute the order between the two clients without needing to relay it to the stock exchange computer. Closing the transaction internally saves the broker costs, and sometimes even makes the broker additional profit from the spread (difference) between the bid (purchase) and ask (sale) prices. A spread of one cent over 1000 stocks means $10 more profit beyond the regular commission that the broker collects from both of the clients making the transaction. To create opportunities where the broker can execute orders in-house, the broker may be tempted to delay execution for several seconds. This is insignificant for the long-term investor, but intolerable for the day trader. In addition, when online brokers relay your order to the market, they will choose the destination cheapest for themselves. Usually these are market makers who will share their profits with brokers. The cheapest destination is not necessarily bad for you and can sometimes be a faster route, but your preferences as a trader are different from those of the broker. You want speed and liquidity; brokers want profit.

SMART MONEY	*Online brokers collect rebates for execution, therefore profit more if they delay execution and route orders to destinations that are cheaper for the broker.*

Should You Trade on Margin?

A margin is a loan that brokers provide to traders. As with every loan, margin bears interest, unless the trader makes use of it only during the course of the trading day, in which case no interest is paid.

When a client opens an account with a broker, the client can choose a **margin account** or a **cash account**. A margin account allows you to buy stocks at a multiple of four times your money: for example, if you deposited $30,000 in your account, you will be able to buy intraday (in one day's trading) stocks valued at $120,000. In other words, the margin carries a 4:1 ratio.

By contrast, if you want to hold stocks overnight, perhaps fearing that the stock price may change in the course of two days' trading, you will need to be satisfied with a 2:1 margin. This sets your buying power at $60,000. If you use this doubled buying power between two trading days, you will be charged interest. Clearly it is worthwhile using the intraday margin during one trading day, as you will pay no interest. I support using margin beyond one day of trading, despite the interest charged, because the trading method that holds for several days is based on aggressive profit goals of several percent, which means the annual interest charged allows a higher expected profit. Margin allows you to work with higher sums than your regular cash balances allow.

SMART MONEY	*Margins are dangerous if you don't know how to use them, but a real gift when you manage them correctly.*

Margin also has its disadvantages. Let's say you deposited $10,000 in your account and bought 1000 shares at $10 each, using all your deposit. In other words, you've used your own deposit without using any margin. A drop of 25% in a stock price from $10 to $7.5 will cause you a loss of $2500, or 25% of your money. On the other hand, if you use a 4:1

margin, buying 4000 shares for $40,000 followed by a drop of 25% in price will cause $10,000 worth of damage and wipe out your account! And what would have happened if you'd slept on Lehman Bros stocks after the Sub-Prime Crisis when they plummeted to $3 and the next day were worth mere cents? When you sleep on a margin of 2:1 and the stock price drops more than 50%, this is the stage in which you are losing not only your own money but that of the broker too. The broker's job, of course, is to prevent risks of this kind. This is why brokers maintain a risk department whose job it is to keep tabs on your account and warn of potentially hazardous situations. In actuality, it rarely happens that a client loses more than the amount in his or her account.

Does margin sound risky? To experienced professionals, not at all. They will never endanger more than a pre-defined sum of money. This sum, which they are willing to risk, will have nothing to do with margin. As we will learn further on, they use **stop orders** as protection, and plan in advance the maximum dollar loss they are willing to absorb. They never absorb losses of tens of percent, and never endanger their trading account. If you remain disciplined and operate according to the rules, you will learn as we progress, and margin will become a gift at your service when wisely used. By contrast, if you are not sufficiently self-disciplined and have a tendency to gamble, beware!

Brokers are at risk and do not share in the profits you can make from margin: so why would they bother to provide you with margin? There are two main reasons. The first is the fact that interest is profit. When you buy on margin beyond the trading day on which you purchased the stock, you pay interest, from which the brokers make a profit. The second reason is that the greater the sum of money accessible to you, the more probable it is that you will execute more transactions with greater volume. Why would you be happy with buying just 200 shares if you can profit from buying 800? In short, margin benefits both sides: the trader can put in just one quarter of the amount needed and enhance his or her potential on each trade by double or quadruple, while the brokers benefit from greater volume of activity which creates more commissions.

As a day trader, I'm very active within the day's trading hours and often use the entire margin capability available to me. I tend not to use the full margin available for purchasing one stock, but for several stocks simultaneously purchased: for example, I might buy stock A without any margin, identify a good opportunity, and buy stock B with margin, and possibly even stock C and D until my money's full margin is maximized.

When I sleep on a stock for a range of several days, it will usually be after successfully taking a partial profit of at least 75% of the shares I bought. The same would apply, too, if I slept on four different stocks: I would use almost no margin.

Summarizing: the disadvantage of margin is the interest it bears beyond one day's trading and the risk of losing four times more than you might have lost if trading without the margin. In actuality, the risk is no higher, as we will learn later, as there is little significance to the sum with which you're trading as long as you use stop orders that limit the amount any transaction can lose. The advantage of margin is that you don't need to make a much larger deposit in order to trade with higher sums. In light of the dangers inherent to using margin, day trading rules prevent brokers supervised by American regulations to provide margin greater than a 4:1 ratio on any single trading day and a 2:1 ratio for more than one day. In fact, the condition for being allowed to use margin is that you are required to deposit a minimum of $25,000 in your account. In any case, even if you do find a way to reach higher margin, as new traders I would advise you to make do with the 4:1 ratio. A too-high margin might go out of control in risky situations where you feel you absolutely "must have" a certain stock. That's precisely when it's best to take a deep breath and minimize the risk. A reasonable margin prevents mishaps of this kind. In short, be satisfied with a little less and you will save a great deal.

How Much Should be Deposited in the Trading Account?

As noted, United States regulations prevent day trading to people with less than $25,000 in their accounts. Day trading is defined as making more than four transactions over five successive trading days. US citizens wishing to operate as day traders must deposit that minimum figure. In actuality, the day trader must deposit more, because the very first loss that brings the total below $25,000 will limit the trader to no more than four transactions over five successive days. This rule does not apply, however, to citizens of other countries on condition that they operate via brokers whose center of activities is not within the US, and on condition that the broker is regulated outside the US.

US brokers offer their services mainly to US clients, and therefore do not match the attitudes of citizens from other countries. In other words, even if you aren't a US resident, you will still suffer the limitations placed on US citizens and will need to deposit a minimum of $25,000 to trade daily. With this in mind, I would recommend that if you choose to open an account with a US broker, you deposit at least $30,000 so that any losses you may absorb will not limit your activities.

SMART MONEY | *The more money you deposit in your trading account, the more you increase your chances of success. "More money" is a relative value based on your changing financial abilities and the risk level you acclimate to.*

Trading CFD's

What is a CFD? A CFD (Contract for Difference) is a contract between a "buyer" and a "seller" certifying that the seller will pay the buyer the difference between the stock price at time of purchase and its price at time of sale. In other words, buying a CFD allows the buyer to profit (or lose) from the difference in stock price without actually buying the stock itself.

Under certain conditions, as described below, and if your broker allows you to choose between stock or CFD trading, choose CFD without a moment's hesitation! CFD is executed in exactly the same way as stock trading. In fact, if your broker does not expressly state what you're trading in, I'm prepared to vouch for the fact that you wouldn't even sense the difference.

So how does CFD trading differ from stock trading? When you buy stocks, you buy them through the stock exchange from a person interested in selling them at the exact same time you've decided to buy. One of the biggest issues with the stock exchange is the scope of supply and demand. But we don't always find the buyer or seller with the required amount, and we often need to "chase the stock." Chasing stock generally costs us both money and health. But when you buy CFD, you're not buying stock at the exchange; you're buying a contract identical to the stock from your broker.

The advantage of this method is that your broker can allow you to buy or sell any quantity without linking it to stock exchange liquidity.

Think of it this way: Let's say you want to buy 1000 shares, but sellers are currently only offering 100. You would have to wait for additional sellers, or possibly pay a higher price for additional stock. When you trade in CFDs you are not limited by quantity, and therefore the instant you hit BUY, you receive the full amount you wanted even if that supply of shares is not currently available in the stock exchange. Similarly, when you wish to sell 1000 shares, you will not have to wait for buyers to take the full quantity. You just sell by hitting the SELL button. If you have experience in the market, as I have, you must agree that it's impossible to tag this method with any description other than "amazing!"

Have you ever heard the claim that students in trading courses who use the "demo" (which allows practicing how to trade without actually involving money) almost always profit? That's a true claim. One of the main reasons explaining their success is the fact that training programs, like CFD trading platforms, do not limit the trader to market liquidity. You press the button – you've bought! You press the button – you've sold! Any quantity, and at lightning speed. Traders in the real market can only dream of such immediacy. Ask any experienced trader what his or her biggest problem is, and probably the complaint topping the list will be speed of execution and liquidity.

More Benefits of CFD Trading

No limit on shorts – In the stock market, some stocks carry limits on shorts. That's not true for CFDs. Nor is there any uptick limit which, in the real market, limits the broker's ability to execute shorts unless the stock rises by one cent.

High execution speed – Buy and sell orders of regular stock go through a long process where the order is sent to the broker, who sends it to the stock exchange, and back. CFD trading is between you and your broker alone, making execution super-fast.

High level margin – CFD brokers are not limited to the usual scope of leverage on stock and can therefore let you margin up to 20:1. How does that translate? If you deposit a sum of $10,000 in your trading account, you can execute trades up to a total of $200,000. A word of warning: high leverage is a blessing to very experienced traders, but can be extremely dangerous for new traders.

What to Check before Choosing Your CFD Broker

Buy/sell spread – You need to check if you broker allows you to trade in regular market spreads. In other words, check that he does not "open" the spread between the seller and buyer price beyond what is shown in the stock exchange where the real share is being traded. I know of CFD brokers who, instead of taking execution commissions, open the spreads by three to ten cents and even more. In this regard I can say that the broker I use, COLMEX, allows me to trade in real market spreads.

Diversity of Stock – Some 10,000 stocks are traded on the American stock exchanges. Of these, for a variety of reasons such as volume of activity, only about 2000 are suited to CFD trading. Check with your broker how many can be CFD traded. Some brokers only offer a small range, some offer dozens or a few hundred, and some, like COLMEX, offer a few thousand, which is all that's needed for trading.

Summing up, I note the interesting fact that CFD trading is legal, accepted, and supervised by the regulatory authorities in most countries in the world except the USA. If CFD trading is so good for traders, why is it blocked to USA traders? Simply, as I explained above, a CFD doesn't trade the stock itself. If all market activity focused on CFDs instead of trading in stock, the stock exchange would lose its main raison d'etre: recruiting capital for companies.

In short, if you live outside of the USA, you might prefer to open a CFD account after checking with your broker that they offer real market spread, a reasonable commission and a broad supply of stock. If you live in the USA, the only way to trade in CFD is by joining a group of **proprietary traders** operating outside America, who may be looking for traders, including Americans, to broaden their trading base.

A Word of Warning

For good reason, the United States has set day trade regulations requiring a minimum of $25,000. In the past, when this standard was determined, commissions were far higher. When the minimum commission stood at tens of dollars per transaction, the trader had no choice but to operate in large amounts of money to offset the impact of these commissions. If a trader did not have a serious deposit in the account, the commissions would gobble up all the trader's profits. Now, with commissions far lower and the minimum currently at about $1.50, the trader can buy and sell small quantities without lessening his or her chances of success. In some countries where Tradenet is active, such as areas of Eastern Europe, the monthly profit target is $1000, which equates to twice the average monthly salary. In short: America is not the whole world, nor is the entire world American.

Nonetheless, relative to the profit levels and your cost of living, years of experience have taught me that the higher the initial deposit, the greater your survivability and reaching success.

Are You Personally Acquainted with Your Broker?

It's completely natural to be wary over depositing your money into the bank account of a broker you don't know. If you want to sleep better at night, knowing your money is safe, check whether the broker you've chosen operates within the framework of regulations. This means your money, like that of others, is supervised, separated from the broker's own ongoing activities, and insured. The insurance provided should not be that of the broker, but of a reliable, external organization. Clients of US brokers are meant to be insured by federal insurance up to a framework of $100,000 in their accounts, while clients of European Union brokers enjoy the automatic cover of the ICF (Investor Compensation Fund) for up to a €20,000 deposit. The ICF covers all of Europe and insures every deposit up to this figure, in every European financial organization.

Broker Support: What You'll Get, and What You Won't

Imagine this: the US Federal Reserve Bank publicizes an important economic notice creating a financial turmoil. Traders, investors, institutions and market makers stream multiple orders into the stock exchange's computers. The outcome: system failure and immense difficulty in getting orders executed. This kind of situation shouldn't bother you in any way, unless you're a day trader holding a particular stock and your only interest is fleeing from it as early as possible.

But bad luck strikes: all systems are stuck and you need to call the broker's client service. Due to the crash, you probably aren't the only ones phoning your broker at that very moment: that means you'll be spending long Muzak minutes until call is finally picked up. Sounds like a nightmare? Experienced traders know these and similar scenarios well.

Admittedly, systems these days are highly reliable. Such situations are rare, but breakdowns can happen. Remember that breakdowns and glitches are part and parcel of the life of a day trader. Try to choose a broker who will respond quickly for no more than the cost of a local call. That's the kind of broker who can save you a lot of money, and help give you peace of mind.

Summary

Whittle down your list of potential brokers according to points you assign each one based on the following:

1. Is the broker well-known and with long-term experience, operating

according to the regulations?

2. Do the regulations under which the broker operates provide for insurance of your money? If so, up to what amount is covered?
3. What is the minimum execution cost?
4. How much will you pay beyond the minimum? (usually a fixed price per stock)
5. Does your broker allow you to deposit less than $25,000 and still allow you to day trade?
6. Does your broker allow you to trade on margin?
7. Does the broker collect a fixed monthly fee for providing a trading platform? If so, how much?
8. Does the broker collect a fixed monthly fee for providing information of any kind?
9. Does the broker's trading platform allow you to observe real time charts?
10. Does the broker's trading platform allow direct access to stock exchanges?
11. Is the broker's trading platform a downloaded, installed, dedicated application, or is it only web-based?
12. Will your broker let you "paper trade", known as practicing on a "demo platform"?

Once you've found a broker of your liking, check his website for where to begin the process of opening your trading account. Once that's completed, deposit your money, receive the trading platform, and continue with the learning process described in this book, while learning the platform you've chosen.

of a broker who will automatically choose the most suitable direct access channel for you in terms of execution speed and cost.

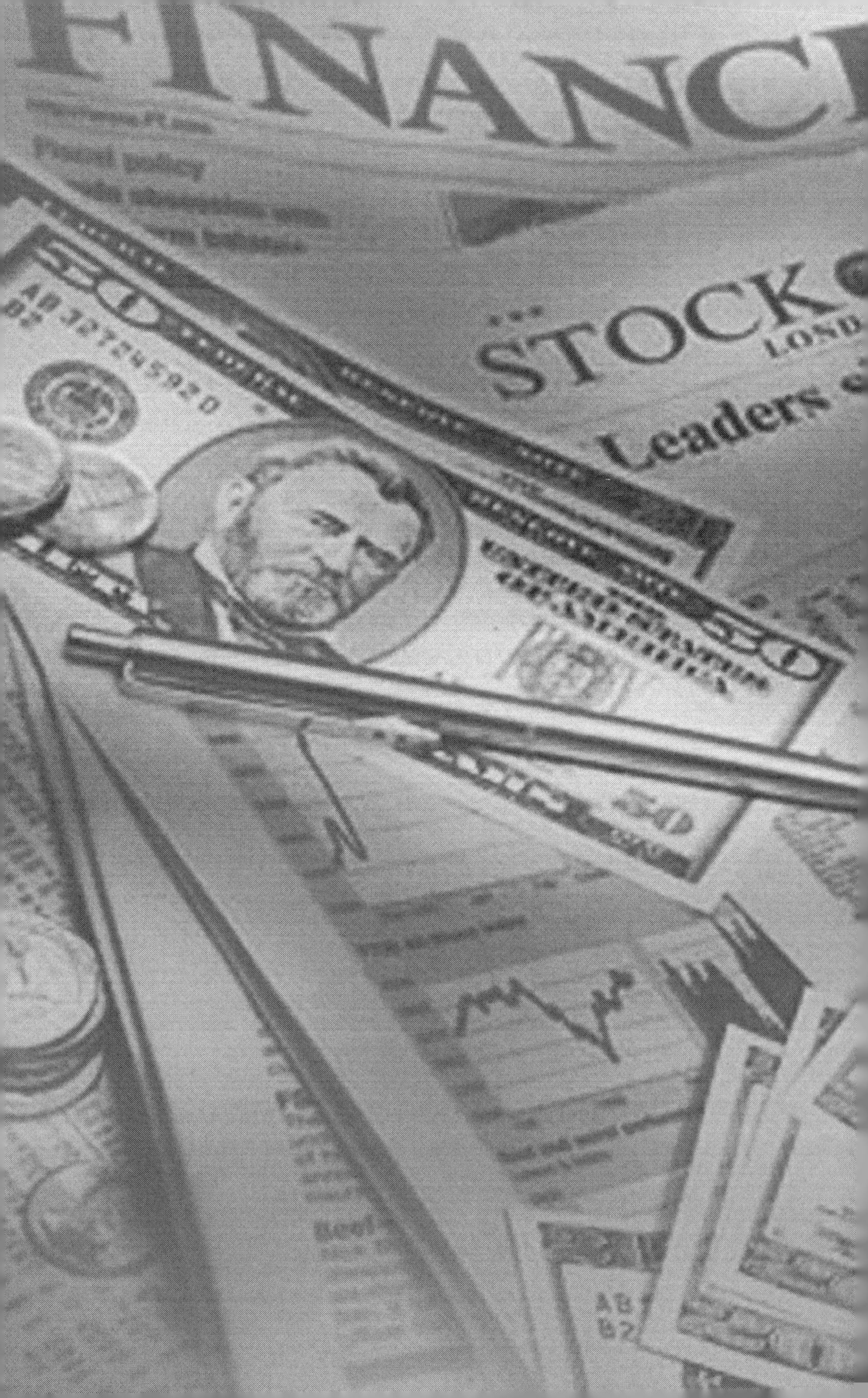
FINANC
STOCK
Leaders

3

Market Analysis

Fundamentals

Prices move in only three directions: up, down & sideways.

The Price Says It All!

The stock market is like a huge giant that constantly changes its appearance. Every trading day is different from the preceding one,and every trading hour is different from the hour before. As the ancient Greek philosopher Heraclitus once said, "You cannot step in the same river twice."

The stock market is the outcome of the sum of all persons operating on and in it. Each has an individual opinion and thoughts, and individually, each pushes the market in the direction he or she is able, whether as a buyer or seller.

Can we nonetheless know what the sum total of persons operating in the market is thinking? Of course we can. A quick glance at that most important piece of information gives us the answer: the price.

A dynamic market which constantly changes is inherently challenging. Our human thinking processes are very standardized. Most people wish to demarcate concepts within boundaries, and sort and catalog things, whereas the market is highly dynamic. To cope with this challenge, you will need to become closely familiar with the market, the principles of stock trading, and how markets behave. This will enable you to establish your own work program, your own rules and limitations, and apply them when you join the market.

The Market Is Always Right!

The stock market's conduct as described has given rise to two similar statements: "the market is always right" and "the price is always right." At any given moment, the market and the price consistently embody all relevant information. Don't try to argue with the market. Many before you have tried and failed. Any attempt to force your opinion or hopes on the market is predestined to failure. Even large players in the stock market, who truly have the ability to slightly shift the market, are aware of the market's forces and consider their moves with due gravity.

Over time, I also learned the purposelessness of disputing the market. For example, one of my rules (which we'll discuss further) is that on any day that I make three consecutive losses, I stop trading. My experience has taught me that if I continue, I just keep losing, since the psychological impact of three losses at a time makes me try to force my will on the market.In that battle, I can assure you, the market will always come out on top.

Market Forces: Bidders and Askers

Understanding the market means first understanding the forces controlling it: in other words, gaining a deeper understanding of the interests of buyers (bidders) and sellers (askers) and the impact of their interests. It is customary to say that if bidders control the market, the price of a stock rises, and if sellers are controlling, the stock price will drop. This is true in general, but too simplified and appropriate to a novice trader or amateur investor. We know that bidders want to buy cheaply, and sellers want to sell for the highest price they can get. For investment banks, who buy and sell for institutional clients and are remunerated according to the bid and ask prices they procure for the clients, buying cheaply and selling at higher prices gets translated into action. We, the small traders, can do nothing but follow in their footsteps.

Let's take a look at the following: one fine morning, a trader in a large investment house on Wall Street is instructed to buy 500,000 stocks of Company X. In anyone's view, that's a lot of stocks... Will Company X's stocks open on that same day with a rise or a drop in rate? The answer depends on multiple factors, but because the bidder wants to buy a huge amount of stocks at the cheapest price possible, the bidder will first try to make the stock price drop. The bidder may start the day by selling a large quantity of stocks as soon as trading opens, igniting a wave of sales. When the stock drops to a price that is sufficiently low in the bidder's view, the bidder will then start buying. Simply put, the buyer's control over the stock caused it to drop instead of rise. A trader following the stock's movement may accidentally think the stock is facing a day of downward-spiraling prices, when in actuality that was only at the start, followed by rising prices for the rest of the day.

"Go in! Go in!"... When Does the Public Buy?

Sunrays are peeping through the window of Average Investor's home. Good morning! Mr. Average heads for the kitchen, makes coffee, and pulls a few cookies from the box. Heading toward the family room, Average detours to pick up the newspaper tossed at his doorstep earlier and eyes the headline: "Hot Stock Exchange: The Five Top Stocks." Actually, that's a good reason to move away from the stocks, but we'll explain that later. For now, Average is sipping his coffee, turns on the television and watches a morning show. The word from the sponsors ends, and the emcee asks, "And how did our money do this week?" We're shown an investment house. The presenter sums up the week's events, ending with the statement: "The stock market is boiling. The public is streaming in." That's actually another good reason to take caution, but more on that later.

SMART MONEY | *The public buys stocks at their peak price. Sometimes the stocks continue to rise, but mostly the publi c holds onto them long enough for them to begin dropping, and the public absorbs the loss.*

An hour passes. The insufferable thought runs through Average's mind: everyone's in and making millions in profit and he's the only sucker still on the outside. That's when the decision comes: "It's about time my money worked for me, too!" says Average to himself, and decides to buy. He puts the cookies back in the box and calls his investment consultant.

Why is Mr. Average Investor buying? Is it because someone recommended that action, or because it's "in the media?" Does Mr. Average know what to buy? When to sell? Which stocks to be wary of? Would you buy a refrigerator or car in the same frivolous way? Perhaps your investment advisor knows what and when to buy? From my acquaintanceship with investment advisors, I'd say that 99% of them have no idea what to buy. In fact, the person has yet to be born who knows with certainty whether a stock will go up or down in the longterm. I don't know, either.

The public tends to buy because of social pressure: others are buying, or a friend suggested it, or for fear of being the only one left out. The public will never be the first one in to buy a stock that has only just begun going up. A stock's potential to rise in the short term is usually identified only by the professionals. The public observes the stock which has already risen and promises to buy if it "proves" itself as strong, and continues rising. Usually the public is only convinced when the stock has already risen too far, proclaiming it a "winner." Then they step in and buy. Who, in your opinion, is selling to the public at the high price? That's right: the professionals. Even if the stock does continue rising, the public will tend to overstay, the stock will start to drop, and the public will absorb the losses.

The Role of the Professional

The pros have a clear role: they take the public's money. And they have plenty of creative ways to do that. Their biggest advantage is the fact that they're pros. That's their profession. The public generally arrives at work in the morning, answers phones, writes e-mails, and believes its money is hard at work. The public receives a salary at the end of the month, because each member of the public has a profession. Each person earns his or her income because of an advantage that has no connection to the capital market.

As with the public, so too with the professional: the pro knows that the public will behave in a certain way. The public feels pressured and sells hysterically when the market comes close to a low, and buys enthusiastically when the market's upward movement is already too tense and about to correct.

Stock exchange trading is my profession. It's a profession that does not require knowledge of economics, but rather of psychology alone. In fact, the less you know about economics, the better off you are. As an amateur psychologist, I know how to predict the public's behavior. The simple outcome is that if both of us invest in the market, the probability is higher than in most cases I will come out the winner. Just as I cannot replace a professional in some other field, there is no reason to assume that such a professional can replace me in my sphere and take my money.

The professionals are not mere stock traders. They are also fund managers and investment bankers and anyone who makes a living from the capital markets. They also have creative ways of taking the public's money. They manage it in return for management fees, commissions, and other kinds of income without ever promising any results! Based on the past, we can see that over the last twenty years, 80% of the world's managed funds earned their clients less than market index yields: in other words, fund managers know they are taking the public's funds in vain, but with every advertisement they continue to promise: "Give us your money and everything will be fine."

One simple and valid conclusion can be drawn in respect to every profession in the world: amateurism costs money, professional brings money in. The dream of money working for you is not realistic, and in best-case scenarios, works solely during occasional periods that can be pinpointed only in retrospect.

In short: no one is prepared to work **on your behalf!** If you want to earn profits, you need to press those buttons yourself. Learning is the key to success. This book is just one part of the process.

Science or Art?

There are four ways to reach a decision on transacting in stocks:
- **Technical analysis**, which is how traders operate
- Fundamental economic analysis, the method for long-term investors
- **Random walk**, the mode of operation for those who claim there is no method
- **Gambling**, the method used by the public which thinks it's found "the formula" for turning a profit

Stock trading is not an exact science. If it were, it would be handled by accountants. No method is complete in and of itself. Even if you learn a 300-page manual on technical analysis by heart, I can assure you that you'll still lose money. The winning recipe is a combination of winning components. The question then becomes: how do I proportion the components? That differs from one execution to another, from one stock to another, from one set of market conditions to the next. Getting the proportions right is, in fact, the art of trading. Stock trading is midway between an exact science and art.

Who's Afraid of Technical Analysis?

Sometimes the very title of a specific field causes people to fear it and feel alienated from it without even knowing that field's content. Too often this is the case with the phrase "technical analysis."

| **SMART MONEY** | *Technical analysis is based on observing past behavior for the sake of predicting the future. Technical analysis is based on outcomes and not on reasons.* |

The word "analysis" indicates a review process that closely studies the details, and often conjures up someone deeply engrossed in meticulously examining mounds of books, articles and papers. The word "technical" generally indicates a practical, mechanical sphere, conjuring up images of engineers in white lab coats bent over blueprints or a complex piece of equipment. Both words merged into one phrase seem to cause strong trepidation.

In fact, the field of technical analysis is far from these images. Yes, it has to be learned, just as any profession must be. Technical analysis, in fact, is simple to understand and easy to apply, especially in the area of day trading which requires only the fundamental tool that technical analysis offers. More importantly, technical analysis does not only relate to dry analysis and comprehension, but actually offers a practical method for stock trading.

So What Is Technical Analysis?

- Technical analysis is a review of graphs showing the behavior of a financial product for the purpose of forecasting future price trends
- Technical analysis focuses on price: i.e., the outcome of the totality of insights of all factors operating in the market
- Technical analysis takes no interest in the reasons for any given price

The technical trader's three basic premises are:

1. *The change in price embodies all market forces.* In other words, the stock price expresses everything that can impact the price as far as economics, psychology, politics, etc. Therefore, all that is needed is to follow the price, which reflects changes in supply and demand.
2. *Prices move in trends.* Trends are cyclical and therefore generally allow predicting their direction.
3. *History repeats itself.* For more than a century, technical analysts have been assisted by graphs plotting stock trends. Accrued information allows identifying recurring behavior patterns. Technical analysts believe that in certain situations the public's emotional reaction can be expected, and therefore the analysts presume that based on past history, future movements can be predicted.

Technical analysis alone will lead you to certain failure. Even if you study all the books ever written on the subject and can quote them by heart, and were you to write software that operates according to their doctrines, you'd still fail.

At the most, 10% of technical analysis components actually work, but not in a vacuum. If you know which of those components to isolate from all those available, and how to integrate them with other components unrelated to technical analysis, you have a good chance of succeeding. But remember, the recipe for success merges experience and art.

Fundamental Economic Analysis: What Does It Incorporate?

A fundamental investor is one who buys a company's stocks in the belief that the main source of price change will be the company's performance, which covers changes in sales turnover, profitability, demand for the company's products, management, cash flows, and more. The main tools these analysts use are the company's balance sheet, analysts' recommendations, information gleaned from the media, and hearsay. A fundamental analyst is also interested in the economic status and the status of the sector to which the stock belongs, such as software developers, semiconductors, and the like. Fundamental investors review market interest rates and try to predict their direction and their scope of change. All this data is weighed, and conclusions are reached.

These are usually long-term investors who do not expect to see their predictions realized in the short term. They therefore keep their positions in the hope of seeing them turn fruitful in the long term.

I use fundamental analysis at the level of media headlines. I don't believe in this type of analysis, but I do believe that the public, and funds, believe in it, therefore I relate to it with due respect and give it some weight in my decision-making processes. For example: let's say the public believes that the stocks of a certain biotechnology company will strengthen due to a diverse set of components. This is good enough information for me to realize I need to focus on technical trading opportunities with biotechnology stocks. In actuality, I'm merging the technical analysis with the fundamental economic analysis.

Random Walk

The theory of roaming negates all types of analysis, whether technical or economic. This theory, developed in academia, sees price change as completely random and unpredictable, and that nothing can be learned from the stock's history towards predicting its future trend. The theory is based on another called "The Efficient Market Hypothesis," according to which prices embody all information available in the market. There are no expensive or cheap stocks because the market calculates all risks and opportunities as an embodied price. The "Random Walk Hypothesis" claims that because markets are random, one should "walk" through them "randomly" [from this point on], and that the best way to profit from a stock is through a "buy and hold" action.

There is indeed a degree of randomness in the market, but to say that all price trends are random is unthinkable. Random walk theory claims that it is impossible to overcome market indices and that one would be hard-pressed to explain the success of famous investors such as Warren Buffet and Peter Lynch. Their claim, therefore, includes me and my successful trading colleagues. A well-known standing joke concerning "efficient market" theories charmingly points to its inherent Achilles' heel:

Two lecturers on economics see a $100 bill lying on the sidewalk. One bends down to pick it up, while the other says, "That's ridiculous. There's no way a $100 bill is just lying there. After all, someone else would have picked it up long ago!"

According to the Efficient Market Hypothesis, someone else certainly would have picked it up long ago, but there it is! Keep in mind that at the basis of both theories, random walk and technical analysis, is the premise that the market manifests all market factors. The difference between these two approaches is that proponents of the random walk see the market as embodying all information at high speed, therefore no one has any advantage in the market, whereas technical analysis claims that important information manifests in the market far earlier than is known to the general public.

Gambling, Anyone?

Well, this isn't actually a method. It is actually the mode of conduct of the public, which rushes to the stock exchange at its peak and flees at its slump. It is the behavioral norm of the public that generally loses money on the stock exchange. It is also sometimes the approach of inexperienced traders who do not operate according to the most basic trading rules, and do not believe in the principles they have set for themselves. Watching such traders from a distance, the observer may think they are real pros, but the dwindling account of such traders tells the true story. Even as a novice trader, be a trader, not a gambler. A sheep dressed in wolf's clothing is still a sheep inside.

Fundamental Economic Analysis Versus Technical Analysis

This long-standing dispute began when the first analyst drew a line between two points representing a stock's price changes over the axis of time, thereby creating the very first price graph.

The essence of the dispute is whether to buy a stock based on company and market performance, such as the company's balance sheet, or based on the stock's behavior as illustrated by graph alone.

Both methods attempt to predict price trends. As already noted, the fundamental economic investor examines the stock's value relative to company performance and market performance, and concludes whether its price is above or below its true value. If, in the long-term investor's opinion, the price is currently below its true value, he or she will buy, and vice versa. The technical trader does not ask "why," but tries to predict price trends according to graphs, that is, results in the real-time field.

SMART MONEY	*Integrating fundamental economic analysis with technical analysis is a winning combination. No method can operate alone, while ignoring the existence and logic of the alternative method.*

At this point, I will cease being objective and say outright that I do not believe in the sole credibility of one or another method. I believe that their integration is the winning method. In reality, I choose to be 80% technical and 20% fundamental. Most technical analysts arrived at this preference through fundamental economic analysis. I can promise you that if you try to earn profits by reading financial reports in newspapers and watching them on television programs, you will discover sooner or later that you're wasting your time.

Why do most people believe in fundamental economic analysis? Because we're educated to invest in the long term. And why is that? Very likely because someone has to make a living from teaching economics in universities, because funds must find legitimate justifications for erroneous purchases, because stock market colleges want to continue existing, because we as humans must peg everything into some kind of mathematical, organized framework, and because none of the educators are willing to admit that basically, they know just about nothing even when history indisputably proves that they've erred throughout the long term! Teaching methods and attitudes have not changed over decades, and sometimes even over centuries.

Most of those involved in the stock market define themselves as purely fundamental or purely technical. In reality, there is no small amount of overlap between the two methods. The problem arises when the two methods oppose each other. History has proven that the technical method has always preceded the economic analysis. Most of the largest market trends occurring throughout history were ascribed no significant explanation according to economic data, yet most could be predicted based on technical conduct. Experienced technical traders learn over time to trust their own considerations, which will often stand in direct opposition to those proposed by fundamental economic analysts. Technical traders will be enjoying the benefits of changes when fundamental investors have long since missed the train.

Would you like an example? Was it possible to profit from hi-tech companies' stocks at the end of the 1990s? Of course, and abundantly! Could even one fundamental investor be found able to justify buying stocks in technology companies that have no income, only expenditures and dreams? Of course not! Technical traders knew where the public's emotions would lead the market, whereas fundamental investors chose to ignore the expected change.

At some point, they nonetheless found justification for joining. Remember the phrase "profit without advertising costs"? Several more illustrious economic concepts came into being along the duration of the hi-tech bubble, meant to justify late-entry into a teeming market. Funds simply could not tell their clients they were not buying when all competitors presented astronomical profits, therefore they invented a financial justification, and happily bought in. Those who wasted their time with analyses of hi-tech companies' financial reports prior to and during the rush, left opportunities wide open for technical analysts to enjoy alone. Those who continued justifying their erroneous fundamental holdings when the stock exchange changed direction and crashed, lost out.

Over time, once the market had absorbed these large shifts, the two methods caught up with each other and once again presented a united front. We ask: must some compromise be found between them? As a novice, I thought the answer was no. Now, with years of experience under my belt, I believe I was wrong. As noted, I'm currently operating on an 80% technical and 20% fundamental mix. I've moved a little to the other side because I found that when sticking with only one approach, the market seems in many cases to operate as though it has a mind of its own. I found that relying on technical data alone did not provide me the advantage I sought. By contrast, it's completely clear to me that relying on economic data alone is nothing more than a gamble. If you've ever tried to watch how a stock behaves after its financial reports are publicized, whether good or bad, you'll understand exactly to what I refer.

Note that I used the very specific terms "fundamental investor" and "technical trader." In the past, when the world was chiefly industrial, it was possible to rely on economic data for the long term. In the past, it wasn't possible to change the rules of the game overnight. When a mega-corporation like General Motors or IBM presented good balance sheets, it was clear that no competitor could surface overnight and take their top status from them. Therefore, these economic data points were reliable for the long term. To compete with GM or IBM, an unimaginable investment would be needed, therefore in the short term, no change could be expected that would endanger the investor too greatly.

In today's technological reality, every young entrepreneur living in student dorms can topple a conglomerate like IBM from the top of the pyramid. Remember when IBM preferred to develop hardware, and some young guy named Bill Gates developed DOS for them? Just check Microsoft's market cap against IBM's to understand how the world can change. And who used technological innovation to topple Microsoft from its top position as the company with the largest market value? Apple, which was dormant for years but reached new peaks with the iPhone and iPad, leaving Microsoft behind at the curve. And what of Google, sprinting ahead? Will Facebook, breathing hard down Google's neck, overtake the lead? In the current business world, any technological or biological innovation can change market structure overnight. The days when our parents would buy a stock such as IBM, place the paper deed (yes, once upon a time a written deed was issued to the stock owner) beneath their pillow and go to sleep knowing all would be fine, have long since disappeared. Nor have we yet begun to discuss the impact of wars and terror attacks…

I believe that long-term investment is dead, together with the world of absolute control and the fundamental economic analysis method. The short term is what to watch, which is why technical analysis is currently the controlling method. We live in a time when we need to trade with fast changes and remain wary of dangerous long-term investments. The technical trader who buys stocks that unfortunately move in the wrong direction (yes, that can happen, too) realizes he or she has erred, sells them and moves on to the next stock. When fundamental investors buy a stock, they hold onto them for as long as it has yet to be proven that the fundamental economic data have altered. Such investors believe that the stock's value is actually higher than its market value, and therefore when it drops in price, it can actually increase their holdings. It's true that not so many years ago, the method did work. Remember the dot-com bubble that burst in 2000? That's where the method stopped working. That's where the technical trader profited from shorts and the fundamental investor crashed in a market which, to date, has yet to fully recover. It was the trader's opportunity, not the gambler's.

If you need further persuasion, let me present another question: is there any link between a company's balance sheet and reality? Older readers may well recall Enron, one of the largest energy corporations in the world. Enron collapsed when its CEO chose to present the balance sheet in a "creative" manner, and made sure he found an accountant who would not stand in his way. Even if we allow that the balance was legitimate, it nonetheless reflected the company's status in the previous quarter, which commenced just three months earlier. Who is interested in it today? I'm sure that most balance sheets presented to us are legitimate and correct, but should we gamble on them with our money?

As traders, we rely chiefly on clear technical data. In the past, we have come across a stock that rose multiple percentages in one trade day, and only the next day the economic data causing the rise become clarified. This does not imply we have no trust in economic data. We just feel that they are already incorporated into the stock's chart.

As if all that is not enough, there's another important difference. Technical analysis can be applied to every stock, sector, and market. Give me a yearly graph for Japan's Nikkei index, and within seconds I can analyze the Japanese market. Show me the yearly graph for the DAX index and in the blink of an eye, I will analyze the German market. Can fundamental analysts, who need to read mountains of material before buying any stock, do that? No! They cannot specialize in every market, sector, and stock. They are limited to a specific sector and even a specific company in some cases, and will never review the entire market, but only a slim segment of it.

Why Do I Never the less Use Fundamental Economic Analysis?

First and foremost, because most of the public uses it. Whether there is any meaning to fundamental analysis or not is as pointless as asking whether there is meaning to technical analysis. As soon as a large enough number of people believe so, and operate on the basis of economic data with predictable outcomes, the experienced trader will know how to take advantage of the predicted movement and earn a livelihood from it. Over the years, I have learned to appreciate the power of the fundamental herd and rein it in for my own purposes. I take no small number of technical decisions based on economic factors alone. For example: I focus a lot on stocks influenced by extreme economic analysis, such as an analyst's upgrade, but then I choose a technical entry and exit point. Using fundamental economic analysis does not in any way indicate that I believe in that method, but I'm definitely a firm believer in the predictable behavioral outcomes of those who do use them. I have no need to deny any kind of prediction. Rather, I need to evaluate whether it will be self-fulfilling.

Technical Analyst or Coffee-Grounds Reader

Is technical analysis an exact science or an art? I think the truth is somewhere in between the two. Senior analysts in Tradenet's trading room often ask me whether it's worth buying this or that stock, and my answer could very well be that it's actually worth selling the stock. If technical analysis were an exact science, there'd be no room for two differing opinions on the same stock. By the way, even within the science of economics, disputes are abundant, and what one economist considers a solid company will be viewed unstable by another.

If that is how things operate, you will surely be asking yourself what function technical analysis holds. At the start of this chapter, I noted that the market is like a giant of tremendous proportions, in a constant state of change. Technical analysis helps create order in the chaos and allows the trader to read the market through stock prices and chart action. Moreover, from the moment traders learn how to read the market, they no longer need to examine it constantly from the technical perspective in order to understand what they see; they simply understand (rather than "read") the market. Technical analysis is therefore a tool that ripens in the trader's awareness: we use it to learn how to read the market, and once we know that, we no longer need it except in instances when reading is difficult. Traders who understand the market can identify market directions at early stages, long before the regular technical signals, and trade accordingly. Obviously, once the technical picture is completely clear, it's clear to everyone, and at that point you no longer have any advantage.

While technical analysis is not an exact science, there are technical analysts, many of whom are well-known, that frequently fail in their analyses. Young traders seeking to coerce technical methods onto the market will fail time after time. When the market is collapsing, there is no significance to technical support levels; when it is euphoric, technical resistance levels are broken without a fight.

Some technical analysts have given a bad name to the field, and threaten the livelihood of astrologers and coffee-grounds readers. Among such analysts you will find charts with so many indices, lines, and figures that you no longer know whether you're looking at a graph or a map of the constellations. Technical analysts who provide forecasts for several months ahead are not professionals, but charlatans.

Leave the Box

The laws of technical trading are known to all trading parties. The specialists and market makers in the New York Stock Exchange know your stop loss order point and your entry orders points, and will often take advantage of this information for their own benefit. Take this into account when you're trading. The resistance line is not a solid wall, and the support line is not stable ground. This is why we first talk about "support levels" and "resistance levels" rather than precise science. Young traders in the trading room often tell me they have sold a stock because it broke the support level, while experienced traders and I have held the stock and in the end, profited. Don't let your hand be too easy with the mouse. Remember that trading is a battle of the minds and always involves two parties: buyer and seller.

This is also why I guide my traders not to place a stop order, but to wait for that moment when the stock reaches the stop and then exit manually. The specialists and market makers know where most traders' stop orders are, and use them to their own advantage.

The Guru of All Gurus!

The world of finance is liberally peppered with gurus. Jim Rogers is one example. He believed with all his heart that China was the next big thing, to the point that he moved to Singapore and his little daughter learned to speak fluent Mandarin, leaving Chinese listeners dumbfounded. And how many gurus predicted the 2008 Sub-Prime Crash? Not long before that collapse, I was invited to participate in a panel of economists at a well-known university.

| **SMART MONEY** | *No one can predict the future of the market or any stock. For every opinion presented by a renowned analyst, we can find a contradicting opinion by an even more renowned analyst.* |

First, the chief economist of a large bank spoke, followed by the CFO of another bank. Both offered solid forecasts: the housing crisis is no more than a simple passing episode, the economy is strong, there is no danger of crisis in the capital market. In short, a message of "Don't worry, all is well."

I'm used to the idea that someone receiving a salary from the bank would not try to frighten the public or drive investors away, but this was over the top. When it was my turn to address the audience, I said very simply, "I don't know what will happen." The moderator persisted, admonition coloring his voice, "We brought you here to tell those present what they should do." So I told the truth, and one which will surely mean that that university will never invite me again to lecture there. This is what I said: "Don't listen to analysts, because they have no idea about the future."

From the reaction of the moderator and the public, I had clearly touched a sensitive spot. The public likes to be told what to do. It likes to be taken by the hand and led, whether to slaughter or splendor, but it does not want to be burdened with the commitment of having to make its own decisions. At this stage of a clearly-explosive atmosphere, I added, "Don't let bankers and funds manage your money, take management fees and commissions, and then tell you 'it will be okay.' The truth is that just like me, they have no idea what will happen in the future."

No matter whom the guru is, or whether he or she takes the form of an investment advisor or analyst, when you read or hear any kind of recommendation in the media, don't lap up those words with thirsty love. Consider them critically, and recognize the fact that even if they are correct, they are known to millions of people, leaving you no advantage.

The Archimedean Point

The Greek philosopher Archimedes is known chiefly for his famous shout, "Eureka!" meaning, "I have found it!" This was his reaction on discovering that the volume of objects can be measured by sinking them into water. Another Archimedean phrase, though less well-known, is "Punctum Archimedis," the Archimedean Point. Archimedes claimed that were he able to grasp the world at a certain point, he could move it.

Some traders seek their Archimedean Point in books. They search for the book or method that will let them "conquer the market." They want someone to take them by the hand until they succeed. I'm sorry to disappoint you, but there is no winning recipe or magical word that lets you profit from every single transaction. The tool closest to the Archimedean Point is the trend, which we will look at more closely in Chapter 5. To identify and take advantage of trends, we first need to learn, in Chapter 4, how to use the graph.

4

The Chart: Money's Footprint

A stock's chart incorporates all its history and points to its future.

How to Read Millions of People's Thoughts

The trader's main working tool is the chart or graph. A chart's function is to present stock price history and indicate its future direction via conclusions based on the past: a kind of financial crystal ball where there is no present, and only the past exists. A nanosecond beforehand is already the past, a second forward is the future. When deciding whether to buy or sell a stock, we cannot be satisfied with only the current price. We must review where that price came from and conclude which direction it is heading. We need to investigate when sellers stopped its rise in the past (resistance lines) and when buyers saved it from crashing (lines of support). Using this and other information, we need to determine how it will behave in the future and at what prices certain actions may occur. We will use as many charts as our computer screens allow to follow the various stocks, sectors and important market indices. Currently, I use nine screens and am considering adding another, but that is mostly to watch the amazed looks on faces of people walking into my work room.

SMART MONEY | *A stock's chart is an integration of fundamental knowledge with the addition of a healthy dollop of human psychology.*

Charts can be weekly, presenting information over several weeks; daily, presenting several days; or intraday, presenting data for the same day at different intervals such as on a one-minute or fifteen-minute basis. These charts provide the trader a look deep inside the market and trace the price changes, which are the outcomes of the constant tug-of-war between buyers and sellers. Stock prices do not rise or drop coincidentally. As a trader, I derive a great deal of pleasure from observing charts showing real-time shifts, imagining all the people seated behind their desks all around the world, buying, selling, and impacting on the price at the very moment I am watching. This is a "war" of control over money and power, with victory going to the person that makes the best decisions based on the information at his or her disposal. I enjoy following the traps that buyers and sellers set for each other. I see the errors and the successes and try to think what I would do in their stead. Even a person with vast experience in the capital market, but none in intraday trading, will find it difficult to understand the logic behind intraday stock trading. Those with insufficient experience might be satisfied with just attempting to understand and analyze the weekly or daily chart. But in fact, intraday trading does have its logic, and plenty of it. The more screen-time experience you gain, the better you will understand what drives the bears and bulls influencing the stock, the more you will become acquainted with the intraday logic, and the greater your self-confidence will increase--to the point where you too will join the war. Every move the day trader makes, whether buying or selling, is based on chart patterns that we will learn, and on outcomes that represent the trader's evaluation of the war's outcomes as plotted on the chart.

Using charts now seems to me the most natural and obvious thing. How can we possibly manage without them? But that is not how things were in the past. Up until one hundred years ago, almost no charts were used. Quotes of stock prices reached the trading room by telegraph, a designated clerk wrote them down on a large board, and the previous price was erased. Successful traders were those blessed with excellent memories. Over time, it became understood that a connection exists between the past and future behavior of a stock price.Some traders began charting the information, seeking recurring outcomes. The use of charts began to make greater headway as famous chart-based theories began developing, such as the **Dow Theory** and the **Elliot Waves**. In the 1960s, charts became increasingly prevalent with the advent of the first industrialized computers.

Several accepted norms exist for presenting prices on charts. Different traders choose different methods, but most of them, especially day traders, almost exclusively use the "Japanese Candlesticks" method which will later be elaborated. Several of the methods are described briefly below, by way of initial introduction

Line Chart

This is the simplest chart, commonly recognized by the public and used most often in financial media. A line chart is created by connecting all the **closing prices** (the last trade price at the end of the day) over a certain period. These are plotted onto the chart, and a line is drawn connecting them. This is the simplest way to present prices, but as we will see later on, it is insufficient, as the information it provides is relevant only to the stock's closing price. For a trader, it lacks the important data such as open price, intraday high price (the peak price for each day) and the intraday low price. This is information that the trader cannot be without.

AAPL – 6-Month Line Chart

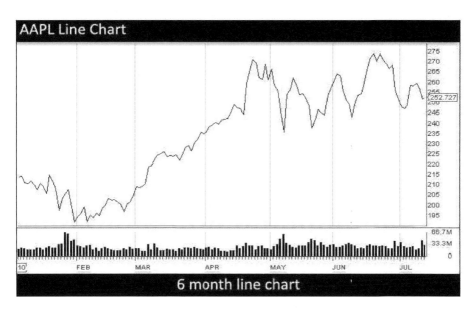

The line chart is useful and most frequently used in the media. It is especially convenient for comparing the prices of several stocks in one chart, or comparing a stock and its sector index. If, for example, we wish to check a stock's Apple (AAPL) chart and compare the AAPL behavior to the hi-tech sector stocks, a line chart makes the job easier and allows determining whether a specific stock is stronger or weaker than its sector.

Summary:

A nice chart, but completely useless to the trader. I use this kind of chart only when I write articles for newspapers or when television program producers request a simple chart prior to going on air that viewers can understand. You've seen it, you've made this chart's acquaintance, and now you should forget it altogether.

Point and Figure Chart

The X and O chart is a very old method first written about in 1898. Its popularity rose in the 1940s with the publication of A. W. Cohen's 1947 guidebook on point and figure stock market timing. By contrast with other price presentation methods where price is dependent on time, the point and figure method marks a rising price as X and a dropping price as O. This method chiefly serves long-term investors, since it presents prices over just one timeframe (for example, the closing prices of a period of trading days).Therefore it sifts out intraday trading fluctuations, based on the premise that intraday changes are no more than distracting noises that cause the investor to implement unnecessary actions. Here is an example of a point and figure chart:

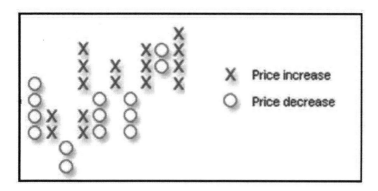

Summary:

If you really want to anger me, read Cohen's 1947 book, which can be ordered online, and try to use this method on intraday trading. There's a good chance that instead of making money, you'll end up in tears. If you're interested in long-term investment, there might be something to gain from reading the book, but long term does not interest me and is not the field we're dealing with here, so it will not be discussed further.

Bar Chart

Now we're moving up a level! Unlike the line chart, the bar chart displays a good amount of useful information and is the most common chart in use by investors. Note that I used the term "investors" and not "traders." On a bar chart, every vertical bar represents price behavior for a specific timeframe, as follows: the uppermost extreme of the vertical bar indicates the highest price for the specific time unit (HIGH), and the bottom point indicates the lowest price (LOW). The small horizontal mark on the left shows the start price (OPEN) and the horizontal on the right shows the (CLOSE) price

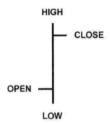

Let's say that the bar chart above indicates price changes of a stock over one day: its opening, highest, lowest, and closing price for one day. Because the closing price is higher than the opening price, we understand that we are looking at a chart showing a day in which the price rose.

How do you think a chart showing an overall drop in price would look? This is how:

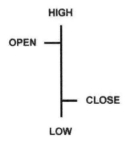

A day in which no change occurred would look like this:

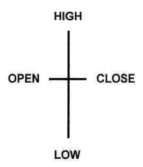

AAPL Chart for 16 Trading Days

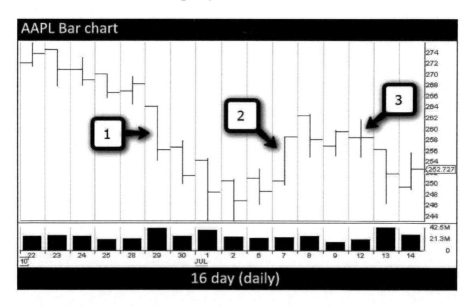

[1] shows the stock price on July 29 starting at its high (peak), dropping, then ending slightly above the low

[2] shows the AAPL price on July 7 opening slightly above its lowest point, dropping, then ending at a high

[3] shows AAPL on July 12 showing no change. The open and closing prices are identical.

A bar can indicate any length of time, from a single day as in the chart above, to a week, a month, and of course much shorter intraday trading periods from five minutes, fifteen, a half hour or full hour. Intraday traders will choose bar charts illustrating from two to thirty minutes. By contrast, an investor wanting to examine a stock's long-term behavior will likely choose bars showing daily or weekly periods.

Note the disparity between the open and closing prices on the AAPL bar chart shown above. Note also that from one day to the next, the opening price is different from the closing price of the previous day; for example, on the day marked [1] you can see that the opening price is lower than the closing price of the previous day.

How is that possible? We call this phenomenon the "price gap," or more commonly just "gap." It is wellknown and important to traders, and will be discussed further. Note that one of the disadvantages of the line chart, unlike the bar chart, is that it does not contain this information!

Why don't traders use the bar chart? On one hand, it is clear and detailed; on the other hand, it is difficult to read. The small horizontals on the left and right eventually drove me crazy, and I'm sure they speed up that inevitable day when you'll visit the optician for reading glasses (I'm not there yet...). Bar charts are generally for older investors who are not willing to learn "new tricks." Bar charts just aren't "cool" enough for young folk like me.

Japanese Candlestick Chart

At last we reach our goal. Up until now, I fulfilled my professional obligation and presented you with several methods aimed at the general public or veteran investors. But they are unnecessary for our purposes, and now we arrive on the shores of the Promised Land. Get ready for a surprise, because it is precisely this Japanese candlestick method which is really retro and amazing, and started in...the 18th century!

The method was developed by Munehisa Homma, a Japanese rice trader (1724-1803) who was one of the first to make use of past rice prices to predict future prices. And the method really worked! Munehisa became very wealthy from the rice trade, and was bestowed the title of "Honorary Samurai." Someone calculated his annual trading profits in modern terms and reached the figure of $10 billion, with a cumulative capital of $100 billion! The principles of this method were studied in the 1970s by several technical analysts, and primarily by Steve Nison who also wrote a bestseller on the method. The result is that the Japanese candlestick method now serves us well.

Munehisa Homma's method allows me to understand the changing prices across an axis of time. Note that I used the word "understand" rather than merely "observe" or "see." Over the years, I experienced an amazing phenomenon. If you, like me, spend several years observing the Japanese candlestick method, perhaps you too will undergo a similar transformation. At some point, though I cannot define exactly when it happened, I managed to comprehend the candle "matrix" (you saw the movie, right?). Now when I look at a complex Japanese candlestick chart, I start talking fluent Japanese. I "understand" the stock without needing to analyze the chart. I can look at it just as a surgeon looks at a brain scan, or as a musician hears music when he or she sees notes. I am in the world of support, resistance, breakouts and breakdowns, and bears and bulls. This virtual world of rising and falling prices is where some of them "respond," too: "Buy me, sell me... I'm willing to keep rising up to the price of..."

You're probably thinking that after so many years of Japanese candlesticks, I've lost my mind. There could be a bit of truth in that. But for those of you who know how to play a musical instrument and who succeeded (unlike me, who was forced to learn piano and is left with nothing to show for it but "Do Re Mi") in moving from just reading the notes to hearing them, you know exactly what I mean. For a musician, this is the stage in which he or she lives within the "body" of the notes. For the stock trader, it is the stage in which he or she feels the stock, senses the fear and greed of sellers and buyers, and knows how to take advantage of this for his or her own benefit. As a novice trader, I needed some ten minutes to analyze a chart comprised of Japanese candlesticks. Now that takes me no more than several seconds.

Below is a typical Japanese candlestick chart showing daily price changes over a period of sixteen trading days. Each candlestick represents one day of trade. Does the chart look familiar? That's because it provides the same information as the bar chart from a couple of pages back. At first glance, it appears a little more complicated, but as I explained above, I promise it'll get easier.

16-Day AAPL Japanese Candlestick Chart

Here, too, each candlestick represents one day of trade: [1] a day of falling prices, [2] a day of rising prices, [3] a day of no change. Take a couple of minutes and compare this chart with the bar chart. Try to understand the way prices are presented in this chart, as compared to the bar chart. I promise you that within a short time, you will understand the concept without having read any explanation. This is important. Please stop reading and make that comparison.

Did you continue reading without stopping? If so, you've just failed the most important test for any trader: self-discipline. This time I'll forgive it, but let's agree that this will be the last time you breach discipline. Without strong discipline, you will pay a costly price.

So how do we read a Japanese candle? As with bars, Japanese candlesticks indicate the movement of prices over a specific period chosen by the trader, which can be a minute, a month, and even a year. But instead of a vertical line with two horizontal bars, the candle has a "'body."

- The top and bottom parts of the body show the opening and closing prices.
- When the candle is a light color, usually green, white or transparent (but other possibilities exist), the closing price was higher than the

opening price. In other words, the price for the represented period rose.

- When the candle body is red, black or any other dark color, it means the closing price was lower than the opening price. In other words, the price dropped.

Most of the candles have a tail, sometimes also called a shadow.

- At the upper end, it is called the topping tail, and indicates the highest price for the period represented by the candle (for example, the day's high).
- A tail at the lower end is called the bottoming tail, and indicates the lowest price for the specific period.

Later we will learn that the length of the tail is very important for analyzing the expected stock price movement.

Japanese Candle Showing Price Rise:

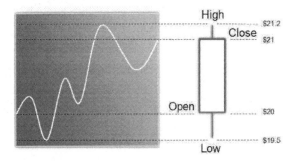

Let's assume this is the candle representing one day of trading. On the left you see a simple line chart describing the stock's behavior over one day. The stock opens trade at a price of $20, drops to a low of $19.5, rises to a day high of $21.2, and ends the day of trading with a close of $21.

To the right of the chart we see a clear candle: that means the price rose. The opening price is the base of the body of the candle, the close is the upper peak of the candle body, and the bottoming and topping tails indicate the day's high and low. Simple, right?

Japanese Candle Showing Price Drop:

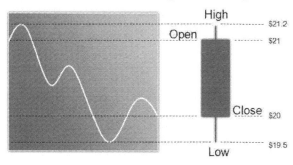

Let's say that this Japanese candle also represents one day of trading. Notice that it is in a dark color. Looking at the bar chart, you can immediately understand that this chart shows a day of dropping prices. To the left of the candle you see the simple line chart describing the stock's behavior over the entire day. The stock opens the day trading at $21, peaks with the day's high of $21.2, drops to the day's low of $19.5, and closes the day of trade at $20.

To the right of the bar chart you see a dark candle, meaning dropping prices. Because the candle is dark, you immediately understand that the opening price is the top of the candle's body, the closing price is the bottom of the body, and the two tails, topping and bottoming, show the day's high and low.

SMART MONEY | *Remember that for a light-colored candle, the opening price will be at the bottom, and for a dark-colored candle the opening price is at the top.*

You might want to claim that the Japanese candle provides the exact same information as the bar chart: the opening price, closing price, highest and lowest prices. This is true, nonetheless there are two differences:

- Because of the different colors, in a split second we can identify whether the stock rose or fell. Compare again with the AAPL chart and see which makes identifying stock price movement easier.
- The second and more essential difference is that Japanese candles developed over time with additional techniques that add a further dimension to the method.

A third reason exists for using Japanese candles: Because most professionals have shifted to using this method, it is very worthwhile that you look at the market exactly the way they do, so that you can operate in exactly the same way they do. If you operate before them, they will not be buying together with you, and your risks increase. If you buy after them, you will be buying at too high a price.

Without a doubt, Japanese candles light the way for traders who know how to use them effectively. Here is another example:

Japanese Candle Showing No Change in Price

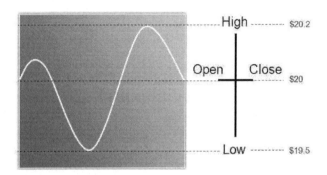

When a stock's open and closing prices are identical, the candle will not be green or red or any other light or dark color, and its "body" will shrink, as you see, to no more than a horizontal line. This candle is called a "doji," and indicates indecision: a perfect balance of power between buyers and sellers. In the chart above, you see that the opening and closing prices are the same: $20. The stock did move around, from a low of $19.5 to a high of $20.2, but in the end, closed with no change.

Presentation of Candles over Varying Lengths of Time

Traders operate within different timeframes than those used by investors, but nonetheless they check every stock chart over the long term and short term, as I will explain. When I want a total picture of the stock I'm interested in trading, I alter the presentation to show different timeframes and change the candles to show different timeframes, as explained further.

One of the stocks I am currently analyzing for potential purchase is "Altria," symbol MO. Altria is the number one cigarette manufacturer in the world, known for Marlboro, Parliament, Virginia, and many other brands. The trade opportunity can be identified easily according to a daily chart, where every candle represents one day of trade:

Altria, MO – Daily Japanese Candle Chart for Three Months

As noted, in this chart each candle represents one day of trading. The size of the chart in relation to the size of this book's page is what prevents me from showing a longer period. However, when I spread the trading platform across my computer screen, the chart is spread across a larger surface and allows me to clearly discern the candles for at least nine months, which is precisely what I would like you to do when you examine a stock. With Altria, I noticed a sharp increase in price lasting for eight days of trading [1] and several days of consolidation [2] around this peak area.

This is one of the technical formations that traders love, and is called the "bull flag." The term derives from the rise in price [1] that looks like the flagpole, and then the stable holding of this price, the consolidation, which looks like the flag itself. The term "bull" means it will charge forward. When people are "bullish" on a stock, they expect it to go up.

In this case, we will want to buy Altria if it goes higher than the top part of the bull flag: this increase is known as a "breakout." In other words, we will buy Altria if its price goes over $21.50. The accepted way of presenting this planned trade is as follows:

MO>$21.5

One of the reasons that Altria's formation appeals to me is the fact that in yesterday's trading, the market dropped sharply by 3%, whereas Altria, as you can see by the consolidation around the flag [2], held up well for its higher range of prices and was not drawn down with most of the market.

Before making my final decision on whether to buy, I want to know a little more of Altria's history. To do that, I will change the chart display to "weekly." Each candle will now represent one week of trading, and I will observe the stock's behavior over a two-year period:

Altria, MO – Weekly Japanese Candle Chart for Two Years

Here, too, if your screen allows it, display an even longer period, preferably of five years. What do we see? Without doubt, Altria has maintained a nice upward trend over the past two years. Yes, I'm still interested!

Now that I like what I see over two timeframes, the daily and the weekly, I want to check its behavior at a closer level. For that, I move to a display of the last ten days of trade and candles showing thirty- minute timeframes:

Altria, MO – Ten-day Japanese Candle Chart at Thirty-Minute Timeframes

When we look closely, we clearly see the consolidation at the top of the flag. Now imagine a situation where the stock breaks out at the flag's peak and rises higher than $21.50. That could be very interesting!

To complete my inspection, I check Altria's behavior over the last day of trading with candles of five minutes. To get an even clearer view, I always prefer to see the last two days of trading:

Altria, MO – Two-Day Japanese Candle Chart at Intervals of Five Minutes

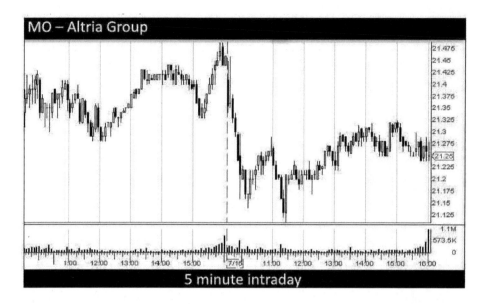

Had I checked only the last two days of trading, I'm not sure I would want to buy this stock. But, having already looked at the past ten days, the past two days fit better within the broader timeframe. Additionally, I keep in mind that the last day of trading ended with a sharp drop in prices in the overall markets, which also affected Altria a bit. I am now very interested. When taking into account the candles for day, week and longer periods, I see clearly that I really like Altria's history and can predict that its future looks good, although not until it moves above $21.50.

SMART MONEY	*Before deciding to buy a stock, you need to check its behavior over periods of five minutes, thirty minutes, daily, and weekly.*

Summary:

When making your decision to buy a stock, and also determining the best entry point (professionally known as a "trigger"), it is vital to switch between different timeframes, examine the stock's behavior using Japanese candles of different intervals, and even elaborate on market activity during the same timeframes. In weekly candles, I see less "noise" than in daily candles, and in daily candles I see less "noise" than in intraday thirty-minute candles, and so on. As an intraday trader, I will make my trade decision within the day's trading according to candles of five-minute intervals, and occasionally according to candles of two-minute intervals.

Swing traders buy stocks for ranges of several days up to several weeks. They will make their decision based on daily charts. Long-term investors, known as core traders, who hold stocks for months and even years, will base their decisions on weekly charts.

The Result

I couldn't resist. Almost three months have passed since I wrote this section, and now, as I make my final editorial adjustment, I decided to complete the picture with the results. Of course, you would not have gotten to see them if I had failed...

Altria, MO – 13% above the Bull Flag

5

Principles of

Technical Analysis

Chart Formations: Mirrors of Fear and Greed

The Basis

Technical analysis is a simple technique as long we don't try to make it complicated. Technical analysis, unlike fundamental analysis, ignores a company's value and focuses wholly and solely on the movement of its price, which is an outcome of supply and demand. The main influences on supply and demand are the human emotions of fear and greed, and market players take advantage of both.

Human emotions can be analyzed psychologically. Technical analysis is nothing more than a mirror of human psychology. Using technical analysis cleverly lets the trader predict buyers' and sellers' moves and take an educated guess at price direction on the basis of its past behavior.

The Trend

We have already mentioned that prices move in three directions: up, down, or forward. The market does not move backwards, because time does not move backwards. The market's directional movement is called its "trend." When the market rises over a period of time, we call this the uptrend; dropping over a period of time is called downtrend, and when it "moves sideways" with insignificant deviations, it is called a trendless market. It is easy to profit when there is a trend, and very difficult when the market has no trend. Generally, those who make money in a trendless market are the brokers who profit from commissions.

Famous Clichés and Trading with the Trend

Several famous clichés are tied to the capital market: "When it rains, everyone gets wet," and "Only when the tide goes out do you discover who's been swimming naked," and "Buy the rumor, sell the news."

But one important cliché describes the most important rule in trading: The Trend is Your Friend.

What does this mean? Trade in the direction of the trend, and only in the direction of the trend. Accompany it and actualize it as long as there are no signs of its ending. The more careful you are about integrating trends, as will be explained later, the better off you will be. The perfect trade occurs when I buy a stock with a clear trend, the sector in which the company operates shows an identical trend, and the overall market shows the same trend.

SMART MONEY | *In actuality, you will try to convince yourselves that "just this once" you will buy contrary to the trend. After all, it "has dropped far enough" and "must" go up…*

Even though I always teach my students to trade in the direction of the trend, it happens that new traders in our trading room suggest buying or shorting against the trend. The basis of their suggestion seems logical: "the stock has dropped enough and therefore must make an upside correction" or "the stock has gone up and must make a downside correction." Yet, other than in very unique cases, this thinking is fundamentally flawed.

Buying a stock on a downward trend, or vice versa, is like swimming against the current of a surging river: there's very little chance you will reach your target, and even if you do, you'll be exhausted. Occasionally, a trader who suggested shorting an upward trending stock later draws my attention to the fact that the stock did indeed drop by so many dollars. I am happy to congratulate his or her success, but also add my generic response, "I guarantee that if you do this ten times, you will fail in at least seven of them." I have spent sufficient years and gained enough experience to guess when a stock is changing its trend, and now am able to relate how I failed in the majority of instances. Don't try it. It's a waste of your time and money.

Trading with the trend allows me to long (buy) strong stocks that are rising and short weak stocks that are dropping. In this way, I preserve the advantage of the trend, and increase my chances of success. Trading against the trend reduces chances of success and misses opportunities in other stocks which are moving in the trend direction.

In *Memories of a Wall Street Analyst*, the book's protagonist Larry Livingstone talks about an old man named Partridge, who had years of stock trading experience. When untrained traders asked his advice about specific stocks, he would authoritatively repeat the exact same answer, "You know, we're in a bull market!" Old Partridge understood and internalized something that even veteran, let alone young traders have trouble understanding: full advantage should be taken of trading with the trend. As long as the market is rising and the stock you bought maintains its upward trend, or as I often say in the trading room, "has done nothing wrong," don't sell it! The same is true when shorting stocks when the market is trending down.

At the start of the school year, I attended a parents' meeting at my daughter's school. Before leaving home, I traded and joined up with my trading colleagues in the trading room. When it came time to leave, I placed protective stop orders into the trading platform. On returning some three hours later, I noticed that the balance in my trading account had risen considerably. The trend did its work and the stocks continued moving. The conclusion is obvious: as long as a stock "does nothing wrong," don't touch it. Go out wherever you plan to go, and don't stay glued to the computer screen. Then you won't be tempted to sell. By the way, my experience has shown that interminably watching those screens does not help a stock's price go up or down.

A new trader might believe that "professional traders" tend to trade throughout the trading day. If that is true, it does not mean that they are constantly buying and selling. Not at all! What it means is that these traders let the stocks do their job quietly, uninterrupted. Trading a whole day does not mean staring at screens the whole day. In actuality, I tend to sit at my computer system for no more than two hours a day, but do come back for brief visits during the trading day just to keep an eye on developments, and chiefly to ascertain no changes in the trend.

In my early days as a trader, I understood that stock trading success lies in increasing opportunities and decreasing risks. To increase my chances, I generally join the majority as far as market trend. How do I know which way the majority is headed? I watch two things:
- the stock's trend (up or down), and
- the stock's volume, which is the number of shares executed between buyers and sellers

Professional traders always prefer volatile stocks which crash or frequently break out, as such stocks behave according to hysteria or greed. These are two states in trading that can bring a lot of money into your pocket if you know how to identify them on time and enter and exit at the right points.

Defining the Trend

The trend is the direction that the market is taking. Because the market, like a snake, never moves in a straight line but always zigzags, the trend is structured from a series of highs and lows.
- A series of highs and lows, where each low is nonetheless higher than the previous one, and each high is higher than the previous one, creates an upward trend. This series is defined by **higher highs and higher lows.**
- A series of highs and lows where each new low is lower than the previous one, and each new high is also lower than the previous one, creates a **downward trend**. This series is defined by **lower highs and lower lows**.

The public generally hears only about rises and drops in the market, but according to conservative estimates, about one-third of the time the market is neither moving up or down, but rather staying the same. A series of similar highs and similar lows creates this movement. In the trading room, we often describe this situation as **moving sideways** or **moving in the range.**

SMART MONEY	*When the market is moving sideways, it is difficult to profit. We can never know in advance if the market will move with the trend or not. Once we notice that the market is trendless, we avoid taking new trades.*

When a series forms of two rising highs and two rising lows, it defines the **uptrend**. In the chart above, we see three rising lows and four rising highs, which is a very clear upward movement. Notice that the fifth high is lower than the fourth. Does this indicate that the uptrend has stopped? No, but it is definitely gives cause to watch for changes.

UpwardTrend:

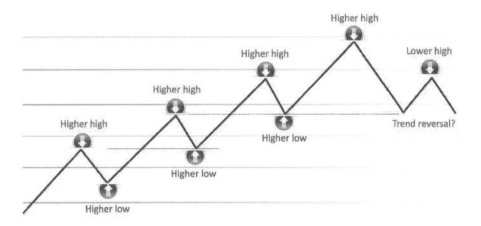

Is there any importance to the time intervals between each high and low? No. The interval during which you trade is the determining factor. If you entered for several days, as a swing trade, because you identified an uptrend on the daily chart (where each candle represents one day), that is the trend you need to "ride." Long-term investors will generally ride trends based on weekly charts (where each candle represents one week), and intraday traders will identify and buy stocks over intraday trends based on five-minute candles.

When should you buy? If you're willing to take risks, buy after the first low. If you tend to be more cautious and are willing to take a little less profit, buy after the second low. We will discuss this in detail later.

Downtrend

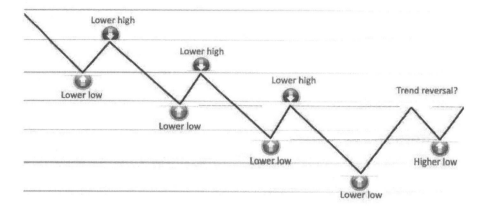

When a series forms of two dropping lows and two dropping highs, this defines a **downtrend**. In the chart above, we see a series of four dropping lows and three dropping highs: a very clear downtrend. Notice that the fifth low is higher than the fourth low. Does this mean that the downtrend has ended? No, but there is definitely room to suspect an upcoming change.

Joy Global, JOYG – Uptrend

Joy Global maintained an uptrend for almost three months, rising from a price of $44 to a peak of $64. Notice the four rising lows and the three rising highs before the stock changed direction, broke the previous low and dropped to a new low. If you had been holding the stock, where in your view should your exit point have been? The correct answer is the trend's break point: that is, the drop below the last high's low, beneath the $58 mark.

Until now, I've explained why it is so very important to trade with the trend, and so important to utilize it fully. (Never forget that!) I also explained the three market trends, but I have not explained what these mean from the trader's viewpoint.

Think for a moment: what does the trader always wish to know?
- A trader always wants to know the ratio of buyers to sellers: in other words, which of these two opposing groups is winning the endless tug-of-war.
- When buyers are winning, we see uptrends.
- When sellers are winning, we see downtrends.
- When there is balance between buyers and sellers, the stock will move sideways, with slight upward and downward movements but no real trend.

What do professional traders do with this information?
- They will want to buy (long) when the buyers are winning: that is, when the stock is rising.
- Thy will want to sell short when the sellers are winning: that is, when the stock price is dropping.
- Sideways movement is dangerous: on one hand, the stock is moving in a range that does not allow for making any profit.On the other hand, a small pull on the rope in favor of one of the sides can lead to losses.

This is why pro traders do not trade during sideways movement, but wait for a clear up or downtrend. Avoiding any action is sometimes the best step to take. Over time, you'll discover that during sideways markets, you will do better when you do nothing! If market conditions do not allow joining a clear trend, don't join. In other words, not joining means not losing money. This will be discussed further.

Support and Resistance

When technical analysts talk about support and resistance, they are usually referring to "lines of support and resistance," but, as is presented further on, support and resistance can also be found at high and low points, in moving averages, and in round numbers. Support and resistance are also linked to another phrase: breakouts and breakdowns.

- A sharp drop in price can be a support breakdown
- A sharp rise in price can be a resistance breakout

Areas of Support and Resistance

In the early 20th century, many stock traders began to acknowledge that a stock needs to break out from, or break down "even the smallest resistance" in order for it to be traded. In those days, traders were not assisted by charts or other technical tools, and only used support and resistance. They remembered and wrote down the highs and lows, and related to them as points of future support and resistance. Even traders on the NYSE trading floor, who in the past had traded using hand signals, did not use any kind of chart. Instead, they used areas of support and resistance. These traders can hardly be suspected of unprofessionalism.

Identifying areas of support and resistance in a stock, then, is vital to traders when analyzing the trend and determining their entry and exit points. As already noted, professional traders are always interested in knowing the balance of power between buyers and sellers, and these areas indicate turning points in the balance.

SMART MONEY | *Who supports a dropping stock? Buyers who believe that it will go up, and "heavy" shorters who realize profit (i.e. are buying back their short positions) during the downtrend*

- The area of **support** is the price where the stock stops on its way down: in other words, the point at which buyers outnumber sellers.

- The area of **resistance** is the price where the stock has stopped on its way up: in other words, the point at which sellers outnumber buyers.

Summary:
In the support area, the majority think that the stock's price is cheap.

In the resistance area, the majority feel that the stock's price is expensive.

Professional traders seek to buy a stock on the way up after it breaks through the area of resistance, and will seek to short (sell) when a stock breaks through the area of support.

I want to emphasize that these are **areas, not lines,** of support and resistance. The term "line" represents a rigid, unfeasible reality. Is it reasonable that all people active in the market will constantly buy at the same support price and always sell at the same resistance price? Of course not. This is even truer for a large market. Additionally, as noted, the principles of technical analysis are known to all people active in the market, and frequently "lines" will be broken out purposely in order to execute automatic buy and sell orders fed into computers, or to tempt innocent traders into buying and selling a stock.

When Support Turns into Resistance, and Vice Versa

- When an area of resistance breaks out, it turns into an area of support.
- When an area of support breaks down, it turns into an area of resistance.

Let's examine this rule using the following charts and try to understand how the rule operates:

Resistance – Turning into Support

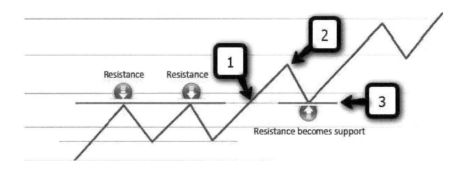

| **SMART MONEY** | *When a stock breaks out of resistance [1], rises [2], and then returns to its breakout price [3], we call the phenomenon a "retest" – in other words, the stock "tests" and certifies the resistance that has now turned into support.* |

Why does resistance become support? For three reasons:

1. Traders like buying stocks that break out through resistance. When a stock breaks out through resistance [1], they buy it, hoping it will go up. When to their joy it does rise and creates a new high [2], they're sorry they didn't buy a larger quantity at the outset... Now the stock is too expensive to make it worth buying more, but they would love to increase the amount they hold if the stock price would drop to its breakout figure [3]. When it does, they buy, establishing support [3].
2. Other traders who missed the breakout see that the stock is rising, and are sorry they missed joining the festivities. They won't buy the stock at its peak [2] because it is too costly, but they're happy to buy it when it returns to the breakout price [3]. When it does, they buy. Buying indicates that they support that price: in other words, they establish support [3].
3. The last ones in on the support list are the "short sellers," who hoped that the stock would not rise, but were caught with a stock that hit new highs [1] and were sorry they did not close the shorts before the breakout. They lose money, but psychologically they have trouble admitting their error and closing the short all the way to the high [2]. Of course they would be delighted if they were given a chance to exit their short position at the pre-breakout price, that is, buy at that price (we will explain later how a short is closed by buying). When the stock does drop down, they will wipe the sweat from their brow, buy, and also be among those establishing [3] support.

Summary:
If a stock drops back down to its "retest" point [3], then all the traders have a common interest: to buy. This shared interest is what turns resistance into support.

Support – Turning into Resistance

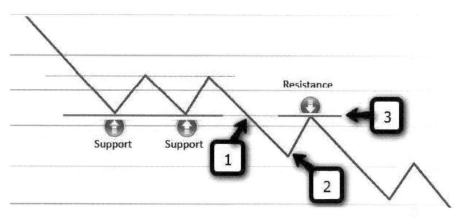

Why does support turn into resistance? For the exact reverse reasons to those detailed above:

1. Traders love to sell short stocks that break down through support. When a stock breaks down through support [1], they execute a short, that is, they sell the stock (more on this later) and hope that it will go down. When, to their joy, it does, and reaches a new low [2], they're sorry they didn't short at the outset with a greater quantity... But now it has gone down too low for them to sell another amount. However, they'd be happy to increase the amount of their short if the price returns to its breakdown point [3]. If it does return, they will increase the quantity of shorts, that is, sell more, and be among those creating resistance [3].

2. Other traders who missed the breakdown [1] see that the stock is dropping and are sorry they didn't join the shorting festivities. They won't execute a short when the price is at its lowest [2] because it has already "dropped down too much," but they would be happy to execute a short (i.e. to sell) if the price returns to its breakdown point [3]. If it does go back up, they will short and be among those establishing resistance [3].

3. The last group establishing resistance is the "long traders" (in contrast with "short traders"). Long traders are those who believed in the stock and bought it before its breakdown, believing it would

go up. Long traders are currently caught with a losing stock: they watch it reach a new low and are sorry they didn't sell it before the breakdown. They are sustaining large losses and have difficulty in admitting their mistake and selling when the stock price is low [2]. They pray that it will go back up to its breakdown point [3] when they will happily sell. When it does, they will also be among the sellers establishing resistance [3].

Summary:

If a stock rises to its retest point [3], it will usually encounter resistance originating in the common interest of all those operating in the market at the time: sellers. This shared interest turns support into resistance.

High and Low Points

The high and low points also serve as areas of support and resistance, both on intraday charts and daily charts.

High – Turning into Resistance

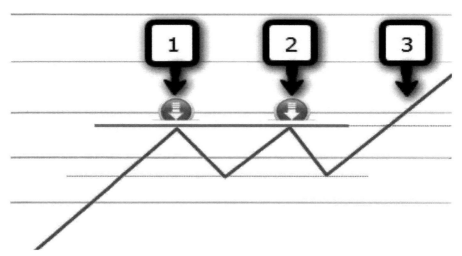

Why does a high [1] create resistance when the price returns to the same [2] point?

To understand this, we need to penetrate the thoughts of buyers more deeply.

Every point on the chart represents both buyers and sellers. The same is true for when the stock reaches its high [1]. Of course, buyers at that point still do not know they have reached the peak price, and in a show of enthusiasm over a strong stock, they buy at this high, hoping the stock will go up. In actuality, when they discover that it is dropping, they are disappointed. They are losing money, and sorry that they were tempted and bought at a high price. They do not want to sell at a loss, so they promise themselves that if the stock returns to the price at which they bought [1], they will correct their mistake and get rid of the stocks at the same price they bought them.

They are not the only disappointed buyers who bought; there are many others who are also waiting to sell at their entry price. If the stock does go back to that first high [2], it will encounter all those waiting sellers.

Can the stock price overcome the sellers' resistance and rise to a new high? Sometimes yes, sometimes, no. The question revolves around the balance of forces between sellers and buyers. In the chart above, we can see that the stock continued rising [3]. In other words, in this case the buyers won.

The retreat from the second high [2] is called **"double top."** When a stock rises to the double top, in most cases it will retreat due to resistance, and drop. In such situations, if you bought a stock that is about to reach its double top, it would be wise to realize some of the profits a little before the anticipated resistance point.

| **SMART MONEY** | *When a stock drops from its high and tries to get back up, it encounters the resistance created by all the disappointed buyers who bought as it rose previously and now wish to sell at their purchase price.* |

Low – Turning into Support

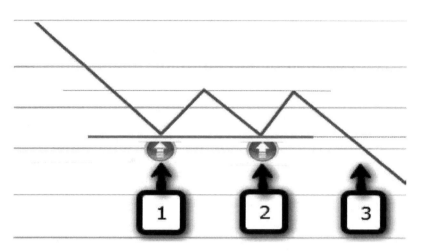

Why does the last low create support?

Here, too, we need to understand the psychological perspective of buyers and sellers. At every point on the chart we will find both buyers and sellers, but in this case, we call the sellers **"short sellers."**

At the stock's low [1], short sellers cannot yet identify this point as the low. In a burst of enthusiasm over a weak stock price, they execute a short, hoping that it will continue dropping.

In actuality, they discover that the stock is rising against their hopes and they are losing, which disappoints them. They promise themselves that if the stock returns to its pre-short price (that is, the same price as the previous low), they will correct their mistake and close the short (that is, they will buy).

If the stock does drop to the same low [2], it will encounter all those disappointed short sellers who are thrilled that the stock returned to their entry position.

Can the stock overcome the support of buyers and drop to a new low? Maybe yes, maybe no... The answer depends on the balance of forces between sellers and buyers.

In the chart above, we see that the stock continued dropping [3]. In other words, in this case, sellers won. The rise at point [2] from the low is called a **"double bottom."** When the stock drops to a double bottom, in most cases it rises again because of the support created by buyers.

How Does a Drunken Snake Crawl?

In a straight line!

Just as a snake will never crawl in a straight line, a stock will never move in a straight line, but always in ups and downs and in highs and lows.

Remember this when a stock is moving in the opposite direction to what you want. Usually a stock moves "against" your wishes because that is its nature, which does not necessarily imply that the trend has changed.

Differentiate between **episodic noise** in a stock's movement and real change in trend. We will discuss "noise" regarding stock prices later.

Analyzing Japanese Candles

So far, we have seen how prices are presented using Japanese candles. Now we will discuss the components of the candle: **the candle body, and the tail.** Each candle contains information about the balance of power between buyers and sellers.

Narrow Range Candle

The **narrow range candle** shows a relatively short distance between the opening and closing price.

Relatively ... compared to what? To the common behavior of the stock being examined.

Every stock has its own "personality." A candle can only be defined as **short (narrow) or long (wide)** if you observe the stock's behavior over a representative timeframe in which you can see the conduct of many candles.

For a stock such as AAPL, a narrow range intraday candle of five minutes might be from ten to thirty cents, although by contrast, for most stocks, it would be considered long range.

- A narrow range candle indicates low volatility.
- A relatively small change in the balance between buyers and sellers indicates, in many cases, sharp movement anticipated in the near future in one or the other direction.
- A narrow range candle also indicates that buyers and sellers hold close to equal force, as occurs with the candle called a "doji." It is not a perfect balance, as represented by the doji, but does have clear significance.

A candle has little meaning in and of itself, but becomes more important when we observe its position in the formation of several candles. For example, a narrow range candle has one meaning if it follows several more narrow range candles, and a different meaning following several wide range candles. This will be detailed later. We will also discuss **trend reversals**. As with the doji, a narrow range candle also hints at an imminent trend reversal, and provides greater reliability to the reversal pattern.

Wide Range Candle

Here are examples of what candle colors and lengths mean:
- When it is light-colored, the buyers are in clear control
- When it is dark-colored, the sellers are in clear control
- The longer it is, relative to the other candles, the clearer and stronger the control

Narrow and Wide Range Candle in AAPL with Five-Minute Candles

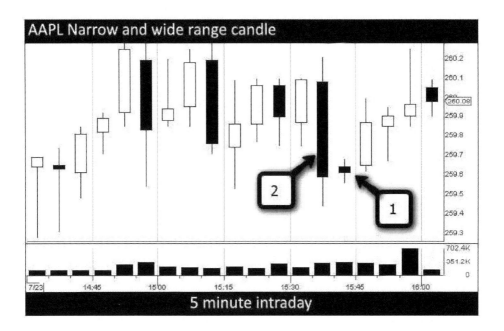

In the narrow range candle [1], the distance between the opening and closing price is very small and almost insignificant. The narrow range, as noted, is a relative term. For AAPL, a range of five cents between opening and closing prices, as we see in this candle, is a miniscule range, but in other stocks such as Microsoft (MSFT), it may indicate a relatively wide range.

When we compare the narrow range candle [1] with the **wide range candle** [2], the narrow and wide ranges become clear specifically for AAPL. In the wide range candle [2], the range between opening and closing prices is 50 cents. Observing this candle relative to adjacent candles, we have no doubt that in that five-minute timeframe, sellers strongly controlled the stock. The very fact that after five minutes of seller control a balance was reached between sellers and buyers, as expressed by the narrow range candle [1], indicates that the battle for control is peaking and could shift to the opposite group. In this case, we can see immediately following the narrow range candle that the buyers did take over. Very often, a narrow range candle does indicate a change of direction, known as **"price reversal."**

What is the stock's trend?

From the chart above, we cannot see sufficient candles to ascertain the trend. But let us assume for now that since the start of trading, AAPL is trending up. Because, statistically speaking, the chances of the trend's continuing upward movement are stronger than the chances of it changing, the narrow range candle [1] has a strong chance of being followed by an uptrend and control would return to buyers, which is what did happen.

The formation of changing direction comprised of a wide range downward candle [2] followed by a narrow range candle [1] and then another rising candle is called **"reversal,"** which we will learn more about later.

SMART MONEY	*We never make trading decisions based on only one candle. Every candle is significant and reliable only within a formation comprised of several candles around it.*

Candle Tail

The tail, also known as the shadow, indicates a change in the power balance between buyers and sellers. To understand how the tail is formed, let's look at the chart below, showing a day of AAPL intraday behavior.

AAPL Fifteen-Minute Candles

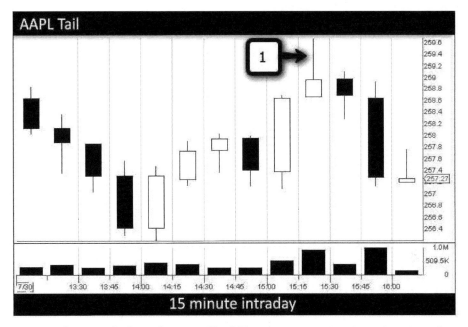

Based on its light color, candle [1] indicates a rise in price: in other words, the stock's closing price is higher than its opening price. But a price rise does not disclose the full story. This candle has more to tell us: it also has a long **topping tail**.

What does the tail signify? As already noted, the tail indicates the stock's peak price in the fifteen-minute timeframe represented by the candle. At some point during those fifteen minutes, the stock price reached the high of the tail, and buyers were in full control. The tail also indicates that buyers did not manage to maintain that high price. In fact, the tail actually shows that sellers took over control of the stock! We see that the length of the tail is almost the full length of the entire candle. Conclusion: there is a high probability of price reversal, i.e. a drop in price, as indicated in the candles that follow [1].

Now, to understand the meaning of the tail even better, let's spread that fifteen-minute interval between 15:15 and 15:30 into candles of one-minute long, and examine what really happened more closely.

AAPL One-Minute Candles

Here the power struggle is more clearly seen. We see a constant, strong increase of clear candles indicating buyer control, and then a sequence of black candles indicating that sellers have taken control. Although at the end of the fifteen-minute interval the stock price rose, the tail's formation shows a shift in control, and therefore an anticipated change in direction of the stock's price. In the previous chart, you can see that this is exactly what happened.

SMART MONEY	*A topping tail indicates that sellers take control, and a bottoming tail indicates that buyers have taken control. Tails are an excellent tool for predicting price reversal.*

Does the color of the candle have meaning relative to the tail? In the fifteen-minute AAPL chart, the candle is clear: this indicates a rise in price. If it were dark, indicating a drop in price, then the tail would even more strongly imply change of control.

A **topping tail** indicates that sellers have taken control. The longer the tail, the stronger and clearer the control. The candle color makes no difference.

A **bottoming tail** indicates an expected upward reversal. Here, too, the position of the candle with the tail within the formation of candles provides the tail with its significance. A long tail pointing down reminds us that there used to be complete seller control, but control has now been taken by the buyers.

Reversal Patterns

Candles very loyally tell us of the battles between buyers and sellers for any given timeframe, but these are just a small part of the total picture of patterns they create.

To understand where a stock originates and to try and predict where it is going, we must look at much more than a single candle within a group of candles, and try to make our decisions based on patterns comprised of several candles. When we learn to identify patterns, we can "understand" a stock with just a glance, and take decisions accordingly.

- **Reversal patterns** are chart formations of a group of candles that help us identify high and low points.
- We use reversal patterns to understand when we should buy or sell stocks which are about to change (reverse) direction. For example: if we bought a stock, we would want to sell as close as possible to its high, but if we were holding a stock short, we would want to buy it back as close as possible to its low, right at the point where it just begins to go up.
- If we want to profit when shorting a stock, we would do that before its price goes up.
- If we wish to sell short, we would want to short when the stock has finished a pullback and is about to execute another drop.

Reversal patterns are usually formed after a significant rise or fall in price. Patterns are subdivided into **bullish**, implying an upward direction, or **bearish**, implying a downward direction.

The patterns I will explain further are common and accepted by professional traders. All these patterns are valid for any timeframe or period. They can be implemented for a group of weekly candles, daily candles or intraday candles, depending on your purposes and the range over which you plan to hold the stock.

Common Reversal Patterns

Doji	A bullish pattern formed at the base of movement when, after several down trending candles, a candle appears showing that the open and closing prices are identical. Doji indicates perfect balance between buyers and sellers: in other words, indecisiveness, and usually indicates possible pattern reversal.	
Dragonfly Doji	A bullish pattern created at the base of movement similar to the doji, but it also shows a wide range bottoming tail indicating that control has been taken by buyers.	
Gravestone Doji	A bearish pattern created at the peak of movement, similar to the doji, but with the addition of a wide range topping tail indicating that control has been taken by sellers.	
Abandoned Baby	A "daily" bullish pattern at the base of movement. The uniqueness of this pattern is that the closing price of the day prior to this doji is higher than the highest price of the doji's tail, and the open price of the next day's trade is higher than the doji tail's highest price.	
Dark Cloud Cove	A bearish pattern where the black candle covers more than half of the clear candle's movement, in the opposite direction to the stock's overall movement.	
Engulfing	A bullish pattern in which the clear candle covers more than the length of the dark candle, in the opposite direction to the stock's overall trend (the dark candle is fully shadowed by the clear candle).	
Evening Doji Star	A bearish pattern where the doji heading the trend indicates pattern reversal, and the dark candle following it moves down to at least below half the body of the clear candle preceding it.	
Evening Star	A bearish pattern. At the trend's peak is a narrow range candle indicating pattern reversal. The candle following it drops to at least below the halfway mark of the clear candle prior to the narrow range candle. The narrow range candle could be clear or dark.	

Morning Doji Star	A bullish pattern opposite to that of the Evening Star. Here the doji indicates pattern reversal after the dark candle, which is followed by a clear candle rising to at least halfway above the body of the dark candle preceding the doji.	
Morning Star	A bullish pattern. At its base is a narrow range candle indicating pattern reversal, followed by a clear candle rising to at least halfway above the dark candle preceding the narrow range candle. The lowest candle could be clear or dark.	
Long Lower Shadow	A bullish pattern. At its base is a candle with a long bottoming tail, followed by a clear candle rising to at least halfway above the dark candle preceding it.	
Long Upper Shadow	A bearish pattern. Its movement peaks with the candle having a long topping tail, followed by the dark candle dropping to at least halfway below the clear candle preceding the peak candle.	
Piercing Line	A bullish pattern. After a dark wide range candle, a white candle forms which penetrates beyond the halfway point of the dark candle's body.	
Hammer	A bullish pattern created when the price of a stock drops significantly, but during the candle's timeframe the price comes back to rise strongly and close with a significantly higher price than the low price.	
Hanging Man	A bearish pattern formed when the stock price drops at the start of the candle's timeframe, but returns to rise strongly at its close with a high price. The strong sales at the outset indicate the beginning of the end for buyer control.	
Inverted Hammer	A bullish pattern created when a dropping stock reverses its pattern briefly and rises, but at the end of the candle's time- frame returns to the bottom and leaves a topping tail. The strong buyer end at the outset indicates the beginning of the end of seller control.	
Spinning Top	A bearish pattern. At the pattern's peak is a narrow range candle with two tails, followed by a dark candle dropping to at least below the halfway mark of the clear candle preceding the peak candle.	

Summary

Patterns are mirrors that reflect the war between buyers and sellers. Patterns help predict the outcomes of this war and allow the trader to choose the winning side.

Try to examine each pattern, and imagine the war. Once you've learned these patterns, your next move is to join the real game. Open a volatile stock price chart, such as that of AAPL, and try to guess, in real time, according to patterns of five-minute candles, what the stock's next step could conceivably be. I believe you'll be presently surprised by your ability to predict the pattern.

Homework

Below is a day of trading in AAPL stock, represented in five-minute candles. Name each of the patterns marked on the chart:

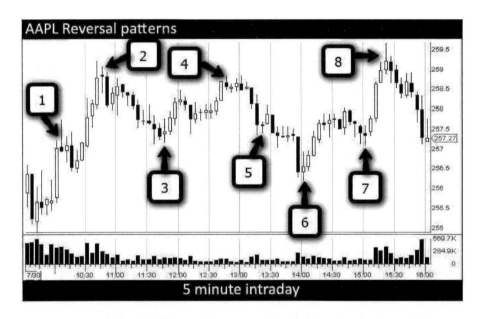

It's not so very difficult, right? So what's the problem? You can make millions this way! But... unfortunately, it's not quite that simple. The question is not only whether you can identify pattern reversal, but how long that reversal will last. For example: if you correctly identify the reversal pattern [1] and execute a short there but do not turn a fast profit, you will find yourself losing when the stock reverses direction toward [2]. Identifying the pattern is the basis, but it is not the entire picture. Later we will also learn that the pattern must be integrating in the stock's trend. In other words, we would not short at [1] because at the start of the day, the stock was running up and therefore the probability is high that the downward reversal would be relatively short compared to the next upward reversal (with the trend) immediately following [1] and before [2].

In fact, the example I chose is a dreadful sampling of a stock that traded most of the day without a trend. If you try to make a profit from the outcomes of these reversals on a day like that, you are destined to failure! In short, don't let me catch you trying to make "fast money." Believe me, I was there, I tried it, I lost enough until I eventually learned that I must never get involved in a trendless stock.

Success requires that you identify the outcomes of reversal patterns in stocks with a clear trend. One good yield from a stock with a clear up or down trend may be enough to provide your daily profits.

Intraday Pattern Reversal for Sears, SHLD

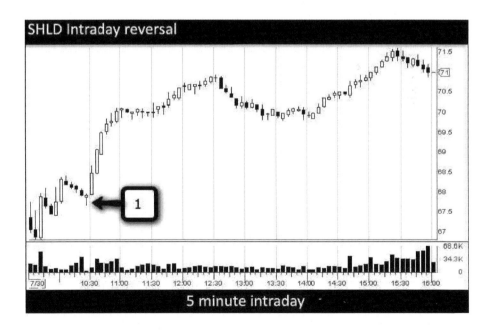

On the day that AAPL went nowhere, Sears began its first hour of trade with a clear upward trend. The day actually began with two dark

candles, but experienced traders know that during the first ten minutes of trade (the first two candles), a stock's trend is still undetermined and derives chiefly from automated orders given by the public to brokers before the day's trading begins. When the third candle rises higher than the high of the two dark candles, we can assume that from here on, the stock will go up.

Has an uptrend been established yet? Absolutely not. We will wait. After the first up trending candle are two dark "corrective" candles. These are then followed by a new high, and we now have two higher highs. Now we can see the trend. Now we await the trend correction, and buy on the first reversal which appears at [1]. At this point the stock is showing the classic reversal pattern with a long bottoming tail and is simply begging us to buy. SHLD closes the day's trading with a high of 4.4% above the open!

Summary:

One trade with the trend is worth a thousand failed intraday attempts at finding the reversal pattern of a trendless stock.

SMART MONEY	*A reversal pattern should be looked for only within the stock's trend. In an up-trending stock, we will look for the bullish pattern, and in a downward trending stock, we will look for the bearish pattern*

Later in the book, we will apply the more common name for these pattern changes: **reversals.**
- A reversal that brings the stock back to trending up is called a **roll-up**
- A reversal that bring stock back to trending down is called a **roll-over**

Homework

Traders will often look at fifteen-minute candles in order to reduce the influence of "noise" on their decisions. On a clean page, sketch a fifteen-minute candle that replaces Sear's first three 5-minute candles. Get the picture?

When to Hit the Button

There is little point in learning patterns if you do not know when to hit the button. In the chart below, I have marked the long and short entries in the accepted reversal formations.

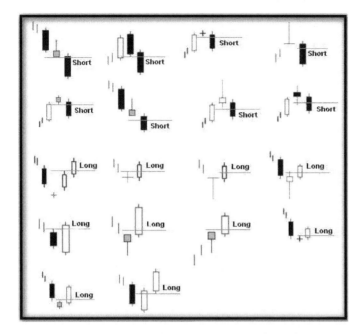

Of course, you need to remember that this is not an exact science. The entry point is more a feeling comprised of many facets tied, among other things, to the general market direction, the trend's strength, the stock's behavior, and a great number of additional factors we will learn about later. At the moment you need to press the button, you will need to assess several factors that may cause you to press early or late, relative to what you see and sense.

As you note in the chart, in most cases I have tried to precede the entry point even before the point where the classic pattern actualizes. When I see a reversal being structured right before my eyes, I try to keep focused on the thought, "What is the probability that the pattern will reach completion?" If I answer "90%," then I'll press the button even before the pattern is fully developed. When I decide to press at this early stage, I base my decision on a lot of experience, but your current status is not the same as mine. My suggestion to the novice trader is to wait until a clear reversal develops. Only later will you acquire the "artistic" component in trading.

The entry points shown on this chart are slightly before the final development of the pattern, but I do think that you can already begin to implement them as shown.

One of the greatest advantages of the online trading room where I trade daily with hundreds of other traders is that I can be heard in real time executing my early entries. If you hear me applying this strategy 50 times, it's highly probable that on the 51st, you'll be able to do it yourself.

Note that so far we have learned when to enter, but not when to exit. In a later chapter discussing trade methods, reversals will be discussed further and we will round out information on money management, aka when to sell.

Breakout and Breakdown Patterns

The function of breakout patterns, like reversal patterns, is to identify the entry point on a stock which is about to make a sharp upward price change. In contrast to reversal patterns, the breakout pattern is not meant to identify the point of reversal, but continuation.

Breakout patterns operate better when the market is stronger and volume is high. It is possible to trade in breakout patterns throughout the trading day, but the best time to do so is during the first ninety minutes of the trading session. Later, we will trade in intraday breakouts providing they look particularly good or are based on the daily chart, and their purpose is for a swing of several days' length.

The reverse of breakout patterns is known as **breakdown patterns**. Everything that has been said relative to stocks breaking out with an upward movement is true for stocks breaking down in a downward movement.

Breakout and breakdown patterns are based on psychological formations of buyers and sellers, on fear and on greed. Every time you identify a pattern, imagine the people currently holding the stock, or about to exit it. Think about the mindset of long traders, short traders, and the disappointment of those who did not succeed in buying or shorting, or those who are currently, like you, trying to enter. By the time you reach the stage where you "understand" the stock, the patterns will be well assimilated in your mind.

Bull Flag

A **bull flag** is a bullish pattern comprised of one or more strong candles that form the "pole" of the flag, and several candles (usually three to five) that consolidate around the head of the pattern, and comprise the flag itself. The long entry will be executed when the price goes over the top of the flag. The pattern's strength derives from the stock price quickly rising to its top, but instead of correcting at its peak as would be anticipated of a stock that has completed a sharp rise, the stock consolidates around the peak and within a short time breaks out beyond that, continuing to move up "without looking back." The significance of rising to a new high is an unequivocal victory of buyers over sellers. Buyers are not waiting for a reversal and are willing to buy at any price. On the other hand, the short sellers, disappointed by the stock's rise and hoping it will correct downwards after the high, are forced to close their shorts when the stock reaches a higher high (i.e. to buy), thus causing further highs.

A bull flag is a strong formation that usually allows us to execute a scalp. The term **"to scalp"** relates to a trading method where the trader executes a speedy entry and exit from a stock. It usually lasts between several seconds and several minutes. We buy at the breakout, sell three-quarters of the quantity at the first signal of weakness, and then hold the remaining piece in the hopes that the final quarter will continue rising. We scalp quickly, since the stock price prior to the breakout was already **extended** upwards and we fear that the breakout will fail.

A Bull Flag Formation for Philip Morris – PM

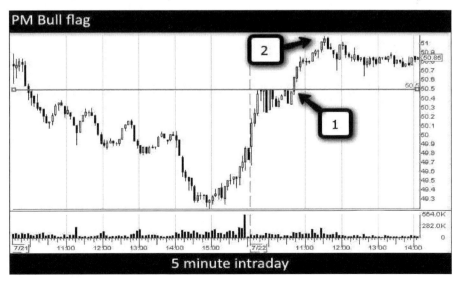

In this intraday chart showing two days of trade, we see Philip Morris rising strongly at the start of trade from $49.7 to $50.5, which is a sharp rise of some 2% lasting for just fifteen minutes. This is the area that forms the flagpole. Now it consolidates around the high and completes the bull flag formation. Note that in this case, we can clearly see over time how the candles around the consolidation become increasingly shorter, i.e. the price is consolidating towards a possible breakout. This is the area of the flag.

Another interesting point is that the stock consolidates beneath the price of $50.5, which we call a **semi-round number**. As we will learn later, at round numbers as well as sometimes semi-round numbers, many sellers inhibit the stock's further rise. The stock breaks out of [1] the bull flag's head (resistance) and rises a little more than 1% [2] "without looking back."

Bear Flag

A **bear flag** is the reverse pattern of the bull flag. The pattern comprises one or more downward trending candles representing the flagpole, and several candles (usually three to five) consolidating around the bottom of the pattern to create the flag shape. A stock will be shorted when the price drops below the flag's low. The pattern's strength derives from the stock price dropping below the low, but instead of correcting upwards, as would be expected of a stock that has completed a sharp series of drops, the stock breaks down under the low. The significance of a new low is an unequivocal victory of sellers over buyers. Buyers are very pressured, do not wait for the correction, and are willing to sell at any price. On the other hand, buyers who prayed for a correction to save them are disappointed by the stock's further drop to a lower low, and sell under pressure, which causes the stock to drop further. The bear flag formation allows us to short scalp (speedy entry and exit), because the stock price is stretched downwards even before the breakdown, and we are afraid that the stock will drop to a new low but then immediately correct itself upwards.

Bear Flag Breakdown, Genzyme – GENZ

In the above example, the stock price of the bio-tech company Genzyme drops at the start of the day's trading, and with one five-minute candle forms the bear flagpole [1]. For the next five candles, it solidifies around the intraday low, hinting that despite the price drop, it has no intention of correcting upwards as would normally occur with a sharply dropping stock. Consolidation around the bottom of the flagpole creates the flag itself. Breaking down the base of the flag leads, as expected, to continued lows.

Cup and Handle Formation

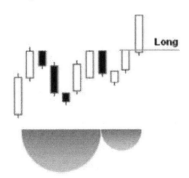

The **cup & handle** formation is a bullish pattern that suggests the shape of a cup and handle. The pattern is comprised of a stock reaching its high, encountering resistance and correcting downwards. The stock returns to the high, and in this way forms the cup. At the high, the stock once again encounters resistance (remember when we learned the term "double top"?) and corrects downward again while creating the shape of the handle. This time, when it returns to a high for the third time, it breaks through the resistance and rises to a new high. The breakout point is the point where we should buy the stock.

What have we learned about the stock prior to its breakout? The stock reached a high, so we realize it is strong. It corrected downwards but returned to the same high, from which we learn that buyers are still in control. The stock drops again, but this time drops less than the previous time and for a shorter period. The stock returns to its high a third time.

Conclusion: Buyers are in control and are even become more aggressive: they are buying after the smallest correction, and they are buying faster. Buyers have begun overtaking the sellers. We conclude that the stock is strengthening and may break out the resistance soon.

Cup and Handle Formation, United States Steel – X

In the intraday chart for X, we can see that the stock is rising strongly at the start of trading and meets resistance at the price of $54.49. It retreats, drops [1] but returns again to the resistance point, and in this way forms the cup. Now it drops to a new low [1], which shapes the handle, but this time the low is higher than the previous low, since buyers are becoming more aggressive. It returns again to its high within a shorter timeframe than when forming the cup. The stock breaks through the resistance [2] and climbs to a new high.

Interestingly, if you track back slightly into the previous trading day, you can see that the area of resistance was formed on that day. You can also see that if you connect the previous trading day's formation to that of the breakout day, you will find a more complex formation called **head and shoulder formation**, which we will study later. Note that the formation does not need to be perfect from the graphical perspective. For example, the line of resistance does not have to pass exactly through the same previous high points.

SMART MONEY	*Patterns do not have to be "pretty" or "perfect" from the graphical perspective. A pattern is valid even with deviations from the precise areas of support or resistance.*

Inverse Cup and Handle

The **inverse cup and handle** is a bearish formation, the reverse of the "cup and handle" described above. The pattern shows a stock dropping to a low, finding support, then correcting upwards. The stock then returns to a low, creating the shape of an inverse cup. It is then supported again at the low point, and corrects once more upwards while forming the shape of an inverted handle. The small handle's shape and the amount of time taken to form it are shorter than the time in which the cup took shape, i.e. sellers are more aggressive. Now it returns to a low for the third time, breaks down through support and continues lower. The breakdown point is where we should sell short.

What have we learned prior to the breakdown? The stock dropped, and therefore we see it is weak. The stock corrected upward but dropped again, from which we learn that sellers are still in control. The stock rises again, but only less than the previous high (this is the handle) and then returns to a low in a shorter timeframe than it took to reach the previous low.

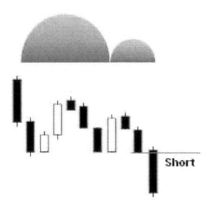

Conclusion: Sellers remain in control and are beginning to sell earlier and lower than at the previous high (the cup shape). The fact that the stock returns to a low faster, and from a lower price, indicates to us that the stock is weakening and that it will probably soon break down through the support line.

Breakdown of Cup and Handle, Myriad Genetics – MYGN

Myriad Genetics begins its trading day with fifteen minutes of sharp lows, finds support, corrects upwards, returns to a low and creates the inverse cup [1]. The stock rises again, drops to a low and forms the inverse handle [2]. The stock breaks down support [3] and continues to drop. Later it reverses direction upwards. The fact that the stock rises after the breakdown formation is of no importance to us. The breakdown succeeded, and with correct money management, as we will learn later, we can profit nicely from that, too.

SMART MONEY	*The success of a pattern in leading to breakdown or breakout is measured in the distance the price moved after the breakout. There is no guarantee that the pattern's success in the short range will lead to a continuation of the trend.*

Head and Shoulders

The **head and shoulders formation** is considered one of the strongest bearish formations. As with the inverted cup and handle, here, too, the structure involves candles consolidating above the line of support in expectation of its breakdown.

The head and shoulders formation, being so powerful, is a favorite of traders and therefore draws the attention of sellers and short sellers more than other formations.

The formation is comprised of a left shoulder indicating the first low price, a head indicating the upward correction and a return to the low, and a right shoulder indicating an additional correction followed by the return of the stock to a low at the support point. The low's breakdown is where support breaks, and also where the short enters.

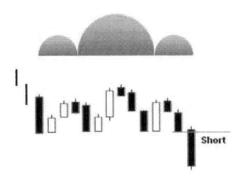

The tractor manufacturer AGCO drops immediately when the trading session opens, corrects a little upwards, and forms the left shoulder [1], corrects and forms the head [2], returns to the support line, corrects again and forms the right shoulder [3], and finally breaks the line of support.

Head and Shoulders For mation - AGCO

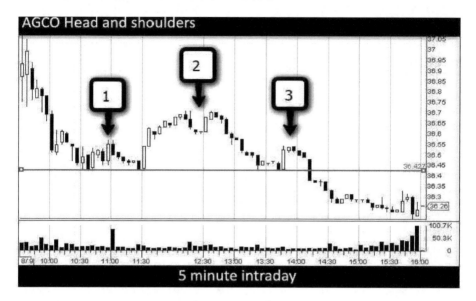

Inverse Head and Shoulders

The **inverse head and shoulders** is a bullish formation, and the opposite of the head and shoulders. Similar to the cup and handle, here, too, the structure shows candles consolidating beneath the line of resistance in anticipation of its breakout.

The inverse head and shoulders, also a strong formation, is a favorite among traders and draws more buyers than other formations.

The structure is comprised of a left shoulder indicating a high price, a head indicating the downward correction and a return upwards to the line of resistance, then a right shoulder indicating a further correction, and a return of the price back to the line of resistance. The breakout through resistance is also the point of long entry.

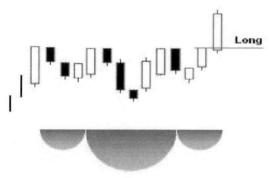

SMART MONEY | *Head and shoulders* formations are "long range" formations structured on multiple candles, and are therefore valid even if they operate against the stock's original trend.

Inverse Head and Shoulders, the Fuel Company – ATPG

ATPG drops sharply when the trading session opens, corrects upwards and forms the left shoulder [1]. It then drops to a new low, but returns to the area of resistance of the left shoulder, and in this way forms the inverted head [2]. It corrects again and forms the right shoulder [3]. It should now be fairly clear that the price is reversing direction. The right shoulder [3] indicates that buyers are no longer panicked, compared to the head [2], and that a breakout of the resistance line should lead to a high.

Pennant

A **pennant** formation can be bearish or bullish. In the pennant formation, the price consolidates while moving in the form of a pennant, as seen in the chart. You need to sketch the pennant in your imagination and then wait for the exit beyond its boundaries, as we see in the chart.

The technical premise is that at the end of consolidation, at approximately 80% of the pennant's expected range, a sharp shift in movement should be executed. Usually the exit from the pennant follows the original trend, in other words: if the stock showed an uptrend before its consolidation in the pennant formation, it is reasonable to assume that the price will break out upward in accordance with the original trend, similar to a bull flag, but without the flagpole. By contrast, if the price consolidates into a pennant while trending down, it is reasonable to assume that a breakdown will occur with a downward movement, similar to a bear flag, but without the flagpole.

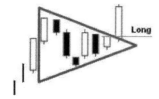

Pennant Breakout, SanDisk – SNDK

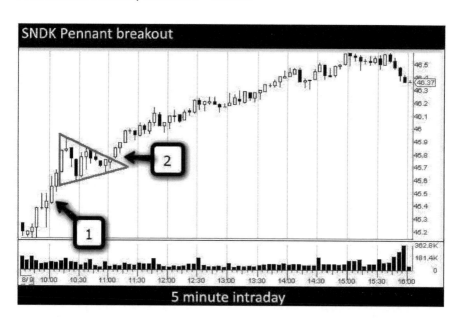

SanDisk rises immediately when the trading session opens [1], encounters resistance, and consolidates in the pennant form. The pennant breaks out [2] and SanDisk continues rising. The buy position can be at the exit from the pennant, or in the transition above the "flag" area. As you see, this breakout formation is very similar to that of the bull flag, but instead of consolidating beneath the upper resistance line, the price consolidates in the shape of a pennant. Personally, I prefer to trade the bull flag formation. It is clearer and simpler to identify entry positions.

6

Indices, Sectors and Crystal Balls

Most stock trends can be anticipated according to the movement of the market and sector to which a company belongs.

How to Predict Movement

Market performance is measured with market indices. Every index represents a different group of companies and is comprised of different market sectors. Indices can be represented on a chart, and we observe the movement of the index through candles. Every index and every sector has a different meaning. Some are more important, some less so, but all are important. A market index does not serve only to show us what the market has "done," but above all else, to predict which way the market is trending. Because the market and sectors are responsible for 90% of price movement for the stocks we trade, it follows that if you know how to predict index movement, you will also be able to predict the price movement of the stocks in which you are interested. Stop for a moment and think about that. Do you really understand the significance of what you've just read? Okay, let's move forward.

SMART MONEY | *The **market index** is no less than the trader's crystal ball. A full 90% of the price movement begins and ends with advance movement of the market index*

We need to recognize the indices in their order of importance and learn how to use them. In addition, and to expand our knowledge, we will relate to some less useful indices, simply because as future professional colleagues, I don't want you to feel ashamed that you're not familiar with them.

As a rule, we monitor several indices. We don't believe in just one index, but rather try to combine information from several of them. Once we get to know the main indices, we will also learn about the sectors comprising each index. Because of the high importance of movement of the indices for the stocks in which I trade, I devote one full screen to indices and sectors and watch them even more, time wise, than I watch the stock prices I am trading.

The Most Important Market Index: S&P 500

The S&P 500 index (symbol: SPX) is the most important index in the world.Without doubt, for traders it is the focal index, the king, the trader's crown and scepter. It was developed by the financial services company **Standard & Poor's**, giving rise to its initials. This index displays the prices of the 500 largest-traded US companies via a formula that calculates the importance and influence of these top 500 companies according to S&P specialists' considerations. Standard and Poor's is considered of highest quality due to its broad range, and it serves as the benchmark for measuring the entire market performance. Of course, the S&P serves managers of portfolios, investment funds, hedge funds, and more in every stock exchange throughout the world.

For example: an investment fund that succeeds in providing its investors with a positive yield of 8% when the S&P rose only 6% will proudly declare that it has **"beaten the market."** On that matter, let me state that research consistently shows the horrific fact that 80% of the world's investment funds do not succeed in beating the market. Therefore, next time you receive your investment fund's annual report, proudly flashing its positive annual return, discover the truth by comparing the results to the market outcomes. In most cases, you will be sorely disappointed. In fact, I have never found a fund that is able to beat the market over the long term.

SMART MONEY | *Do you want to beat 80% of the funds? Buy **market basket ETFs**. Research over a twenty-year period shows that 80% of funds worldwide do not succeed in beating the market index.*

Note: from this point on, whenever I refer to "the market" or "the market index," I will be referring to the S&P 500 index.

The rise and fall of indices are measured in percentages, but stock market specialists on TV channels such as CNBC or Bloomberg will usually be heard saying something like,

"The S&P rose today by 18 points."

These specialists expect you to know at any given moment the index point value. Currently, for example, the market is around 1,800 points, so you will need to understand that a day's rise of 18 points is an increase of 1.0%. The index's value in points is the normalized price of 500 different stocks, but it is not a tradable index. In other words, you cannot buy and sell that index itself. To trade in index-linked values, the **"Exchange Traded Fund" (ETF)** was invented, and will be explained further.

Previously, I noted that the S&P 500 is the most important index for the intraday trader. Why? Because 60% of a stock's movement will be dictated by index movement. In other words, the stock you have bought will rise or fall **after** the S&P 500 has risen or fallen, and you will profit or lose chiefly by being dependent on market direction.

Would you like proof? Observe the index in the chart below, where you can see the connection between the S&P and the stock:

Comparing the Intraday Behavior of Apple (AAPL) and S&P 500 (SPX)

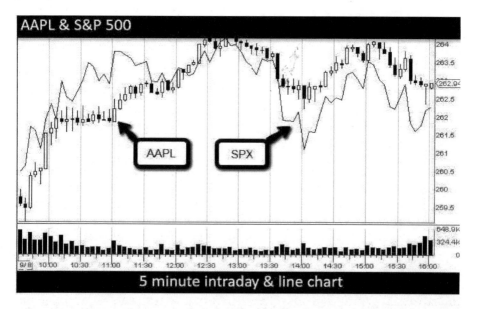

In the chart above, you can see Apple's intraday movement in five-minute candles. If you thought Apple had a life of its own...you were

wrong! All intraday movement is determined at the outset by the market movement. The market moves first, and individual companies' shares follow. Certainly an important stock such as Apple carries serious weight in the market index, but its weight is still relative to 499 other companies comprising the index. In other words, Apple does not have the power to move the index on its own. This is not true for the NASDAQ 100 index in which Apple is currently a 20% component.

I can well imagine how you are taking a deep breath and saying, "Just WHAT does he mean? Am I supposed to know in advance when a stock is about to rise even before it has?"

The answer is: Yes!

Is it easy to make money this way?

The answer is: No!

Apple should move in the direction that the market is trending, but you can never know how much the market will move, how far behind it Apple will move, and when the market will reverse.

How can we nonetheless take advantage of this information? In several ways:

Buying

Let's assume Apple is about ready to break out through intraday resistance and you are weighing the risk of buying at the breakout. Now let's assume that just before Apple breaks out, the market also broke out to a new high. Does the market breakout help you decide whether to buy Apple in the breakout? Of course! Let's also assume that the market showed a strong breakout. Would you now consider buying a larger quantity than what you might have initially intended? Yes! You would have considered entering Apple because of a nice technical formation, but you reached that decision and the quantity you chose because of the market's "support." Think about the reverse case: You are considering buying Apple at the breakout, but just before Apple's breakout, the market breaks down. What would you do? Yes, you must forego entering.

Turning a Profit

Let's assume that simultaneous to the market rising, you bought Apple, the stock rose, reached the area of profit you set, and now you're trying to "squeeze" a fraction more profit from the uptrend. Your finger is poised on the mouse, and you wonder whether you should press that sell button. The market stops moving up, and suddenly begins to correct down. This will usually occur just before Apple will also correct. Is this the time to sell and turn a profit? Of course it is. Because we have already learned that 60% of Apple movement is tied to market movement, so Apple will almost certainly drop following the market's drop. It is true that stocks do very occasionally "have a life of their own" and Apple could go up even if the market is dropping, but the risk in trading will be much higher.

SMART MONEY	*Don't fight the market. Don't buy stocks moving opposite to the market direction, because you will almost always lose money. Go with the market direction. Going against the market direction is tough and lies in terrain where only extremely experienced traders dare to trade-- and even then, very rarely with success.*

Sideways Movement

Let's assume that you're interested in buying a stock that is about to break out, when the market starts moving sideways. Should you buy when the stock breaks out? I have no perfect answer, but if there is no market support, the breakout will be much weaker, and the risk high to very high. The wisest decision in such cases is to buy smaller quantities.

Trend

Let's assume you wish to buy a stock which is up trending when the market is downtrending. Should you buy? Most likely, you should not. The most feasible eventuality is that the market will continue trending down, and sooner or later your stock will follow the market direction. Institutional investors buy only in accordance with market direction, and if they don't help you, it is better that you don't buy.

Exceptions

Sometimes I break my rules on purpose. If, for example, I believe something special is happening to a stock and its chances of rising are particularly high, I might buy it even when the market is down trending. Of course there is high risk when I buy against market direction, and therefore my stop order, which is my protective backstop, will be closer to the buy price, and of course I will buy a smaller quantity.

Independent Stocks

There are very few stocks which have what is known in professional jargon as **"a life of their own,"** meaning that they are not influenced by the market direction. They are usually stocks with low volume in which institutional funds do not invest, and are therefore less sensitive to the moods of institutional traders as these moods manifest in market direction. Usually these are stocks priced at less than $10, which we will learn more about later. Be wary of these stocks unless you have gained a lot of experience.

Sometimes a stock will have "a life of its own" when special announcements are made. An example would be the publicizing of an important announcement concerning a stock, when an analyst's recommendation goes live or is changed, when quarterly reports are made public, and so on. In such cases, the stock may move irrespective of market direction, though it will still be affected by market direction. For example, the market may drop while a specific stock rises. Nonetheless, if you compare the stock's movement relative to that of the market, you will see that every time the stock executed an intraday reversal, it was closely synchronized with the market's intraday reversal. In other words, when the market corrects down during a downtrend, the independent stock will correct down even though it is showing an uptrend. This means that even if you are trading in a stock that is moving against the market trend, you still need to examine every move in the market's trend.

Note:

All the principles noted above are also relevant in reverse for stocks that are in a downtrend, i.e. for shorts instead of longs. If, for example, the market is rising and on that same day, a certain stock in which we wish to execute a short is dropping, **it is still moving according to market direction.** While it is dropping, despite its direction being the opposite of the market direction, it will correct up each time that the market index goes up, and will go back to dropping each time that the market index drops. By the end of the day, the market could end with highs and the stock with lows, but the intraday movement will be strongly influenced by market direction.

Index Symbol

Different trading platforms may present the same index under different names, but with the same basis. If you wish to find the SPX index, you may need to search for an identical or closely similar symbol: SPX, $SPX or SPX$ - the same symbol with a dollar sign before or after it. If none of these symbols matches your graph software, use the symbol search field to look for the term: S&P 500.

Summary

The market index known as the **S&P 500** represents not only the market direction but also the mood of private and institutional investors, and of traders. Institutional traders do not buy stocks when the market index drops, but wait patiently until the index downtrend causes the stock they are waiting for to drop, allowing them to buy it at a cheaper price after the correction. When you buy a stock, you should look for support from the institutional investors. You want their mood to be as happy as possible, and you want their money to enter the stock you have just purchased. Don't expect that to happen when the market index is dropping. Don't fight the direction of the market!

SPY – The S&P 500 ETF

As noted, the S&P 500 market index, symbol SPX, is not a tradable index but denotes in points the state of the stocks that comprise it. Because many investors, especially those disappointed by funds, are interested in finding a simple way to link their money to market yields, i.e. to "buy the market," the solution for them is to buy the S&P 500 ETF (Exchange Traded Funds) that follow the market and are known as SPYDERS, bearing the recognized symbol **SPY**.

ETFs are financial instruments traded exactly like stocks, and are therefore given symbols just like stocks. The SPY price is very similar to its value in points with the deletion of one zero. In other words, if the SPX stands at 1500 points, the SPY price will be in the vicinity of $150. ETFs are more sensitive to supply and demand fluctuations.

Unlike the SPX, the SPY can be graphed to show volume, which does not exist for an index.

ES – The S&P 500 Futures

If I haven't yet confused you with the difference between the non-traded index represented by **SPX** and the tradable ETFs represented by **SPY**, I will likely succeed in confusing you now when I present **the most important variation of the S&P 500**, represented by **ES**.

The ES is the S&P 500's futures contract, or as it is professionally known: **E-mini S&P 500 Futures.**

Without going into a detailed explanation at this point of "future contracts," I do wish to differentiate between a stock and a futures contract: a futures contract is a "financial product" which can be bought and sold just like stocks, but with one difference: its expiration date is at the end of each quarter.

The price of the futures contract represents the "anticipated future" of the S&P 500. In other words, the ES represents the anticipated market direction. In actuality, the ES is a tradable contract, traded by a crazy bunch of experts in the **CME – Chicago Mercantile Exchange**. These traders operate in transactions with a volume of billions of dollars daily. It's commonly accepted on Wall Street that futures traders know better than anyone else on the face of the earth whether the market will go up or down. If you check the ES at the end of a day's trading, you will see that it precedes the SPX or SPY by several seconds, and therefore allows you to note market direction earlier, too. Since we have already understood that the S&P 500 is THE most important index for the day trader and determines 60% of the direction of stocks you are trading, if you also use the ES, you will definitely know before others which way the market is moving. In short, it's worth money.

Not every broker or chart provider allows display of the ES, since they need to pay for the information coming from the Chicago Futures Exchange. If your broker does supply this information, you will likely be charged some $50 per month for it.

Another advantage of the ES is the fact that it is electronically traded almost 24 hours a day (it closes for 15 minutes at 4:15 pm EST) except on weekends, which goes far beyond normal trading times of stock exchanges, operating between 9.30 am to 4 pm EST. This means that the ES is traded before other trading sessions open. Therefore, if you look at the pre-market chart about one hour before the start of trade, which is what I do, you will know whether the market will open positively or negatively as compared to the prior day's close. But of course, you are not the only ones able to check the pre-market chart: every decent financial site or television channel, such as CNBC, will keep you updated prior to the trade session opening as to what kind of opening the futures are "signaling," adding a warning statement such as: "Futures do not always represent market direction."

Should You Trade in Futures?

Futures trading is not for everyone. Futures contracts behave like stocks, but with heavy leverage of 1 to 20. This means that you get a lot more bang for your buck trading futures contracts. Even if the price of futures shows no volatility, the movement of money in the accounts creates the illusion of real volatility. This illusion, accompanied by the thrill it arouses of seeing money in the account, attracts "gamblers" who usually very quickly lose their money. Veteran traders like me also trade (but not exclusively) in futures. I would recommend that novice traders with less than three years' experience do not even try. Everything in its own good time, and patience pays off.

What is the ES Symbol?

Futures expire every three months, at the end of the third Friday of any quarter. Simultaneous to their expiration, new futures contracts are being formed and traded: their expiration date will be at the end of the third Friday of the next quarter. Unlike a stock which carries a fixed symbol, each future has its own symbol. Your broker can help you find the current symbol of a future, but you can also do that yourself, as will be explained.

An example of a futures symbol with an expiration date of the first quarter of 2013 would be **/ESH3**.

Explanation of the Symbol

The slash always precedes the letters "ES," which are the two letters in the symbol that will never vary. The "H" represents the quarter, which in this case is the first quarter of the year, i.e. this future expires at the end of March. The digit indicates the year, i.e. 2013. The digit will always be single: 3 is 2013, 4 will be 2014, 5 will be 2015, etc.

The quarters are represented as follows:

H – futures contracts expiring at the end of March
M – futures contracts expiring at the end of June
U – futures contracts expiring at the end of September
Z – futures contracts expiring at the end of December

I taught myself to remember which letter represents which quarter by linking it with the name of a much loved food, "hummus," as well as the fact that the letters are in alphabetic order.

Question: It is currently September 2, 2013, and you wish to view the relevant futures charts. What symbol will it carry?

Answer: You can already view futures expiring in December 2013, but they will show lower liquidity than those expiring in September, and therefore you will choose futures expiring in September. After the third Friday in September, all trading volume will be on the December contract, although most professionals "roll" to the new contract more than a week before expiration.

The symbols will be:

Futures expiring in September: /ESU3

Futures expiring in December: /ESZ3

Summary: SPX, SPY, ES

The market index is the most important index for intraday traders. If I'm on holiday in Thailand and forced to forego my entire array of screens in my trading room and make do with my 12-inch laptop, the only index I will display, other than the chart for the stock I'm trading, is the five-minute intraday SPY chart or the five-minute intraday ES chart. Every market index movement will be important in helping me decide whether I need to buy or sell a stock. I will use the SPX only when I need to quote a change in the market for a professional article I am preparing for the media.

I choose not to waste expensive paper on samples of the SPY or ES charts, since they will look identical to those of the SPX, and you will only see differences when you starting tracking them in real time.

NASDAQ 100: The Second Most Important Index

The NASDAQ stock exchange also receives a good share of display space on my computer screens. The NASDAQ 100 index, with its **NDX** symbol, is the second most important index for day traders. The index was developed by the NASD, National Association of Securities Dealers, which established the NASDAQ stock exchange. This index represents the price of the leading 100 NASDAQ companies. Since the NASDAQ stock exchange contains a very high proportion of technology companies, the index closely reflects the state of affairs in these companies. A unique phenomenon for our times, in light of the sharp rise in price of Apple's stock [AAPL], developed when Apple covered some 20% of the index's movement. We often joke that if you buy NASDAQ 100 ETFs, you get Apple, plus a bonus of some 99 other stocks…

At this point it is not necessary to list the entire 100 important companies represented by the index, which you can find easily on any financial site, but you surely realize that in addition to Apple, the NASDAQ 100 includes other well-known companies such as Microsoft [MSFT], Intel [INTC], and Google [GOOG]. As with the S&P 500, here, too, each stock carries a different weight. If Apple goes up some 3%, it will have stronger influence on index performance than a similar rise by a less important stock.

Since the S&P 500 contains the 500 most important stocks in the market, clearly a significant proportion of NASDAQ 100 stocks will be among the S&P 500. This explains why the S&P is considered more important and reliable than the NASDAQ 100. Why, then, do I give this index a central position on my trading screens? Is the S&P 500 not sufficient?

The answer relates to the volatility of the NASDAQ 100. It is comprised chiefly of stocks from technology companies. It is well known that these stocks show high volatility relative to the lack of volatility typical of most of the "solid" stocks in the broader S&P market index. Technology stocks are more volatile because the "dream element" embodied in their price is higher than the same "dream element" in a company unrelated to the sphere of technology. For example, the impact of a new electronic gadget on Apple's stock price will be more significant than on shares of Ford [F] when it announces a new model. A volatile index cannot necessarily be relied upon, therefore the NASDAQ 100 is given second place in the list of important indices, but its second place is by virtue of its volatility.

As noted, 60% of market movement is dictated chiefly by the S&P 500. Therefore, it is important for me to analyze index direction. Since the NASDAQ 100 is more volatile than the S&P 500, the NASDAQ index will often indicate the expected direction **before** the S&P. As an example, let's assume that the NASDAQ 100 breaks out first to a new high. Does that mean the stock I bought will also reach a new high? No. As we learned, it will move chiefly according to the S&P 500 rather than the NASDAQ 100, but the NASDAQ breakout may certainly hint at the direction that the S&P 500 will take. To summarize: an early NASDAQ 100 breakout causes me to suspect that the S&P 500 will follow suit. The NASDAQ 100 early breakout is often like an advance warning system of what will happen with the S&P 500.

NASDAQ 100 Symbol

The NASDAQ 100 symbol is **NDX**. As with the SPX, it may appear on your charts with a $ sign before, after, or absent from the symbol: NDX$, NDX, or $NDX. If one of these symbols does not match your trading platform, use the symbol search field to find the symbol by entering this term: NASDAQ 100.

The NDX, like the SPX, is not a traded index, which means you cannot see its volume. It moves only during trading hours, as it is computed based on the price of the 100 stocks that comprise it and are traded in real time.

NASDAQ 100 ETF: QQQ

The NASDAQ 100 NDX index is not a tradable index, but many individuals are interested in linking their money to NASDAQ 100 yields (which is very dangerous!). As a result, the ETF (Exchange Traded Fund) came into being. It tracks the NASDAQ 100 and is known as **"the Q's"** or by its familiar symbol, **QQQ**.

As with the ETFs for SPY, which track the S&P 500, the QQQ is also traded as though it were a stock. It has its own symbol, buyers and sellers.

Being a traded ETF, many traders prefer tracking the Qs than the NDX, because with ETFs, "money talks." ETFs are more sensitive to changes in supply and demand, and a displayable volume is created.

NASDAQ 100 Futures Contract: NQ

The NQ is the NASDAQ 100 futures contract. It is professionally known as the **E-mini NASDAQ 100 Futures contract**. Just as the ES represents the S&P 500's expected future, so the NQ represents the NASDAQ 100's expected future.

The NQ is a contract traded on Chicago's CME. If you watch the NQ during the trading session, you will see that in actuality, it precedes the NDX or QQQ. Paying your broker for the ES package should automatically include all E-mini indices, thus the NQ will be in that package too. It is electronically traded almost 24 hours a day. Checking its chart just before the trading session opens will show you whether the NASDAQ will open up or down, long before many others know.

The NQ Symbol

As with the ES, NQ contracts expire every three months on the third Friday at the end of each quarter.

An example of the symbol for futures expiring at the end of the second quarter would be **/NQM3**. The slash and the letters "NQ" will always remain part of the symbol. The rest decodes precisely the same way as for the ES: "M" represents contracts expiring at the end of the second quarter, and "3" represents the year 2013.

The Forgotten Index: Dow Jones, DJI

The **Dow Jones Industrial Average [symbol: DJI]**, also known simply as the "**Dow,**" was developed by Dow Jones & Company. It is the most veteran and famous of indices on Wall Street. The index is comprised of thirty of America's larger companies over a variety of sectors and is meant to act as a "bell weather" index for the economy. Large numbers of investors worldwide view the Dow as the main tool for following the US market's mood. It is most often quoted in financial media, but the Dow is the last index that needs to interest you as traders. Stock exchange traders are often smug when they come across investors who mention the Dow, which these traders often call "the forgotten index." The only reason it ranks in the third (yet still highly respectable) position is not because you are meant to use it, but because you will hear it abundantly quoted.

Keep in mind that Dow Jones & Company publicizes hundreds of different indices relating to diverse sectors and various states. The DJI is indeed the most famous of them all, but it remains only one of the many indices.

Why do we not use the DJI? Firstly, because it is comprised of only 30 stocks, therefore is not truly representative of the market. Secondly, the thirty stocks comprising the index are often the most "tired" stocks of mega-companies which are highly lethargic. As traders, we need volatile indices representing future expectations and not old histories of mega-corporations. The Dow simply does not deliver the goods.

How is the Index Represented?

The DJI may appear in your trading platform without the $ symbol, or preceded by or following the letter symbol: DJI, DJI or DJI. If one of these symbols does not match your trading platform, use the symbol search field to find the symbol by entering this term: Dow Jones Industrial Average.

The DJI, like the SPX and the NDX, is not a tradable index, so you cannot see any trade volume. None exists. The index moves during trading session times and is a derivative calculated for 30 stocks traded in real time.

The Dow Jones ETF: DIA

The Dow Jones Index [DJI] is tracked by the **"Diamonds" ETF, symbol DIA.** The DIA is meant for people, of which there are a great many worldwide, wanting to link their money to this index's yield. Just like SPY and QQQ, the DIA is traded like a stock. In other words, it has a symbol, and supply and demand.

The Dow Jones Futures Contract: YM

The YM is the Dow Jones futures index and is professionally known as: **E-mini Dow Jones Industrial Average Futures contract.** As with the other futures described, the YM represents the expected futures outcomes of the Dow. It is also electronically traded 24 hours a day on the Chicago CME.

The YM Symbol

This, too, follows the pattern of the ES and NQ. The YM expires on the third Friday of the last month of each quarter. An example of a YM for the fourth quarter of 2010 is: **/YMZ0.**

Rebalance: How to Profit from Index Updates

Once each year, the research organizations Standard & Poor's, Dow Jones, and NASDAQ undertake a joint review of the composition of companies included in the indices they manage. When a specific company is encountering difficulties and its stock has plummeted, it is highly probable that this company will be removed from the list and replaced by a "new star." Stocks such as Apple and Google did not always appear on the index, but made their entrance due to strong successes and to ousting stocks that were doing poorly or were completely inactive.

Why does this need to interest you? For two reasons: first, never believe a person who says something like, "If you had invested $1000 in the Dow Jones 30 years ago, you'd be rich today." That's no less than fraud, used by Wall Street salespersons and fund managers trying to solicit you into a long-term investment. In actuality, the index changes annually since stronger stocks replace those doing poorly. If you'd have invested in the *original* index, you'd have lost a lot of money by now.

The second reason is based on a known trading method: many funds link to an index. For example, a fund may promise its investors that it will only invest in stocks belonging to the S&P 500 index. When a stock is removed, the fund is forced to sell it and instead buy the stock moving into the list.

So far, so good. Do I need to detail how money is made from this activity? Since the information concerning stocks being removed and entered into the index is publicized several weeks before the actual update, the funds are forced to sell and begin buying in advance. In other words, a stock being removed from the index will **drop**, since the funds are forced to sell it; a stock entering the index will **rise**, since the funds are forced to buy it. It's that simple. Type the term **"S&P Rebalance"** into your search engine to find the dates and precise list of stocks leaving and joining the index.

Summary: Market Indices

It's time to make some order out of all the information above.

If you're working with just one screen (which I hope won't be for too much longer), the chart that needs to cover nearly one-quarter of the screen is the ES if you have access to futures, or the SPY if not.

If you have two or more screens, devote between one-third to half of one screen to the ES alongside the NQ (or the SPY and QQQ). I allocate about three-fourths of a 23-inch screen to these two indices.

Display the information in five-minute intraday candles. The larger your screen is, the more trading days you'll be able to display at once. I suggest your display covers at least three trading days. Showing a three-day history helps me search for the support and resistance points over the last few, most current days.

Spot Test

Answers follow.

1. You are about to buy a stock that is about to break out, whereas the ES index jumped a few minutes ago to a new high. Should you buy?
2. You want to buy a stock currently running up, whereas the S&P 500 is trending down. Should you buy the stock?
3. You want to buy a stock, and at the same instant, the S&P 500 breaks out to a new high. Should you buy?
4. You want to execute a short on a stock, and it looks to you that the S&P 500 index is about to break down to a new low, whereas the NASDAQ 100 is trending up in a reverse pattern to the market index. What should you do?
5. You want to buy a stock just as the NASDAQ 100 is breaking out, but the S&P 500 has not broken out yet. Should you buy?

Answers:

1. As noted, 60% of a stock's movement is dictated by the movement of the market index. If the index has gone up and your stock didn't jump higher together with it, something doesn't sound right. Maybe a large-quantity seller is preventing it from going up? Maybe other buyers aren't interested? It is reasonable to assume that the market will self-correct fairly soon for at least part of the highs, which means the stock will likely drop rather than rise.

   Conclusion: don't buy, or buy only a small amount with a close stop order, to protect yourself.

2. In your first three years of trading, I do not permit buying stocks moving in the opposite direction to the market's movement. If you do, or if you execute a short on stocks not following the market direction, the chances of you losing money are at least 60%. Once you have amassed experience, you will learn how to operate against market direction in some cases, but only under unique circumstances and in specific stocks which show extreme movement and ignore market conditions. First, gain much more experience.

3. Of course! If you're about to press the buy button just as the market breaks out to a new high, buying is a correct move that reduces risk and significantly improves opportunity. It is reasonable to assume that the market will strongly impact your stock and the price will go up, even if you've made a wrong choice.

4. The NASDAQ 100 very often precedes the market index. If the NASDAQ 100 is rising when it looks to you as though the market is about to trend down, there is a reasonable chance that the market will not break down, which increases your risk. Wait for the market index's breakdown to occur, and only then press the short button. If the stock breaks down before the market cooperates, short for a smaller quantity and be constantly on the watch for reversals.

5. Since it appears that here, too, the NASDAQ 100 may precede the market index, it is indeed better to buy, but with great caution. Buy, for example, half the total amount you might want in the hope that the market index will also break out to a new high. If this does occur, buy the second half of the quantity you had in mind, on the condition that the stock's price has not run too far ahead.

Sectors and Industries

So far, we have learned that 60% of price movement is influenced by the market index (S&P 500) movement. But this is only partial information. Of the remaining, 30% of the influence on movement is derived from the movement of the sector to which the stock belongs. Only 10% of the time will a stock "take itself into its own hands" and make its own way in the market independently.

Stocks belong to industries, which together comprise a sector. The financial sector, known simply as **financials**, is subdivided into four industries: banks, various finance organizations, insurance companies, and real estate companies.

Let's assume you wish to buy a bank stock, such as Citigroup, symbol C. We already know that the S&P 500 is responsible for 60% of stock movement, so before you click "buy," you would glance at the market index and make sure it is trending up. Now I would ask you to also glance at the chart for the industry to which the stock belongs: in this case, the banking industry. I assume there is no need to remind you that during the 2008 Financial Crash and afterwards, banks were the weakest market industry: in other words, the market index might be moving up, but the banks dragged far behind, and may even have been trending down. A stock belonging to an industry which is not functioning correctly will find itself in difficulties even when the market is optimistic in general.

When you are about to buy a stock, first check to which industry it belongs. This may take a few seconds before you reach a decision, but they are definitely a few seconds well spent. Over time, you will come to recognize most of the stocks and will not need to check each one's industry. For example, to which industry does TEVA Pharmaceuticals (symbol: TEVA) belong? Drugs. To which industry does INTEL (symbol: INTC) belong? Semiconductors. The next time you encounter these two, for instance, you should be able to remember them. Within two to three years, you should be fluent in the sectors for 70% of the stocks in which you trade.

SMART MONEY	*I do not always check the sector or industry before taking a trade. Stocks belonging to a marginal sector are not checked.*

A good proportion of the stocks we trade will belong to one of **four main industries: banking, technology, semiconductors, and biotech.** On the screen which displays the two most important market indices, I also allocate space to relatively small charts showing five-minute candles for three of these industries: banking, biotech, and semiconductors. Of course there are many more sectors, from stocks related to aircraft and flight to the production of paper, but the impact of those sectors on the market is negligible, therefore I do not allot them screen space.

Exercise in Comprehension:

On the daily chart, Southwest Airlines' (LUV) stock shows a nice pattern while trending up, and you wish to buy for a range of several days (remember that several days is called "swing"). You're waiting for the best possible conditions.

When the trading session opens, you notice that the market is rising strongly and the **Oil & Gas sector** is rising even more strongly than the market. You check the reason and discover that fuel prices are rising. An immediate outcome of rising fuel prices is a drop in **Airline sector** stocks which are highly dependent on fuel costs. Conclusion: today is not the right day to buy Airlines sector stocks.

On days when the market is trending up, the associated question is which sectors also rose, which of them rose more strongly than the market, and which dropped despite the market's move. On a day of highs, we can assume that between 70% to 90% of the sectors are also rising. On the other hand, as noted earlier, some sectors will almost always move in opposite directions to each other, such as the contradictory movement of the Airline sector to the Oil & Gas sector, because of the strong impact of fuel prices on airline profitability. When the market index drops, for example, the price of gold will almost always rise. When the price of **gold** goes up, the **Mining sector** will also rise. We see that gold and mining companies often move in opposition to market direction. On a day of sharp upward movement in the market, would you want to bury your money in a stock belonging to a dropping sector? Of course not. So, check sector direction before entering the market.

Here is a list of the main industries and their symbols:

Symbol	Sector/Industry
DJI$	Industrial
BKX$	Banks
NBI$	Biotechnology
SOX$	Semiconductors
MVR$	Retail
NDXT$	Technology
DJUSEN$	Oil & Gas
QNET$	Internet
DJT$	Transportation
DJUSAR$	Airlines
DJU$	Utilities
DJUSAP$	Autos
DFX$	Defense
RXS$	Pharmaceuticals
IXTC$	Telecom

Note that sectors and industries tend to mingle: banks, for example, are an industry within the Financials sector, but because their weight in the sector is varied, traders tend chiefly to follow the banking industry.

Multiple Symbols

To check the status of banks, it is possible to follow several different symbols, sourced in the various indices developed by the different companies. Dow Jones, for example, has its own banking index, which is different from the index produced by Merrill Lynch. This simply means that the Dow Jones analysts grade certain banks differently from Merrill Lynch's analysts. The symbols in the table above are the most commonly used among traders, but individual traders may have other preferences.

Integrating Tools

The most successful formula calls for cleverly integrating all the tools described above. The ideal trade will integrate buying at the correct technical entry point for the stock, while monitoring the market and the industry to which the stock belongs. If you choose to buy a stock that is stronger than the market and that belongs to an industry showing strength on a day of an up trending market, you will greatly enhance your chances of success.

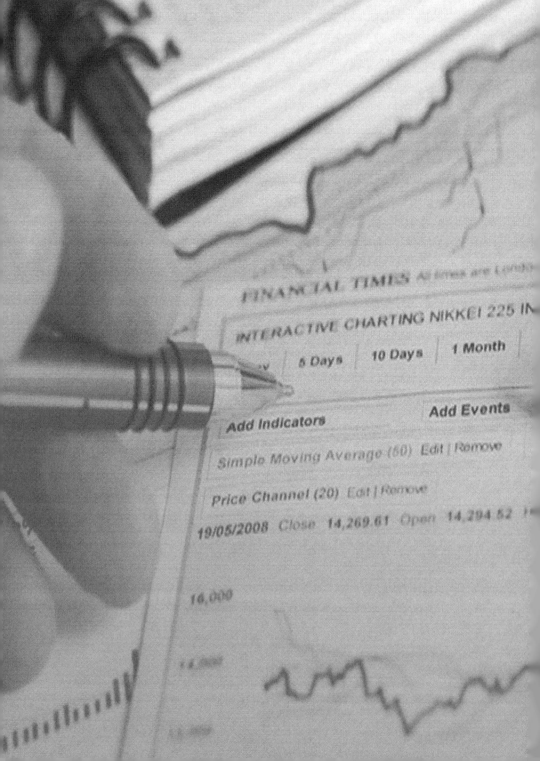

FINANCIAL TIMES All times are London

INTERACTIVE CHARTING NIKKEI 225 IN

| 5 Days | 10 Days | 1 Month |

Add Indicators   Add Events

Simple Moving Average (60) Edit | Remove

Price Channel (20) Edit | Remove

19/05/2008 Close 14,269.61 Open 14,294.52

16,000

14,000

7

Indicators:

The Trader's

Compass

Indicators, like a compass, show the direction but not the path.

Reading a Million Individuals' Thoughts

We have learned about trends, chart patterns, and indices, and now we will discuss indicators, which are generally derived from the trend.

Indicators do not usually add new information which cannot be learned from the chart, but sharpen and clarify the information inherent in the chart. Let's say, for example, that you have bought a stock running up, and you wish to know when to sell it as close as possible to its high. What defines the high? How can you use the index to identify the high?

SMART MONEY	*An "indicator" is an assistive tool for decision-making. Indicators do not add new information, but help us decide when to hit the buy/sell button.*

There are, in fact, no small number of indicators which claim to provide you with the absolute answer. I would say that indicators are what their name implies: they provide orientation, but they are not the absolute final factor upon which your decision should be based. Using indicators is similar to navigating with a compass. The compass shows which direction you are facing, but cannot instruct you how to arrive at your destination. You need to decide which path to take, and often that path will not be what the compass has shown. If stock trading were as simple as using an indicator, any computer could replace me successfully!

When I started out as a trader, I relied strongly on indicators. Now, after many years' experience, they are well-embedded in my subconscious and I hardly look at them anymore. Furthermore, to save screen space and "clean up" the charts of stocks in which I am trading, I removed all the indicators from the display. Do I suggest you do the same? Of course not. After many years of screen time, I have reached the stage of "understanding" the charts just as Neo "sees" the matrix. If you're just starting out, and even some years into trading, you still need to use indicators to base your understanding upon and to gain guidance. Over the years to come, I believe that you will also reach the advanced stage of freeing yourself from dependence upon indicators. Until such time, use them, understand them, but don't take them as given, and do not operate mechanically as though they are the only instructing factor.

There are many technical indicators, including the RSI, MACD, ADX and more. The more that technical analysis develops, the more indicators and new technical tools develop. But a professional trader is assisted by very few indicators, since during trading there is no time to read multiple indicators, and because the trader is concentrating on the chart from which the indicators are derived.

The most important indicator for analyzing a trend is the **volume**, as it is one of the few technical tools not derived from the trend and provides the trader with an important, additional perspective on a stock's status. Trade volume is a unique indicator that I am never willing to forego.

Volume of Trade

The volume of trade, or as it is simply known, volume, notes the number of shares being traded at any given moment. Volume is marked by bars at the base of the chart. Beneath each Japanese candle is the volume bar appropriate to that timeframe. If the Japanese candle represents five minutes, the volume will present five minutes, and if the candle is green, the bar will also be green. Occasionally, according to the trader's choice or the platform's limitations, the color of all volume bars will be identical and it will not be possible to distinguish between down volume and up volume.

Volume for TEVA in Five-Minute Candles:

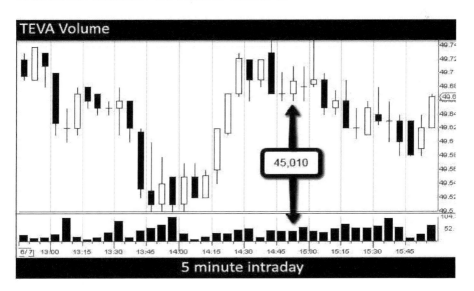

For the five-minute candle marked on the chart above, beginning at 14:50, volume shows 45,010 shares. To see the volume for each candle, position the mouse on the candle and press the mouse button (this may vary, depending on the platform).

Volume indicates the strength of the trend. Some claim, however, that because every transaction involves a buyer and a seller, or in other words, someone who thinks the stock is cheap and someone else who thinks it is expensive, the sum total of opinions in the market is zero and volume has no significance. There is some degree of truth in this claim, but those who hold this view ignore the identity of both buyers and sellers. Since institutional buyers are usually the smart ones in the market, their opinion holds greater weight, which makes it harder to claim that the sum total of all opinions is zero. As a result, it is important to identify volume changes deriving from the activity of these institutional buyers.

Volume Precedes Price

One of the most well-known clichés concerning volume is that "volume precedes price." Why would volume precede a rise in price? Institutional traders who receive instructions from large clients wishing to buy millions of a certain company's shares do not feed a buy order into their platforms for the entire amount in one go, as that would completely expose the client's intentions, jump the price higher, and reduce the bonus the traders receive for buying cheaply. Traders will therefore be interested in buying cheaply in order to receive the client's full remuneration, since the traders' bonus increases the lower the net price that they get for their client. Traders will therefore conceal their intentions, enter and exit the market repeatedly, each time buying a relatively small quantity. In this way, traders can hide their intentions, and may succeed in preserving the stock's low price, but the scope of purchases as manifested in the volume cannot be hidden. The volume may therefore reveal that stocks are being collected prior to a price spike. The same is also true for drops in price. Large sellers, usually investment funds, receive information prior to it reaching the public and begin operating in large volumes before the stock has moved.

SMART MONEY	*Buy and sell orders can be hidden, but volume can never be hidden. An increase in volume always indicates a reason: someone knows something that you do not yet know.*

Average Volume

It is important to check the average daily volume of trade before entering a stock, for two reasons:

1. Identifying Relative Increase in Volume

A significantly large intraday volume compared to that of the day before indicates some special activity involving that stock. We love to locate and follow up on stocks showing volume increases, especially with a double leap, or even much higher. Stocks with increased volume can be easily found using simple screening software or while glancing at the stock's chart. We can easily discern the growth in volume if we compare the charts showing the prior and current day's volumes. Of course, a comparison is only possible after at least midway through the current trading day, and must be made for the same timeframe of the previous day. When I consider buying a stock and see a relatively noticeable growth in volume, I can make the decision more easily. I may even increase the quantity of my purchase, based on the premise that the increased volume indicates increased interest and therefore increased chances of success.

2. The Possibility of Buying and Selling at Any Time
Traders will buy a stock only if they are certain that they can buy and sell at any time, at any price, and for the entire quantity purchased. When the average daily volume of trade is low, for example only 100,000 shares per day, the spread between the bid (buyers) and ask (sellers) will usually be more than one cent. This makes it difficult for you to buy and sell at your desired price. For example: you bought a stock and wish to sell immediately, but find that you're forced to sell at a considerable loss because the closest buyer is too far beneath your buy price.

Furthermore, stocks with low volumes carry no "meat," and their buy and sell liquidity at any price, even if buyers do exist, will be relatively small. Because of the large spread between bid and ask, and the absence of "meat," just one large transaction is enough to strongly impact the stock price. It could suddenly go up, which is great if you bought it. By the same token, it could suddenly drop, leaving you no time to sell with minimal loss. In short, light volume stocks are not for the fainthearted or those who hate high risk, like me.

SMART MONEY	*With time, you will recognize most of the stocks you are trading and will not need to check whether they match volume requirements. You will get to a point where those checks are needed only for a small range of stocks.*

Conclusion
A professional day trader will usually not trade stocks with an average volume of less than one million shares per day. Not to worry: there are

thousands of stocks with a day volume in excess of that figure.

In summary, a professional trader looks for stocks trading over one million shares per day on average, but also with volume better than the prior day's volume.

How can we know, after an hour of trading, whether the day volume is going to top one million? Switch quickly from the intraday five-minute candle chart to the daily chart, and check the volumes over the previous few days. With just a glance you should be able to see whether volume is only several thousand shares, or above one million. If the volume is borderline, compare the volume of the current day's opening with that of the previous day's opening, and try to assess the current day's potential on that basis.

Pay attention to another phenomenon which may mislead you. Sometimes, a considerable portion of the volume derives from several trades, or one single large trade. In other words, you might believe that the intraday volume is large enough, but in actuality most of it derives from one trade of hundreds of thousands of shares. To check if this status is relevant, check the volume indicator and look for a single candle that represents an extremely high volume.

What Volume Changes Mean

A wise rule states: "Buy the rumor, sell the news."

Sometimes rumors can be exposed by identifying volume increases. Volume changes, if interpreted correctly, can in certain circumstances constitute an important index for buy and sell decisions. For example: when a stock rises and breaks over resistance, the breakout should be typified in a noticeable volume growth and thereby indicate increased interest of buyers. A rule of thumb says that volume increase is considered significant when the five-minute candle showing the breakout doubles relative to the candles preceding the breakout. Later we will examine several rules that we need for interpreting volume changes as the stock moves.

We need to differentiate between volume increases prior to **daily breakout** (in one-day candles over several days) and volume increases preceding **intraday breakout** (in five-minute candles during the trading session).

How to Interpret Volume Increase Prior to *Daily* Breakout

When the volume of activity for a stock increases before the **daily breakout**, we should suspect something significant happening to the stock. Daily volume grows for a reason. Sometimes, it indicates news that has yet to be publicized formally but has already leaked to "those in the know." It could also indicate a large institutional buyer who has accumulated shares. As is customary in funds, once 90% of their target is reached, the institutional buyers release the brakes and want to let you know, by making large purchases, that they are interested in supporting the stock. The trader is hoping that you, and many others like you, are noticing that volume increase, and will join in and help drive the stock price up.

Growth in daily volume can be simply identified using free Internet screening software such as Yahoo Screener or Stock Fetcher. For identifying intraday volume change, you will need to buy a more advanced program such as Metastock. Most new traders should not feel the need to buy these software packages and do all of the work themselves. Trading is enough work. Use professionals and the tips that they are willing to share to find stocks until you become successful enough to try to find stock patterns for entry yourself.

One of the differences between the professional and amateur trader is the former's ability to correctly identify the entry price. Volume growth helps us locate the entry price. An amateur will analyze several indices (usually an unnecessary action) and make the buy decision with a delay, only after his or her confidence level is sufficiently strong. It is a known fact that the amateur's confidence rises in direct relation to the stock's price rise, so that in most instances, the amateur's entry price will be lagging. A pro trader knows how to ignore extraneous indices and reliably evaluate the correct entry price, with the stock about to break out. Volume growth right before breakout is, in many cases, the earliest sign of the impending breakout. Amateurs join later, while professional traders are watching the stock's price rise. To a great extent, this is also the difference between profit and loss.

Big breakout volume represents the point of change in the public's perception of the stock's worth. During pre-breakout consolidation, very few are interested in buying the stock. The more the volume grows, the greater the number of newly-interested parties. The more buyers there are who believe that the stock will continue its new trend, the greater the chances of success.

A stock that breaks out with a small volume does not catch the "radar" of traders, and its chances of succeeding in the new trend are much lower. After the breakout, investors are more skeptical, seeking additional "proof" supporting the move. Large volume is definitely one of the more important signs assisting us in deciding whether to hold the stock. A stock not showing a volume increase will generally encounter intraday institutional sellers for up to three days from the breakout. Institutional supply will create a new area of resistance which the stock will find hard to break.

Breakout Volume Increase for Caterpillar, CAT

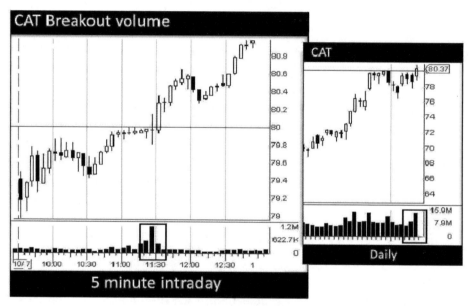

In the daily chart on the right, you can see how Caterpillar broke to a new daily high of over $80. You can also see, at the base of the chart, that the breakout involved almost double the volume of that of the preceding days. On the left, the intraday chart shows how the stock consolidates below $80, and when it breaks the resistance, volume jumps to 1.2 million shares in just one single five-minute candle! Without a doubt, a lot of interest was shown in this stock, which increases its chances of continuing to trend up. Caterpillar's potential breakout was identified in the trading room several days before the actual jump, and we followed it closely in the hope of buying at breakout. This trade was definitely a highlight.

<table>
<tr><td>

**SMART
MONEY**

</td><td>

*Funds hold stocks for the long term and are therefore not
sensitive to intraday price changes. Traders buying before
the intraday breakout are highly sensitive to even the
slightest price change.*

</td></tr>
</table>

How to Interpret Volume Increase Prior to *Intraday* Breakout

As noted, a differentiation must be made between volume increase prior to a daily breakout, and prior to an **intraday** breakout. At the intraday level, volume increases prior to the breakout are not usually a good sign, as it is generally caused by independent day traders rather than institutional traders. As we will study in depth later, traders buying stocks prior to intraday breakout may be particularly sensitive to even the slightest drop in price. A large pre-breakout volume indicates that there are multiple "new hands" buying the stock. These new buyers, unlike the veterans who bought the stock when it was much cheaper, are still in a dangerous position. They have not yet profited and are therefore far more sensitive than the veteran traders. If the stock should break out and correct even slightly, there is a reasonable chance that the new buyers will flee quickly, causing a temporary price drop. Usually these drops correct rapidly and the stock resumes the upward trend. Experienced traders will even take advantage of the temporary low to buy cheaply.

Buyers Fleeing Caterpillar, CAT

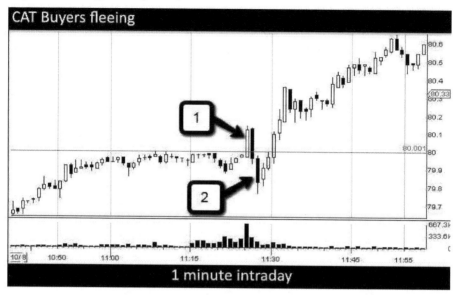

1 minute intraday

Looking at Caterpillar's $88 breakout at the one-minute candle resolution, we see Caterpillar's buyer shakeout precisely at the breakout. The price broke with a large volume of 600,000 shares in one minute (most of whom are new buyers like me) and rose by 15 cents [1]. So far, so good. A high volume integrating breakout on the daily chart and a nice technical breakout in the trading session should succeed, but pay attention to the pre-breakout volume increase. The problem occurs when many of those "new hands" feel pressured, and start selling after the price rose by just 15 cents, creating a snowball that within two minutes sends the stock to a pullback of 38 cents [2]. Many years ago, I, too, would have been among those feeling pressured, selling at a loss and gaping when the stock turned back up and reached new highs. Many years of experience later, with many insights gained into human behavior, on this occasion I doubled the quantity I bought at $79.89 and enjoyed watching the continuing uptrend. An amazing trade instead of a burning loss!

How to Interpret Volume in an Uptrend

Since volume increases indicate the trend's strength, we would want to see volume increase every time the stock returns to moving in the direction of its trend. If volume does not grow as the trend develops, perhaps a reversal is about to occur, which brings its reliability into question.

When trying to decide whether to buy a stock trending up, we need to examine the behavior of volume at the points of price change within the trend itself.

Example of Intraday Change in Volume of Akamai, AKAM

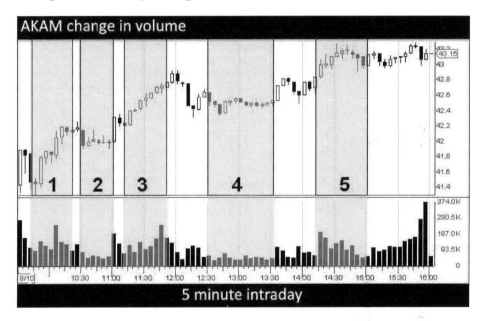

In the chart above, notice Akamai's strong day of highs shown in five-minute candles. Notice also that the volume during the first trading minutes and last trading minutes is higher because of automatic buy and sell orders from individuals and institutional traders; therefore, these points have no technical importance. In the area marked [1], the stock is trending up with a (relatively) large volume. In the area marked [2], Akamai is dropping with a small volume: this is a sure sign of lack of enthusiasm over the drop. In area [3], it is running up again strongly with large volume. In area [4], it trends down once more with small volume, and at [5], it peaks at a new high with large volume. The conclusion is simple: more enthusiasm during the upward moves than the downward moves indicates that the trend's chances of continued highs are greater than its chances of dropping.

What might have occurred had we seen the volumes grow during lows? Would we have sold? Not immediately, but we would definitely have started being "suspicious" about the trend's continuation, and begun planning our exit point should the reversal strengthen. Sometimes increased volume is no more than coincidental "noise" that means nothing.

SMART MONEY	*A stock trending up needs to show increasing volume when trading upward (indicating enthusiasm), and smaller volume when trading downward. A down trending stock needs to show the opposite.*

How to Interpret Volume in a Downtrend

The behavior of a stock in a downtrend is slightly different from that of a stock in an uptrend. It is more difficult to interpret the volume of a stock when it is trending down compared to when trending up. Sometimes, when the stock breaks support, the breakdown is not typified by large volume since many investors tend to deny their failure and continue to believe in the stock even though it is a losing trade. Amateurs tend to remain true to a stock in much the same way as they stay true to a football team on a losing streak. Have you ever seen a football fan leave his or her losing team? Amateurs will always offer the same response: it's good, it'll come back, it's got good products, its management is good. Pros, on the other hand, know when to cut their losses quickly. Amateurs will deny their own failure, and are sometimes drawn into big losses that cause emotional paralysis, preventing them from functioning logically. Paralysis and denial may reduce volume of a stock during initial lows.

Another reason for low volume is the absence of demand. A losing stock is dropping due to lack of demand, which does not enable sellers to sell. At a more advanced stage when the stock continues falling, fear takes over. The public is beset by panic, and volume increases when sellers begin vying for demand, selling aggressively at any asking price. On the other hand, this is also the stage when some institutional traders begin accumulating the stock again.

Generally, three to five days before a stock falls, when the volume grows, the stock will find support and possibly even return to a high. Price correction with small volume chiefly indicates that "flea market players" have joined the short-term trade, seeking bargains. Usually they will fail, as the stock will usually continue to trend down, but this never prevents them from bragging about their amazing success. I meet such players frequently at conferences where I lecture. They always boast of the latest stock they bought. It sounds something like this: "I just bought Citigroup when it was at $2 and now it's at $11." Almost always, they recall their rare successes rather than their multiple failures. They conveniently forget that they also bought Lehman Bros. at $3 and discovered the next day that it had dropped to zero, just as happened to any number of other trades they executed, all of which lead to the eventual closure of their trading account.

How to Interpret Large Volume without Any Price Movement

Large volume without any significant price movement can come about from an institutional trader's demand. The decision-making processes of institutional traders are very different from those of day traders or private investors. Institutional traders will give some weeks, if not months, of consideration to buying a stock. During that time period, they conduct an in-depth economic study, known as fundamental research, on the company and its products, its financial reports, its market status, and much more. As institutional traders manage huge sums of money, they need to purchase extremely large quantities of stocks, typically in the hundreds of thousands if not millions of shares, in order to "move money." That kind of quantity, if bought in the market from random sellers, will create high demand and cause price spikes before the fund has managed to collect the required amount.

The solution is arrived at through several avenues. First of all, the fund will try to locate sellers holding large quantities and buy them direct in "out of exchange" transactions. These usually cover hundreds of thousands of shares in one transaction. Large-quantity buyers are prepared to pay a little more than the market price based on the premise that if they try to buy within market activity, the price will be pushed up. A seller approached by an institutional trader knows that if he or she tries to sell a very large quantity within regular market activity, it will force the price down, and the seller will then receive much less than the price offered by the fund.

However, by law, these out-of-exchange transactions must be reported to the stock exchange, which means that the trade volume will appear on your trading screen without its impacting the balance between buyers and sellers, and therefore does not affect the stock price even if the trade was executed at a price higher or lower than the price currently traded on the market. A fund will try to obtain 80% of the total planned quantity in this way. It will then go about trying to purchase the remaining 20% slowly, carefully, quietly, in small quantities each time, direct from stock exchange sellers. This volume-dependent process may take from several days to several weeks.

The next stage is of great interest. The fund is already holding a large quantity, and is now interested in signaling its interest to the market, which causes the stock price to rise. The fund starts buying in the market, creating volume and price highs which arouse interest and draw the stock price to greater highs. The price trends up even more strongly, and additional buyers, noticing the resonance, join the trading. This in turn thrusts the price to even higher highs. Since a large portion of liquidity is already held by the fund, the path has been paved for the stock to climb virtually without resistance.

Does this sound a bit fishy to you? Who said the stock exchange is the epitome of fairness?

How to Interpret Large Volume at the Daily High

When a stock breaks to a high on the daily chart, we can often see at the high an extreme volume increase, known as **climactic volume**. It usually takes some time until the public is convinced there is a real story behind the breakout, and begins to buy. The reason for the climactic volume is public enthusiasm. When, usually with some delay, the public is finally persuaded and buys en masse, the "big money players" move in: these are institutional sellers taking advantage of the highs and large volumes in order to be rid of large "blocks" of stock while the uptrend is at its highest. We call this phenomenon **"selling into the power."** Sellers cause resistance to continued highs, creating the climactic volume. Large supply invites short sellers, and price correction begins to appear. The last group of sellers, the public, is the biggest loser. They feel pressured, sell, the stock drops to near support level where it is again accumulated cheaply by the institutional traders, and begins to reach highs again with large volumes.

| **SMART MONEY** | *The public does not buy a stock as it starts to rise. The public always buys with a delay, after the stock has "proved itself" as strong.* |

How to Interpret Climactic Volume at the Intraday High

Climactic volume at the high is usually a warning signal for an anticipated correction.

Intraday Climactic Volume Correction, BBT

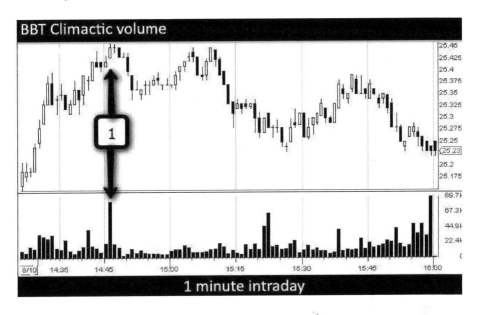

On this sample day above, BBT is hitting highs at the trading session's opening, approaches the high and adjacent to the high, volume grows noticeably [1]. As we learned, volume that grows during the uptrend is a positive sign. This is usually true, but not for a sharp jump in volume, as in the example above. This is an irregular volume. Veteran buyers are taking advantage of the high to realize profits and to sell into the power, while less-experienced buyers are chasing the stock, continuing to buy close to the high. Now, many new buyers enter the market, and at this point, before even earning a cent, they are highly sensitive to any small change in the stock's price. Just one tiny correction of only a few cents will be enough to pressure them and cause the stock to return down with a sharp plummet. This process is similar to the first failed Caterpillar breakout we analyzed earlier.

Moving Averages

As we learned, stocks do not rise in a straight line, but in zigzags. This is the nature of the trend. Part of the natural process of reaching highs involves pullbacks. A stock in an uptrend and correcting is still a stock following its trend, and this is how we should view it.

Of course, not every low will be accepted with forgiveness, which means we need an assistive tool for defining the trend. **Moving averages (MA) are tools that assist in defining the trend and warning of possible reversals.** Their role is to flatten the zigzag and make it easier to read the trend. Unlike other indicators that will be described further on, the information provided by the MA is unequivocal and makes reaching conclusions easy.

The MA is computed according to the **averages of closing prices** for a defined period, and appears on the line chart as a continuous line. By way of reminder, the "closing price" is the price at which the last trade was made for the period being examined. For example, this could be the closing price for the trading day if the timeframe is in days, or the price of the last trade if the timeframe is five-minute candles.

The average is called **moving** because the average of closing prices is computed for each time within the period being checked. An example is a moving average known as a "10 period MA" on the daily chart. The average of closing prices for the past ten days is computed. In this way, the average "moves" each day according to the closing price of the day being added on to the previous nine days. The closing price is the basis for calculating the MA, since the closing price is the most important data.

Sample Calculation

Exercise: Calculate the 10 period moving average (**10MA**) at the end of the 10th day for a stock that rose from $10 to $20 with a spread of $1 per day over 10 consecutive days.

Answer: Let's add up the closing prices of the past ten days:
$11 + 12 + 13 + 14 + 15 + 16 + 17 + 18 + 19 + 20 = 155$
The average for 10 days is $155/10 = 15.5$
In other words, the MA at the end of the tenth day is 15.5, and is written

as follows:
10MA=15.5

If we also knew the trading data for a few days prior to this group of ten, we would be able to calculate the MA for the 9th day, the 8th day, and so on, connect all these results using a continuous line, and arrive at the MA for 10 periods.

Example of Moving Average (MA) for FFIV

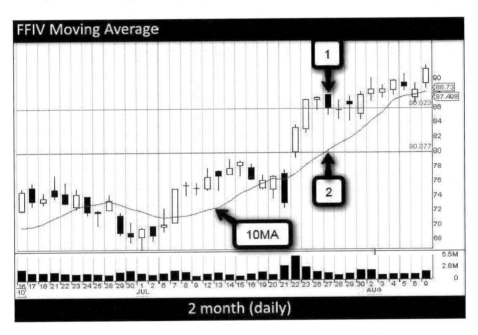

I have added to the FFIV daily chart the moving averages line for ten periods (10MA). On July 27, 2010, the trading day closed at $86 [1], and for that day, the 10MA was $80 [2]. If we add the closing price for July 27 [1] to the closing prices of the preceding nine days and average them, we arrive at $80.

Traders tend to use two of a variety of moving averages: the **Simple Moving Average (SMA)** and the **Exponential Moving Average (EMA)**. No need to panic! Understanding both, and the differences between them, is not overly difficult.

| SMART MONEY | *For intraday trading in five-minute candles, use a moving average of eight or ten periods. For swing trading (one-day candles), use 20, 50 and 200 periods.* |

The Achilles heel of moving averages is that the data is historical, i.e., it relates to information from the past and is therefore known as a **trend-following indicator,** or **"lagging" indicator.** The more we distance over the axis of time, the data used to calculate the average at the start of the period becomes much less relevant to the present. For this reason, instead of being assisted by a simple moving average giving equal weight to each timeframe, many traders use the **exponential moving average,** which gives greater weight to the timeframe closest to the present. In other words, closing prices of the more recent timeframes are considered more meaningful than those of the more distant timeframes. There is some logic to this approach, of course, but we need to keep in mind that the essential use of the MA is to act as an indicator alone. Interestingly, traders using the regular MA will reach the same conclusions as those using the EMA. It's more a matter of habit, preference, and experience than anything else, so just go ahead and use whichever MA appeals to you most. New traders will generally prefer the EMA, but even then they tend to use the SMA when relating to 200 timeframes. Why? That's the norm, so that's what you should follow too.

"Fast" and "Slow" Averages

A long-range moving average, such as 200MA, is less sensitive to recent closing price differences, since the weight of each timeframe is relatively small, and therefore changes will be "slower." A short-range moving average, such as 20MA, shows higher sensitivity to recent closing prices, so changes will be "faster." As we will see, integrating the slow and fast MA can be a good indicator of trend direction.

Within the trading session and using five-minute candles, we would prefer to use the 8MA or the 10MA. For longer-term trade, such as when reviewing the chart for the purpose of entering a swing of several days, we would use the 20MA, the 50MA and the 200MA. Later, we will practice their correct application.

How to Apply the MA

As noted, the MA assists us in defining the trend. Identifying the trend and its reversals can be done in two ways: examining the link between

MA and the Japanese candle chart, and examining the links between the MAs. In addition to trend analysis, the MA also serves to define the entry and exit points, as we will learn later.

When analyzing the meaning of MAs for a stock that is trending up, remember that the explanation in reverse is valid for a down trending stock.

- **Rule 1:** A stock's ride above the MA indicates a continuing trend. A drop beneath the MA signals the trend's end.

Daily Chart Trend Development for Akamai, AKAM

In March, Akamai leaves a long period of moving sideways and begins to rise [1]. Notice how the stock "rides" the 20MA. In some cases, you can see the stock drop beneath the 20MA line, but these are all intraday lows which began and ended in the same trading day. The first suspicion of a trend change occurs towards the high when it breaks the 20MA, but finds support in the 50MA. Eventually it breaks down [2] and abandons the uptrend.

What You Should be Anticipating

First and foremost, you should expect an up trending stock to ride the 20MA exactly as Akamai does over several months, starting at [1] and up until the breakdown of the moving average. Riding above the 20MA is considered a classic uptrend.

The 20MA line is therefore the line of support. When I look for an entry point on a stock trending up, I need to find it as the stock is close to the 20MA. This assumes that a strong stock will separate from the 20-period line of support but will return back to support as it continues to trend up. When the stock drops clearly below the 20MA line, we expect it to be supported by the 50MA line, but this is also the stage where we begin suspecting a reversal may be occurring. Breaking down under the 50-period line almost always means a trend reversal. Additional support should come from the 200MA line.

For upward trending stocks, when the chart crosses below the 20MA line, it means the uptrend could be about to reverse. Similarly, for stocks trending down, when the chart crosses above the 20MA line, it means the downtrend is about to reverse.

A formal reversal can be defined when both the slow and the fast-moving average lines converge: for example, in the chart of Akamai, we see where the 50-period and 20-period lines converge at [2]. The significance of the reversal is that in the short range of 20 periods, the stock has dropped, while at the longer range of 50 periods, the stock is still holding the uptrend. Some traders wait for this convergence point to sell, but in my opinion that is already too late. Checking the Akamai chart, we see clearly that the decision to exit could be made long before then.

Moving averages that parallel each other and are known as **"railway tracks"** indicate a long, continuous trend. Distancing of MA lines from each other indicates a strengthening trend, while closeness indicates a weakening trend. At [1] we see the start of distancing (divergence), and near [2] we see signs of closeness which ends with convergence of the lines.

SMART MONEY	*Divergent "railway tracks" indicate a strengthening trend. Tracks that begin to converge indicate the potential danger of trend reversal.*

Why Calculate a 20-Period Line?

There are two reasons. First, it has become the normal conduct for the market. Second, it is a self-fulfilling prophesy. Many traders assume there will be support at the 20MA and therefore buy stocks supported by this line, which is considered the technical support point.

What's Up? What's Down?

In a stock trending up, you will want to see the stock riding above the 20 period line, which is above the 50 period line, which should be above the 200 period line. This is the classic definition of an uptrend.

Can the 200MA line be above both the 20MA and 50MA lines? Of course it can. Imagine that the stock has trended up for 50 consecutive days, meaning that both the 20MA and 50MA lines are beneath the stock price. However, checking 51 or more days previously reveals that the stock crashed from an extreme high, and therefore the 200MA line would be higher than the 20MA and 50MA lines.

When to Buy?

Once you've identified a stock trending up and you wish to join its continuing trend, you need to buy when the price is reversing, as we learned in the previous chapter. The entry (buy) point needs to be on, or fractionally above, the 20MA line, but not too far distant from that line.

When to Sell?

You sell when the stock's closing price for two consecutive days is lower than the 20MA line.

When to Buy or Sell within the Trading (Intraday) Session?

The same rules apply for intraday trade, except that the period you follow is ten periods of five-minute candles, although some traders prefer only eight periods. In actuality you will discover, as we will later learn, that your intraday buy or sell decision will not be based only on the behavior of the MA, but will also integrate other factors.

The Unique Significance of the 200MA

The 200MA is known as either a strong area of support or of resistance, depending on the direction from which the stock price approaches it. When a stock is down trending, it will find very strong support along the 200MA line. By contrast, in instances when the 200MA line is above the stock price, the stock will find difficulty in crossing it on its trend upwards. Even traders who prefer using the exponential moving average (EMA) will almost always use the simple moving average (SMA) when relating to a period of 200 timeframes.

Remember that you, too, should follow the behavior of the majority of traders. If you choose to work with an MA that is different than what the majority of traders use, you won't receive the support of that majority. **Example of 200MA Resistance for TEVA Pharmaceuticals, TEVA**

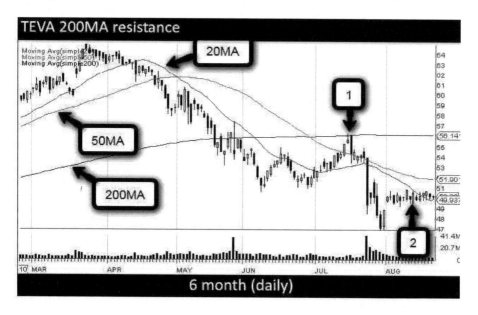

TEVA maintains a clear downtrend right beneath the 20MA line. The 50MA line is properly positioned above the 20MA line, and finally, the 200MA finds itself between them. At [1], TEVA tries to reverse trend, crosses the 20MA line, crosses the 50MA line, and then rams its head against the 200MA ceiling. The 200MA line's resistance is an amazing phenomenon that recurs several times. What does it mean for you?

Let's say you wish to buy TEVA because you believe it will move higher. Don't buy it when it is just below the 200MA line, since the stock shows difficulty in crossing that barrier. If you bought the stock much lower than the 200MA, it would be wise to realize some of the profit as it approaches that line.

While we are already paying close attention to TEVA's current status, we should also notice the beautiful consolidation at [2]. The stock is "picking up steam" and is about to move sharply in one of two directions, up or down. Both of them are suitable for trading and it is likely that both would make good trades. I followed the stock with the intention of trading if and when it decided to leave that short range area.

In the end, I couldn't resist. Here is the outcome, just weeks after I wrote the paragraphs above: a jump of 9% within several days. Sometimes it seems that this game is just too easy...

Oscillators

The oscillator is a technical tool that assists in identifying **overbought** and **oversold** statuses, and signals that the current trend is reaching its end before the change shows on the chart. In other words, the oscillator is a kind of indicator which helps identify when "**stupid money**" is entering the market, contrasted with "**smart money**" leaving the market; and vice versa.

When overlaid on a chart, oscillators are very useful for identifying the extreme points and overbought and oversold prices of stocks. Sometimes, though, oscillators can be too effective and cause unnecessary and even mistaken trade activity. This is why an initial signal for entry is insufficient, and it is best to wait for the second, confirming signal. When the oscillator does not move in the same direction as the trend, it is alluding to an approaching trend reversal.

Unlike trend-following technical tools, oscillators are very effective when the stock is moving sideways. As the field of technical analysis develops, there are increasing numbers of oscillators. In general, because I am a total fan of "understanding the stock" and because I don't like a lot of "noise" on the chart during the trading session other than volume, I tend not to use oscillators. At the outset of my trading experience, I was far from understanding the stock and needed oscillators just as you will during your initial stages. Hopefully, over time, you will no longer need them either. Some years down the line, when you're completely free of dependence on oscillators, you will be able to operate faster and more effectively.

Despite the above, however, when it comes to screening stocks, there is no substitute for oscillators. Identifying candidates for trade at the end of the trading session, before the new session opens, or during the trading day all require using oscillators to help you prepare a filtered, useful list of choice stocks.

Now is the time for an important cautionary note: sometimes new traders attempt to use multiple oscillators simultaneously, magnifying the "noise" as they work: usually, the result can be summed up as "not seeing the forest for the trees."

The Relative Strength Index – RSI

The Relative Strength Index is an oscillator that measures the force of any stock's acceleration, rather than comparing two or more stocks, as "relative" may possibly appear to indicate. It does this by checking the average of changes occurring in closing prices over a specific timeframe. The indicator was developed during the 1970s by Welles Wilder, and is meant to assist in identifying the overbought and oversold points.

Any oscillator you display on your charts will need to be defined to retroactively check a predetermined period. The normally accepted timeframe for the RSI is fourteen days for swing traders. Some traders define it for shorter terms of nine days, and others for even longer periods such as twenty-five days.

- The shorter the predetermined period, the more sensitive, or **fast**, the oscillator is, and the greater the possibility of multiple false signals.
- The longer the predetermined period, the less sensitive, or **slow**, the oscillator becomes, but then there is a higher possibility that you will get the buy and sell signals after the move has begun.

Sample of RSI Oscillator Feed in My Screening Software

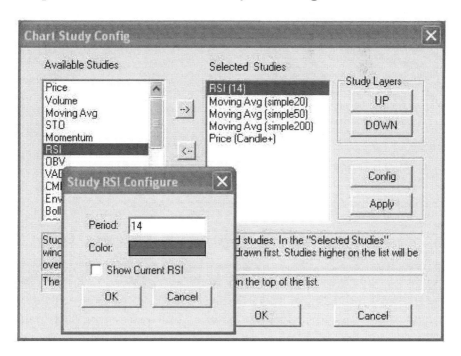

In my trading platform (COLMEX Pro), as with other similar programs, I need to click the chart to choose the type of oscillator I want to add to the chart. As you can see, I have added a total of five features: price in Japanese candles, the three moving averages discussed earlier (20, 50, 200), and the RSI for a 14-day period. Double-clicking any oscillator opens a window where I can change that oscillator's parameters: for example, its timeframe and color on the chart. It's that simple.

- The RSI oscillator operates on a 0-100 scale.
- Once it goes higher than 70, we need to suspect a possible overbought status, i.e., a signal that the stock is about to drop.
- Once it drops under 30, this could be indicating oversold status, i.e., a signal that the stock is about to reverse to highs.
- In addition to signaling the optimal buy and sell area, the oscillator also indicates lines of support and lines of resistance even before they are clearly seen on the chart.

Example: Finding an Extreme Point on Net Ease Daily Chart, NTES

I have added the RSI calibrated to fourteen periods to this NTES daily candle chart for six months. Figures on the right of the chart are the indicator reading and not the stock price. I also added the horizontal lines which are the two RSI lines of extremes at 30 and 70. As seen in the chart, you can find three points where the indicator is warning of transition, above or below the extremes. At [1], the indicator fractionally crosses over 70, i.e., it is indicating a top, and it is right. At [2], the indicator drops beneath 30, warning of an expected bottom, and it is right again. At [3], it is again hinting at expected drops.

Is this the time to short? I can promise you I have no intention of shorting a stock that is trending up, so why use the oscillator? We use it as an advanced warning system. If you are currently holding a stock, you should be concerned, but you do not necessarily need to sell unless other indicators, such as trend, volume, reversal configurations, and more, are supporting that decision. In short, the RSI is only an assistive tool. And, it is only one of many.

The MACD Index

MACD stands for Moving Average Convergence-Divergence. Analysts dub it the "Mac-Dee." It serves as both an indicator and oscillator. The MACD is displayed on the stock chart as two lines moving adjacent to each other and signaling buys and sells at the points where they cross over each other.

You don't necessarily need to read what follows, but if you really want to get tangled in a technical explanation, clench your teeth and read the rest of this paragraph. The MACD is comprised of two lines. The first is derived by deducting the exponential moving average for 12 days (12EMA) from the exponential moving average for 26 days (26EMA). Alongside this line is the second, which is the exponential moving average for 9 days (9EMA). When this second line crosses the first, by moving either up or down, the relevant buy or sell signals are produced. Remember that we discussed the moving averages that cross each other and indicate trend reversal? The MACD is a slightly smarter use of these moving averages.

Examining the MACD on the Same NTES Chart

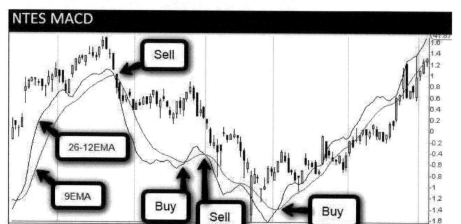

The result is interesting, without a doubt, especially if we compare the MACD buy and sell instructions each time the 26-12 EMA cuts across the 9EMA with the buy and sell readings for the RSI. Food for thought: will integrating both these indicators improve the outcome?

Fibonacci Sequence

The Italian mathematician Leonardo Fibonacci (1170 – 1250) wished to find a mathematical depiction for the way rabbits reproduce. From his experiments, he created a mathematical sequence bearing his name. The sequence is as follows: 1, 2, 3, 5, 8, 13, 21, 34 and so on. The sequence is based on several interesting rules: from the third number on, each new number is the sum of the two previous numbers; from the fifth number on, the ratio of any number to the preceding number is approximately 1.618, and for any number and the number following it, the ratio is 0.618.

So what is fascinating about 1.618? It is known as the "golden ratio," and amazingly, it can be found in multiple areas of our lives, from natural phenomena to artistic works, and all the way to the behavior of stock prices.

| **SMART MONEY** | *Does Fibonacci really impact your stocks? In my opinion, this is no more than a self-fulfilling prophecy, but since it is so, I have no choice but to give the indicator its rightful place.* |

Followers of the "golden ratio" theory will claim that the ratio is highly common in art and architecture. In actuality, it is a little difficult to prove or refute this claim, chiefly because of the difficulty in measuring it. Among buildings claimed to have been structured according to the golden ratio are the ancient pyramids of Giza, the Athenian Parthenon, and even the Dome of the Rock in Jerusalem. Since the pervading opinion for many years now is that the golden ratio is the most proportionate and hence attractive balance perceived by humanity, architects and artists have adopted it in their works of art and structures. It is known that Leonardo da Vinci applied it to several of his most famous works, among them the facial features of the *Mona Lisa.*

So just what is the connection between rabbits, culture and art, and stock trading? The trader Ralph Elliott published a theory in 1932 known as the "Elliott Wave Principle." I won't describe the theory in full detail, since I do not consider it important for short-term stock traders, but will mention that according to this theory, the most common ratios between the market waves are 38.2%, 50% and 61.8%, the latter being the golden ratio. Being able to recognize this ratio assists in estimating how the next wave will look, and determining the appropriate entry and exit points. From that time on, the golden ratio in short-term trading also grew in importance, as will be explained further.

Main Application: Price Correction

The main application of the Fibonacci ratio in short-term stock trading is to calculate price correction: for example, take a stock that has reached its high and begins to return downward. Where will it find support? According to the Fibonacci ratio, that should occur at several points: when it drops 31.2% from the high, 50% from the high, and 61.8% from the high. So if the stock rose by one dollar, it should find significant support if and when it drops by 31 cents, 50 cents, or 62 cents from its high. The view is that buyers will wait for the Fibonacci correction and buy based on the assumption that the Fibonacci point is the point of support. The opposite will be true for a stock trending down and returning upwards.

In light of the great many Fibonacci aficionados, I must admit that very often, the ploy succeeds. But as you may have understood from the tone of my remarks, I am not counted among this indicator's followers. On the other hand, we should never argue with buyers or sellers waiting patiently for the designated support point, even if I personally feel the method is worth little more than fortune-telling in a coffee cup. So, I have no choice but to give Fibonacci waves their due respect. Here are two examples:

Example of Price Correction for Bank of America, BAC

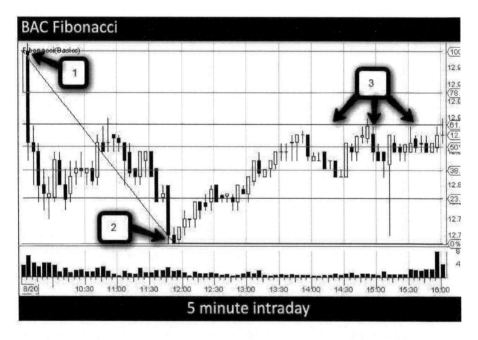

Bank of America stock is dropping during the day's trading from point [1] to point [2]. The distance between the two points is 100% of the drop. How far will the stock correct upwards? It corrects precisely up to the Fibonacci point indicating 61.8% [3] of the low. Is this a coincidence? No. The greater the number of people believing in the method, the easier it will be for the prophecy to self-fulfill.

Additional Application: Setting Targets Using Fibonacci Extensions
When a stock price breaks resistance and rises to a new high, some traders plan the breakout target price according to the Fibonacci

principle. In such a case, the high prior to the breakout up to the line of resistance is 100%, and the price target should the stock break out is 131.2% or 161.8%. For example, if the stock rose one dollar and stopped at the line of resistance, the breakout target will be 31 or 62 cents. This is called a Fibonacci extension, rather than a Fibonacci retracement.

Example of Breakout Target Calculation for Cephalon, CEPH

Cephalon consolidates below the line of resistance in a classic cup and handle pattern. The distance from the base up to the line of resistance is 100%. When the stock breaks out, it reaches the precise Fibonacci target of 161.8%. Another interesting case? Or, perhaps just a large number of traders who believe in the method and take profits at the commonly accepted target point. Were they actually the ones inhibiting the stock's progress at that level because they believed it would be resistance?

Bollinger Bands

These were invented by John Bollinger at the start of the 1980s. Bollinger's concept was simple: he drew a moving average line across the chart and sketched two bands, one above and one below it. In this way, a kind of "tube" was formed, outlining the stock's movement. The premise for creating a tube around the stock's movement is that the stock can be expected to move in the future within the same frame in which it moved in the past.

"Tubes" are not a new concept and certainly preceded Bollinger. The problem with this method is its reliability: in various market conditions, such as crises, stocks tend to be more volatile and therefore break the boundaries of the framework more frequently. Bollinger's innovation was to set the bands a variable distance from the MA. He did not set the distance on the basis of a fixed percentage, but on a known statistical method which you might well have learned years ago, called "standard deviation." Standard deviation is a calculated statistical value representing the volatility of data. Using the standard deviation, we can measure stock volatility, and thus use deviation to set the distance between the bands and the MA in a way that adapts to stock volatility. The beauty of the standard deviation is the fact that the distance between the bands expands when stock volatility increases, and lessens when stock volatility drops. In actuality, Bollinger created a tube that shrinks or expands according to volatility, and thereby significantly and successfully increased the method's reliability. An exhausting explanation. This is likely the stage when you wish to know its application.

If we commence with the premise that in the vast majority of cases, a stock will move between the bands, then when the price reaches the upper line, this means the stock is in a state of **"overbought"** and therefore should return downward. By contrast, when the stock price drops to the bottom line, it means that the stock is in a state of **"oversold,"** and there is a reasonable probability that it will now return upwards.

When you define Bollinger bands on your charts, you will need to take into account the following data: the MA should be set to ten periods and the SD (standard deviation) should be set at 1.5. In other words, the Bollinger bands wrapped around the movement of the stock you are watching will be calculated according to volatility over the past ten trading days. The mathematical value of the SD is that 90% of the stock's movements will be captured between the two bands.

When I take into account in advance that the Bollinger bands according to the parameters above will encompass 90% of the stock's movement, should the premise not be that a stock which has gone beyond these boundaries would not return inside them? Can this mathematical fact not define a trading method with more than 90% success rate? Yes, of course it can. We will learn more about this in the chapter on trading methods.

Bollinger Bands for Visa, V

Note how 90% of the stock's movement is caught between the two bands. Notice also that the distance between the bands widens as volatility increases. In my personal opinion, Bollinger bands are the most interesting and useful of all indicators that I display on my intraday charts.

TRIN

As discussed in the chapter on market indices, to determine market direction and evaluate its continued direction, we tend to rely chiefly on the S&P 500 and are assisted also by the NASDAQ 100. These two indices are excellent tools which allow evaluating market direction, but they do have a disadvantage: when the market rises or falls, it is difficult to know the force of buyers and sellers. This is because charts show market direction but do not show an additional, important component that influences our decisions: volume. Completing the picture requires that we know the force of the trading volume flowing into rising or falling prices. The **TRIN**, also known as the **Arms Index** after its creator Richard Arms, is meant to improve this state of uncertainty. The function of the TRIN is to measure declining trading volume compared to rising trading volume.

The symbol for TRIN on your charts differs from one broker's platform to another, but will generally be $TRIN, although the dollar sign may also be after the letters. We display the TRIN indicator in five-minute intraday candles.

The premise behind the TRIN indicator is that we should not relate only to market direction. For example, imagine a situation in which the market is rising on low volume, but more and more trades are actually being executed for dropping stocks. In other words, the rising stocks show no buyer enthusiasm compared to stocks that are dropping in high volumes. This state indicates there is no change of direction at that particular moment, since the quantity of rising stocks is still higher than the quantity of dropping stocks, but the rise in trade volumes of dropping stocks definitely seems to indicate an approaching pattern reversal.

The TRIN examines trade volumes of stocks on the NYSE and is an extremely useful intraday tool for the short term. The fact that it represents only stocks traded in the New York Stock Exchange is of no significance, since these stocks represent the overall market. In other words, if you are trading a stock linked to the NASDAQ, there is no need for concern: the indicator also represents the anticipated behavior of your stock.

Below is an explanation of the formula by which the TRIN is calculated:

$$TRIN = \frac{\text{Volume of trade of falling stocks}}{\text{Volume of trade of rising stocks}}$$

Analyzing the components of this formula, we understand that:
- When the TRIN is greater than 1, it means that the trading volume of dropping stocks is higher than the trading volume of rising stocks. In this case, the risk of purchasing the stock is greater, and conversely, the chances of succeeding with a short are also greater.
- When the TRIN is less than 1, it means that the trading volume of rising stocks is higher than the trading volume of dropping stocks. In this case, the risk in short selling is greater, and on the other hand, the

chances are better for buyers.

In most cases, when you look at the TRIN indicator in a dropping market, the TRIN will be above 1, and in extreme cases, around 3 or 4. When the market rises, the TRIN will be less than 1 and in extreme cases, around 0.3. Mathematically, the outcome of the formula can never be less than zero.

SMART MONEY | *In a normal market, the TRIN will show a scale between 0.7 and 1.3. In extreme situations, the indicator may move from 0.3 on days of sharp highs to 4 on days of sharp lows.*

Why do we need the TRIN indicator if we can see market patterns and guess fairly clearly where the TRIN is? Very simple: Because the TRIN allows examining two main variables:

1. **Points of extremity**. The points of extremity for the TRIN are higher than 1.4 for a falling market, and lower than 0.6 in a rising market. The meaning of the TRIN reaching these extremes usually shows an extreme market. Let's say that the market is rising quickly and the TRIN shows a reading of less than 0.6. This indicates that the market is about to reverse and return downward. By contrast, when the TRIN shows a reading above 1.4, it means that the market is exhausted on the downside and is about to reverse upward.
2. **The TRIN trend**. When the TRIN shows a reading of 0.7 (a rising market), and continues to rise continuously for approximately 30 minutes toward a reading of 1, there is a reasonable chance that it will continue the trend (as you remember, we learned that the trend is our best friend) and cross a reading of 1 into territory that represents a downtrend. This means that the number of buyers is lessening and the number of sellers growing. In other words, the market may reverse its uptrend and switch to trending down.

TRIN Behavior in Five-Minute Candles

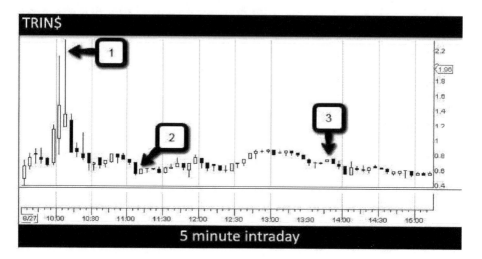

Let us analyze the TRIN without looking at the market chart:

At the start of trading, the TRIN rises and we understand that the market is trending down. About half an hour later, we find a jump to 2.2 [1]. This means it is reasonable to presume that a sharp low has occurred, with high volumes of trade. A 2.2 reading is very extreme, and indicates that the market is in a state of downward tension (a state of oversold) and we can expect a correction. The TRIN drops to below 1, indicating that the market is moving back into highs. At [2] we see the trend of highs stop, and the market begins moving sideways. At [3] the TRIN drops slowly, indicating a further try for highs, but its slow movement indicates that the market is rising in small volumes which are not creating enthusiasm.

Now we will examine **the SPY at those same points**:

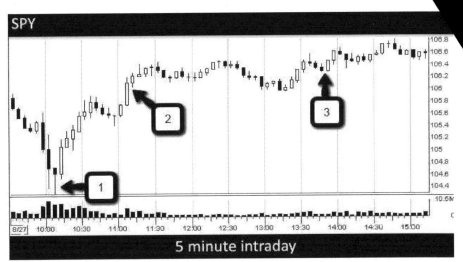

5 minute intraday

Examine the TRIN and the market chart and try to "understand" the relationship between these two indices. I do not expect you to reach conclusions at this stage, but I do expect that when you start trading, you will carefully observe both and try to understand the balance and influence on anticipated trade patterns, especially at the points of extremities.

Reservation: the TRIN is not a reliable stand-alone indicator. It is only one of several indicators which together provide insight for a trader. The TRIN must be integrated with additional indicators, and all the information weighed to create a more informed comprehension of anticipated market patterns.

Further note: The TRIN operates well on normal days. On days when Wall Street is really riled up, many indicators, including the TRIN, may show extreme outputs such as a 3 reading. The trader needs plenty of experience to know just when to use the indicators for a market that is beyond normal activity and operating chiefly on the emotions of fear or greed. Such days can indeed be highly successful for your trading account, as they are days on which it is relatively easy to guess market patterns without the use of indicators.

TICK

A tick on a stock is a change of one cent. The TICK is a simple but important indicator that examines the "ticks" at any given moment for

inus the "ticks" for dropping stocks on the NYSE, and
1me, i.e., the difference between the quantities of rising
's.

. example, that at a given moment, 2500 of the
..ely 4000 companies trading on the NYSE are rising, and at
_uy the same moment, 1500 companies are falling. The indicator's result will be 1000, according to the following calculation: 2500 minus 1500 = 1000. In other words, at that particular moment, more companies' stocks are rising than there are stocks falling. The indicator can show an up outcome like that of the example above, or a down outcome, where the quantity of companies with falling prices is greater than those with rising prices. Ticks can move very speedily between up and down readings even when the market is rising or dropping, since they represent momentary outcomes. During an upward pattern reversal, the number of stocks rising will be higher for that moment than those falling: the tick will show a positive number even if the market overall is trending down. When the tick is negative, the quantity of falling stocks is greater than that of rising ones. When the market is moving sideways, the tick data is around the zero mark.

| **SMART MONEY** | *During an uptrend, the tick's highest highs will be higher in absolute value than the tick's lowest low when the market returns downwards.* |

The symbol on your charts will be $TICK, although the dollar sign might be on either side of the word. Displaying the indicator can be a problem. Few platforms know how to display it properly, since the regular chart usually is unable to display a negative outcome. For this reason you may need to make do with only the positive TICK results. We display the TICK in five-minute intraday candles.

Even though the TICK indicator shows NYSE data and not NASDAQ data, you should relate to it as though it represents data for the entire market.

Exercise

The market is rising, the trend is up, and the TICK shows a strong up reading of 1000. The stock you want to buy has just reached the trigger point. Should you buy, or not?

We can utilize the TICK in two ways:

1. **Point of extremity.**

A reading of minus 1000 is an extreme reading. This is an extreme negative status in which the quantity of stocks falling is **greater by 1000** than the stocks rising. Conclusion: the market is showing an exhaustion low and should therefore be reversing upwards.

A positive reading of 1000 also represents an extreme status in which the quantity of rising stocks is 1000 more than those falling. Conclusion: the market is showing strong upward exhaustion and may therefore be returning downward shortly. In rare instances, the reading may reach a positive or negative 1300. Generally around the 800 to 1000 mark, it will turn around as the market pattern reverses.

Did you understand the answer to the exercise?

An extreme high or low point can occur several times a day and generally correct within several minutes. Following the pattern reversal, the TICK returns to the sideways area of between -500 to +500, an area in which the indicator is basically telling us nothing.

SMART MONEY | *An extreme reading will not stop us from entering the market for a long-term swing of several days, where brief intraday fluctuations have no effect.*

Answer to the Exercise:

How does an extreme reading affect our decisions as traders? Very simply. If you plan on buying a stock trending up, believing that it will continue to trend up, you need to buy it at the optimal time and not at the point of extremity which holds a greater feasibility of it dropping. Therefore, before buying, it is worth checking the TICK indicator.

Let's say you saw the indicator display a positive reading of 1000. As we learned, this is an extreme reading meaning that the market anticipates an impending reversal. It is very reasonable to presume that the stock you are about to buy will also correct with the market trend. The market cannot withstand a positive reading of 1000, so it is worth your waiting until the stock reverses, together with the market, and perhaps buying it at a lower price as it reverses. The same is true for the opposite direction: an extreme negative reading usually indicates a reversal, and this correction will cause the stock you are about to sell short to rise.

I frequently present this same exercise to my students, and almost all of them miss the correct answer. They interpret the positive 1000 TICK reading as indicating a strong market, and are interested in buying. Big mistake! Now you can see how, while it is indeed a very strong reading, it indicates that the market is nearing exhaustion and a correction can be anticipated. Market support is important for your stock's breakout, and therefore while it is reversing, the chances of failure are even higher than usual. Wait patiently for the reversal and buy cheaply. A stock price may not always drop, but it is better to lessen the risks and increase the percentages of success.

2. TICK trend

TICK in Five-Minute Candles

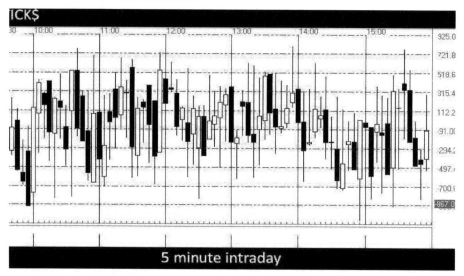

5 minute intraday

- When the market is showing an intraday downtrend, the TICK will often move between negative readings of minus 1200 (enthusiasm over lows) and positive readings of plus 800 (non-enthusiasm over reversals).
- When the intraday trend is up, the TICK will move between minus 800 to plus 1200.

Every so often during the day, you need to examine the TICK trend. For example: while the market is trending up, is the TICK showing readings of more than 800 with increasing speed? In other words, is there increasing enthusiasm?

I am aware that the chart above looks like a complete mess, but if you try to decode it according to the TICK trend, you will find that the market rose at the start of the trading session, moved sideways, and then dropped towards the end of the day. In actuality, when you observe the TICK in real time, you will understand it much better than the chart above. I do not expect you to comprehend the chart at this stage, but definitely do expect that when you observe the TICK and the market direction in real time, you will try to understand the relationships and influences of the TICK on anticipated trade, especially at the points of extremities.

Summary

The TICK primarily warns of points of exhaustion where the market is about to undergo a short-term reversal lasting some minutes. Since the market direction influences 60% of the movement of stocks you are trading, you need to know if the stock you are buying is at the point of extremity and about to return.

In special cases, despite the explanation above, we may buy a stock for intraday trade even though a TICK reading hints at an anticipated reversal. In such a case you need to relate to the action as a **scalp**, which is buying and selling for a brief period of seconds to minutes. In other words, you must be aware of the fact that the stock may suddenly return and you must be more attentive and take some profit at the first moment of weakness, when the stock appears about to reverse. With a little luck, it won't return.

The VWAP Indicator

The Volume Weighted Average Price, or **VWAP**, is one of the most important tools available to the intraday trader, since it very reliably represents the moves of many institutional traders. As we have learned, institutional traders are responsible for 80% of the volume of stocks in which we trade. If for a moment we disregard the public, which constitutes just 20% of stock volume, we see that at any point in time, institutional buyers and sellers are not acting for the purpose of short-term trade profits, but are operating on clear instructions: "buy cheaply" and "sell at high prices." This is where an essential problem surfaces: it would be easy to check traders' successes if they sold the stock on the same day they bought it. However, when institutional traders buy stocks in order to hold them over the long term, how can we know if these traders bought at high or low prices? How are "expensive" and "cheap" defined over a day of trading? This is the function covered by the VWAP. It allows defining expensive and cheap relative to a stock at any point.

The first platform to present the VWAP indicator was from a company called Instinet, which included the new tool on the trade screens of many institutional traders.

The VWAP calculation. Take a deep breath, and then read this twice: the VWAP is the average intraday price of a stock as a function of volume at all levels of price. To calculate the VWAP at any given moment, a sampling of the price of every transaction made up to the calculation point is taken, the price is multiplied by the volume of each transaction, all values are added up to the sampling point, and the result is divided by the accrued number of shares traded up to that same point (volume). If this explanation is too complex, don't try too hard to understand: skip it and just make do with the example below.

Example: Let us say that when the trading session opens, the first trade in the stock of ABC is made at $30, for a quantity of 100 shares. Multiplying those two figures produces 3,000, therefore the VWAP (dividing the outcome by volume) is $30. Let's say that the second trade in ABC is at $30.10 for 1000 shares. The result of multiplying those two figures is 30,100. Now the sum of those two first trades is [3,000 + 30,100 =33,100] and the total trade volume is [100 stocks + 1000 = 1,100]. Dividing the accrued result of 33,100 by the trade volume of 1,100 produces a quotient of $30.09.

Had we calculated a regular average of two trades without encompassing the different volumes of trade for each transaction, the result would have been $30.05. Does this figure reliably reflect the stock price? Of course not. It is clear that a transaction of 1000 shares carried far greater weight than a trade of 100 shares. The VWAP produces a higher average as a function of including the volume in each trade. It produces what is known as **"the fair price"** for ABC.

Now let us return to the institutional traders: when they receive an instruction to buy 100,000 shares "on the cheap," their clients and managers are hoping that they will be able to make most of the purchases at the lowest possible price below the intraday "fair price." If we draw the VWAP line across the stock chart, it will show us the price above and below which 50% of the stock's volume occurred. In other words, if institutional traders succeeded in purchasing the stock at lower than the VWAP line, they will enjoy a bonus, and if they bought it at above that line... perhaps they need to find a different job.

| **SMART MONEY** | *When a stock trades for a long time around the same price, we call this "dynamic fair value" or "balance of power."* |

Over time, the VWAP became a favorite among institutional traders, especially when large hedge fund buyers began using it to review the intraday successes of the traders they employed. Currently, an institutional trader's worth is measured by his or her ability to "beat the VWAP." Every transaction the traders make is compared in real time to the VWAP indicator. Traders are considered successful if they beat the VWAP, i.e., if the trade's average buy price was lower than the VWAP at that moment. The more a trader beats the indicator, the greater that trader's worth. From here to calculating trader remunerations was a very short path. Interest peaked in the VWAP when it eventually became the tool by which bonuses were calculated for traders.

| **SMART MONEY** | *Do you understand the amazing significance of this indicator? Knowing what institutional traders are about to do at any given moment is vital and highly useful information!* |

The VWAP was first recognized as important, and adopted broadly by traders, at the start of 2003. Originally, it came about as a need by groups with big money and by funds. The latter were assisted by institutional traders when buying and selling very large quantities of stocks. The only way they could supervise the effectiveness of transactions was to instruct traders to beat the VWAP. Funds generally remunerated institutional traders on the basis of a 2.5 to 3.5 cent commission per stock. However, a trader beating the VWAP could receive a bonus of 10 to 12 cents per share instead.

Most of the activities of institutional traders occur during the first 90 minutes of trading and the last hour of trading. Traders currently operate multiple algorithmic platforms geared to promoting activities connected with the VWAP price, such as the program that buys stocks when they suddenly drop lower than the VWAP and sells them when they move above the VWAP price.

Now that we know how the institutional traders operate, let us review several practical ways for utilizing the VWAP in intraday trade.

Practical Applications

From our viewpoint, the VWAP indicator begins to get interesting only after the first half hour of trading, once significant volume has already been traded. Our starting point is that a stock being traded above the VWAP can be expected to "return" to the VWAP. This is because institutional traders instructed to buy the stock will not buy when its price is above that level, and institutional traders instructed to sell receive incentives for selling above the "fair price," i.e., above the indicator level. The opposite will occur when the stock is beneath the VWAP: it will receive support by institutional traders buying "cheaply," while on the other hand sellers will wait for it to go over the VWAP. For us, the meaning is clear and simple: a stock above the VWAP can be expected to drop, and a stock below it can be expected to rise. The VWAP therefore serves as a magnetic point over the course of the day.

Reviewing the Intraday Chart Showing VWAP for Apple, AAPL

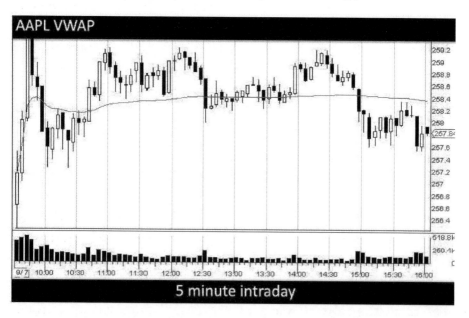

Notice the VWAP line. Why does Apple constantly return to it? Simple: when the stock is above the line, which makes it considered "expensive," institutional traders instructed to sell do so; and when it is below the line, therefore considered "cheap," institutional traders instructed to buy do so.

Additional Practical Uses

When a stock showing an uptrend pulls back, i.e. returns down, how far will it go? You have probably answered correctly: to the VWAP. At this point, institutional traders will start buying again, and it is highly probable that this is also when the price will begin rising again.

What happens if the price is not supported but continues trending down? If the downtrend leads below the VWAP level, it is reasonable to assume that the stock has reversed its pattern. Buyers who had been the victors are now defeated. In the balance of power, buyers and sellers have changed places. The clearest support for that assumption is that even the institutional traders are not buying.

PIVOT POINTS

Pivot points are actually intraday lines of support and resistance. We can display them on the stock or index chart we are following. When the price drops down to the pivot line or rises up to it, the line serves as support or resistance.

Pivot points are based on a calculation that averages the highest price, the lowest price and the previous day's closing price. Later we will learn how the calculation is made.

- Pivot points are represented on the intraday chart by five lines: S1, S2, PP, R1, R2.
- S = support, R = resistance

Pivot points have two functions:

1. They allow us to determine market trend. A breakout of the first resistance line, R1, indicates a good chance of a continued uptrend; vice versa, a breakdown through the support line, S1, indicates a downtrend.
2. They determine entry and exit points. For example:
   o When the pivot line is broken, the next anticipated resistance line is at R1. Therefore, at this level, it is worth taking some profits or buying above it.
   o If this first line of resistance, R1 is also broken out, the next goal is R2, and there, too, it is worth taking profit or buying above it.

o The same follows for the opposite situation, trending down: the lines of support at S1 and S2 may delay a drop in price, therefore profits should be realized at the S1 or S2 support lines, or shorts should be entered beneath those two lines when they are broken.

Impact of the Pivot Points on Shares of the Steel Trading Company, X

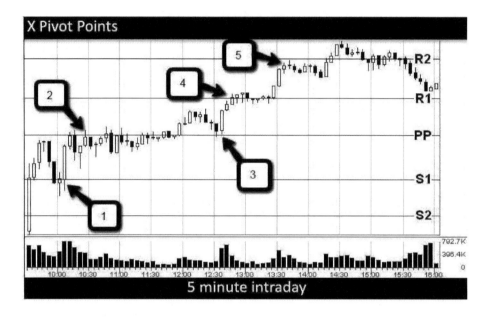

X is trending up strongly when trading opens, and stops very close to the pivot point (PP) line. As you will understand from the calculation below, the pivot point line is considered the intraday axis of movement of the previous day's trading, which in that respect makes it also considered a "fair price," like the VWAP.

This means that when the stock opens below the pivot point, buyers will be found who are ready to buy the stock. Of course, they will buy only up to the stage when the price reaches the pivot point, which currently serves as resistance.

The price then drops and is supported at S1 [1]. Buyers return to the scene, and the price trends up but encounters resistance at the pivot [2]. It succeeds in breaking through the pivot and returns down, supported by the pivot which now serves as support [3]. The price continues up to the next line of resistance at R1, stays there a while as expected [4], and then continues trending up to the next resistance point R2 [5].

How to Calculate the Pivot Point

No need for panic: even though the calculations appear complex, finding the pivot point is simple, even very simple, and in truth, fairly unimportant. In short, skip the following explanation if such things bore you!

- Pivot Point (PP) is the average of the highest price, the lowest price and the closing price of the previous day's trading:

$$\text{Pivot Point} = (\text{High} + \text{Low} + \text{Close}) / 3$$

Once the pivot point is calculated, we use this to calculate the support and resistance points. Note that there is importance to the order of the results:

- S1 is the first (1) level of support (S) and is the pivot doubled, minus the high of the previous day:

$$S1 = (PP \times 2) - \text{High}$$

- R1 is the first level of resistance, and is the pivot doubled, minus the low of the previous day:

$$R1 = (PP \times 2) - \text{Low}$$

- S2 and R2. Once the first levels of support and resistance are calculated, we can calculate the second levels of support and resistance:

$$S2 = \text{Pivot} - S1 - R1$$
$$R2 = \text{Pivot} - S1 + R1$$

Summary

What is the true meaning of the support and resistance lines calculated relative to the previous day of trading? As with Fibonacci, the pivot lines would be meaningless if the institutional traders and market makers would not have made increasing use of these methods. They are again a kind of self-fulfilling prophecy. The original use of pivot points began when floor traders would receive lists of pivot points on paper charts at the trading session's opening. The nature of their work required constant movement, shoving each other out of the way with their elbows and shouting over each other's heads. They simply could not move around with intraday charts, so were forced to glance at a ticker of numbers running across the screens covering the trade hall walls. When the stock they owned moved up and reached one of the pivot points, what did the traders do next? They sold. That's all there was to it. Most of the trading halls have closed, and traders still physically inside them are apparently using iPads now, but pivot points have stayed with us. Since institutional traders buy and sell according to pivot points, it leaves you little choice but to follow their lead, and give pivot points their due.

Which Indicators Should You Use?

Too many cooks spoil the broth, says the proverb. Too many indicators are not helpful, but harmful! If you try to reach decisions using a number of indicators, it is probable that I would buy and sell a stock before you've even managed to say "Fibonacci." While still novices at trading, I suggest you use the following indicators:

- On the intraday chart in five-minute candles:
  1. Volume
  2. Moving Averages for 8 or 10 periods
  3. VWAP on one chart and Pivot Points on a second chart

- On the daily chart with one-day candles
  1. Volume
  2. Moving Averages for 20, 50, 200 periods

- On a second daily chart for analyzing stocks:
  1. Volume
  2. MA of 20, 50, 200 periods
  3. MACD or Bollinger or RSI depending on the type of analysis

8

Shorts: Profit

from Price Drops

Crises always provided the best opportunities.

The History of Shorts

The first known incident of shorting is attributed to a Dutch trader named Isaac Le Maire, who in 1609 sold "more shares than he owned" in VOC, a Dutch company. By this act, he did something unique in the capital markets of that time.

This deal also led to the first regulatory law in history prohibiting execution of shorts for a brief period of two years. Since then and to date, short sellers have drawn the ire and fire of regulators, politicians and the general public. Short sellers were blamed for the infamous collapse of the first-ever "public stock" company in history, the East India Company. They were also blamed for the crash of the Dutch tulip market in the seventeenth century, for the Great Crash of 1929, for the fall of the British Pound in 1992 when George Soros, the world-famous Hungarian investor, sold £10 billion and profited by billions overnight. Short sellers were also blamed for the Dot-Com Crisis of 2000, and even for the Sub-Prime Crash of 2008. Napoleon called short sellers "the enemy of the people," President Herbert Hoover denounced them, and FBI head J. Edgar Hoover opened an investigation against them. That's a lot of people opposed to short selling!

Short sellers have never been liked by either the public or legislators, since they are known for profiting from other people's losses. No one likes to hear about financial success stories when he or she is on the losing end, and everyone needs a scapegoat upon which to heap the woes of the world. On the other hand, shorters, as they are known, gained the blessing of famous investors such as Warren Buffet, who support their positive influences on the capital market. Shorters can be credited with one simple fact: when they find a bubble, they will do all they can to expose and explode it! Usually the bubble will burst much faster than it would have if left alone, but on the other hand, bursting bubbles prevents additional investors from bringing their money into the market and afterwards losing it all. Shorters are the oppositional force to investors, a kind of contra-balance in bubbles and overpricing of all kinds. In short: they are the ones who monitor the market, bring in liquidity, and warn of mishaps waiting to happen. They hold an important role, and are aptly rewarded. In addition, once the bubble is burst, they are the buyers preventing the stock from going to zero!

Shorting: Why?

Two-thirds of the time, the stock exchange trends up, and one-third of the time it drops. Sometimes the periods of dropping markets are long, and as with the Dot-Com Crash of 2000, can last for several years. Crises occurred in the past, and crises will occur in the future. Even during periods of dropping markets, a trader has to earn a living. During such periods, I have no intention of looking for a new job in hi-tech. This is when shorting comes into play. When you buy a stock, it is called going "long." A "short" is the opposite action.

- We use shorts to try and profit from down trending stocks.
- Usually the laws of entry for long buying are valid in reverse for shorts.

We will learn more about this later. In this chapter, we will examine how shorts operate.

Shorts: the Potential

The potential for profiting from shorts is far greater than from longs. In fact, most of my profit as a trader derives from shorts. Why is there greater chance of profit? For two main reasons:

- First, because stocks fall faster than they rise.

  Why? A pressured investor will sell faster than it took a greedy investor to buy a rising stock.

- Second, shorts are a superior means for making a profit, since 99% of the public does not understand them nor knows how to execute them.

As usual, the big money is where the public doesn't know what to do.

| **SMART MONEY** | *The majority of the public does not know how to execute a short sale. The big money can be made where the public does not know what to do!* |

How Do Shorts Work?

We execute a short on a stock that we think is about to drop.

Technically, when we buy a stock trending up, we hit the BUY button. A short is no more complex to execute. In the trading platform, next to the SELL button you will find the SHORT button. All you need to do to execute a short is press it. You still don't understand how to do it? Just press the button: everything will work out fine.

Here's an example from real life. When we execute a short, we are selling a stock that we do not own for a high price, with the intention of buying it later cheaply.

How can we sell a stock we do not own? Very simply. Here is a description of a familiar situation: Let us say that you enter an exclusive furniture shop and buy a sofa on special order, upholstered specifically to your taste. Since this is a custom order, it is reasonable to assume the sofa is not in the store's warehouse, and you will only receive it once your wishes have been carried out. Let us say that the shop assistant sells the sofa for $5000, takes your money and promises delivery within several weeks. Once you have left the store, the salesperson phones the manufacturer and orders the sofa for less than what you paid: for example, $4000. Some weeks later, the sofa is delivered as promised.

Does this sound like a common-enough situation? Note, however, that in the first stage, the salesperson sells a sofa that the store **does not have** for $5000, and only after you have left, the store actually buys it for $4000, making a profit of $1000. In stock market terminology, the store has executed a "short" sale: in other words, the sofa was **first sold at a high price, and only afterwards bought for a low price**. The exact same procedure holds for stocks as for sofas, cars or any item ordered which you do not receive immediately on paying for it. The system works. So, how can I sell stocks I do not own?

Example of Short Sale of Checkpoint, CHKP

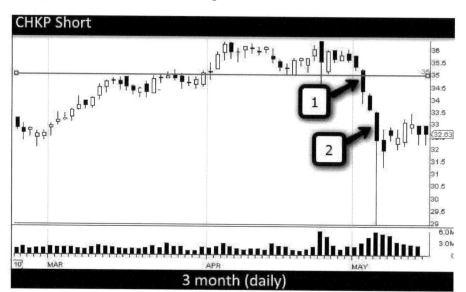

Checkpoint sank below the line of support at $35. Let's say I want to sell 100 shares short, and I press the short button at [1]. What happens? I have just sold 100 stocks I don't have!

How can I do that? Very simply, because my broker loaned them to me. How does my broker have 100 Checkpoint shares? The broker manages the accounts of multiple clients. Since Checkpoint is a high-volume stock, it is reasonable to assume that some of the broker's clients hold Checkpoint shares.

Now let us say that one of the broker's clients, a fellow named David, holds 300 Checkpoint shares in his account. David bought them two years ago, and believes in their long-term future. When I pressed the short sale button, the broker took 100 of David's shares and sold them for me according to my instructions.

In actuality, I sold 100 authentic shares, but they are not mine. If David were to suddenly check his account, would he find 300 or 200 shares? Since no one bothered to update David that I sold 100 shares belonging to him, David still thinks he has 300 in his account, even though in reality there are only 200. What would happen if David decided to sell all 300, right then? The broker would simply shift 100 from someone else. Legal? Absolutely.

In one of the conferences where I taught, a young woman raised her hand and said in all seriousness that she felt the system of selling short did not withstand the test of integrity. Perhaps not; but it definitely does hold up to the test of the market and the law. Markets are not socialist by nature. The market is not intended to assist anyone, and no shorter gives consideration to the best interests of the public, only to his or her own interests. We can think about that situation in the following way: I borrow David's shares and sell them. David has an interest in his shares going up in value, but by selling his shares, I increase the supply and cause a drop in stock price. Not only does David have no idea he is helping me, but by selling his shares, I cause him damage. Pure capitalism.

Does that sound dreadful? The truth is that compared to other services we have become accustomed to accommodating, shorting is not so horrible. For example, you know, of course, that when you deposit money in the bank, it is used as the basis of loans for other people. It is the Capital Adequacy Law that makes it legal for banks to lend nine dollars for every dollar you deposited! Shorts are child's play by comparison to the regular banking system.

When I execute a short on Checkpoint, I sell 100 shares for $35, receiving $3500 for them. Actually this is not my money, and the value of the shares is counted against me to ensure that I return David's 100 shares as soon as possible. Remember that by selling 100 of his shares, I owe him those shares in return. There is only one way to exit a short, whether that incurs profit or loss: at some point, I must buy 100 shares and return them to David.

To my great joy, I discover I was right and that Checkpoint has plummeted to $33, as I had anticipated. At this point, I decide to exit the trade and realize the profit. How is that done? I buy 100 shares at [2]. Since the price is now $33, the cost of my purchase is $3300. The 100 shares I bought are now returned to David's account, and the trade comes full circle. I now owe David nothing.

Examining the process, I bought at $3300 and sold at $3500, therefore am left with a profit of $200.

The difference between a short and a long is the order by which the process is conducted. With a short, we start by selling and end by buying. We sell for a high price, and try to buy for a low price. This is known as **sell high, buy low.**

What could have happened if my prediction turned out to be a failure, and the stock price rose to $37 instead of dropping to $33? Under such circumstances, I would be forced to buy 100 shares for $3700. Since I sold them for $3500, and now have to buy back for more, the process ends up being sell low, buy high and a loss for me of $200.

Summary

When we expect a stock to rise, we can buy low and sell high. When we expect a stock to drop, we still buy low and sell high but in reverse order: **first we sell high, then buy low.** As you see, no one has yet come up with a better way to make a profit other than the ancient method of buying cheaply and selling at a higher price.

SMART MONEY	*The difference between a short and a long is the order of actions. To execute a short, we start by selling, and end by buying.*

Are Shorts Riskier than Longs?

In light of the fact that stocks drop faster than they rise, shorts work better and are faster and more reliable than longs: from my point of view, intraday trading in shorts is less risky. The risk in shorts may ambush you if and when you swing trade a short, holding it for days at a time, since you can never know what the situation will be when you wake up. We execute shorts on weak stocks. When a weak stock reverses, the effect of the upward correction can be sharp. (Later we will learn about the "short squeeze.")

Another aspect is the potential for loss. If you are holding a long position, the maximum potential for loss is the value of the stock. A stock worth $20 can drop to $0, so the maximum loss is limited to $20 per share. By contrast, when you hold a short, the potential for loss is unlimited since a stock worth $20 can also rise to $200, or in theory, "to infinity." This occurs in very rare cases and your likelihood of ever experiencing such a situation is very low, but it is definitely a risk that must be taken into consideration and recognized.

Summary

During the day's trading, shorts are not any more risky than longs. However, if you choose to hold shorts for several trading days, they can definitely become dangerous and will require a high level of skill and caution.

How long does a broker let you hold a short? This varies from one broker to another. Some require closing shorts within three trading days, while others set no limitations.

Shorts for Advanced Traders

So far, I have reviewed the principles of short selling, why they exist (the need to profit from dropping stock prices), and how the procedure is conducted. Now it's time to look deeper.

You know that when executing a short, you are selling shares that are not yours in the hope that when the stock drops, you will buy it back at a lower price than what you sold. Up to this point, it sounds simple, and for many traders and investors that is all you need to know. But from the viewpoint of those who like to understand how trading works, there is a lot more to learn.

Can short selling be executed with every stock? What might happen if you were interested in shorting on a stock your broker does not hold? In actuality, you will discover that you cannot execute a short on all stocks. The limitation is tied to the stock's public ownership and the number of open shorts on it. In other words, a stock with low public ownership will not be held by a great many clients, and therefore the possibility of your broker loaning it to you is limited. A second limitation often occurs when a stock with high tradability drops sharply, usually as a result of a newsworthy event. Sometimes the quantity of shorts on a stock is so large that all available shares have been leant to other shorters. However, for 95% of the stocks with high tradability, which is the only type in which we trade, shorts can be executed and any limitation is actually fairly uncommon.

Example of a Stock that Temporarily Cannot be Shorted

In this daily chart, you can see a rare example of a large percentage crash in Goldman Sachs (GS) stock, resulting from the publicized criminal investigation into the company's conduct based on the fear of investor fraud during the 2008 financial crisis. In the Tradenet trading room, we shorted at the start of the process, when the stock dropped to below $174. Two days later, when we saw that the downtrend was continuing and we wished to increase the quantity of shorts, we found that this was not possible because all available shares had already been taken by other shorters.

Regulatory limitations can occur, although very infrequently. In cases such as the financial meltdown of 2008, shorts were prevented, based on political considerations. Once every few years, usually during crises, the public's voice rises to a shout against shorters, and a moral argument ensues concerning the contribution or harm shorters wield on market stability. In some rare instances, shorts were prohibited on certain financial stocks for several weeks. In actuality, the limitation was set only towards the close of the crisis at points in time that no healthy shorter would execute new shorts. So in actuality, the prohibition barely affected traders. As traders, we have become accustomed to the resurfacing every few years of the time-honored dispute between supporters and detractors of shorting. Each side has its "justifiable reasons," but in the final run, history has proven that the voice of logic overcomes opposition.

How can you know that it is not possible to execute shorts in a certain stock? When you press the SHORT button, the trading platform will display a message, usually of one word: **Unshortable**. Some trading platforms allow accessing this information even before you give the order.

SMART MONEY	*An alternative to shorts in cases where your broker does not hold the particular stock is the PUT option. We will not learn about the put option here, but it is not a complex process.*

Is it possible that one broker will allow executing shorts in a certain stock, and another will not allow it? Yes. In actuality, it is not your broker who lends you the shares, but the **clearing bank**, which is a central organization working with a great many brokers. The different brokers themselves work with different clearing banks. Although the clearing bank your broker works with may have no shares of that stock, another competing clearing bank may have shares. If you really insist on executing a short in a stock that your broker's clearing bank doesn't hold, you can request to trade in stocks labeled **HTB (hard to borrow),** but you will need to pay almost double the commission for each short executed. Usually this makes using HTB stocks less than worthwhile. There are also interest charges for borrowing shares, especially if you hold the position overnight.

The quantity of shorts allowed on a stock is supervised by the Regulator to ensure that brokers, craving their commissions, are prevented from shorting quantities larger than the amount of shares they actually hold. Once each month, all brokerage companies must report the quantity of shorts in their clients' accounts. By way of example: a company has 100 million issued shares. Is it possible for the public to borrow from brokers all 100 million and sell them short? This is a highly unfeasible situation, but it is technically possible. To borrow the entire quantity, they must all be purchasable. But every company holds shares that cannot be purchased. Some are held by company owners and defined as **Restricted**. Some are held physically in the form of paper deeds by people who have purchased them. Since they are in the owners' homes or safes, and not deposited with brokers, they are not available for lending. The quantity of a specific company's shares open to short selling can be viewed on a range of financial Internet sites, such as Yahoo Finance.

Reviewing Current Short Status on Yahoo Finance for Checkpoint, CHKP

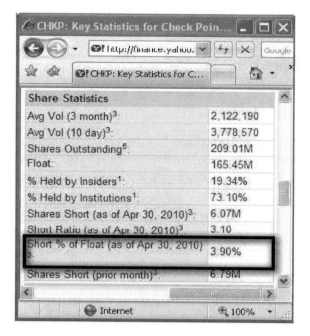

According to Yahoo, the quantity of CHKP shares sold short for the particular date checked is 3.9% of all CHKP shares. Is that a lot? Not much? It makes no difference. Firstly, the information is not precise: it relates to data received via brokers several weeks earlier! Secondly, this data contains no details that allow you to reach any conclusions about the stock's anticipated direction.

Example

Let's say a company called ABC has a high quantity of shorts.

- Does the large quantity of traders executing shorts on the stock mean that the stock must drop?
- Or does it mean that with so many shorts executed, the shorters eventually needing to buy the shares in order to return them to the owner will cause the stock to rise?
- The answer is: both situations can occur, and it all depends on timing. The truth is that for a company losing value, with its price plummeting

towards zero, it may get to that point irrespective of the quantity of shorted shares. The reverse can also occur: if there are a large number of shorters and for some reason the stock begins to rise, shorters will panic since they will need to buy high. As a result, **short covering** may begin: shorters, pressured by the need to return the shares and seeing the price rising, will need to "cover" open shorts. You can never know what is happening behind the scenes without checking the stock chart. And this issue brings us to the next, very important topic.

Short Squeeze

Occasionally a situation called a **"short squeeze"** occurs. Let me describe a true event concerning a stock that for a very long time traded at around the $2 to $3 mark.

The company was known to be having difficulties, and therefore, as can be expected, there were a large number of shorters involved who believed that the company would close and the stock price would drop to zero. In a surprise announcement, some good news surfaced and the stock shot up overnight from $3 to $5. This panicked the shorters, who had entered close to the $3 point. Some, especially those using a high margin, woke up the next morning to find they were holding a losing position and were forced to close those positions by buying while the price was rising. The more the price rose, the stronger the avalanche of shorters closing trades. Every price rise caused increasing numbers of shorters to close losing trades. As a result of the shorters needing to buy no matter what, the price was pushed to a peak of $15 in just two days.

Did reasonable investors reach the conclusion that the stock was worth $15, and buy in? No; in fact the opposite was true. It was clear to everyone that the price would return to zero. It was mainly the panic of short sellers forced to buy at any price that caused the spike. Once their pressured actions eased off, the price increase ended and the stock dropped back to a value of several cents.

Every so often, players with deep pockets will try to increase the quantity of their shorts as the price is rising in order to **average up** a losing trade, but even they have limits. Shorts come under great pressure when these heavy players try to borrow shares from the broker and execute more and more shorts as the price trends up. At some point, though, they cannot receive any more shares on loan from brokers because the brokers themselves hold only limited quantities, and using them "on credit" from the original client, cannot be stretched any further.

What drives the stock price? This is what we should always be asking ourselves. Is the stock being driven by fundamental data that improved overnight? No: prices spike when an imbalance develops between buyers and sellers. An imbalance results from there being more reasons to buy and fewer reasons to sell. Thus, until the stock reaches its new balance, it will continue rising.

An amazing phenomenon can sometimes be observed during trading: a stock that hits the heavens! What should you do as you watch this happening? Should you join in? If you are not extremely experienced, the answer is a definite "no"! This is very dangerous territory. The long-term core investors have no fundamental data to infuse confidence in the stock, and short-term traders usually find no good technical formation that helps them decide whether to enter or exit. The clamor can stop at any second, and without any warning.

| **SMART MONEY** | *It is best not to trade extreme intraday price spikes. This is when the game gets too dangerous. You can never know when the spike will peak, and usually you will not be able to see a valid technical entry point.* |

Summary

So far, we have learned how shorts operate, the fundamental principles, and what happens behind the scenes. You now know that:

- The purpose of shorts is to profit from dropping stock prices.
- Selling a stock short means borrowing shares from the broker who in turn borrows from one of his or her clients.
- If the broker cannot lend them, such as when they are out of stock, we cannot execute a short, in which case the opportunity must be waived.
- "Short squeeze" means that a stock is rising sharply usually due to some good news about the company, which sets into action a wave of shorters rushing to close their position, which in turn causes the price to jump even higher disproportionately to the company's true value.

Is the explanation now complete? No. It gets even more complicated.

Naked Shorts

We will now take a look at the dark side of short selling and learn about the phenomenon known as "naked shorts," so called because they have no real cover. The phenomenon occurs when a large organization, usually a hedge fund, interested in shorting a very large quantity, **sells shares it cannot borrow**!

How can it do this? After all, we have just learned that shorts cannot be executed on shares that cannot be borrowed. But as we know too well, nothing stands in the way of those who really desire something, and market makers can make that something happen. They do this by selling shares they do not have, and transferring these "naked shorts" from one account to another for periods so short that the regulatory body cannot follow the trail. They can also do this by executing shorts in stocks of US **dual-traded companies** which are simultaneously traded on stock exchanges outside America. These foreign stock exchanges are not concerned with enforcing the regulations.

Why would organizations make a naked short trade? It often creates big business, especially during periods when the economy is weak and the dollar has dropped heavily compared to its competitors. In such times, company values drop, they weaken, and eventually are forced to issue more shares in order to recruit funds. This works in the shorters' favor. Even shareholders may eventually be forced to sell more shares which until that point had not been in circulation in the market.

Naked shorts are not listed anywhere, so if you look at Yahoo Finance and see that a company with 30 million traded stocks has 3 million shorted, you can be sure that 3 million actually means nothing, and has the same probability of being correct as incorrect. Perhaps millions more shares are shorted with almost no one knowing, since the trade is not registered.

Let me close this section by saying that this is yet further proof that examining data on shorts in the market is not a good basis for making your trade decisions. Those should be based on checking the stock chart. Charts do not lie. People definitely do.

Summary

The bulk of the public loses money during economic crises. You and I will also lose when the economy collapses, inflation runs wild, and the funds in which our money is invested are negatively affected by a dropping market. In short, during crises we all lose out, and we have no control over that. By contrast, however, as traders we must learn how to profit from dropping markets, and not merely profit, but profit big. The learning process is long, and you will not be able to start it during the next crisis or just weeks in advance of it. You need to prepare for the next crisis years before it happens. In other words, you need to start preparing right now.

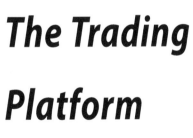

9

The Trading

Platform

Practical steps to choosing, configuring, and operating your trading platform

My Trading Platform

Most how-to books do not provide instruction on trading platforms. I think that's a mistake. A trader must know more than just how to choose the right stock. Traders must be able to choose their platform and know how to use it. I recall my early days as a trader and the shock of opening the trading platform for the first time, with no idea where to begin, what to look at, or how to click the button. Even when I learned the basics on my own, no easy feat at all, I was still very far from being able to configure the charts and the platform I currently use. I also remember how on the first time I visited Chris, my mentor in Phoenix, Arizona, I very precisely recorded every chart and window and their exact positions on his screens. The purpose of this chapter is to save you a lot of effort in figuring out, by trial and error, how to make your monitors work best for you.

The trading platform is the trader's pipeline to the market. The platform must be fast, effective and reliable. It does not need to be overly sophisticated, since such platforms tend to be slow and cumbersome to operate. Have you ever seen a racecar driver's cockpit? If not, you're likely to be disappointed the first time you do. We tend to think of racing drivers as needing special, smart controls with a whole gaggle of electronic devices. The opposite is true: the driver needs very little. What the driver needs are speed, agility and dependability. The same is true of the trading platform. Don't look for unnecessary platform "toys." Just like the racing driver, you need a fast, dependable foundation. In the long run, the trading process is based on just three buttons: BUY, SELL, and SHORT.

During my years as a trader, I have used just seven different platforms.

The first was from "Ameritrade," an online platform that required no installation, but did not provide the performance speed needed for trading. As a web-based platform, it was ideal for long-term investors, but was far from supporting the intraday high speed execution needs of a day trader. The second platform I used was the wonderful CyberTrader, which unfortunately was bought out by Charles Schwab, a company that specializes more in investment than active trading, and therefore killed the platform.

My next choice was a top-of-the-line technology called Trade Station. It was advanced and smart, containing endless "toys," but it created a "too many trees to see the forest" situation and was unsuited to day trading. Three months later, I realized I needed to be like racecar drivers, who can't compete in a luxury Mercedes model. I set out to look for the next platform.

My fourth choice was an excellent one, but it had no charts. Its execution performance system was excellent and fast, but to check charts I needed to link with an external program. The charting program was also excellent. However, needing to integrate two platforms required not only an additional payment of several hundred dollars per month to the charting company, but it was unwieldy. Even though I really liked the platform, I realized it was worth letting that one go as well.

My fifth attempt lasted no longer than two weeks. The platform was slow as a turtle and highly sensitive to my Internet speed. It would crash, get stuck, and stutter several times a day. When I sought service for it, I came up against a stone wall in the form of an employee in New York named Chang with a service awareness that left much to be desired.

I finally reached a good "resting place" when I began using the COLMEX Pro platform, which adapts well to novice traders and experienced traders alike. At last, I had found a real "cockpit" for stock trading, with a few extras, but no bells and whistles.

Choosing a Trading Platform

In Chapter Two, I detailed the characteristics required of a trading platform, and therefore I will only repeat the main points:

- The platform must be of the Direct Access type, allowing the trader to buy and sell shares directly for every target according to the trader's choice or an effective automatic router.
- The platform must be installed on your computer and not web-based, since only the installed programs are fast, reliable, and can be

personally configured.

- The platform must be simple and user-friendly, with the ability to simultaneously display at least 20 different charts over several screens.
- The platform must display over several screens and provide the ability to save the installation configurations, so that each time you reopen it, it will return to the multi-screen configuration you defined and saved.

Download and Installation

First, you need to open an account with a broker and deposit money in it. This issue was covered in Chapter Two. Once you have completed the account opening process, which should take no more than a few minutes, you will have to wait for the broker's authorization, which could take a few days. You will receive an e-mail congratulating you for joining, and a platform download link. The download process is simple and identical to that of any program, and therefore needs no explanation. The questions begin to surface after installation and with the first time you open the platform, since at this stage you still have no clue, really, about what to do. More on that later.

First Activation and Screen Configuration

All trading platforms are very similar. This explanation is structured around the COLMEX Pro platform, but will not vary greatly for any platform. When you first open the platform, you will find a **window layout** which the broker has chosen for you. Since brokers do not understand much about day trading but understand a lot about trading commissions, you will generally find that the configuration they offer is nothing like what you need. It is no more than a place to start. If this is your first day of study and you are using only one screen, you will need to start with the basic windows configuration I demonstrate later.

The trading platform allows you to arrange various windows across your screen, each of which has a specific function. You will configure the position and number of windows according to your needs. Further on, I will recommend several basic configurations and explain their components. Once the windows are set up the way you want them, you will need to save the display configuration (Save Screen, Layout, or Page) under a name. I tend to save several configurations: suited to one screen, to two, to three and so on. I also save my favorite configurations on a USB stick on my key ring, so that if I need to trade when I'm away from home, I can easily install my platform on any computer and upload the screen layouts (Open Screen) that I prefer.

Screen Configuration

The Most Basic, Simplest Trading Platform Configuration

The screen configuration I will demonstrate below is the most basic, suited to a 12-inch screen. I use this one with a laptop when I am away from home. The configuration comprises seven different trading windows (to be explained). The larger your screen, the more windows you will be able to add.

Example of Basic Configured Windows on One Screen

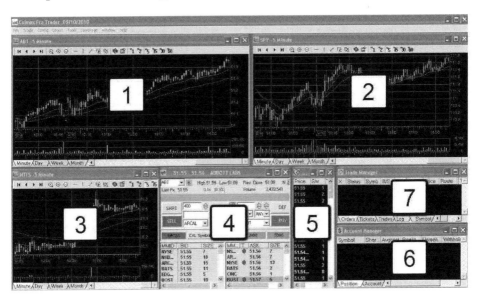

1 – The Main Stock Chart

On the main stock chart, I display the stock I am following at the time. It shows five-minute candles [1] of [2] intraday data for a range of two days. Notice the dashed line [3] separating the two days of trading on the chart. To see the stock's daily formation over a longer period, I simply click the DAY button to the right of the intraday MINUTE button [2].

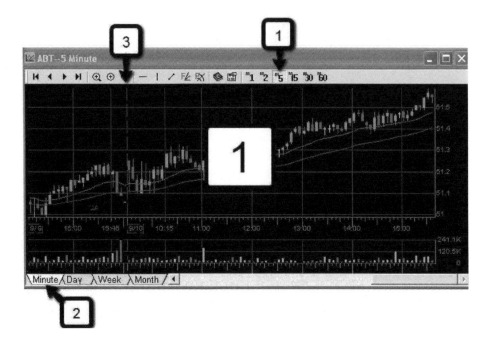

2 – The Market Index Chart

On the market index chart I display the SPY, which as we have already learned is the most important index for traders. The chart will display intraday information and five-minute candles for a two-day period. Note the perforated line separating the two days.

3 – The Secondary Chart

On the secondary chart I display the stock I am following. I may be watching a new stock on the primary chart [1], while simultaneously following up on a stock I have just bought on this secondary chart.

4 – The Trade Window

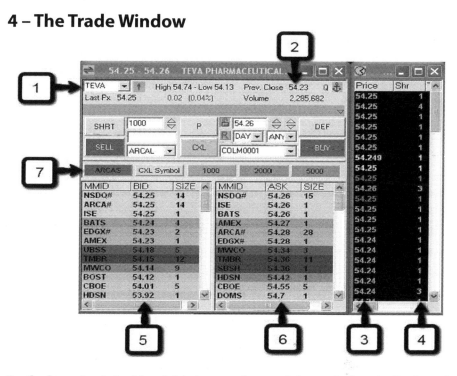

On the broader left side of this image, the stock box window is displayed. On the narrow right side is the Time & Sell (T&S) window, on which I will expand later. Both these windows must always be side by side. In some trading platforms, they even appear together in the same window. The stock box is a trader's central execution tool. In the top left corner of the stock box, we can type in the stock symbol [1]. In the upper section we find information known as Level I data [2]. This is data such as the previous day's closing price, the highest and lowest prices of the current day (high and low), the current day's trade volume (number of shares), the price of the most recent trade (Last Px), percentage of rise or drop of the stock relative to the previous day's close (0.04% according to this image), and the price change in points (0.02; in other words, the share price rose today by two cents).

On the stock box's right, we can see a small anchor. If you drag it with the mouse into the T&S box on the right, a link will be made between the two windows, so that from now on any stock you display in the stock box [1] will have its data displayed in the T&S. In the same way, you need to link the stock box and the primary stock chart, so that every time you change the symbol in the stock box [1], the relevant data will immediately display in the primary chart and in the T&S. In this way you can create a link between a large number of windows and charts.

Beneath the Level I upper data area are the buy, sell, and short buttons, as well as additional commands to be explained later. Beneath them are buttons [7] that can be personally defined. I use them (from left to right) for feeding in protection orders (ARCAs), cancellation orders (CXL symbol) or for fast purchases of 1000, 2000 or 5000 shares. You can set both the text on the buttons and the commands linked to them.

Level II

Beneath the personally defined buttons is the data area known as Level II. It displays buyer demand [5] and seller supply [6] or, as it is known by traders, "market depth."

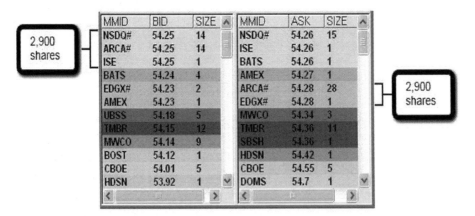

In the instance shown above, you can see that the best purchase, known as BID (on the upper left) stands at $54.25, whereas the best selling price, known as ASK (upper right) stands at $54.26. In other words, the difference between buyers and sellers, known as between ask and bid, and called SPREAD, is one cent. To the left of the price column is the MMID (market maker ID) column. This contains identity details of the buyer or seller. The buyer's or seller's source may be an ECN, as with ARCA or NASDAQ; or a market maker like SBSH (Salomon Smith

Barney). Sometimes, you can find the market maker for both parties: for buyer and seller simultaneously. In the case that both a buyer and seller are available on an ECN, this usually indicates different clients of the same ECN, and in the case of a market maker for both parties, the market maker is trying to profit from the one cent spread. One cent, in very large quantities that only market makers generally see, can end up being a lot of money!

The market depth (that is, the quantity of buyer demand and quantity of seller supply) is very significant. We see how the buyers (the bid) at $54.25 spread across three lines which are emphasized with the same color. Each price layer receives its own color. The total demand quantity at that level of demand is 2900 shares. Notice how the accepted display form of quantities is in units representing hundreds. In other words, 14 + 14 + 1 = 29 represents a demand of 2900 shares at $54.25. Demand, in this case, is divided among three different buyers. On the sellers' (ask) side, you can see a relatively smaller supply of 1700 shares at $54.26. The meaning of larger demand than supply is clear: when there are more buyers than sellers, there is a good probability that the stock price will rise. On the other hand, if the surplus demand has caused you to decide to buy, then it is first worth glancing at the number of sellers found at two cents above the current supply price. Notice that at $54.28, two sellers are trying to sell a quantity of 2900 shares. In other words, if you buy the stock and it goes up only two cents, it may have difficulty in crossing the resistance of the next batch of sellers. Have you already cancelled your buy order? Or is it worthwhile buying only if it passes $54.28?

Let's say that despite the resistance, you are considering buying. Before that, you must check your escape path. If you check the buyer depth, which is below the price of $54.25, you will discover that demand is very low. In other words, if you purchase several thousand shares, you will find great difficulty in exiting at a reasonable price. The solution may be in buying a smaller amount, or perhaps not buying at all. On the other hand, if you are planning to execute a short on the stock and when pressured, may need to exit the short (that is, buy), you can rely on a large number of sellers from whom to buy. Every stock has a different tradability, which means you need to check each one from the point of view of quantity you are willing to risk, and adapt it to the number of bids and asks as displayed in the Level II market depth.

Hiding information

Large quantity buyers and sellers tend to hide the real quantities they are offering since they do not want others reading their intentions. For example, when I want to sell a quantity of up to 1000 shares, I use a command known as RESERVE which displays a sale of only 100 shares even though the amount in actuality is far larger. The buyers, who do not know they are watching a large quantity seller, buy a small amount each time, until eventually they buy the entire amount I intended to sell. What might happen if I displayed an amount of 3000 shares, for example? Without doubt I would scare away small buyers who would avoid buying, since they know that if they buy a small quantity, the stock will not move until a large buyer would come along and purchase all the stocks I am trying to sell.

Sometimes, when you hold a stock whose price has stopped at a certain position and refuses to continue trending up when you are long, or refuses to trend down when you are short, try to discover in the MMID column who the seller is, insisting on adding quantities, or in the case of a short, who the buyer is that insists on renewing quantities. The phenomenon is very common in cases when the stock is trending up and reaches a round number, and heavy sellers can often be found who are not interested in revealing the true quantity they are offering for sale.

Market depth exercises

The opposite situation occurs when large scale market makers who have accumulated shares may wish to display a large quantity for sale, and which they have no intention of selling. They hope that the large quantity will deter potential buyers and even translate into seller panic. They hope that displaying a large amount will reduce the stock price and make it easier for them to accrue more for a cheaper price. This is also why, sometimes, you will find the same market makers on both sides of the transaction: on one hand, the market maker will sell, or at least display like a large seller, and on the other hand, the market maker will buy.

Until a few years ago, market depth manipulations using the Level II are were a common phenomenon. Many traders tried to decipher the nature of market maker behavior, and act according to what they felt the market maker was about to do. This was known as "find the bull": traders would spend entire days seeking the bull that would take them to their promised land. Thick books were written on this activity, and thousands of traders tried following market makers as a way of making profits. Over time, the methods by which market makers could display or hide orders became increasingly elaborate, the market depth exercises dissipated, and all the books on that subject were sent to paper recycling. Market makers can rout their orders exactly the way any trader can through an ECN, so that you will never know who is on the other side, and any attempt to try and understand the other side's 'methodology' of actions is doomed to utter failure. In short, do not waste your time on this: time is too precious. Focus on the quantity of buyers and sellers, and the market depth as displayed in actuality, and just accept the fact that it is rarely the full range of information concerning true depth. Look for reasons in the shape of a large seller renewing stock, give the seller a few seconds or minutes, try to understand if that seller is about to disappear, and then make an informed decision.

Varying layers of colors
As noted, each layer of color represents a different price level. When the first layer representing buyers is broader than the first layer representing sellers, there are more buyers than sellers. Note that a larger quantity of buyers does not necessarily mean a larger quantity of shares, but the larger the quantity of different buyers and sellers, the better the market depth is, since the supply or demand are divided among a large number of traders. If you were considering selling, what would you prefer to see on the buyers' side: a single buyer, buying a large quantity of shares, or three different buyers simultaneously purchasing that same quantity? I would prefer the latter: the division among multiple buyers is better than one single buyer.
The purpose of these colored layers is to allow you to catch, at a glimpse, a visual image of the pressures felt by buyers and sellers. Over time, the changes in color will be an inseparable part of your overall awareness over the strength or weakness of a stock at any given price.

5 – The T&S Window – Time & Sales
The Time & Sales window is a separate part of the attempt to understand a stock's direction. Some time ago, I invited a friend with a year's experience in trading to sit with me during one of my trading sessions.

He was a little amazed that alongside each stock box, I always positioned the T&S window. I was equally amazed to hear that until now, he had never used it. After spending a short amount of time with me, he realized its need. The T&S window shows every transaction executed for a stock. The usual display is for the latest trade to appear in the window's upper section. As you see, the latest trade occurred at $54.25 for a quantity of shares listed as "1", in other words, 100 shares. The trade before that was for 400 shares. If you look a little further down, you will find a trade at $54.249, a transaction that only market makers are capable of making as they "cut" the price between buyers and sellers, and it is the first in the list between the spread. This is their advantage area, since you and I have no legal ability to perform trades with fractions of cents.

Why is the T&S window so important to me? For several reasons.

- The first reason is explained with this example. Let's say a large scale buyer is not interested in showing the quantity of shares she or he wishes to buy at $54.25, and therefore I cannot see the true quantity that the buyer seeks. But the information that the buyer cannot hide from me concerns the number of transactions, ie: the volume of trade occurring at that price. In the T&S window, I see every trade and the rate at which they are being executed. This information, together with the quantity of shares displayed in the market depth window, will give me a reliable and realistic image.

- The second is the following: the T&S window has an additional important characteristic: the color used to display each transaction. When a trade occurs where a buyer is willing to pay the supply price, known as ask, which in this case is $54.26, the color of the line in the T&S window, representing the quantity being sold, will be green. Green means buyers are more aggressive than sellers: in other words, they are willing to pay the full price requested by the stock's sellers. On the other hand, when a trade goes through at the demand price, ie, the bid, it means sellers are capitulating to the buyers' demands, and they are willing to sell at their price. The transaction color in the T&S window will be red. A sequence of red colored trades tells us that buyers are under pressure, and a sequence of green colored trades tells us the sellers are under pressure. If the spread between buyers and sellers is greater than one cent, a transaction might be executed at some intermediary price, which would be colored white. You can define these colors yourself on your trading platform, and even add additional colors for various other types of signals.

Some years ago, when I was explaining the meaning of these to one of my students, he asked: "And what does the yellow color stand for?" Well, it turns out I am color blind. For years, apparently, I've missed out on seeing another color...

Practical examples

- A sequence of green trades: the stock is strong, and trending up. Buyers are pressuring.
- A sequence of red trades: the stock is weak. Sellers are getting rid of the merchandise at any price.
- A sequence of red trades but the stock price is not dropping: a large scale buyer hiding a large amount.
- A sequence of green trades but the stock price is not rising: a large scale seller hiding a large amount.
- A sequence of white trades: market makers are trading at an intermediate price. It is hard to interpret the meaning of this, but it is interesting to know that market makers are involved.

Executing orders

The main use of the stock box is to execute buy, sell, short, and additionally, more complex orders such as defining profit and protection targets.

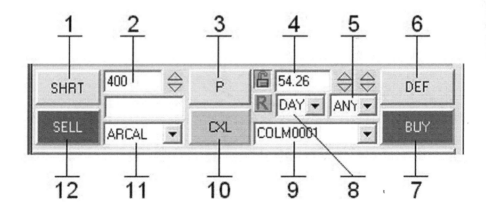

1. The "short" button
2. The amount of shares sought. You can define your default amount.
3. Instruction to display in the window [2] the quantity of shares you are holding – called POSITION
4. The LIMIT price at which you are willing to execute the trade. This

order will be explained later.

5. Two possibilities: ANY, which is an instruction during buying or selling to execute the trade for any quantity that can be obtained. For example, if you wish to buy 400 shares and only 350 are being offered, the trade will be executed for 350. The second option is AON, standing for All Or Nothing, an instruction to execute the trade only if all the quantity of shares you want is available. In other words, if 400 cannot be bought, then buy nothing. I don't recommend doing that.

6. The DEF (Default) button will bring you back to the default status if you have changed any parameters in the meantime.

7. BUY button.

8. Order validity limitation. When DAY appears, the order will cancel at the end of the trading day. When GTC appears, standing for Good Till Cancelled, the order will remain open until you manually cancel it.

9. The trading account from which you execute orders. If you have several accounts, such as portfolio managers do, you can use this window to toggle between them.

10. Cancellation of any waiting order for the specific stock.

11. Order routing to different liquidity targets. We will learn more about this later.

12. The SELL button.

6 – The Account Manager Window

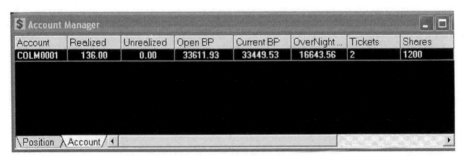

Account	Realized	Unrealized	Open BP	Current BP	OverNight...	Tickets	Shares
COLM0001	136.00	0.00	33611.93	33449.53	16643.56	2	1200

The account manager window contains two tabs in the lower bar: one is the open positions marked as POSITION, and the other is the ACCOUNT tab. In the first, you will be able to see the profit and loss status of every open trade. In the account tab, you can find a summary of all open or closed activities. The image above shows a realized profit of $136; buying power available to the account during the trading day, where BP stands for buying power; the overnight BP; the number of trades, which here is two, and is also known as **Tickets**; and the volume of trading day sales and purchases, here showing 1200 under the **Shares** tab, which in this case refers to a purchase of 600 shares and a sale of 600 shares.

7 – The Trade Manager Window

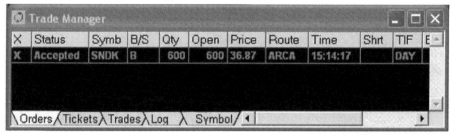

The most important and useful tab in the trade manager window is the open orders tab, labeled **Orders**. In the image above you see that my trading system is currently in a buy status (B) for 600 SanDisk (SNDK) stock at $36.87. The time of the order is also displayed, as well as its validity, DAY, under the TIF (time in force) tab. This means the order will cancel at the end of the trading day if it has not been executed. The order can be cancelled by clicking the button marked X on the left of that bar.

• **the Market Watch window**

Symbol	%Change%	Change	Volume	Last
DJI$	0.38	39.84	93,321,084	10455.08
COMP$	0.21	4.8	1,252,034,174	2241
SPX$	0.44	4.83		1109.01
NYA$	0.46	32.16		7066.53
RUT$	0.36	2.28		636.9
TYX$	0.73	0.28		38.73
XAU$	0.73	1.34		184.83
MID$	0.38	2.92		764.43
XAX$	0.9	17.551		1966.7165
IIX$	0.02	0.042		259.6641
XMI$	0.47	5.352		1147.755
TOP$	-0.14	-3.27		2277.8
VIX$	-3.9	-0.89		21.92
AMGN	0.95	0.51	3,351,157	54.3
CSCO	-0.49	-0.1	38,163,014	20.51
ORCL	3	0.733	35,513,264	25.0632
IBM	1.4	1.78	3,186,349	128.14
QQQQ	0.24	0.11	50,777,805	46.54
AAPL	0.17	0.45	11,603,979	263.52
INTC	-0.5	-0.09	54,138,569	17.91
BBBY	2.3	0.91	1,991,601	40.38
ESRX	1.5	0.69	3,442,911	45.62
MOT	-1.1	-0.09	20,468,101	7.89
TEVA	-0.04	-0.02	2,314,885	54.21

This window allows following up on stocks or indices. You choose which stocks or indices to feed into the window. You can also choose the columns setup. In this image, you see the columns I have chosen: symbol, change as a percentage, change in points, volume, and last price. In the upper section, I chose symbols of important market indices and sectors. Beneath them are several stocks I am following. You can open several such windows and save different types of stocks in each, according to various follow-up categories. For example, stocks on the verge of breakout, stocks trending up, stocks trending down, and so on. Right clicking with the mouse on a symbol opens that stock's chart and allows you to quickly check a long list of stocks or indicators. Your trading platform updates every symbol and indicator in real time. This means that the more symbols you add to your tables, the stronger your internet bandwidth needs to be. For this reason, most brokers limit the number of charts offered to several dozen, and the number of symbols for follow-up to several hundreds.

- **the News window**

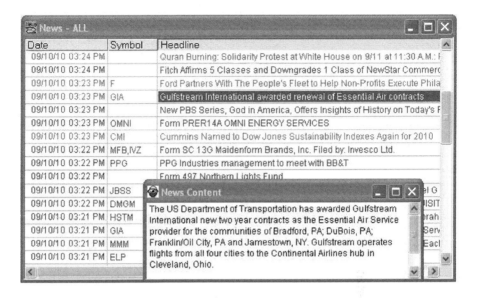

This window displays real time information derived from various data suppliers. The window shows the notification's time, the stock's symbol, and a summary of the information. Clicking the button on the summary line allows me to see an image, opening an additional window displaying the detailed information. I do not tend to follow market notifications. The rate at which they enter is very high and it is difficult to efficiently scan them and focus only on the important, impactful notices. For me, working with this window wastes precious time. On the other hand, perhaps I am not providing a good example, since one of the traders in our trading room insists that he absolutely makes his living from the real time information coming through. So the choice is up to you.

- ## The Alerts window

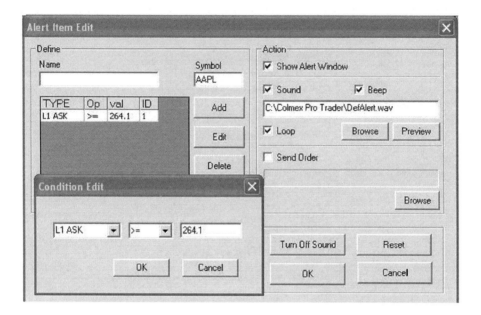

When you plan to buy a stock if it reaches a specific price, but you are following several other stocks simultaneously, it is wise to feed in an alert. In the case above, I fed in an alert that will activate when the ASK for AAPL is equal to or more than $264.10. If and when Apple reaches this price, a warning will pop up on the screen and play a sound. You can set any number of warnings, but I recommend using this tool in a very measured way, since too many alerts disturb trading procedures with all their noise.

The Trading Orders

Limit

The limit order is very common and very useful. Its simple meaning is "Buy (or, sell) at this price limit." The two commands are called buy limit order and sell limit order.

Here is an example: when I look at the Level II window, I see that the ask (ie: sellers) are offering stock of TEVA for $54.26. I decide to buy 1000 shares at no higher than that price. To do this I will use the limit order, which I feed in and execute in the stock box as follows:

1. I enter the stock symbol TEVA [1]
2. Enter the amount of shares wanted: 1000 [2]
3. Enter the limit ($54.26) in the order execution window [3]. It is also possible to choose this price by clicking on it in the Level II window on a seller at that price.
4. I choose the limit order [4]. For example, ARCAL. There are several limit options possible, which will be detailed later.
5. Lastly, I click the BUY button [5]

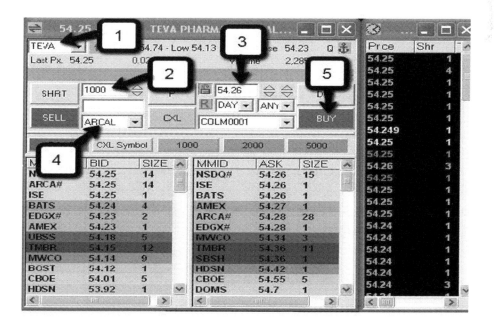

- **Notes**

If there are sufficient sellers to supply the 1000 shares I seek, I will receive the entire amount. However, if someone else hit the buy button faster than I did, the full size that I want might not be available. For example, if someone else gets to 300 shares before me, I will be executed on 700 shares and an open buy order is created for the 300 shares I still want. My demand for 300 shares will now appear as the highest BID and will wait until sellers come along. At any time, I can cancel the bid for 300 shares by clicking the cancel button.

- **Practical example**

In the market depth image (Level II), you see that the number of sellers at $54.26 stands at 1700 shares. What would happen if I wanted to buy 2000 shares with a limit of $54.26?

Answer: since only 1700 shares are offered there, that is the maximum quantity I could buy at the limit price I have set. The only way I can receive all 2000 is if there are sellers hiding their real supply.

Outcome: since there are insufficient sellers at $54.26, the ASK price will go up by one cent to $54.27 and the BID price will also go up one cent to $54.26. My bid price will display as an open order for 300 shares. It will remain open until someone is willing to sell at my limit, or until I cancel the open order.

What would happen if I tried to buy 2000 shares at a limit of $54.27? Note that at this price, one seller is offering 100 shares. In other words, I would receive 1800 shares total: the 1700 shares at $54.26 and 100 at $54.27.

What would happen if I had set a limit of $54.28? Judging by the number of sellers at $54.28 you can see that I would have received the whole amount of 2000 shares from the moment I clicked BUY. I could even have received more than 2000, if I had wanted them.

Would it not have been worth buying some of that quantity of 2000 shares from the beginning, at the higher price? Not necessarily; it depends on how much you really want the entire amount. It is usually better to take the smaller quantity, and wait a few seconds, or a little longer, for more sellers willing to meet your lower limit.

Additional uses for the limit order

- **Buy limit**

Let's say I decide to buy a stock if it goes higher than $30. I prepare a buy limit at $30.01 and when the price reaches that limit, I click the buy button. The buy order is executed at the requested price if a seller is found at that price. The meaning of a limit order is to let me limit my bid at $30.01; in other words, I am not willing to buy at a higher price. So in this case, I am placing a Limit order that is already at least partially executable by the sellers displayed in the market.

The advantage: I fix my maximum price.

The disadvantage: I take a risk that there will not be enough sellers at the price I set, and the trade will not be executed at all, or will be executed for only part of the amount.

Possible solution: I can enter a limit for $30.03.

This is the order you would usually use, but it depends on the nature of the stock. For stocks with low volume and high volatility, you may need to increase your limit price, buy at a higher price than you had originally wanted, and increase the risk. By contrast, with stocks of high volume, you may be able to manage with a more precise limit, since the chances are higher of receiving the stock at your bid price.

- **Sell limit (SHORT)**

I decide to sell a stock when its price drops below $30. I prepare a sell order at $29.99 and when the price drops below $30, I click the Sell/ Short button. The sell order will be executed at the requested price on condition there is a buyer for that price. The meaning of the limit is that I limit the sale price to $29.99. In other words, I am not willing to sell for less than that price.

The advantage: I fix the minimum price I am willing to accept.

The disadvantage: I take the risk that there will not be enough buyers at that point and the trade will not be executed.

Possible solution: setting the limit at $29.97. This means I want to sell when the share drops below $30, but limit the sell price to $29.97.

Every limit must be planned according to the nature of the stock. For stocks with low volume and high volatility, it is worth increasing the limit's spread, but then I might be selling at lower than I had wanted. By contrast, for stocks with larger volumes, it is usually not necessary to increase the limit's spread, since there is reasonable chance of selling the stock at the requested price.

- **Pending Limit buy order**

   I am watching a stock trending strongly up, and intend to buy. I don't want to buy it at a high price, but rather I want to wait for it to pull down so that I can buy if and when it drops. For example, the stock price reached $30.60 and I want to buy if and when it drops to $30.25. I enter a buy limit at $30.25 and click the buy button. The order is ready for execution, but is not immediately filled when I hit the button. Instead, it waits for the price to drop to my limit, and is then executed when someone sells shares to me.

- **Pending Limit sell order**

   I bought a stock at $30 and plan to sell if it rises by 30 cents. I enter the sell limit order at $30.30 and click the sell button. The order is waiting in the system and will not be executed immediately, but only when the sell limit is reached.

Market order

   The market order, by contrast to the limit order, indicates: "I want to buy or sell now, no matter what the price is!" This order is executed immediately when the button is clicked, hitting all shares available for sale until I am filled. For example, if I try to buy 2000 TEVA shares via a market order, I will immediately get the quantity I want, but at what price? According to the supply we saw in the Level II window, I will receive 1700 at $54.26, 100 more at $54.27 and 200 more at $54.28. That's not bad for shares with high liquidity. If I try to buy 2000 shares with low liquidity using the market order, I may in extreme instances jump the stock price by tens of cents, and then discover that when I want to sell, there are not enough buyers. The market order is therefore very effective and fast, but useful only when you want stock with high volume.

Example of order execution

   I want to buy 1000 TEVA shares by a market order. I enter it into the stock box as follows:

1. Enter the symbol TEVA [1]
2. Enter the quantity of shares wanted, in this case 1000 [2]
3. Choose the "market" order in the window [3], eg: ARCAM
4. Click the BUY button [4]

Advantage: This is a fast way to enter a trade because you don't have to enter a price, skipping one field of work, but you must use this order only for stock that allows a broad "market depth", ie: are of high volume.

Stop order

The stop order is conditional upon the stock moving up or down to a certain price before it executes. One example would be when I do not hold a certain stock and want to move to buying it if it rises above a certain price. Another case might be when I hold the stock and want to sell if it drops beneath a certain price. The stop order does not stand alone: it is always linked to another execution order.

For example: if the stock rises to price X, then buy, but at no more than Y cents above price X. In other words, this is a stop + limit because I am only willing to pay up to a certain price. I might also choose a buy stop + market combination, such as buy above price X at any price.

Confused? We will clarify this further with additional examples.

- **Stop loss order**

    The most common type of protective stop order is called a "stop loss". As with all stop orders, this one too indicates a change of status, i.e."I hold a stock and wish to sell when it breaks under a certain price."

    For example: I bought a stock at $30 and want to define in advance my exit point at a loss if the stock drops below $29.70. In other words, if the stock drops to $29.70, I want to sell it, lock in my loss, and "stop" it from getting worse. To do this, I need to use a stop order. When entering the order in the trading platform, I will first need to click STOP, and in the window that opens, enter the stop price of $29.70. I now define what I want to happen when the stock falls to the stop price. I need to choose between selling at limit of X cents (which means, "I want to sell but for no less than price Y") or selling at market (which means, "If the price drops to $29.70 I want to sell immediately and for any price".)

    The outcome: if the stock drops to $29.70 it will sell at my limit or at market. The advantage of the stop limit order is that it ensures the sale will not be executed beneath the defined price. The disadvantage of the stop limit order is the fact that if there is a shortage of buyers, I might find that the stock has gone further below the limit and dropped to a level which is far lower than I had wished, and now I am still in the stock, waiting to sell it higher than the current market. Hence, the advantage of the stop market order is that I will know clearly that I exit the stock when it drops past the stop price.

SMART MONEY	*Not all stop loss orders are orders that stop losses. The stop loss is also entered in cases where you want to limit a stock's drop in profitability.*

Since, from the outset, we are trading in stocks with a good liquidity, I would recommend you always use the stop market order.

One of my ways of coping with large quantities is to enter several sale orders in the form of stop market at spreads of 5 to 10 cents. For example: if I want to protect 3000 shares from drops in price, I will enter 3 different orders at measured intervals of several cents per 1000 shares per sale. Obviously for stock with high liquidity, this would be an unnecessary step.

Entering the Stop Order

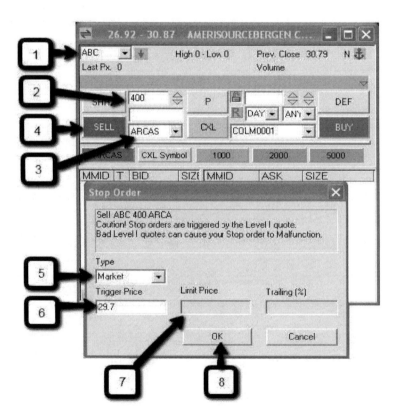

Let us say you are holding 400 shares of ABC and are interested in entering a stop market order if the stock drops to $29.70. The sequence of actions you need is as follows:

1. Enter the stock symbol [1]
2. Enter the quantity of shares you want to protect in case of falling prices [2]. You don't need to enter the entire amount you hold.
3. Choose the order type [3]. In this case, ARCAS was chosen. We will learn more on this later.
4. Click the SELL button [4].
5. An additional window will open: enter the type of order – market or limit – to be executed if the price drops to the stop price [5].
6. Enter the stop price [6], which in this case is $29.7.
7. If at step [5] you chose a limit order, now you need to enter the limit (e.g. $29.67). Not recommended!
8. Authorize the execution by clicking OK.
9. Check in the trade manager window, under the Orders tab, that the order was lodged. If it does not appear, check why in the Messages box and correct any errors.

• **Short Stop Loss Order** - When you short a stock, you are selling a stock you borrowed from the broker, and you will want to protect your account should the stock price go up. Your stop order will be a BUY rather than a SELL (step 4 above), and your stop price (step 6 above) will be higher than the stock's current price. Other than that, the procedure is identical. It implies that if the stock price rises to price X, please buy according to your choice of a limit or market.

• **Stop Order for Buying a Stock** - A trader intending to buy a stock breaking out is not always interested in following the stock for hours until the breakout, if at all. It is possible to enter a conditional buy order.

For example: Let's say that ABC is consolidating beneath the resistance line at $30. You want to buy ABC only if it breaks out above $30. This is the procedure:

1. Enter the stock symbol ABC.
2. Enter the quantity of shares you want to buy at the breakout: let's say 400.
3. Choose the stop order, for example, ARCAS.
4. Click the buy button. Remember that the order is not executed immediately.

5. A window opens for the stop order. Enter the type of order (limit or market) to be executed when the price rises to $30.01.
6. Enter the stop price, which here is $30.01.
7. If at step 5 you chose a limit order, enter the limit price, e.g. $30.03.
8. Authorize the action by clicking OK.
9. Check in the trade manager window under the **Orders** tab if the order has been lodged.

The opposite is valid for a situation where you want to execute a short in a stock if it drops beneath the support level.

• **Trailing Stop Order** - The trailing stop order is very attractive to new traders, but is less interesting to veteran traders. The order links the stop order position with the stock's changing price. Let's say that you bought a stock for $30 and want to enter a stop order for a price drop of 30 cents. Of course you can do this the regular way with a stop order for $29.70, but you can also enter instead a trailing stop for 30 cents, or if you prefer (I never do!), as a percentage, in this case 1%.

SMART MONEY | *The trailing stop order is problematic since it does not take into consideration support and resistance levels, reversals or any other technical behavior. Generally it is not recommended.*

With a trailing stop order, the stop price moves up with the stock. In other words, the stop will always maintain the distance of 30 cents below the stock's peak price, no matter how much it goes up. In other words, you can enter the trailing stop and go on vacation. This, by the way, is the only time I would recommend using the trailing stop – when you are on vacation. Its disadvantage is that it is based on nothing: not on areas of support or resistance, and not on intraday or daily reversals. If you're going to be away from the computer for several hours, enter a stop order at one single, lower price for a while, according to the stock's behavior, and suited to the right technical area. A trailing stop is usually a bad idea.

Entering the Trailing Stop Order

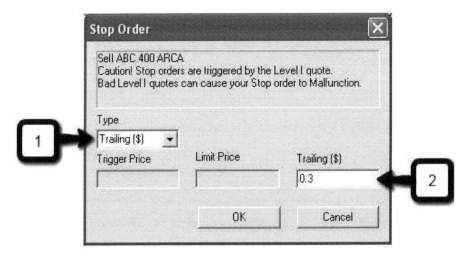

This is a relatively simple process and very much like entering a regular stop, except that in window [1] you need to choose "trailing" through one of two ways: either as $ or as %. I have chosen $ in the image above. Now enter the range. In this case I chose $0.30 [2]. Authorize the order by clicking OK, then check to make sure the order is listed in the trade manager under the Orders tab. That's it.

Complex Orders

Not all trading platforms are able to execute complex orders, but the COLMEX Expert system can. These orders are structured from several different steps that, when activated, cancel other steps. For example, Stop Limit +TTO does the following: (1) buys the stock at a specific price (stop price), but not for more than a defined price (limit), and then (2) if the stock was bought, activates a profit or loss order. Then, (3) if the price goes up to profit target, sells and (4) if the price drops to the stop loss, sells. When either the stop loss or profit target is reached, it cancels out the other.

The significance of this complex order is clear: it makes defining all parameters of the trade possible by defining both the trigger price, controlling the maximum execution price (the limit), and then the target or loss prices. These orders can be entered before trading hours, and then you can go on vacation. Amazing!

Here is an example of a complex stop order for buying 1000 SanDisk shares, SNDK:

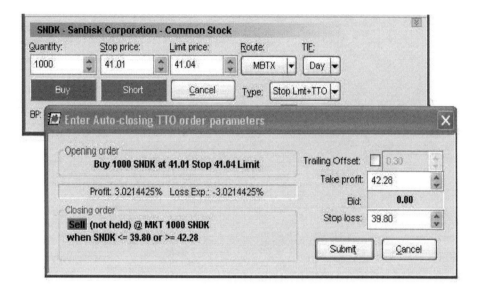

The order will be executed if SanDisk reaches $41.01 (stop) but at no more than $41.04 (limit). If the stock reaches the trigger price and is bought, then two further conditional orders go into action: it will be sold if it reaches the profit target of $42.28, or if it reaches the stop loss of $39.80. Note that both these actions are set at "market."

Order Routing

Routing to Different Destinations

When you buy or sell a stock, you need to decide how you want to route the orders. **Routing** is a topic on which entire books can be written. At this stage, I do not suggest you delve too deeply into it, since it is particularly interesting for those who trade in very large quantities of thousands or tens of thousands of shares.

First, we need to understand what routing is. In Chapter 1, we learned that when you are interested in buying or selling a stock, you need to find a buyer or seller willing to take the role of the other party in the transaction. One possibility is to route your orders to the market makers. We learned that they make their profit within the spread between buy and sell prices. We also learned that we might encounter the specialists, the NYSE version of the NASDAQ market makers. Another routing option is direct to the ECN (Electronic Communication Network). The ECN is a network of computers that links buyers and sellers and in which you can set buy and sell orders without the agency services of market makers.

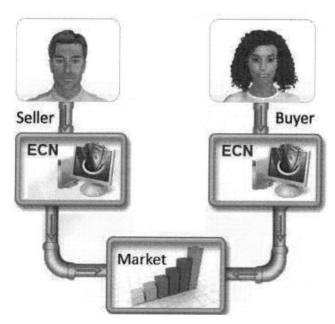

As stock traders, in contrast to investors, you need to use a Direct Market Access (DMA) trading platform. This allows you to route your orders to whomever you choose: direct to market makers, or to the ECNs. The advantage in market makers is that they do not take commissions for executing the order, but they will be a little slower. By contrast, the ECN options are much faster, but if you remove liquidity (to be explained later), they will take a commission which is currently $3 for every 1000 shares.

Automated Routing

If you trade in small quantities and find it difficult initially to understand how to use the routing options, ask your broker if he or she can provide you with automated routing. The broker, through the automated routing program, knows how to choose the cheapest, fastest destinations with the highest liquidity, which are really the best options when dealing in small transactions.

Manual Routing

If nonetheless you want to route direct, for example to an ECN called ARCA, you will need to choose the ARCAL order when setting the limit, or the ARCAM order for an order directed at the market. When I want to execute a stop order, I can choose ARCAS. In other words, the last letter indicates the type of order: limit, market, or stop. If, for example, you want to route a limit order to market makers, you can use SBSHL (Salomon Smith Barney), or NITEL, or a range of other routes to various market makers, according to the routing options offered by the broker you have chosen.

Choosing the Appropriate Route from the Available Options

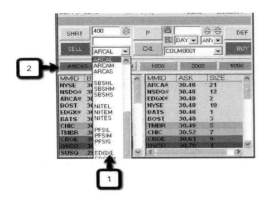

When I open the routing dropdown list [1], I can choose my order type (limit, market or stop) and where to route it. As you see above, the first three orders are the ones I generally use. If, however, I want to direct my orders to other destinations, I can choose from many options.

Why might I want to change the destination? Notice the amount of sellers on the ASK side. You can see that the first seller, with an amount of 2100 shares, is ARCA, and the second, with 1200 shares, is NASDAQ. If I am interested in buying up to 2100 shares, I would choose the ARCAL navigation, click the button and buy the shares direct and fast via ARCA. On the other hand, if I want a larger quantity, I would need to buy shares via the other, NASDAQ ECN marked as NSDQ.

The advantage of ARCA over many other ECNs is the speed and nature of its operation. If the entire amount sought is not on ARCA, they commit to finding it for me from another ECN or market maker. In other words, they will supply me with 2100 shares which they are holding, and then buy the rest from another ECN. In my opinion, ARCA does the work better and faster than other ECNs, although if you are buying very large quantities, you may need to route your orders direct to different destinations.

Adding and Removing Liquidity

ECNs compete with each other and try to attract traders to their services. The more one ECN's market depth increases relative to a competitor, the more traders will use its services and pay its commissions. When I buy stock displayed by a buyer in the ASK column, I am "removing liquidity," meaning that I reduce the number of sellers of the stock I bought, which is not good from the ECN's point of view. When I sell shares to a buyer on the BID side, I am removing liquidity of buyers, which decreases market depth. For removing liquidity, I pay the ECN a commission of $3 for every 1000 shares. This commission is in addition to that which I pay to my broker, and the broker passes that extra commission down to me. These are known as **pass through commissions** and are collected separately from the regular commission agreed upon between me and my broker.

Another cheaper possibility is to position my buy order on the BID side and wait for a seller to offer shares to me, instead of buying direct via the ASK. When I do that, I am actually **adding liquidity,** and for that the ECN gives me $2 for every 1000 shares, which the broker also passes along to my trading account. In other words, I have just reduced the costs of my trade. The advantages of this method are dual: I receive a commission instead of paying it, and I buy the stock at one cent less, which is a saving of $10 for every 1000 shares. The disadvantage of adding liquidity arises from my needing to wait until a buyer comes along who is willing to sell the shares at my BID price.

From my experience, if you want to exit, it is almost always preferable to remove liquidity and pay the surplus commission, since in most cases the price will just "take off" and you could be left with even greater damage.

Summary
Order Routing

Working directly with the ECN, adding or removing liquidity, is usually the most appropriate mode of operation for advanced traders operating with large quantities of shares. It is reasonable to assume that as you start out, you have sufficient other details to pay attention to, therefore I recommend once again that you choose the automatic routing provided by your broker. If you have no such option, choose the ARCAL default.

Trade Orders

You can't see the forest for the trees? The bottom line is very simple. This is the best way to get ahead: your trading platform should always be set to the **limit** order, since you will be using it 90% of the time. In special cases, you will use the **market** order, and generally, only after you have bought a stock or are planning a complicated entry, will you use the **stop** order. As you accrue experience, you will find that it's not as scary as it sounds.

The Trading Room

So far, we have gotten acquainted with the trading platform, its windows, and how to use them, but we still have not learned how to position the platform's windows, especially if you are trading with more than one screen. To explain this, we need to take a few steps back and observe the bigger picture: arranging the screens and the trading room.

My trading room is my fortress. Woe to whoever dares step foot inside during trading hours. I am far from user-friendly, including to my wife, three daughters, and even our dog, whose bond with the family trader earned her the name "Shorty." In other words, my door is closed. I would even lock it quite happily if this were not considered exceedingly antisocial. Pleas from the inner depths of our home, such as "Daddy, the TV's not working" or even screams of fear along the realms of "Daddy, come quickly, there's a huge cockroach!" gain no traction during trading hours.

As worthy of the most important room in the house, I devoted a good deal of thought and effort to planning this room to suit my needs. Your trading station must also match your available space, equipment, and budget.

My trading room

Scary? Since taking this photo, I have added another screen, which is outside the frame. Together with the projector, I use no less than ten screens. Sometimes I do wonder if I need them all, or whether I buy them just to impress the pool cleaner who, with every visit, tells me how he dreams of being a trader, "but never finds the time for it."

I use a lot of screens because I like to see what's happening in the market. Sectors, indicators, and dozens of stocks can be displayed at once. As the head analyst of the Tradenet trading room, I must be constantly up to date in real time with every event. In addition, this is my profession and my hobby. Every professional invests in good work tools, whether that's a quality drill which is effective, reliable and therefore saves time, or any other kind of tool in constant use. Similarly, I invest in quality computers and screens. Can you guess how much it costs to set up three desktops, two laptops, seven 23-inch screens and a projector? Approximately $4000. A builder/renovator's toolbox costs a great deal more!

If you've made the decision to become a trader, invest in the infrastructure. You can start with a computer linked to two screens, although very quickly you will move to a desktop linked to four. Trying to save money? Like the "chicken or the egg" argument, buying cheap will end up expensive. If you do not invest in a quality infrastructure, you may never succeed. If you are still unsure whether this is the profession you want to pursue, start with just two screens but be ready to add more fairly quickly.

My Screen Setup

Let's start from left to right. The projector is hooked up to my old laptop which should long ago have made its way into the trash can, but it serves well for displaying content from financial sites. The projector is also linked to the cable converter, and occasionally, when there is important news or when planning the trading day, I display CNBC on it. The other screens display the following information:

1. Charts of the two market indices: SPY and QQQ, as well as three sector charts: Bioteck (NBI$), Banks (BKX$) and semiconductors (SOX$)
2. Screens 1 to 4 are operated by two dual screen cards in one desktop computer. Screen 2 follows 15 stocks. In the lower quarter of the screen are my Account Manager and my Open Orders.
3. Two stock boxes, each linked to a Time and Sale (T&S) window and the chart for their relevant stock. Along the right of the screen are charts for four stocks for intraday follow-up. That section of the screen is where I usually display several open trades.
4. Two stock boxes, each of which is linked to Time and Sale (T&S) and their relevant charts.
5. This screen follows stocks trending up: charts for some 16 strong stocks I am following during trading hours. These are stocks for which I seek opportunities to enter in reversal in an up trend, or buy at breakout. This screen is linked to a laptop for which screen 6 is its main screen.
6. Stock box linked to the Time and Sale (T&S) window and a chart showing the stock, my second account manager (my second brokerage account), and orders. It displays the leading 20 rising or dropping stocks: my Top 20.
7. This screen follows stocks trending down: charts for 16 weak stocks I am following during trading hours. These are stocks for which I seek opportunities to short a reversal in a down trend or short at a

breakdown.

8. A stock box linked to the Time and Sale (T&S) window and chart displaying the stock, my third account manager (my third brokerage account), and orders; a follow-up list for sectors; and a real-time stock scanner operating to predefined parameters, meaning stocks that have risen or dropped by certain percentages and stocks reaching new highs or lows.

10

Winning Trades

It's time to click the button: best entry and trade management methods

How Many Times Will You Need to Read This Chapter?

Before we start the most important chapter of this book, let me share some of my concerns with you. I am afraid you might miss something important, something huge! Why? Because naturally, the first time you read this book you will not understand its significance in the same way you will after several months of experience. When I ask myself what the chances are of you reading this chapter a second and even a third time, I fear the chances are slim. And I am fairly certain that on a first reading alone, you will not grasp the real meaning of this chapter.

SMART MONEY	*A successful trade comprises the right entry point and money management. Only the right combination of the two leads to continued success.*

I hope I'm wrong, so prove me wrong. Reread this entire section: every word and every trade idea appearing in it will become etched in your mind as to what makes a profitable trade and what makes a loss. Every word is carefully weighed, and every sentence and trade idea contains the experience of many years of trading. I wish to emphasize that this book, and particularly this chapter, were not meant to be read just once. They are geared to second, third and fourth readings, separated by some months and years. Many topics covered in this chapter will become comprehensible once you've traded for several months, and, in the hope you continue successfully as a trader, will become clear once you've traded for several years. I can virtually guarantee that each time you reread this chapter, you'll be sorry that you didn't read it just a short while earlier. The earlier you begin to analyze and internalize, based on your experience, the more you will reduce losses and begin to see a dramatic boost in your chances of surviving as a trader. That's enough of my emotional input for now. Back to business...

Integrating Tools

We have learned why we need to trade with the trend, the meaning of the important trading indicators, and what to be careful of, but does that now imply that we can find any stock trending up and buy it? Can we enter the stock at any moment while it is trending up and the indicators support continued uptrend?

No!

The market direction and use of indicators are important components, and even critical to success, but they are not enough. To succeed, we need to choose the right stocks under the right market conditions, and most important, at the right points!

You need to know when to click the button and when to get out. The purpose of this chapter is to integrate these tools, trends, indicators, and most vital of all, entry points.

Remember! The right entry point is responsible for 80% of your trade's success.

How to Be a Breakout Winner

Trading at a **breakout** is a basic trade strategy. It is the most important and the most used by traders. At the breakout, we expect to see fast movement of prices beyond the technical formation. The assessment is that the momentum of the breakout will lead the stock price to new highs which will allow the trader to realize a profit. The breakout will always be in the trend's direction and never against it. Breakouts are usually accompanied by high volume.

A **breakdown** is the reverse price action of a breakout. With breakdowns, we execute shorts. Breakdowns also always occur in the direction of the trend and never against it. To make the explanation more accessible, I will focus on breakouts, but remember that the explanation in reverse is valid for breakdowns.

In the section discussing formations, we learned that the breakout is based on transitioning beyond the familiar technical formation. We must plan the breakout at the stage where the formation is taking shape, and we must remember that not every development ends with a breakout.

When we identify the breakout formation taking shape, we can plan the entry point and the appropriate trade strategy. Intraday breakout is planned for a short interval of seconds, minutes, or several hours, and usually will be based on a technical formation comprised of five-minute Japanese candles.

Swing traders planning on holding a trade for several days will plan their breakout in the same way, but using daily candles instead.

Intraday Breakout, PCAR

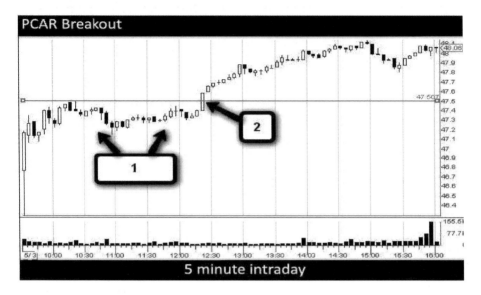

In the image above, we see that PCAR begins the day's trading at $46.40, rises, encounters resistance at $47.5, and consolidates [1] beneath the upper price range until the breakout [2]. The interesting point in this breakout is the fact that the volume did not increase. The reason is simple: notice the time that the breakout occurred. It was at the start of the lunch hour break, when most market players (usually the institutional traders) have gone out to eat.

Why Do Breakouts Occur?

Breakouts occur when there are more buyers than sellers and the price **breaks over resistance.** Naturally, our purchase point will be one cent above the line of resistance. We can imagine a breakout as a large quantity of water held back by a long dam. The dam wall is the line of resistance. What happens if and when the dam wall breaks? Obviously, not only you and I know the answer to that. A large number of buyers are waiting for the breakout, and many others with less experience will join the move at later stages, fueling it a little further. To a great degree, breakouts above resistance are self-fulfilling prophecies.

Most Breakouts Fail

A breach of the dam will certainly lead to flooding. Unlike the dam, a breakout from a technical formation does not always succeed.

Statistically, no less than 80% of breakouts fail!

Despite this high percentage, we should not conclude that buying at breakouts is unwise. On the contrary: we need to understand the stock's behavior at the breakout point, anticipate when and why it may fail, and manage it such that we are assured of our profit from the initial move, even if the breakout eventually fails.

SMART MONEY	*Eighty percent of breakouts fail. Failure does not have to lead to loss. We need to acknowledge the fact that most breakouts fail, and instead learn how to take advantage of them.*

A **false breakout** is defined as a state in which the stock breaks the line of resistance but returns to it and even below the breakout price at a later stage. Does a false breakout necessarily lead to monetary loss? No! The conclusion we should reach is that we must acknowledge the fact that most breakouts are false, and learn how to take advantage of them even under those circumstances. If you know how to handle a breakout, you can leave the losses to less-experienced traders while you realize a comfortable profit, even as the breakout is failing.

Consolidation

The more a stock consolidates prior to its breakout, the stronger the breakout will generally be. A well-known snippet of wisdom states: *the longer the base - the higher into space.*

Simply put, consolidation is the breakout's energy source. The longer the consolidation, the more attention people will pay to the stock; the more people there are following the stock, the more people there will be buying it at the breakout, thus increasing the chances of success. As the consolidation lengthens, one can almost feel the steam building up and waiting to burst through!

Planning and Execution

The entry point is simple and clear: we buy a stock that has gone up in price one cent above the breakout formation.

Later, we will learn that it is occasionally possible to buy even before the breakout if we are able to assess that there is a strong chance the breakout will occur. Breakout buying is a very common method of trading, but requires nerves of steel, the concentration of a fighter pilot, and high-level technical skills.

Prior to breakout, we need to plan our target price. We estimate this in cents, and not in percentages: in other words, how many cents will the price rise after breakout? Estimating the target is based on integrating market direction and market force, the stock's force on the breakout day, and the stock's history of breakouts. Its history refers to its intraday behavior over the past two or three days.

It is reasonable to assume that if we look back, we will see that this is not the only breakout over the past few days. By how many points did it jump in the previous breakouts: 20 to 40 cents, or perhaps 50 to 70? Every stock has its own unique "'personality," and you need to get to know your stocks "personally." For some, an amazing breakout is just a few cents, and therefore will not tend to interest us. Others breakout often with a range of tens of cents.

What is the Stock Volume?

Low volume is dangerous since it becomes more difficult for us to realize quick profits. By contrast, stocks that trade millions of shares per day, such as Citigroup (C), will tend to have more trouble moving and breaking out. We will therefore look for breakouts in volumes of more than one million shares per day, but be less interested in those stocks that trade many millions of shares per day.

The Personality of the Citigroup Stock, (NYSE: C)

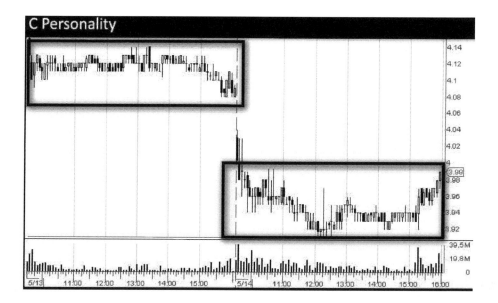

Notice how the Citigroup stock locks within a short range of 4 to 6 cents over two consecutive trading days, with a volume of hundreds of millions of shares per day?

The large volume of buyers and sellers on each side does not allow the stock to move, and ruins all chances of a big breakout. This unique "personality" trait damaged the price and only changed when company management understood the problem and implemented a **reverse split** at a 1:10 ratio to the stock price.

A 1:10 **reverse split** means that for every 10 shares held, the holder receives only one without incurring damage to his or her capital, because all shareholders are adjusted accordingly. The price of the stock then adjusts naturally, so if the price had been $4 per share, it would now be $40 per share since only 1/10th of the shares now exist. The outcome was immediate: volume sank and the stock's nature altered overnight.

How and When to Click that Button

The correct entry price is one cent above the line of resistance, i.e. the moment you see that the first trade goes through above the breakout formation.

Stocks tend to breakout fast, and you need to remember that you are not the only one waiting for the breakout. At the breakout point, you will be competing with other traders who will also try to buy.

You can use two kinds of orders:

- If you use the LIMIT order, limiting to 3 or 4 cents above breakout price, there is a fair chance you will not get your shares, or perhaps only a much smaller quantity than you had hoped for. For stocks with low volume, use only the limit order.
- If you use the MARKET order, there is a far higher chance of successfully entering the trade. The risk is that the MARKET order carries a "buy at any price" condition, and you may be buying at higher than you intended to pay. This is a possible, though very rare, scenario with stocks having high volumes.

In most cases, you will get better results with the limit order.

Do not expect at this point to understand what you have just read. Practical experience will make it all make sense.

Buying Before Breakout

As we have learned, the correct technical entry point is one cent above resistance, but in many cases we try to buy the stock before the breakout. This is a point in time where, in our assessment, the chance of breakout is good.

How do we **define good chances?** Generally, greater than 80% is considered a good chance.

Why not wait until the first trade above the line of resistance, and only then buy? For two reasons: to decrease competition with other traders after breakout, and the possibility of improving our risk/reward ratio because the purchase price is lower.

In principle, you should try to predict the breakout and buy before it actually occurs. To do that, you need to closely follow the stock's behavior in the seconds prior to breakout. Your trading platform should be providing you with all the necessary data. You must follow the chart, the volume, and the balance between buyers and sellers manifested in the BID and ASK, for every single cent in which the stock is being traded beneath the breakout point.

Where a price consolidates in the short range, you will see that the balance between the bid and ask is identical, since the nature of consolidation is that neither side is victorious in this "war." However, when the price approaches the breakout, you can see how the balance is breached in favor of the buyers, and that the volume of trade begins to soar. Once you see that the volume is increasing and that the **sellers' liquidity** is almost depleted, that is the point to click the button.

- **Seller's liquidity** refers to the number of shares appearing in the ASK dropping to zero.

Over time, as you gain experience, your success rate at predicting breakout moments before they occur will improve.

What happens if you buy pre-breakout and the price does not breakout? This does not mean the stock will not breakout later on. Most stocks eventually do, and the only question is if you are able to cope with the loss until it does. The solution is simple: before the breakout, buy only half the total amount you had planned on, and at the breakout, buy the rest if you can. When you estimate that the chance of the price breaking out is not as good as it initially seemed, you can generally sell at a loss of just a few cents.

Which order should you use when buying pre-breakout? When I buy pre-breakout, I tend to use the LIMIT order, limited at most to the ASK price. If I feel that the price is about to break out within seconds, I use the LIMIT for up to 3 cents higher than breakout price. If you realize you have clicked the buy button too late, the stock has passed your limit and you are left with no merchandise, leave the limit order open another ten seconds following the breakout. In many cases, the price pulls back slightly prior to its continued trend up, making it possible for you to join the breakout. Don't leave the order open for too long, since you don't want to get it filled hours later if the stock returns to the breakout price after making a good initial move.

Pre-Breakout Volume

Would you want to see an increase in trading volume prior to breakout?

I imagine your answer would naturally be "yes," that increased volume indicates strong interest, and strong interest prior to breakout would lead to a stronger breakout, right?

In fact, this isn't necessarily true. Once on the verge of breakout, the price has already taken the long journey up to this point. The price has risen, is resting, and we await the next leg of its journey.

SMART MONEY	*Large volume prior to a breakout is not a good sign, since it indicates a change of ownership. Nervous buyers, who may flee at the first sign of weakness, take the place of veteran, relaxed shareholders.*

When you watch a stock's chart, try to decipher the state of buyers and sellers. Try to imagine who they are, what they are thinking, and what you would do in their place. Let us analyze the situation: veteran investors are the ones who bought the stock a long time before it reached its current breakout point, and can therefore be defined as "the strong hands" of the game. They profit nicely and are not sensitive to slight fluctuations in price. By contrast, new buyers, who bought around the consolidation point prior to the breakout or immediately following the breakout, are the "weak hands" since they have not yet earned a cent. They are highly sensitive to every loss, and any small change in price may pressure them to exit, contributing to a failed breakout.

Large volume during consolidation and pre-breakout means multiple buyers and sellers and a lot of shares changing hands. We need to assume that veteran investors are realizing profits, whereas nouveau buyers are the "weak hands." The conclusion is simple: when large amounts of shares change hands, ownership moves from strong holders to new, weak holders who will likely panic at the slightest fail.

Compare the situation to a residential neighborhood where you live. Let's assume a large number of real estate transactions occur there. A lot of homes are changing hands. In a few years' time, will it remain the same neighborhood you know so well? Of course not. The population changes, and the nature of the neighborhood with it. The same happens to the stock you are buying. Large volume prior to breakout means a change of ownership. That, in turn, means changed behavior of the stock. The change may cause higher sensitivity or jitteriness, and even a failed breakout.

The Fear of Clicking the Button

A common phenomenon among new traders is the fear of clicking the button. The price breaks out and new traders watch it, paralyzed, trying to gain confidence while the stock rises cent by cent. By the time new traders buy, they will usually pay too high a price. It is a familiar phenomenon. I was there, and extricated myself. No doubt you will experience it too.

Summary of the Buy Process

During consolidation, you do not want to see a particular high volume. You want to try and predict the breakout and buy, if possible, a fraction beforehand. After the breakout, you want to see increasing volume. Volume that is dying down indicates loss of interest, and raises the danger of a failed breakout.

When to Sell?

Entering a breakout is a precision technique. It does require no small amount of experience, technical ability, and psychological stamina, but it can be clearly defined. By contrast, identifying the exit point is far more a matter of "artistry" than precise information.

As we learned, you should try to estimate the breakout target in advance. This estimate will be based on past price behavior and market conditions, but during the breakout, you need to examine several variables in real time:

- Has there been a reduction in volume following the breakout, indicating decreased enthusiasm?
- Are buyers increasing their buy orders during the uptrend? When buyers chase a stock, its chances of success are greater. You can watch the pursuit in the form of renewing quantities in the BID.
- As the price trends up, can you see a large seller displaying a serious quantity in the ASK?
- Is that seller renewing quantities each time he or she successfully sells?
- What is the market direction? Does it assist you? Go against you? Or is it going nowhere?
- What is the direction of the sector to which the stock belongs?

All these factors need to be taken together to present you with an overall status of the stock and its chances of lifting off to new heights, or the immediate need to click the button and realize your profit. As you see from the bulleted points above, there is no precise, black and white answer, as you may have wished. A rule of thumb generally says that most breakouts end with taking a **partial**.

- The first profit-realizing point, which is a partial profit, is known simply as a **partial.**

A first partial can be taken at between 14 to 30 cents from the breakout point. High-priced stocks, however, may allow you to take a partial of a half dollar, dollar or even more. As you see, there is no hard and fast rule.

How Much to Buy? To Sell?

Every trader must operate within his or her limitations: the amount of money in the account is one factor, and the other more important limitation is his or her psychological ability to gain or lose money.

There are several more factors that dictate the correct mode of operation, and which have nothing to do with your own limitations. The minimum amount of a breakout purchase must be 400 shares, and the maximum is generally thousands of shares and dependent on liquidity and the amount of money in your account.

- Why the minimum of 400? The main reason that I like to use 400 shares is because I prefer to take a partial of at least three-quarters of the amount bought at breakout. An amount of 400 allows you to execute a partial with a round figure of 300 shares. A smaller amount, such as 300, will not allow you to sell three-quarters which would be 225, and a round figure of 200 is not three-quarters but only two-thirds.
- Another reason to use 400 shares is the dollar profit target: an amount of 400 shares should contribute an average of $100 profit at breakout. If you are day trading, you should not be satisfied with less than this.

SMART MONEY	*At breakout, realize three-quarters of the amount you bought and put that money deep into your pocket. Remember: we never return our profits to the market!*

After closing out 300 shares, you need to continue managing the 100 shares that remain. I tend to realize three-quarters of the amount in the first partial, since I am a firm believer of "putting that money in my pocket" when I am shown to be right. I am also aware of the fact that holding the remaining 100 shares is like a gamble without any apparent advantages, since the real advantage was reaped at the breakout. The rest depends on the trend and fate. Sometimes those remaining shares will allow me to reach a greater profit than the partial, and sometimes they will drop beneath the entry price and cause some minor damage. In any event, the 100 shares left after a partial of 300 are never meant to bring you to a loss. Remember this fundamental important rule: **We never return our profits to the market!**

What Happens When a Breakout Fails?

You've bought at the breakout. The price goes up several cents, and to your sorrow, begins to drop. Why did the breakout fail?

The answer is simple: there are more sellers than buyers. But that is not enough an explanation, so let us look a little deeper at who these sellers are. There are two possibilities: the first is that you have simply made a mistake and gone for the wrong stock at the wrong time. In other words, the stock you chose was weak, or the market or its sector dropped at precisely the breakout moment. In such cases, you should exit as quickly as possible and absorb the loss. Another explanation is that the big players are trying to **shake out** buyers like you. The big players, who know your entry point and know how pressured you will be over a drop in price before making any profit, may take advantage of the expected volume at a strong breakout in order to sell large amounts, which would otherwise be difficult to sell. The result is a drop in price that snowballs and brings the price down to where large market players are buying up again, much more cheaply. Perhaps from that point on they will allow the stock to rise safely.

When I find myself in this situation, I tend to wait until the hysteria has died down, and then happily increase the amount of shares which are now 15 to 20 cents beneath my entry price, before the stock price begins to pull back to the breakout level. This kind of situation generally occurs within several minutes. If the stock does not return to its high within several minutes, get out!

How to Short at Breakdowns

As noted, shorting at breakdowns is essentially identical to buying at breakouts, but in reverse. The goal, of course, is to take advantage of the down-trending momentum of the price. Whereas breakouts are nurtured by greed, which by its nature weakens once the object is attained, breakdowns are fed by the fear that fills the investor who sees a stock crashing before his or her very eyes, and wants to be rid of the holdings as quickly as possible.

Hysteria takes hold very quickly, and therefore breakdowns are a favorite of mine, more so than breakouts. Since breakdowns are speedier, you will need to be faster in your reaction, keeping your finger on the mouse, but you will generally receive good remunerations faster, too.

The second difference between breakouts and breakdowns is the timeframe that breakdowns last: which will be as long as the hysteria continues, and the nature of hysteria is like a house catching on fire. It erupts fast, but dies down even more quickly. The "festival of lows" will generally end within one to two hours of commencement, and then a stock that broke strongly will tend to pull back, or **retrace**, a considerable part of its fall. This is also why I generally will not "sleep on" shorts with the same quantities as I would if I were holding longs for a swing of several days.

Breakdown Short, Estee Lauder Cosmetics, EL

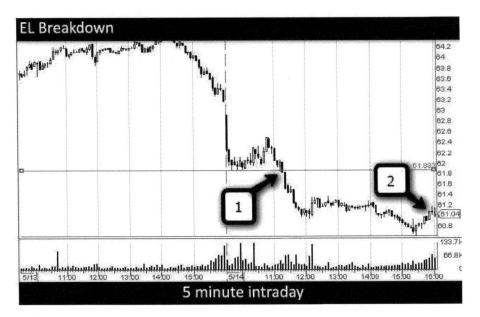

At [1], EL breaks down with the classic inverted cup formation. We see a lot of enthusiasm, large volumes and eventually, the calm. Notice how after the first breakdown the stock continues to move sideways, and by the end of the trading day [2], ends at the price level of the first low. In other words, the hysteria has lessened and the stock has "calmed down."

Winner Reversals

Buying at a breakout is the fastest but also most dangerous method. Buying a reversal (change of direction) is based on patterns of direction change, which we learned about in previous chapters. It is simpler, slower and far less risky. Relative to other methods, it is definitely a method recommended for beginners!

Reversals are based on continuing trend. The classic definition is a change of direction within the trend. This describes a stock's movement from highs to lows and back to a high (or from low to high and back to low).

- A reversal that brings the stock back into the uptrend is called a **roll-up**
- A reversal that brings the stock back into its downtrend is called a **roll over**

When are Reversals Preferable to Breakouts and Breakdowns?

During the opening hours of the trading day, when the trade volume is relatively high, both methods work well. However, the closer it gets to lunch hour, the volume of trade decreases, together with chances of breakouts and breakdowns working. This does not mean we cease trading breakdowns and breakouts in later hours of the day, but as time passes and volume decreases, we will also lessen our risks by trading in smaller quantities.

For this reason, beyond the first ninety minutes of trading we prefer not to enter a stock at a breakout or breakdown, but wait for it to pull back, knowing that almost certainly the correction, or **pull back**, will occur. Stock prices never rise in a straight line. They always pull back, which allows you to buy them more cheaply. Buying at pullbacks reduces the risk of loss and provides a greater range of security. When the stock has ceased pulling back and once again reaches the breakout point, we are already in a position of good profit. The stop point is still a way off, and the chances of a second breakout where the stock will peak are much higher.

Entering a Reversal: Market Rules

For a successful trade, we need a market helping us in its general direction. This means we need to enter a reversal with a trending up stock only when the market, as embodied by the S&P 500, supports continuation of that trend (or the reverse for a trending down stock). Of course, we must ensure other fundamental market conditions as with any trade, such as an appropriate risk-reward opportunity ratio, a reasonable stop point, and changes in volume that match the trend direction. For example, when a trending up stock pulls back, we must check that the volume is decreasing as the stock drops, but when the stock returns to its initial trend, we would prefer to see volume increase. The meaning of increasing volume is that you are not the only ones identifying the opportunity, so you benefit from the assistance of other traders.

The Entry Point

The correct entry point is responsible for 80% of a trade's success. The entry point in reversal is not a precise science, but I will try to define it in a way that allows you to come as close as possible.

We buy a reversal only when the stock has made a real pullback from its peak. The way to "feel" the right entry point is to try and imagine when you might sell the stock if you had bought it at its peak, but it trended against you. Observe the entry point and imagine where you would feel pressured and want out. If the stock has dropped below that point, it means that most of the weak buyers have already sold, and that this is therefore the correct position for clicking the button. You need to do the exact opposite of what pressured buyers who bought at the peak did.

Intraday Reversal for the Fuel Company Occidental, OXY

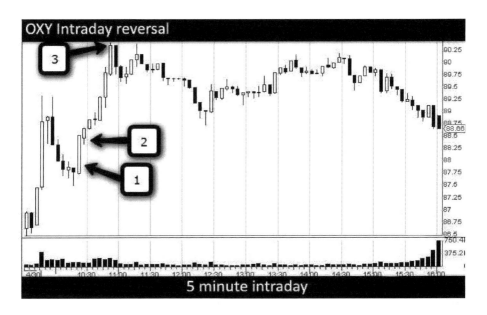

OXY Intraday reversal

5 minute intraday

In this example, you can see the intraday reversal traded in my trading room. OXY opens strongly and rises when trade begins for four five-minute candles, from $86.50 to $89, a rise of 2.9%. A stock rising almost 3% in 20 minutes with a volume of hundreds of thousands of shares has a strong chance of reaching higher peaks. OXY did display strength at the start of the day. Remember that a stock chart rising a half-percent looks similar to the stock chart for a stock rising 2.9%, but they are not identical at all. Most stocks will be traded with sharp highs or lows during the first ten minutes of trading, which says nothing about what will occur later. However, a stock's rising more than 1% in large volumes causes me to understand that something positive and not coincidental is happening. Clearly the stock wants to keep rising, and its chances of preserving the uptrend are very high. OXY pulls back for about half its high, displays a classic reversal at [1], and then easily goes higher than its first peak.

Since I tend not to buy stock during the first ten minutes of trading, and definitely do not "pursue" a stock rising quickly, I waited patiently for the painful pullback. Why "painful"? Read what I wrote at the start of this section: imagine a situation where you made the mistake of so many novices and bought during the stock's first jump, or even at its peak at $89, then saw the stock drop halfway back to its starting point. How would you feel to watch a pullback of $1.50? Would you stay steadfast, or sell? Would you feel pressured? Try to imagine where you would feel pressured: that is the buy point! If you also need visual assistance, you can use the Fibonacci lines for entry at pullback with a range of 30% to 60% from the peak.

Once the pullback is established, the stock shows a classic reversal in five-minute candles, and indicates its willingness to bounce. In the trading room, I announced an entry at $88 [1]. We entered, sold half the quantity at [2], and another quarter at the peak [3], totaling some $1.40 above the entry point. We left the last quarter until the end of the day, and one-eighth was transferred to the next day when, to our great joy, the stock continued trending up.

What would have happened if I had entered at the wrong point and suffered a loss of 20 to 30 cents? The answer is simple: I would not have exited. I would wait for the reversal in five-minute candles even at the lower price, and pray for the stock to rise. Why? Because the stock rose several percent in just a few minutes. Without doubt, something positive is happening there: after all, it's a strong stock. The fact that I bought at $88 [1] says nothing. I could have been wrong. The stock might have dropped several tens of cents and only then begun to trend up. No one can promise that my entry point is the correct one, even if I were buying according to the best of rules. But the formation of the five-minute candles led me to believe that chances were good for this being the best entry point. You need to keep in mind that the stock is strong, and therefore in most cases, it will end up, even if it temporarily drops below the buy point.

In some cases, however, the price will not recover and I will lose money. When that happens, it is definitely not pleasant, but it is part of the statistics which overall work in our favor. It pays to absorb a few losses if more frequently we generate handsome profits. It is better to occasionally suffer and frequently profit. Remember that intraday changes of direction, even if based on clear reversals in five-minute candles as you see in the stock chart, are significant but do not necessarily indicate the correct entry point. It is enough for one large seller to want to drop a large quantity at the click of one button to change the chart's ideal status. My suggestion is simple: believe in the stock, even if it continues to drop after you bought it. Remember that when that happens, it has still done "nothing wrong." That's what stocks do. The stock does not care whether you have erred in estimating the entry point and bought a little too high. You must keep in mind that strong stocks reverse back to highs in most cases. Period.

SMART MONEY	*Have you entered a stock that is not working in your favor? Before fleeing at a loss, check the chart carefully and ask yourselves honestly: "Has it really done anything wrong?"*

When can we nonetheless start "getting angry" at a stock? When does the concept of "it's done nothing wrong" no longer apply? Look at the chart and imagine a situation where you bought at [1], but the stock did not return to its uptrend, and instead continued trending down. Where is the point at which you'd start to get angry, or begin to doubt whether it would reverse and trend up? My answer would be at around $87.25. At this point, I would begin to realize that "something wrong" has taken the place of the strong start, and I would exit. You can definitely be assisted by the Fibonacci line of 61.8% to determine when the price pulls back a bit too much. I would not exit precisely at the 61.8% level, but I definitely would not stay with a stock that dropped much below that.

Why did I exit so quickly at [2]? In retrospect, it is clear that I should have waited a little longer, but in real time I had no idea that the stock would rise by almost $1.5 from its reversal point. Secondly, I needed to put that trade behind me as quickly as possible. Remember, I want to see profits. In this case I realized **"half my size"** in order to get to the point where the other half was a **"free trade."** In other words, following the initial realization, I am at the point where I cannot lose on the trade even if the price drops below the entry point. Selling half the quantity, even at a smaller profit, helps me let the second half reach a peak that I am not sure I would have psychologically been able to allow had I been holding the "full size" and fearing I might lose out on the entire process. Realizing profit does not have to be logical from a purely mathematical viewpoint. When it is psychologically logical, it becomes mathematically logical, i.e. within the range of profit.

Should we buy only after a clearly displayed reversal in five-minute candles? The example above is clear and simple, but many other stocks do not offer a chance to wait for a classical technical direction change such as the lower doji. In such cases, you need to develop sensitivity and buy the stock during its downtrend at the point where you estimate a suitable change of direction. Clicking the buy button will occur before the classical reversal shows on the chart in five-minute candles. To improve your estimated entry points, carefully examine the quantity of buyers and sellers noted in the BID and ASK areas of your trading platform. When it seems to you that the stock is at its optimal point and the number of buyers is greater than sellers, click the button. In cases such as these, which are naturally less clear than the classic reversals in five-minute candles, I will usually buy using half-size and wait for clearer technical indicators in order to buy the second half. I will also buy that second half even if the price is lower than my initial entry point, or if the price rises immediately, than at a higher entry point that is not significantly higher than my initial entry. In other words, I am willing to admit my error and understand that I bought the half-size at a slightly too high price, and add the remainder at a lower price. However, if it becomes clear that I have bought at the right entry point and the stock price rises, I am not willing to chase the price and buy at significantly more than I originally paid, and will therefore make do with just half the size. Being in control of this procedure requires a good degree of skill, experience, and "artistry," and is not suited to new traders. As long as you are still new to trading, seek classical reversals, and if there are none, forego the trade and wait for the next interesting stock.

Summary: Reversals

Unlike buying at a breakout or shorting at breakdown, buying at a reversal is a more correct and calmer entry point, less risky, and with a better risk/reward ratio. Its disadvantage is its psychological strain. It is far more natural and simple to buy at the breakout of a new high. At the breakout, we buy a stock reaching new highs, while in reversals we buy stocks trending down during their overall uptrend. Buying a stock trending down will always be more difficult psychologically than buying a stock trending up. We need to overcome our natural emotions and hesitation, understand that strong stocks almost always pull back, and that their chances of returning to highs are far greater than their chances of continuing to drop. Be courageous, and click the button. Don't worry: with a little practice and experience, it will all become clear.

Trading Gaps

First we need to define the term "gap." It is the difference between one day's closing price and the next day's opening price. When a gap forms, the first trade of the day will be higher or lower than the closing price of the previous day.

- A **GAP UP** forms when the stock opens at a higher price than the previous day's close
- A **GAP DOWN** refers to an opening price which is lower than the previous day's close

In fact, a gap almost always forms, and the first trade of the day in any stock will be different even by one cent than the previous day's close. Small gaps are insignificant, so we will describe how the more fundamental gaps come into being. These are usually in the range of a half-percent or more.

Why would a price open differently than the previous day's close? Usually this is the result of news or rumors circulating between closing time and the next day's opening of trade, such as when a company publicizes its financial reports during the after hours. In other cases, it may be no more than a pullback from a day of sharp lows or highs, or due to market news that is not related to the stock itself but to the mood of investors.

Gaps Almost Always Close

Gaps have expectable behaviors. This means you need to learn how to handle them, whether you are holding stock you bought the day before and which opens the new day with a gap, or whether you are planning an entry into a new stock opening with a gap.

SMART MONEY	*Most gaps fill: 80% of gaps fill on the day of trading in which they come into being, and 90% close within ten days.*

The most important information you need to know concerning gaps is that 80% of them fill on the same day they developed, and 90% are filled within ten trading days. For example, if a stock opens with a gap up, it is likely that during the same day of trading it will drop to the previous day's close, thereby closing or filling the gap. The opposite is true for a stock opening with a gap down. It is reasonable to assume that during the current day, its price would climb to the previous day's close and the gap would close.

Gap Up for Baxter at Opening of Day's Trading, BAX

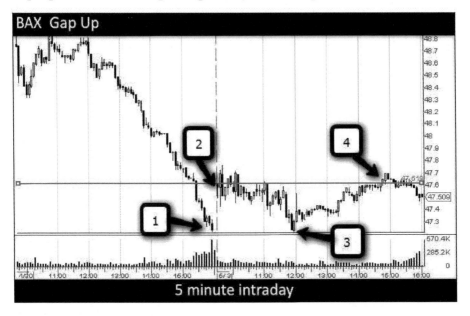

5 minute intraday

Baxter ends the day's trading at $47.24 [1] and opens the next day at $47.61 [2], showing a gap up of some 0.8%. Here we see the common phenomenon resulting from negative information which led to the previous day's drop, followed by opening the next day with a gap up that somewhat pulls back from the previous day's sharp low. Note that in this particular case, the gap created on the second day of trade is "trapped" in the range of the first day of trading. The fact that the gap is trapped further increases the chances of the gap closing. As you see, during trading, the price drops and closes the gap [3] and immediately thereafter changes direction and rises back to the opening price level [4].

The gap-closing phenomenon, especially when relating to a gap trapped in the previous day's trading range, is well-known and carries an 80% intraday chance of success.

Important note: the above is valid for gaps less than 3%. Higher gaps will not close to the same degree, and in many cases will continue moving in the direction of the gap rather than towards closing the gap.

Why Do Gaps Form?

Generally, a gap already forms at the pre-market stage, because buyers are willing to pay a higher price for the stock than the previous day's closing price, or sell for a lower price than the previous day's closing price. The pre-market open price is set by the market makers in accordance with supply and demand, as conveyed to them several hours prior to trading. When demand is greater than supply, the stock will gap up; when supply is greater than demand, the stock will gap down. As we will learn, stocks are also traded during pre-market hours!

Why Do Gaps Close?

The explanation begins with the previous day's trading, where an institutional buyer received instructions to sell a large quantity of shares (in the current example, BAX).

Firstly, we need to keep in mind that institutional traders buy or sell large quantities of shares and therefore scatter their sell orders across several days so as not to adversely affect the stock price. Their goal, of course, is to sell at the highest price possible, since if they do so (relative to the stock's behavior on that particular day: see the section on VWAP), they receive handsome bonuses.

Let us assume that the institutional trader who sold BAX on the first day of trade has not yet completed his or her task, and still holds several hundred thousand shares which must be sold the following day. At the start of the next day, the trader tries to complete the task and sell more shares.

Keep in mind that the trader was willing to dispose of them for yesterday's close of $47.27 [1]. To his or her great joy, the second day of trading opens and the trader finds that buyers are willing to pay $47.61 [2], some 0.8% more than the previous day's closing price! For the institutional trader, this is a gift sent from heaven! The trader knows that if he or she sells for more than the previous day's close, a fine bonus awaits. What does the trader do? Rub his or her hands with glee and sells! How far down will the trader sell? For as long as the price remains **above yesterday's closing price:** in other words, for as long as he or she can earn a bonus! Institutional traders do not rush. They know they have the ability to flood the market, but they do not want to see sellers changing market direction too quickly. So they sell a little, wait until buyers return,

324

PART 10 - Winning Trades

sell a little more, and so on. We need to keep in mind that the institutional sellers are also competing with other institutional sellers. Within a short time, buyers run out of steam and only sellers remain. This is when the stock begins to move "south," or to drop. For as long as the price remains above yesterday's close, institutional sellers keep selling, which earns them a bonus. The instant the price drops to yesterday's close, there is no bonus anymore. The institutional seller sells until the price drops to $47.27 [1], and at this point stops. This is when the stock frees up from the institutional traders and begins to rise again [4]. The outcome: the gap has filled.

Most gaps close by the first hour of trading. It all depends on the quantity of institutional traders taking advantage of the chance to profit from the gap, and the competition among themselves as to who will sell first.

We must also remember that at every price level are non-institutional buyers and sellers. When a stock opens with a gap up at the start of trading, it does not arouse automatic buy orders. This is because buyers generally do not lodge automatic buy instructions when a stock is rising and goes above a certain price, but sellers do set automatic orders. Let us say, for example, that you bought BAX at the bargain price of $47.27 [1] and set an automatic sell order in order to realize profit, should the stock reach $47.61 [2]. Admittedly, you expected to earn your profit by hard work, but happily you woke up in the morning to a wonderful new reality: with the opening of trade, you discover the price is $47.61 [2]. What happens to the automatic order you set before the day's trade began? It is immediately hit! In other words, as long as we are above yesterday's closing price, we are in the territory of private sellers joining the institutional traders until the gap closes.

Clearly, all the conditions relating to a gap up apply in reverse to a gap down, where the stock price opens lower than the previous day's close. In the case of a gap down, the price will be pushed up by the activities of institutional buyers. In this case, the number of buyers who began purchasing the previous day will discover that the stock price is lower than it was at yesterday's close. For them, this spells a bonus! They will buy until the gap closes, or at least 80% of the time.

Closing the Gap, BBBY

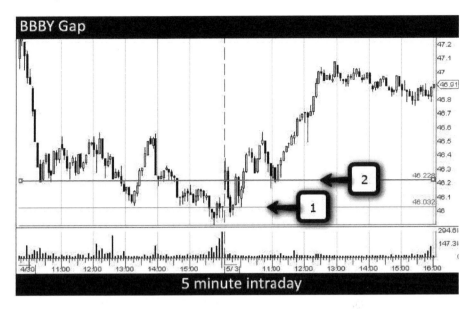

5 minute intraday

In this chart, we see the gap up for BBBY which closed its prior day of trading at $46.03 [1] and opens the second day at $46.22 [2]. Notice how it dropped and closed the gap within just fifteen minutes. The point where the gap closed [1] is the point where institutional traders ceased selling and the stock receives the "green light" to keep trending up. Remember that 80% of the gaps close on the day of trading itself, and over 90% close within ten days!

Never Chase Gaps

Let us say you decided prior to trade that you wish to buy BBBY if it goes higher than $46.3. You check at the start of trading and find it opens with a gap up, and in just a few more cents it is likely to reach your trigger price. Looking wonderful! Should you buy?

At this point, an alarm should sound in your mind. Remember the saying: **"We never chase gaps!"** Even if your heart says "buy," the hours of study we've spent together should be enough to loudly ring "stop!" Why? Because the chances are high that the gap will close.

| SMART MONEY | *Do you want to buy a stock? Not if it opened with a gap up. Remember: we never chase gaps* |

326 PART 10 - Winning Trades

Gaps in Dual Stocks

Breaking the norm are stocks traded on more than one stock exchange, such as Toyota, which is traded on both Wall Street and the Tokyo Stock Exchange. These are known as **dual-exchange traded stocks.**

Since the trading times on Wall Street and Tokyo do not overlap, Toyota will almost always begin the day with large gaps in accordance with the closing price of the other stock exchange.

SMART MONEY	*Gap formations in dual-exchange traded stocks are not valid! In general, we avoid trading in most of the dual-exchange traded stocks.*

Note how easy it is to determine that Toyota (TM) is a dual-exchange traded stock:

In the daily chart above for Toyota, we can clearly see that every trading day opens with a gap. This is a distinct formation indicating a dual-exchange traded stock.

Market Index Gaps

Since the S&P 500 market index represents the 500 leading stocks, it will display the cumulative gaps for all the stocks it encompasses. When the market index opens with a gap up of a half-percent, what does this imply for all the stocks comprised on the index? The cumulative meaning must also be a gap up of a half-percent. Of course, some stocks may open with a greater gap up, some with less, and perhaps even some with a reverse gap, but the average must be at least equal to a half-percent.

Let us presume that the 500 top Wall Street stocks open with a gap. What should happen next? Eighty percent of the money in those stocks belongs to institutional rather than private players. Since the institutional players, as we have learned, are interested in selling as long as the gap is open, in most cases the market index gap will close exactly the same way as the gap for a single stock comprising the index will close.

Gap Close for the ETF – SPY

Notice the openings for the last six trading days on this chart. They all open with gaps, and they all close. Days 1, 3, 5 and 6 already close perfectly on the same day, and days 2 and 4 close partially the same day and complete the close by the next day. Based on these gap closings, can we define a winning trade strategy? Of course we can!

Strategy Label: Closing the Gap for the ETF – SPY
- Entry point: at opening of trade, long or short in the direction of the gap closing
- Entry conditions: the SPY must open with a gap of at least 20 cents,

on condition that the gap is no greater than 85% of the range of movement of the previous day's trading (the difference between the highest high and lowest low of the day's trading), nor less than 15% of the previous day's trading. Reason: a gap that is too large indicates extreme events which may lead the market into sharp movement, increasing risk. A too-small gap is not interesting.

- Exit point:
  1. Sell at the end of the day's trading if the gap has not closed; OR
  2. Sell when the gap closes.
- Outcomes: during the three years between October 2007 and October 2010, 471 gaps upheld these criteria.

Assuming you had invested $16,000 in each trade, these are the results:
  - o Maximum profit per trade: $373.9
  - o Maximum loss per trade: $778
  - o Average profit: $55.86
  - o Average loss: $145.01
  - o Success rate: 81.95%
  - o Weighted success rate: 63.62%
  - o Overall profit for three years: $9,236
  - o Average annual yield: 17.58%

Summary

The method works. The method's Achilles heel is the 18.05% of cases where the gap does not close: days when the market opens with a gap and keeps moving, or as the phenomenon is known, **Gap & Go**. On rare days when the market "escapes" us, the average loss is far greater than the average profit, thus the weighted success rate is lower.

Trading the QQQ

In the chapter detailing indicators, we learned the importance of usi[...]
Bollinger Bands. We also learned that when a stock price reaches the
upper band, it is in a state of **overbought** territory and must return down.
By contrast, when it drops to the lower band, it is in **oversold** territory
and there is a strong chance of it retracing upwards.

We also learned that you need to define the band data in your
trading platform to calculate 10 periods and a standard deviation of 1.5,
which means that the Bollinger Bands will be calculated according to
stock's volatility over the previous ten trading days. The mathematical
significance of a 1.5 standard deviation is that 90% of the stock's
movement will be caught between the two bands.

Based on the above, we should be able to assume that a stock or ETF
which moves beyond the boundaries of the bands will return to these
boundaries. Here is an amazing trade method which takes advantage of
this premise:

Daily Chart for NASDAQ 100 ETF – QQQ

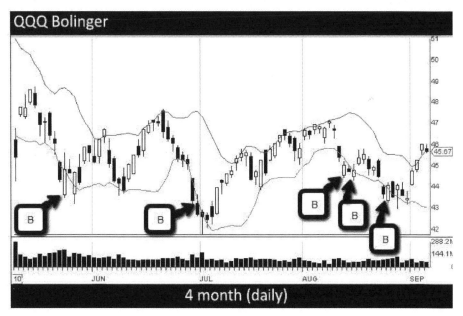

For four months, I wrapped the daily chart for QQQ (known as the Qs)

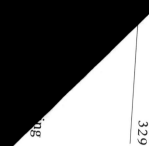

...ccording to the definitions above. Notice how the ...act as the Qs' volatility increases or decreases. You ...; "wrap up" most of the Qs' movement. Notice also ...break the bands, they return.

...dge funds use similar strategies. The advantage of the
...for hedge funds is in the large volume, which allows
reliable entries and exits with large sums of money.

MONEY

329

Strategy Label: Daily Pullback for QQQ

- When to buy? When the Qs drop beneath the lower band
- Indicator: Bollinger, 10 periods, SD 1.5 (standard deviation)
- Buy point: Buy the day after the closing price was lower than the bottom Bollinger Band. Buy the ETF at the opening price of the next trade day ONLY if the opening price is still lower than the bottom band.

Why do we NOT want to buy at the previous day's closing price? Buying on the day after the first drop is meant to ensure that hysteria has passed and the dust has settled. During periods of hysteria, the opening price of the second day is likely to be far beneath that of the first day's close. On the Qs chart, five buy points which uphold these criteria are marked "B."

- Sell point: Sell immediately when one of the following conditions appears:
  1. At the end of any day of trading when the NASDAQ QQQ closes higher than your buy price (even if that is the same day on which you bought); OR
  2. At the end of 20 trading days (one month).
- NOTE: as long as a trade is open, do not enter another trade. Close the open one first. The purpose is to prevent a large loss during periods of extreme hysteria when the market may not "return" as anticipated.
- Exercise: in the Qs chart, analyze the buy and sell points according to the rules we learned. You will find that we have a 100% success rate. In four of the five instances, the sell point occurred at the end of the same day that the buy was made, and in one case, we were forced to wait for five trading days.
- Outcomes: in the three years during which I checked this strategy, January 2005 to end 2007, I documented 45 events in which the NASDAQ QQQ provided buy opportunities according to the strategy

above. Here are the details:
o Successful trades: 41
o Failures: 3
o Success rate: 93%
o Average profit per trade: 0.4%
o Average hold time per trade: 5.07 days
o Overall period profit: 17.6%
- Parameter change: the Achilles heel of any trade strategy is its sensitivity to minor changes. A slight change of parameters can bring about considerable change to outcomes, but may impinge on the method's reliability. If, for example, you change this method's parameters to 20 periods and SD 1, you will find that the success rate stands at over 90%!
  Is this method also valid for single stocks? Yes. Instructions follow:
- Buy point: Buy the stock that belongs to the NASDAQ 100 the morning after it closed beneath the lower Bollinger Band, on condition that its new opening price is still lower than that band.
- Sell point: Sell immediately when one of these conditions is met:
  1. At the end of any day of trade when the stock closes higher than your entry point (even if that is on the same day you made the purchase); OR
  2. When 20 trade days (one month) have passed.
- Outcomes: during the four-year period I checked, from January 1999 to January 2003, a total of 3,870 trade opportunities upheld these criteria. Details for that period as follows:
o Successful trades: 3,684
o Failures: 186
o Success rate: 95.19%
o Average profit per trade: 2.77%
o Average holding time per trade: 3.06 days
o Sequence of successes: 121
o Sequence of losses: 3

Summary
Not bad at all!
Results can be improved if one is willing to increase the risk and operate as hedge funds do, using margin to double and even quadruple their outcomes. No large investment is needed to execute 44 NASDAQ QQQ trades over a period of three years. Any sum of money is suitable,

and the risk is relatively small.

On one occasion, a man who recognized me in a public place approached and said, "You don't know me, but I owe you a lot of money!" I was amazed to hear his story. It seems that based on an article I'd penned describing this strategy, he'd tested the method, reached favorable outcomes, established a hedge fund, and recruited tens of millions of dollars from investors. Although the fund now employs diverse strategies, this is still its leading, most successful one.

Scalping

Traders can be divided into three types: **swing traders, day traders, and scalpers.** The three methods can be integrated, which is my preferred mode of operation.

Scalping refers to very short-term trades. Swing traders hold stocks over to the next day, and day traders generally try to get as much from the stock as possible within one day of trading. Both swing and day traders generally base their systems on technical analysis with a touch of fundamental analysis.

Scalpers are based one hundred percent on technical analysis. Their goal is the very short term. Changes of just a few cents for several seconds up to some minutes are sufficient. This means that in order to earn a livelihood from the market, scalpers need to trade in relatively larger amounts than day or swing traders. Scalpers with little backing (which is, sadly, the case for most of them) make up for what their pocket lacks by trading in financial products which can be leveraged more than the typical leverage of the world of stock trading. These may include **futures**, leveraged twenty times more, **options**, and of course **FOREX** (foreign exchange) which can reach leveraging of up to 500 times more, expressed as **500:1 margin.** The absurdity is that trading in these strongly-leveraged products is harder and incredibly more risky than stock trading. Nonetheless, the dream of "striking it rich quick" draws people with no funds and no experience into the hardest areas of trading, where they will often begin, and almost invariably end, their trading careers.

Here is a classic career-end scenario typical of most of the leveraged-futures traders I know:

Note What Happens to the SPY Within Several Minutes:

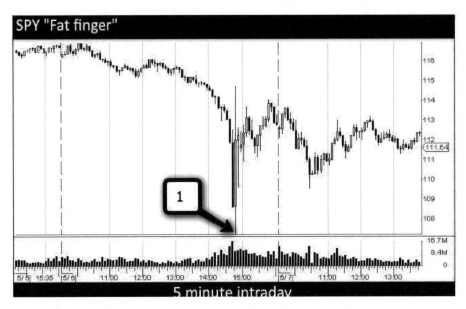

On May 6, 2010, for reasons that remain unclear, a large fund accidently sold a huge amount of S&P 500 futures in one sad click of the button. In recent years, in light of increasing usage of algo trading platforms, such events occur with increasing frequency, so much so that the name "fat finger"was invented for the phenomenon. In this case, the fat finger sold S&P 500 futures and crashed the futures index (ES) by 10% within seconds.

It was a shocking event, known as the "Flash Crash," which kept traders worldwide glued to their screens, thinking for a moment that the end of the world had come! And indeed, the end of the world had come for some of the larger futures traders who use 20:1 margin. In actuality, by what would become understood as the halfway point of the drop, when the ES fell "only" by 5%, their entire accounts were wiped out, since 5% at 20:1 = 100% ! When their accounts reached a zero balance, their brokers automatically closed the accounts, and when the market pulled back just several minutes after the fat finger had made its move, those traders were left in complete shock, with accounts showing a perfectly round zero. That was the last day many futures traders I know ever traded, and I'm sure the same is true for thousands more whom I do not know.

| **SMART MONEY** | *Leveraged scalps are guarantors of failure: if not today, or even next year, their day of judgment is bound to come.* |

As I hope you now understand, trading with margin is extremely dangerous, since scalpers tend to "stretch" their accounts using leverage to the very furthest boundaries possible. They can, in fact, profit hugely and for long periods, but it is enough that just once every few years they encounter one single fat-finger incident or other extreme phenomenon (such as the 9/11 tragedy) to wipe them out of trading forever.

In my experience, scalping can cause you far more harm than benefit during your first years of trading. I wondered if I should even devote any space to scalping activities, fearing that you may be influenced by reading about them and be drawn to trying the method out. I chose a compromise: to describe the activity while emphasizing the extreme dangers. A successful trader needs a high level of self-discipline. If you have that, read, internalize, and please stay clear of scalping until you are very far advanced in your development as a trader.

When are Scalps Executed?

There are several ways to execute scalping. One occurs when we estimate that a sharp price movement is about to occur. The goal will be to enter and exit quickly. Why exit quickly, rather than stay a little longer and improve the results? The answer depends chiefly on the timeframes, of which there are several that are suited to very short-term scalping:

- **When trading opens**

During the first ten minutes of trading, most of the volatile stock prices are seen on our screens as "going crazy," and in most cases, this is because of private investors who have given their brokers pre-market buy or sell orders. These are executed at market price during the first half hour of trading, and can agitate stock prices strongly. If you follow a particular stock, such as Apple (AAPL), you will learn how to gauge its start-of-day behavior and find, over time, that with a surprising degree of reliably you can predict its behavior. Apple can go up as much as one dollar during the first five minutes, retrace the entire price rise in the next two minutes, and continue to any direction afterwards, regardless of those first minutes. Can you profit from a fluctuation of one dollar in either direction? Of course, on the condition that you have a lot of experience, the nerves of a fighter pilot, and a lot of money to waste until you "perfect" the method.

- **Lunch hours**

    Often enough, I encounter a winning formation during New York's lunch break (11:30 to 13:30). During this timeframe I do not expect considerable market movement and therefore I know that if I buy a stock at the breakout, I should not expect continued strong movement in the breakout direction, but rather a very short breakout often followed by quick failure. Lack of trust in the breakout continuity does not mean I am unwilling to take a profit of 10 to 20 cents and quickly flee before the stock breaking out changes its mind! Lunch break is also the time when the "one cent traders" are most active: more on that method later.

- **Close of trading**

    For scalping, this is the best time possible. During the last hour of trade, and especially during its second half, volumes grow due to end-of-day institutional fund activity. The problem with this last hour is the lack of continuity. Continued movement cannot be expected, so developing profit can't either, since the day's trading simply ends. During this timeframe, reverse formations are usually most successful: for example, a stock that rose strongly may pull back for part of the high since many investors may wish to realize part of the profits, lessen risks, and "go to sleep" with fewer open trades. The reverse occurs with a stock price dropping strongly, when short sellers that pushed it down all day begin to realize profits (i.e. they are now buyers) and the stock pulls back part of its drop.

Example of Scalping with DOW

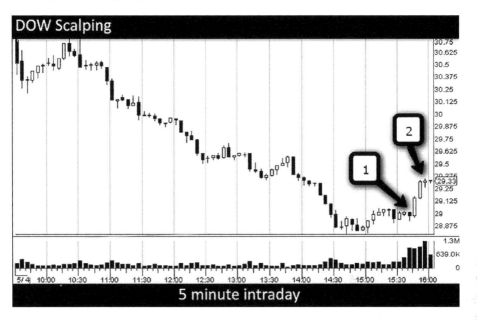

This is a classic scalp, executed on May 4, 2010 in our trading room, during the last half hour of trading. DOW, a leading chemicals firm, crashed with the entire market as a result of rumors publicized on that date that Spain would be the next European country reaching insolvency. Whereas the market indicator dropped by 2.5%, DOW dropped some 8%. We estimated that shorters, who enjoyed a field day with the stock for almost all the trading hours (note the perfect downtrend), would close some of the shorts towards the end of the day: i.e. they would buy. At [1], for the first time that day, the stock changed trend in five-minute candles. We anticipated this change several seconds beforehand, and entered a long at $28.95. At [1] the trend change showed as strengthening, and at [2] we realized a profit of 40 cents. Also note the high trading volume just before the stock changed its trend. A large amount of shares changed hands during those minutes, which considerably reinforced our assessment that a pullback can be expected.

The Scalping Technique

The first condition: you need to keep your finger on the mouse, and your eyes glued to the screen. You need to give your full attention to the stock.

You must buy and sell with precise LIMIT orders. You must absolutely NOT chase the stock, because with scalping, profit or loss is measured in just a few cents. In many cases, I place an exit order in advance. For example: if I buy 3000 shares at $20 and anticipate an increase of 30 cents, I will set a sell limit order in my trading platform of:

o   1000 shares at 20.15
o   1000 shares at 20.25
o   And wait with my finger on the mouse for the first sign of weakness in order to sell the remaining 1000 shares

SMART MONEY	*Scalps are meant to be short term, and are therefore not executed in small quantities. Trading in small quantities of shares causes the "small-money syndrome" and leads to failure.*

Scalping is not executed in small quantities of shares. New traders scalping in small quantities, such as 300 shares, find themselves caught in the trap of negligible profits, or as the phenomenon is known, the "small-money syndrome." Selling 100 shares for a profit of 15 cents seems like too small a yield, so they will try to drag the trade out for a few more cents, and usually discover that they have waited too long before selling. The stock pulls back down by 10 cents, so it does not pay to sell because the profit is even less now, and they wait a bit longer. Then the stock returns to their entry point, or even below it, and the scalping ends in a loss!

With large quantities of shares, by contrast, a decent profit is earned with each partial trade locked in, without the need to cope with the small-money syndrome.

Note: the terms "small money" and "decent profits" are relative and will differ from one trader to another, depending on each one's monetary backup and psychological makeup relative to profits or losses.

The One Cent Scalp

Cent scalping is a trading method geared at making profits of one or just a few cents, from light intraday fluctuations in stocks with "locked prices." Stocks with **locked prices** are stocks in which hundreds if not thousands of traders are operating, executing bids and asks at one cent above or below the stock's traded price. This is not a classic trading method based on noticeable intraday fluctuations resulting from breakouts, breakdowns, or direction changes. In contrast with everything we have learned so far, scalping for one cent is based chiefly on lack of volatility. I wish to emphasize that this is not my area of specialization, or even a method I like too much, but in certain market conditions detailed in the next section, it can be applied successfully.

One Cent Scalping and the Commission Barrier

The first condition for participating in this method is to have a large trading account. If you want to profit from the movement of one cent and still overcome the barrier of commission, you need to operate with no less than 10,000 shares. A profit of one cent on 10,000 shares is worth $100, from which commission must still be deducted. The commissions with this method are the key to success or failure.

Here is an example: let us say that you profited one cent on 10,000 shares, producing $100. Let's assume that you pay a commission of one cent per share, and you bought 10,000 shares. That totals $100 profit, cancelled out by the commission, and when you sell, that costs another $100. Altogether, a loss of $100. Even if you paid commission of one-tenth of a cent, totaling $20 for both buy and sell executions, you have still left 20% of your profit with the broker.

This may sound reasonable to you, but you must also take into account the sad fact that when you lose (at least 30% of your executions will end up as losses), the loss plus the commission will total $120. The weighted average is definitely to your detriment.

The solution: unlike the method of charging one cent per share, which will only be worthwhile if you operate in quantities of up to 2000 shares per click, when you trade in large fixed amounts, you need to ask your broker to define a different commission system based on the **Per Trade Commission Plan** rather than the **Per Share Commission Plan**. If you trade in large amounts, it is probable that you will be able to close on a price of $3 to $6 per click of the button, unlimited in quantity.

In actuality, large-scale traders usually receive commissions rather than pay them. How? When you set your bid and ask orders and wait for their execution, you are adding liquidity to the market! When you do that, as we have already learned, you receive a commission of $2 per 1000 shares from the ECN. With a simple calculation, you can understand that the relatively small quantity of 10,000 shares will bring you an ECN return of 0.2 cents per share, which is $20, while you paid only $6. What would happen with a quantity of 100,000 shares? The ECN return is worth $200, while the commission you pay is still $6. Can you see where this is going? I am familiar with traders who make their living from buying and selling a share at exactly the same price, for profits of hundreds of dollars from the ECN return alone. If they're lucky, they also manage to earn another cent per share.

Sound easy?

No, it isn't easy at all!

One Cent Scalping: the Method

- **First find a low-priced stock**

This should ideally be in the $5 to $10 range, with low volatility and a volume of tens of millions of shares per day. The candidates change during different periods of market activity, volatility, and price. Remember that volatility is this method's worst enemy. Just imagine how much you could lose if the stock moved ten cents against you! This is also why you MUST operate according to the following rules:

1. The stock must be moving sideways with no trend, or in industry terms, the stock must have a **locked price**
2. The stock must show no volatility and movement of up to 5-10 cents per day
3. The market is moving sideways with no trend (generally occurs during lunch hours)
4. The stock is priced up to $10. You can buy cheap stocks in large quantities even if your name is not Warren Buffet
5. The stock shows large trading volume of tens of millions per day

The simplest way to choose a stock is to fish it out of the list that always contains the "top ten" high volume stocks traded on NASDAQ or NYSE. Notice that I do not relate to stocks that made it into the list by chance, but those which are on that listing constantly. On some days, you might choose Bank of America (BAC) or Intel (INTC), Microsoft (MSFT) or others. Citigroup (C) used to be the scalpers' favorite as long as its price hovered around the $4 mark in volumes of hundreds of millions of shares per day, before the reverse split was executed, as already described.

When you bring these stocks up on your screen, you will see intraday volumes of tens if not hundreds of millions of shares, and enormous numbers of bidders and askers. Many of them are playing the one cent game.

Who in fact shifts the stock if no one wants it to move more than one cent? Of course this would not be the scalpers working at the single cent level, because they are basically locking the price and preventing movement. The real change comes from the public and from funds bidding and asking with long-term investment in mind, and they are not interested in whether the stock has gone up or down one cent.

Let's assume you have chosen your stock and it's time to trade. The operation itself is fairly simple but requires a good deal of experience. First, even if the price is moving sideways, examine the overall market trend and the stock's trend. If the trend is up, you will want to execute a long rather than a short, and vice versa. Now you need to enter your buy limit order in the BID, and wait patiently until sellers hit your bid. The moment you have bought the desired quantity, you enter a sell limit order on the ASK side, with a profit target of 1 to 3 cents, and wait for buyers to hit your ask in the reverse direction.

Notice that there is no need to use the short order, since for most of the trading platforms the regular SELL will operate exactly like a short. Now that you have sold the quantity you bought at a profit, and added to that sale a double quantity, you are in a short and therefore need to position a double quantity on the BID side with a targeted profit of 1 to 3 cents, repeating the cycle. Once the market becomes more volatile, and based on the premise that you are on the right side of market direction, you need to cancel the exit order and try to profit from a few more cents beyond the original profit target.

I wish to stress, yet again, that this method *sounds* simple. In reality, it requires a great deal of patience, self-discipline, and deep familiarity with the market. You need to follow the stock chart in one-minute candles. You also need to watch the market chart which will indicate if you need to flee the trade with an unexpected loss, or cancel an exit order and let the market take you to unanticipated profits of a few additional cents. For the same reasons, you need to be following the stock's sector chart. You should be avoiding any trade when the stock is at a breakout or a breakdown point which may shift the stock into dangerous territory.

Example of One Cent Scalping with Citigroup, C

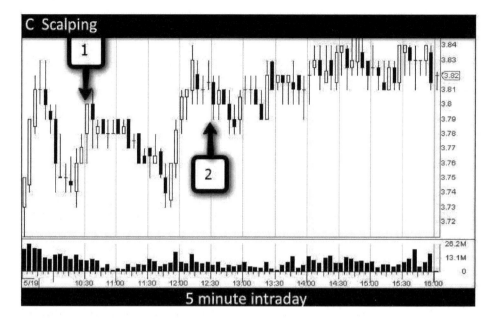

Citigroup (C) is trading with high volatility up until the end of the opening hour [1], making it an inappropriate time for cent scalping. Citi slows at 12:30 during the lunch hour [2], and from that point up to the end of the day, it fits the scalping criteria. Notice that in addition to the high volume during the opening hour of trade, which does not include scalpers, the volume from point [2] up to the end of the day shows an average of ten million shares in five-minute candles. Notice how the stock price is locked in the range of just 4 to 6 cents fluctuation.

A good reason for scalpers to work Citi hard prior to its reverse split was the fact that its price was so low! To buy 10,000 shares at $4 required them to provide a relatively small capital of just $10,000 which, leveraged at 4:1, allowed them buying power of $40,000. Some time ago, I watched a trader whose entire trading involved scalps of one cent on Citigroup shares. For several hours I watched how an account of $100,000 and a quantity of 100,000 shares per trade brought him to a profit of $32,000 by the end of the trading day. The next day he did return some $18,000 to the market when Citi moved a few cents against him and did not pull back, but for the most part, he held that positive balance over time.

But the story is not all rose-colored. He was forced to change brokers once every few months, because sooner or later the new broker would realize that this person is involved in what is known as **toxic trading.**

More on that later.

Types of Orders

Generally we do not route orders direct to market makers, but for quantities of tens of thousands of shares, you will find that it is the market makers who will provide the fastest execution. Market makers are pleased with large quantities, so you should consider executing your orders through businesses such as NITE (Knight Capital Group) and SBSH (Salomon Smith Barney). For example, with a quantity of 100,000 shares, it is preferable to place two separate orders of 50,000 with each of these two market makers, and during trading, observe which of them fills the order faster. The advantage of this method of using market makers is execution speed; the disadvantage is that you will not receive the ECN's refund commission.

How can market makers fill orders faster than the ECN? Because they themselves are trading within these small spreads. The role of market makers, as we have learned, is to provide the market with liquidity, which they do not do in return for a guaranteed place in heaven. They provide liquidity since they want to profit, just like you do, from the gaps between the bid and ask prices. What you are doing with thousands or tens of thousands of shares, they do with millions. Relative to stocks traded at locked prices, they do this best and easily because they have one advantage over you: they are allowed to trade in fractions of a cent.

The phenomenon of trading in fractions of a cent will anger you deeply. For example, you may be waiting to get rid of a stock with a one cent profit. Let's say you bought at $8.01 and are planning to sell at $8.02, but in your trading platform you notice thousands of shares being sold at $8.019. In other words, someone has "overtaken" you at a better price of just one tenth of a cent. This is one of the market makers' advantages, and you will simply have to wait your turn patiently. On the other hand, since they're playing in the gap, they will most likely be the ones who will buy from you and sell to someone else. At some point, they could very well buy your stock at $8.02 and sell it to other market makers in the gap for $8.019, aiming to profit from a little less than a cent, but in gargantuan quantities.

One Cent Scalp Trading is Toxic

As noted above, scalping at one cent profit is not a standard trading practice. It is doing no more, in fact, than taking advantage of market inefficiency. Up to the end of 1999, scalp traders benefitted from a different structure of the market, since stock prices were not traded in increments of one cent but in eighths of a dollar: $8, $8 1/8, 8 2/8, and so on. In those times, locking the price of a stock between the bid and ask yielded a profit of 1/8 of a dollar, which is 12.5 cents in either direction. Intraday scalpers flourished, but since then the method is in decline, since the stock exchanges are looking to be rid of anyone specializing in this method. Professionally, the supply and demand that such traders add to the market is defined as **toxic liquidity**.

Market makers who identify you as providing toxic supply will block access to your broker, who in turn, fearing what may happen, will block your account. This is usually why retail traders cannot operate alone using this method. The retail trader needs to join a trading room operated by companies specializing in trade of this kind. These companies are actually brokers themselves, and hold private ECNs in order to overcome the limitations. This is not trading you can do from home in your spare time. It is an office job. You need to work with the platform and services of a specific company, and you actually become a kind of salaried robot living from the boring fluctuations of one cent per share. If you shut down the air conditioners in these trading rooms, you'll probably discover they're more like a third-world sweatshop than pleasant stock trading centers. Nonetheless, if your financial situation does not allow investing in studies and making an initial reasonable deposit in your trading account, these companies offer you a work environment, studies, and capital that can help you start out as traders. While still young, within certain financial constraints, and despite other kinds of disadvantages, this may be a good starting-point choice.

| **SMART MONEY** | *One cent scalps are defined as "toxic trading." If that is the ONLY method of trading you're using, expect your broker to close your trading account!* |

This explanation on how to utilize scalping is to show that under certain conditions and in the right proportions, the method can be made to work for you, but I do expect that your main operational method will be the classic forms of profiting from volatility, market and stock trends. I believe that if classic trading is your main method, you will be able to earn an income under any market condition with any broker and without exploiting market failures. Nonetheless, in non-volatile market conditions during the NY lunch break, and with sufficient experience, scalping will help you take home a few hundred dollars more. A broker will not forego working with you if you integrate a reasonable level of scalps in your regular trading activities.

The Little Red Riding Hood Trap

The term is clearly borrowed from the world of criminal behavior. Red Riding Hood is a trap in which a candidate for elimination is invited to a seemingly innocent event, only to discover that it was the biggest and last mistake of his or her life. In short: seduction, deception, destruction.

In the world of trading, we apply the term "red riding hood" to an enticing formation that rouses our inherent greed, draws us into entering a stock full speed ahead, and usually leads to scathing losses.

What identifies a red riding hood formation? It's usually one that looks too good to be true: for example, when a stock consolidates at a distance of just a few cents from the breakout line for several long minutes, or even a few hours, it may look as though it is consolidating nicely in the short term, readying for the perfect, full breakout. But in many cases it is a trap. When you see a really good-looking formation, try to ask yourself what is making it so attractive. A stock stuck in the narrow range beneath the line of resistance is a very clear sign of one thing: a large seller. The stock wants to rise, but the seller is not done just yet. Even if the stock breaks resistance, there is a good chance that the seller will renew quantities, buyers will panic, unload their merchandise, and the stock will fall enough to shake you into a loss.

What should you do in this case? First, thoroughly examine the resistance point. Take a careful look at the Level II window, check the quantity of shares being offered for sale, and try to identify the seller. Is this a market maker attempting to refresh stock all the time? Since it is often difficult to access clear data through the Level II window because sellers can hide their sell orders, carefully check the T&S (time and sales) window where you will find the flow of trades actually being executed. No one can hide the amount of shares being sold at the resistance point! If you see a large quantity changing hands without being able to identify a seller renewing stocks, you will understand that this is a smart seller concealing sale instructions.

How Do We Make Money from this Situation?

As noted, buying a red riding hood at breakout is not a good idea, but buying it after its failure is a whole different story. Wait for the breakout, wait for the failure, and buy when disappointed buyers are getting rid of their stock at a loss of 12 to 25 cents beneath the breakout point. In most cases, the stock will return to the resistance level where you will be able to sell at one to two cents below the original breakout point. You may be able to do this several times, as long as the stock has not broken out. It is a nice, simple intraday scalping method with relatively high success rates.

Be warned, however: the method requires psychological stamina, since it involves buying as a stock is trending down. If this is a strong stock, it will want to go up. The reason for its temporary drop beneath the breakout point is because a large number of buyers have suddenly fallen in love with the formation and bought before the breakout, then panic when the stock direction moves against them by a few cents. You need to train yourself to operate against your natural instincts and buy precisely when inexperienced traders are selling at a loss. On the other hand, if you bought the stock at the breakout and it gets stuck at up to ten cents above the resistance point and seems to be showing signs of dropping beneath your buy point, flee it as fast as you can. Exiting a stock which is not doing what it should be doing is also a tough psychological demand, since we tend to convince ourselves that "if we just wait a little longer, it will be ok."

Example of Red Riding Hood for Textron, TXT

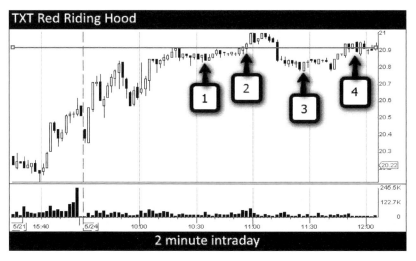

Textron rose strongly in trade's opening hour. The stock encountered resistance at $20.91 and consolidated [1] beneath the resistance line for 45 minutes. Without doubt, a lovely breakout formation! Several problems I found with this formation led me to pass on it. First, the stock was consolidating beneath the resistance line for too long and too perfectly. That already makes it suspicious. Second, I noticed that sellers were renewing supplies all the time, and that was also the reason why the stock did not break out for 45 minutes. Thirdly, even if the stock would break out, it was too close to resisting the round number of $21 (see section on "round numbers" further on). The stock had risen just 9 cents, encountered sellers waiting for the round number, and dropped. Who were the sellers that caused it to plummet?

Throughout the consolidation process [1] prior to the breakout, a large quantity of shares changed hands, and "weak buyers" who had not yet locked in their profit were entering. When the large sellers continued selling shares beyond the breakout point, weak buyers felt pressured and at a certain point dumped their merchandise, causing a drop in price of 15 cents below the breakout level [3]. This is the point where you should buy, and then sell at [4] when the price returns to the breakout level. If you familiarize yourself with these rules and this method, it becomes child's play!

Pre- and Post-Market Trading

Wall Street is open to regular trading for six-and-a-half hours, between 9:30 am to 4 pm in New York (EST). These are busy hours which start and end with the ring of the bell, but these are not the only hours of activity. In addition, it is possible to trade during periods of minimal activity before and afterthe official trading hours.

Some brokers allow their clients the opportunity to utilize pre-market and post-market trading. The NASDAQ stock exchange, for example, allows trading in stocks from 4 am and until 8 pm, New York time. It is probable, however, that your broker does not provide services at 4 am. You need to check pre- and post-market trading times with your broker. While they will differ from one broker to the next, the usual timeframe is two hours each way beyond the formal trading day. These extra hours are set by the exchanges as an opportunity for those that wish to be able to exit and enter stocks due to news outside of market hours.

Why would we want to join pre- or post-market trading? For the greater majority of stocks, no major volume changes are noted during these hours. By contrast, when well-known companies publicize quarterly reports or convey important information outside of normal trading hours, their stocks will show lively activity. This means that you, too, can join the pre- or post-market trading. The theoretical advantage is that you can be among the first reacting to financial announcements, long before the general public reacts. In actuality, if you wish to listen to my advice, keep a safe distance. I strongly recommend that you **never** trade out of regular hours. I can pretty much promise you that in the long run if you ignore this advice, you will lose far more than you will make.

The Dangers of Pre- and Post-Market Trading

1. **Low volume:** Unlike during regular trading hours, there are very few active buyers and sellers during pre- and post-market timeframes. This means that you might not obtain the shares you want, or find a buyer for shares you wish to sell.
2. **Wide spreads:** Due to the low volume, spreads between the ask and bid tend to be wide. This means that at the moment of purchase, you

have already lost the spread should you wish to exit the trade.

3. **High volatility:** Again due to low volume, volatility may become particularly high but generally will not show a clear trend. In other words, one moment you may be profiting, and the very next you could be losing, fleeing in fear, and the cycle continues.

4. **Price uncertainty:** Pre- and post-market prices are not always linked to the regular trading hours prices. You may often end up paying much more than during the regular trading day.

5. **Limited use of trading orders:** Before and after regular trading hours, it is only possible to use LIMIT orders for immediate buying and selling. This means that if the stock shows sudden movement, you are likely to miss the entry or exit point you wanted, especially dangerous when you do not have any stop order to protect you.

6. **Competition with professional traders:** Most of the traders at such hours are professionals or large funds who are better informed than you.

7. **Faulty platforms:** Online trading carries the risk of faulty trading platform reaction times. During pre- and post-market hours, the level of service you will receive from your broker will generally be very poor.

8. **High commissions:** Brokers tend to charge higher commissions for trades executed outside normal trading hours.

Summary

I realize that on the face of things, trading before and after regular market hours--especially following financial announcements--sounds exciting, and indeed it is. That's also why I tried my hand in pre- and post-market trading. I developed my own special techniques, got enthused over financial announcements, bought and sold, and in the end... lost! I am well aware that you might very well succeed, unlike me, but I strongly recommend avoiding unnecessary problems. So I stand by my initial advice: steer clear of these hours. You can believe me when I say they're nothing but big trouble. Save your time, and you'll be saving a lot of money over the years. After my cumulative experiences, I developed my own special rule: never touch the button during pre- and post-market trading, no matter how seductive the situation looks.

I recall instances where I held stocks over from the previous day's trading, and during pre-market trade saw them being traded for amazing profits or searing losses. In both cases, the psychological pressure requires bringing the situation to a close as quickly as possible. The brain demands that you realize the profit or the loss, driven by just one thought: get past the pressure! Wrong! That's about the worst mistake you can make. In the greatest majority of situations, you will receive a better price during the first five to fifteen minutes following the opening of trade.

SMART MONEY	*Pre- or post-market trading inherently contains multiple risks and in the long term does not pay. We do not trade before or after trading hours, period!*

In 2010, with the stock exchange reaching peak prices over a 14-month period, and after eight straight weeks of unstoppable price rises, I was invited to a television financial program in my capacity as analyst. While all other analysts predicted continued increases, I predicted a 10% pullback. The next day, the market rose another 1.1%. The next day, the wheel came full circle. I was spot on! Within several days, the market dropped by 8% and provided us with an amazingly successful week of shorts. By the weekend, I realized that the drop had been extremely sharp, and must retrace at least a little. For the weekend, then, I positioned myself in three stocks which I estimated would retrace upwards more than all others: Apple (AAPL), Goldman Sachs (GS), and TEVA. I waited patiently for the opening of trade on Monday. An hour before trading opened, I took a look at the pre-market status. I couldn't believe what I saw on the trading platform: the market was opening with gap up, the size of which I had never seen before...4.5%! For my account, the gap established a pre-market profit of $28,000! That's when my hands started to sweat and my pulse began to race: what to do next, sell at pre-market or wait?

I have already taught you that at this stage you must never sell, but instead wait. But just for this one occasion, I wondered if I should bend my own rules. That would require no more than hitting the sell button and all the pressures would evaporate. And such a lot of money! I didn't give in. I waited. One hour later, some ten minutes after the opening of trade, the profit jumped to $36,000 and I locked in almost all of it. For the first time that day, I took a deep breath. Not bad for one hour's work. What might have happened if I were a novice trader? I have no doubt that I would not have been able to withstand the pressure, and would have sold in the pre-market. Remember that pre-market buyers buy in the pre-market because they believe they will see a better sale price during regular trading hours. They are usually the top level professionals, and they are almost always right.

Notice What Happened on that Day to Apple, AAPL:

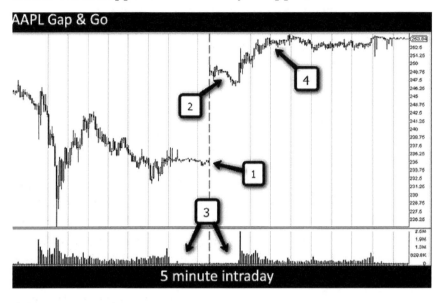

The chart above shows regular trading hours as well as pre- and post-market trading [3]. Apple ends Friday's trading at $235.63 and is traded post-market with a slight downward bias [1]. I buy 900 Apple shares before trading ends, assuming that on Monday they will open at a higher price. During Monday's pre-trading [2], I am happy to see Apple traded between $247 to $249. Pressure is increasing! The question is: to realize profits or to hold the stock? Notice the low volumes of trade [3] in the post- and pre-market. I managed to stay in control, and sell after the initial price spike at opening of trade, around $251, for a profit of $15 per share [4].

Using VWAP at Opening of Trade

In Chapter Six, we learned that institutional traders use the VWAP indicator during intraday trading. Now we will learn how to use this index for short-term trading, right out of the trading gate.

Often, and usually as a result of some news item, we expect strong volatility in a stock during its first seconds of trading. One technique customarily used when we wish to take advantage of strong volatility in a stock is the Pre-Market VWAP test, applied several seconds before trading opens. As we know, orders can be executed prior to the official opening of the stock exchange. Based on pre-market trading activities, the VWAP can be measured prior to the opening of trade, for example: a stock opens with a large downward gap before trading begins. As a result, an institutional process occurs when trade opens, known as "finding the price." Institutional traders, with their huge quantities, check the levels of support and resistance during the minutes prior to the start of trading, looking for the "fairest" opening price at which they will begin shifting large quantities of shares. If the stock opens with a downward gap and in its first seconds of trading is below the **pre-market VWAP**, we know that sellers are dominant when the market opens. The probability is therefore great that the price during the first seconds of trading will fall. If the opposite situation exists, where the stock opens with a downward gap, but during the first seconds of trading is above the pre-market VWAP, we can assume institutional buyers are busy, allowing us to take advantage of the situation and buy immediately when trading opens. The pre-market VWAP allows us to enter orders earlier than other traders who are trying, a little later in the day, to estimate the initial market direction through changes of price and the momentum several minutes after trading opens. By nature, the act of waiting and the altered prices at opening create greater risks for those who wait. Using the VWAP will reduce the level of risk for professional traders, giving them certain advantages.

One of the toughest problems of trading based on pre-market VWAP is the question of when to enter **stop loss orders**. That's not a simple matter. Sometimes stocks tend to go a bit "crazy" when trading opens, which is why I request and stress that it is an activity best -suited to experienced traders.

Taking Advantage of Round Numbers

Stocks find difficulty in going beyond round numbers. When a stock is trending up and hovers below a round number, it will generally encounter resistance and withdraw. Round numbers serve as precise points for resistance and support. The "rounder" a number is, the stronger its support or resistance will be. Numbers ending with fifty cents, such as $28.50, also serve as areas of support and resistance. A figure such as $40 is rounder than $35, while $50 is rounder than $40, and so forth.

Why do stocks stop at round numbers? They hold psychological significance. We view them as stronger and more whole, even though there is no mathematical basis for this view. Think about that next time you're considering a purchase priced at $9.99.

Let us presume that an average investor has bought the ABC stock at $44.28. Generally, following the purchase, the broker or banker will ask that investor, "If the stock rises, at what price do you wish to realize your profit?" Most likely, the investor's answer will be a round number, such as $50. Can you imagine a situation in which the investor will tell the broker to sell at $49.98? Since the majority of investors makes the same exact mistake and sets their sale orders at round numbers, when the stock reaches that number, a stream of sell orders accrued by brokers over anywhere from months to years is automatically set into motion and the large supply of sellers at the precise round number stops the stock from moving. When that happens, buyers who bought at the peak begin to lose their patience and sell. The number of sellers eventually outweighs the number of buyers, and the most likely outcome is that the stock price will drop. How far might it go down? No one knows that.

Behavior of TEVA at a Round Number

In the daily chart, we can see the behavior of TEVA over three years. Twice on its way up, it ceased progress at the round number of $50. The first time, in January 2008 [1], it dropped back to $43; the second time, a month later, it dropped back to $36 [2]. The third time, 18 months from the first attempt to break the $50 mark, buyers finally succeeded in outweighing sellers and the stock rose. Automatic orders fixed at the round number by sellers succeeded in holding the stock back for a full year-and-a-half!

How do we, as traders, make use of the round number phenomenon? If you bought a stock and are considering when to execute a partial (lock in part of the profit), you need to consider the option of setting your order at one or two cents below the round number, staying wary of the fact that the stock may be likely to fail there. As it reaches the round number, you need to keep your finger on the mouse and check the quantity of buyers and sellers carefully. Give the stock a chance to move past the round number, since if it does, the momentum of success may send it into highs of several tens of cents. But at even the most minimal sign of failure, lock in the gain immediately. On the other hand, if you have decided to buy a stock which is currently being traded just below the round number, it is preferable to wait until that round number is passed.

Intraday Round Number Breakout – MFB

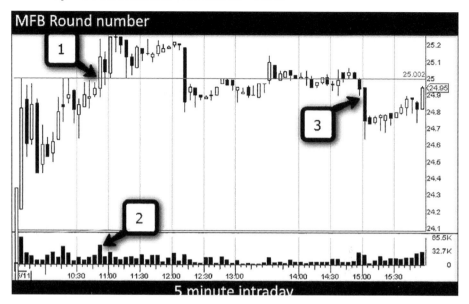

We bought MFB in the trading room when it broke out above the round number of $25. Before the stock broke out, it reached the round number and stopped there several times [1]. The breakout sent it upwards by 30 cents, allowing us to take a good partial of three-quarters of the quantity bought. Notice the increase in volume [2] at the breakout point. The final quarter was closed at a loss of ten cents [3]. Not a big trade, but definitely some nice clean work there, taking advantage of the round number breakout in the correct way.

SMART MONEY	*Round numbers serve as points of resistance and support. We try to buy above round numbers, and realize profits below them.*

When a stock drops towards a round number, things turn around. Usually there will be a large number of buyers at the round number, therefore if you are in a long, it is better that you let your stop order remain beneath the round number in the hope that the stock will find support and return to highs. If you're planning a short, it's best to execute it only when the price drops below the round number. If you're already in a short with a stock dropping towards the round number, consider taking a partial several cents before it reaches the area of support at the round number and turns around.

Summary

When we are in a long, we should consider realizing profits a little before the anticipated round-number resistance. When we plan to buy a stock trading just below the round number, it is preferable to buy if and when it gets past the round number resistance point. When we long a stock, it is preferable to enter a stop order a little below the round number. Traders wishing to short will prefer to execute the short below the round number, and place their stop orders a little above the round number.

Trading Small Caps

Special significance is applied to trading in low-priced stocks. Many traders love them because of their high volatility. Known as "small caps," some such stocks move through ranges of tens of percentages during a single day and are highly popular among risk-loving traders. Small cap trading requires the trader to be highly proficient in the technique, and is therefore not suited to novice traders with insufficient experience who could easily be drawn by the low price and theoretical potential of large profits arising from high volatility.

SMART MONEY	*We define "low-priced stocks" (small caps) as stock being priced below $10. Most funds worldwide are prohibited from buying stock priced at less than $10, which accounts for their high volatility.*

What is a "small stock" or "small caps"? There is no absolute definition, but the currently accepted explanation defines it as stock from a company with a market value of between $300 million to $2 billion. To calculate a company's market value, its stock price is multiplied by the number of shares issued.This information is available from sites such as Yahoo Finance.

The definition of small caps has changed through the years. For example, stocks currently considered "small" may have been considered of mid to high-market value twenty years ago. Before entering the stock during trading hours, should we perform a multiplication exercise to assess the company's market value? Of course not; that is why we search for a common denominator that makes checking fast and easy. The simplest solution is to fix a price: almost all stocks traded below $10 are "small caps."

Why are small caps more volatile than others? Two reasons apply: due to the higher risk in small caps (their title being indicative of their inherent risk as issued by small companies), and because for the greater majority of international funds, a standing prohibition prevents them from investing the public's money in inherently volatile stocks. Funds buy in large quantities; the movement of stocks held by large funds is gentler, since a drop in price will often lead them to increase the amounts they hold. When a stock rises sharply, however, they will take advantage of the large volume to sell. Small caps, which do not receive the support of institutional investors, are dependent on the whim and will of private investors who can buy or sell with one click of the mouse.

A second reason for high volatility in small caps relates to something we have already discussed: stocks move in cents rather than percentages. The smallest possible gap in trading is one cent, whether the stock price is $5 or $50. At breakout, traders will push a $50 stock upwards by tens of cents in just the same way as they may do with a $5 stock.

Very few funds are permitted to trade in small caps (under $10), but generally all funds are prohibited from trading in stocks with a price lower than $5. When a stock price drops below the $10 mark, traders anticipate that institutional traders will begin releasing their holdings, creating expectations which tend to become self-fulfilling, causing the stock to drop sharply.

We can use this knowledge to our advantage in two directions:

• Use the dropping price to short a stock beneath the $10 mark I am so fond of. These breakdowns often turn out to be particularly strong when they integrate a downtrend together with a breakdown beneath the round number of $10.

Short in Dean Foods Company below $10, DF

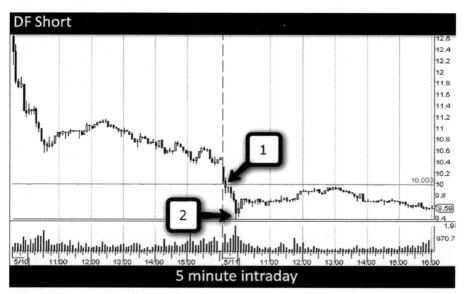

5 minute intraday

Right at the start of trading, our trading room team executed a short on Dean Foods below the $10 level. The stock had shown weakness the previous day, and it seemed natural that it would continue dropping. At breakdown the stock dropped by 61 cents [2] for five consecutive five-minute candles, virtually without looking back. It was a great trade to start the day.

Trending up: when a stock traded for a lengthy period beneath $5 begins to climb and looks as though it will break out above the $5 level (being the price at which some funds may begin buying), a situation is created where traders familiar with institutional behavior starting "pushing" the stock upwards in large volume, assuming that fairly soon the institutional funds will start purchasing.

Important: When I am considering whether to trade in small caps, I relate to stocks that belong wholly and solely to the stock exchange's **main trading list.** These stocks show daily volumes of above one million shares. It is absolutely forbidden to trade in stocks not on this list, such as **pink sheet** stocks, which you will easily recognize by the PK suffix next to their symbol. I also believe you should keep away from "Penny stocks". Penny stocks is one of the most dangerous scams in trading. They are cheap for a good reason. All institutional funds and big traders never trade or invest in them. Beginners get attracted to penny stocks because they think that they can profit easily and because penny stocks are cheap. In reality, penny stocks are easily manipulated by scammers, very volatile and very risky to trade. Scammers use junk emails, one page "Stock Picking" websites and forums to push traders to invest in penny stocks. When the beginners are buying the scammers are the sellers. Sometimes scammers go as far as offering "Penny Stock Courses" or sell "Penny Stock Picking" services, which is even more dangerous. In fact, novice, unexperienced traders, are paying in order to be scammed.

How Can Small Caps Be Found?

Small caps are generally dormant stocks that "awaken" for a few days. When they do, they can be identified on the first significantly volatile day based on volume increase or sharp price changes, or on the following day. We can expect that the momentum will keep them moving for some days. Every day you should make a list of the small caps that appear interesting on that day. You can identify them in various ways: by a follow-up list, or by using free, simple programs called **stock screening software** which we will learn more about later. Define these programs according to the following filters: stocks priced $3 to $10, with trade volumes growing exponentially, and which rose in one day by more than 10%. To find small caps during trading, I use my COLMEX Pro tool called the **Top 20** which identifies and displays the leading 20 stocks in the market at any given moment, many of which are small caps.

What is the Best Time for Trading in Small Caps?

You can trade in small caps throughout the day, but my preferred time is during the lunch break, which is 11:30 am to 1:30 pm, New York time. Regular stocks are "resting" because the institutional traders have gone out to eat, but by contrast, the small caps generally traded by the public are much more active and provide interesting trade triggers.

What is the Entry Point for Small Caps?

Use the accepted formations, especially breakout and reversals, according to your personal preferences. Choose the stock based on volatility and volume considerations: in other words, choose stocks traded in volumes that are no less than one million shares per day. You must also be sure there is a reasonable spread of no more than 3 to 4 cents and an appropriate risk-reward ratio.

The Russell 2000 – Market Index for Small Caps

Just as we do not trade in regular stocks without checking the market direction as embodied by the S&P 500 intraday behavior, we do not trade in small caps without a strong backwind from the small caps index, known as the **Russell 2000**, symbol RUT$. Just as we use the SPY for following the S&P 500, we are similarly assisted by the **IWM**, the Russell 2000 ETF. In actuality, when a small cap breaks out in large volumes, the Russell 2000 direction will have no effect on it. By contrast, if you wish to understand the nature of small caps on any particular day and their chance of breakout on that day, check the Russell 2000 for an overview of the direction and market force of small caps. Clearly, then, we do not use the Russell 2000 in the same way that we use the S&P 500, which is an intraday tool for certifying breakouts and breakdowns and for reaching decisions on profit realization. We use the Russell 2000 only for insight on the "nature" of the small caps.

Should We Short on Small Caps?

The volatility of small caps in cents is very similar to that of larger stocks. As we learned, stocks move in cents rather than percentages, and therefore you should not try to buy 10 times more in small caps than you would for regular stocks, since you will still be increasing the risk tenfold! As a rule of thumb, we trade in small caps in exactly the same quantities as regular stocks. In actuality, you must check the stock's volatility in real time and decide on the spot as to the best quantity, according to stock volume and behavior.

SMART MONEY	*The volatility of small caps in cents is similar to that of large stocks. Therefore, we will usually buy small caps in the same quantities as we would buy large caps.*

Summary

To reduce risk, professional day traders will generally trade in large and medium caps with high liquidity and narrow spreads. It is definitely possible to trade in small caps, but prior to entering the stock, be very sure of your choice and handling decisions. Professional, precise handling will generally produce higher yields relative to the stock's price.

Reciprocal Range Play

This method is applied to a stock which opens trading with a considerable gap (opening price is significantly higher or lower than the previous day's closing price – see previous sections on this topic). The objective of this method is to enter the stock after the gap is closed, when it technically appears that it may continue moving to an equal distance in the opposite direction.

Reciprocal Range Play for Myriad, MYGN

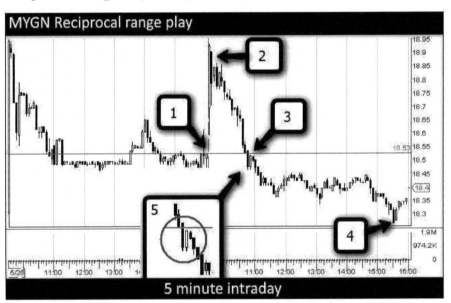

The chart shows MYGN's behavior over two days of trading. MYGN closed the first day at [1] and opened the next day with a gap up [2]. Several minutes after trading opened, it became clear that the stock was moving down to close the gap. We have already learned that there is a clear tendency for gaps to close on the same day of trading. Experienced traders know how to take good advantage of this known opportunity, and many execute shorts, "helping" the stock drop further.

As we see in the chart above, closing the gap is only half of the stock's movement. Sometimes, as in the case above, a "bi-directional" or

reciprocal opportunity forms when the strong gap-closing momentum breaks after the close [3] and causes the stock to continue trending down [4]. Note how the distance between points 3 and 4 is identical to that of between points 2 and 3.This is the basis for the term **reciprocal range.**

Analyzing the process: At the start of trading, the stock opens with a gap up [2]. Within minutes, bears take control and the stock begins closing the gap. Long players, who had hoped that the stock would continue rising (Gap &Go) find themselves trapped on the wrong side of the game and set their exit point (stop order) at the most reasonable point: this is the gap-closing area [3]. Short sellers who sold at [2] are aware that stocks have a good chance of changing direction after closing the gap [3], and they therefore set [3] as their profit target. When the stock closes its gap [3], we can expect a reversal of direction, or at the very least a slight retracement upwards. Indeed, a little below [3] we find the upward retracement [5]. The entry trigger into reciprocal range trading is where the **bear flag** at [5] breaks just below the midway point.

What happens when the bear flag breaks? Everyone has a common interest in selling: new short players will enter shorts when the bear flag breaks, short players who entered at [2] will be sorry they closed their shorts and some will execute new shorts, buyers who entered at [2] when trading opened understand that the closing gap will not save them and they sell. Other aggressive buyers who bought when the gap closed [3], assuming that the stock would begin to rise once the gap had closed, find themselves on the wrong side of the action and are also forced to sell.

Who are the losers? Buyers are, of course, are the biggest losers; not only the aggressive ones entering when the gap closed [3] in the hope that the stock would reverse and begin an uptrend, but also those who bought during the previous day and now find themselves trapped in a crashing stock. The coming together of energies created during the down movement, together with the closing of new and old longs and the entrance of new short sellers, leads the stock to a further sharp drop which, in most cases, can be expected to bring it down to its double-distance target [4].

To increase the success rate of this process, it is best if the gap-closing point [3] is in the vicinity of the previous day's **pivot point.** This is true for the case above. As we have learned, the **pivot point** is a mathematical calculation of the price at which most of the previous day's trading volume occurred. As can be seen in the previous day's chart, most of the activity occurred around the point where the gap closed. The pivot point is generally referred to as **Fair Value**. This indicates that the majority of buyers bought during the previous day at the average found at [3]. When the current day's price drops below [3], all those who were caught in the wrong direction get trapped. The closer the gap-closing point is to the pivot, the more disappointed buyers there will be seeking to exit the stock if it keeps dropping, which pushes the reciprocal range process along even better.

SMART MONEY | *The entry point for reciprocal range trading will be at the breakout or breakdown of the technical formation emerging above or below to the gap-closing point.*

Analyzing reciprocal range trading in the opposite direction is exactly the same. When a stock opens with a down gap, rises to close the gap, reaches the closing price, and continues rising, it is reasonable to presume that it will allow us a chance for good, long reciprocal trading. In such a case, the trapped ones are traders who entered into a short around the previous day's pivot point, and are now forced to buy when they move into a loss.

Trading at Financial Reports and Announcements

At the start of each quarter, public companies must report to the stock exchange, investors, and to the public on the outcomes of the previous quarter, together with their forecasts for the months ahead. Quarterly earnings reports are typically publicized during April, July, October and January, as soon as the quarter ends. Most companies issue their quarterly reports before or after trading hours, although this is not a requirement. As such, earnings reports will almost always cause a gap in the stock's price. The gap direction can never be known. Even if you have in-depth financial knowhow and can analyze any company's financial reports for yourself, do not imagine even for one moment that you are able to predict the gap direction. It can happen that great reports lead to equally great drops, or vice versa. I have never yet met an economist who was surprised by the stock's direction following a quarterly report. That is odd, but in retrospect, the explanation goes something like this: "Yes, outcomes were excellent, but in clause [...] of the balance sheet, the company informed of its reduced expectations." In short, the market is comprised of two kinds of people: those who simply do not know, and those who have no idea that they do not know. Nor do I ever know with any certainty which way the price is going to move. So how do we nonetheless profit from quarterly reports and announcements?

Company balances are detailed and contain a great deal of economic and business data. For short-term traders, this data holds no interest, but the short-term outcome on long-term investors interests us a great deal!

During the "earnings season," institutional investors closely follow the stocks in their portfolios, and decide whether to hold or dump them. Two important, if not the most important, factors in the institutional investors' decision-making processes when considering whether to increase or decrease holdings of a specific stock, are:

- Forecasts by analysts reviewing the stock
- Analysts' predictions on whether the company will increase profits and revenues during the coming quarter

These factors, together with several others, have the power to drive institutional investors to take action. Such action includes extraordinary announcements, changing recommendations, and macro-economic announcements which influence the market in general and the stock's specific sector in particular.

Generally, the stock price will rise proportionately to sector and market movement, and any "moving outside the lines" will generally be possible only through significant economic triggers. During crises or fear of an upcoming crisis, the market "punishes" stocks which do not follow their predictions, thus a careful follow-up on stocks showing sharp daily movements can create good short-term (days) and medium term (weeks) opportunities.

To find opportunities during the quarterly reports period, you need to check the date of the particular stock's report, or simply ready yourself for any day's trading by preparing a list of all stocks that interest you. If you wish to locate the stocks according to the date of their report, a wide range of financial sites can help. My personal favorite is Yahoo Finance.

Locating Report Dates Using Yahoo Finance

Locating Report Dates Using Yahoo Finance

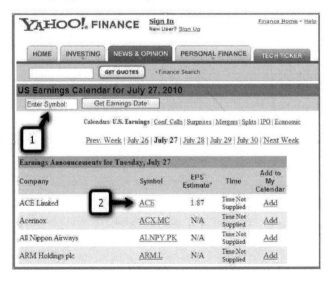

This page presents all the stocks for which reports were publicized on July 27, 2010. I chose to have the results displayed according to alphabetically-arranged ticker symbols [2]. If you wish to check the report date of a specific stock, you can enter its symbol into the field [1].

SMART MONEY	*We do not "go to sleep" holding stocks about to publicize reports, since even if the report results match our trading direction, the stock's actual behavior can be unpredictable.*

Allow me to clarify: it is absolutely prohibited to "go to sleep" holding stocks about to publicize a quarterly company report. If you plan to buy a stock for a swing of several days, you must always clarify its report date. If that date occurs tomorrow pre-market, you are taking an enormous risk! In fact, even if the report is due out the next day after the market or even the day after, it is enough for a rumor or two to cause a sharp gap even before trading begins. In a best case scenario, the situation might bring you a handsome profit, but in the worst case scenario, you might experience a scathing wipeout. It is important to keep in mind that the gamble has 50% odds of the price going either way. Even if you believe that the report's results will be far better than analysts' expectations, and even if you are proven right, it is still a huge risk. Stocks tend to surprise, without any connection at all to the reports. Good reports can be followed by a crash, and vice versa. Even if you are right, the market may not want to support you.

The only situation in which I am prepared to hold a stock during the reports period is when I have sold at least three-quarters of it for a very good profit, and the additional 25% no longer endangers me. Below is an example with the Lexmark [LXK] company. I bought its stock for upwards of $46. The profit target for selling three-quarters of the quantity was 3%. I knew that in several days the company would publicize its quarterly report, but predicted its stock would reach the profit realization point beforehand. Indeed, that is what happened. The stinging slap on my face came with the report's appearance. Notice what happened to Lexmark:

Publicizing the Quarterly Report for Lexmark, LXK

Lexmark breaks out above $46 [1], and within four days reaches the planned target price. On reaching a 3% profit I sold 75% of the quantity I had bought, knowing that the quarterly report would appear the next day. During the day following the report's publication, I discovered that Lexmark had opened with a wild down gap of 9% below my entry price. The stop order intended for the entry price of $46 executed at the shocking low of $42, and the 25% of shares evaporated at a huge loss.

Now check the bottom line: a profit of 3% on three-quarters of the stock together with a loss of 9% on one-quarter of the quantity of stock leads to the grand total of...zero! Overall summary: I didn't lose, I didn't win. Moral of the story: very simply, do you want to take huge risks and sleep on a stock right before its quarterly report is publicized? Make sure that you have realized a handsome profit beforehand for the greater portion of the shares you are holding and take a calculated risk only on a very small percentage, if at all.

What might have happened had Lexmark not reached my profit target before the report's appearance? I would have sold the entire quantity. In the long term this is not a problematic phenomenon, since statistically in half the instances, when a gap is to your detriment, you will lose; whereas in the other half of instances, when the gap benefits you, you will profit. The cumulative result of dozens of such gaps will, most likely, be zero.

By contrast to quarterly earnings reports, the outcomes of analyst recommendations can be fairly well predicted: for example, a "strong buy" recommendation by a Goldman Sachs analyst will generally cause a price spike. The "sell" recommendation, or a significant legal claim, will generally cause drops in the stock's price. The problem with financial announcements is that you can never know when to expect them. Here, too, statistics comes to your aid. Unlike the completely unpredictable market reactions to the publication of quarterly reports, when you buy a strong stock which is rising, it is highly presumable that one reason for its uptrend is a positive announcement which until publication had been known only to a few with insider knowledge who began buying before the public. True, they are not operating legally, but do not be naïve. If you have bought the stock because it is demonstrating strength rather than because you know a positive announcement is about to go public, then following the announcement the stock will generally continue moving in the direction in which you are trading.

So far, we have analyzed a situation in which you "sleep" on a stock for a swing of several days. Next, we will relate to intraday trading.

Intraday Trading at Announcements

Our goal is to profit from a stock's volatility, whether derived from a quarterly report or an announcement, rather than guess the stock's direction. Before the start of trading, we will check several financial sites for stocks expected to make reports public at the end of the day's trading, and look for stocks expecting changes due to changed analysts' recommendations. They will be fed into a follow-up list, and if you have sufficient computer screens, I strongly recommend displaying each one with its own chart and following them all over the course of the trading day.

When should we buy, or execute a short? First of all, remember that we are not going to enter any stock before we have seen its actual direction in real time. We will examine its direction and hit the button only when the acceptable technical formation develops. Notice that market direction will have much less impact on stocks in the news than on other stocks. In other words, even if the market is trending up and the stock you have chosen is "suffering" from the analysts' changed recommendation, you can still short it. The success rate of the short will increase if the market is behind it, but in this particular situation of reports and announcements, the market direction is not vital.

Macy's (M) on the Day it Announced Profit

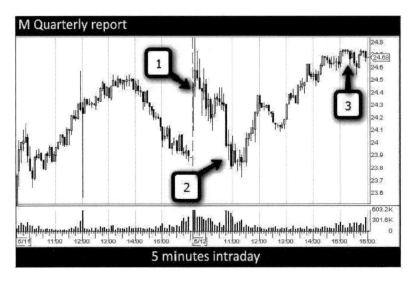

M Quarterly report

5 minutes intraday

On May 12, 2010, following an excellent quarterly report, the retail giant Macy's opened with an up gap of 2.2% [1]. In addition, a positive review was also publicized relating to Macy's growth in sales. Immediately after the trading day opened, Macy's dropped sharply and closed the gap [2]. As we have seen, the gap-closing point is very often also the point where direction changes, which was true in this instance. Macy's recovered and closed at the highs [3]. What would have happened if, following publication of these positive reports, you would have bought the stock at the opening of trade [1] in the hope that it would continue rising? Most likely, with a drop of more than 2% towards the gap-closing point, you would have found yourself with a loss. The conclusion is that a stock's behavior following publication of financial information is erratic and cannot be anticipated. Everything is possible, and anything can happen. If the stock moves up, it can be bought long if it also shows a satisfactory technical formation, and backed up by a reasonable stop order.

Question: Can you identify a good technical intraday entry point for a long? I see the "inverted head and shoulders" formation at $24.40. Can you also see it?

How to Identify a Bottom

Crises are an inseparable part of stock exchange life. Once every few years, the stock exchange crashes due to one crisis or another. Statistically, the average investor experiences at least three major crashes during his or her lifetime. During the past decade alone, markets crashed due to two mega-crises: the Internet Bubble of 2000, and the Financial Crisis of 2008. Second-level shakeups appear as mini-crises, such as with the collapse of the Twin Towers on 9/11, or the Dubai crisis, the Greek crisis, the Japanese tsunami, and other events which I have already forgotten.

At the peak of the market's reaction to the March 2009 Sub-Prime Crisis, very few people actually identified the bottom. Nor could they have even imagined in their wildest dreams that in just over a year, the market would lurch from the bottom with a meteoric rise of 100%, with hardly a backward glance. Buyer opportunities at the bottom are extremely rare, but allow us, if we identity the bottom correctly, to utilize trading methods for longer than the short term to which this book relates. I believe that as traders, we must be open to all types of opportunity, even if it sometimes deviates from the limitations of our short–term approach. We must operate as day traders, yet hold stocks for periods of several days to several weeks using swing methods, and in special instances, try to profit from longer-term volatility of several months.

Since 90% of the public loses in the stock market, we need to conclude that the public tends to buy stocks when they are at peak, and dumps them when they reach "rock bottom." What can we conclude? That we need to do exactly the opposite to what the general public is doing. The way to do that is to identify the peak or bottom, neither of which are simple tasks. I will try to provide you with several rules for identifying a bottom. They are not perfect mathematical rules, but they will help you consolidate your views when you next encounter a crisis.

These rules are very simple, but somewhat difficult to master. The greatest difficulty is psychological. Our brains tell us it is time to act, but our hearts resist. This resistance may derive from fear of loss, from social pressure, from being spooked by the unknown, and more. Resistance derives from the simple fact that we are human. Although the physical distance between mind and heart is short, for most people it presents a gap that cannot be bridged. Success requires you to undergo a mental shift that merges thought and emotion into a single path. It is a tough mental process which generally takes some years to internalize.

- **Rule 1: Blood first needs to flow in the streets**

When you are looking for a stock's bottom, try to imagine how you would feel if you bought it at its highest price before it plunged. If you think you could handle the drop without fleeing, then it's not the time to buy! If you feel you could **not** withstand the pressure, that you would break and sell, then that IS the time to buy. This is an important rule, but notice that it does not apply to all stocks. You need to focus on stocks with good fundamentals, where no one quite understands why they have dropped, rather than on those which are trending down because of negative earnings reports. You will be looking for stocks dropping as a result of overall market hysteria.

Usually, I do not buy stocks because of their fundamental value. That's a game best played by the funds. I am sufficiently experienced to know that there is no link between book value and stock price; but sometimes, when a stock is being traded shockingly below its real value, that's the time to buy.

Within the framework of this rule, you also need to check which sector the stock belongs to: for example, during a severe financial crisis (2008 Sub-Prime Collapse, for example), if you would have considered buying a bank stock traded at a dreamy 1:6 Price to Earnings ratio (PE) based on the next year's profits, I'm not sure you would have been making a good trade. It is more reasonable to assume that over the next year, the bank would not make even half of that PE ratio. By the same token, I would also not recommend looking for bottoms in dotcom stocks during Internet crisis years. Remember that the more pain caused by the drop in price, the higher the chance for a successful bounce.

- **Rule 2: Don't listen to analysts' recommendations**

Pay no heed to technical analysts, financial analysts, financial sites, hocus-pocus software that forecasts the future, fund managers, and especially not to economists who claim they have identified the bottom.

They are all no more than background noise, and you need to keep your distance. This is not an easy game to play. It is not about reading a newspaper article. Fund managers who claim to be "bullish" on a stock are virtually declaring that they have already invested in it. Remember the first rule: the greatest pain is at the bottom, and the situation needs to seem hopeless before you enter as a buyer. If too many people tell you that the market will go up, you still haven't seen the bottom. The less you listen to people speaking "with authority," the greater your chances of success. The faster you conclude that no one can assist you, especially the economists, the better off you will be. Most economists will not admit, despite years of formal education, that they are unable to explain why the market rises and falls. But to justify their academic degree and their career status, they will find convincing explanations. Ask them if they have put their money where their mouth is!

- **Rule 3: Analysts have to lower their rating**

When searching for the bottom, you need to do precisely the opposite of what the analysts are recommending. Most of their recommendations are misleading. In many cases, funds use analysts to recommend stocks which the funds have just stocked up on. Companies also lead analysts and feed them internal information from morning to night. Did you ever wonder how an analyst knows how to "precisely calculate" a stock's anticipated profit? The analyst receives a precise figure from the company's finance manager.

SMART MONEY	*When a stock at a low is "suffering" from a lowered recommendation or downgrade which does not cause the price to continue falling, that is a sure sign that the weak sellers are already out of the picture, and usually indicates that the price will now start trending up.*

The stock you are buying must be "suffering" from an analyst's downgrade. In all my years as a trader, I have yet to meet an analyst who upgraded the rating to "buy" at the bottom. Almost without exception, analysts will lower ratings at the bottom. A stock which had been rated a "strong buy" will become a "strong sell." The problem is the method: most analysts rate stocks based on the ratio of anticipated profit and real profit. When a stock realizes its forecast, analysts will upgrade their recommendations, and when it does not uphold the forecast, they will downgrade. When the stock fails even slightly or temporarily, they will downgrade. When a recommended stock crashes, analysts will shamefully downgrade. In other words, this is all part of a cop-out. Things get worse after a crisis, because crises catch most analysts by surprise. They get caught at the peak of the crisis with too many "strong buy" recommendations. The outcome: the stock exchange regulator fumes. Regulators do not like situations where analysts recommend and the stock exchange is crashing. In response, regulators issue instructions to lower expectations. The outcome: if you are hoping for "buy" ratings at the bottom, forget it. To buy a stock at bottom you need to see that a decisive majority of analysts reviewing the stock recommends selling. But pay attention: if the removal of the last remaining "buy" recommendation does not topple the stock price further, this is a sign that all the weak sellers are now out of the picture, and the stock price reflects all the negative expectations. From here on, the only way left is up.

- **Rule 4: The volume at the bottom must be large**
  Before deciding that the bottom has been reached, you need to be sure that the weak investors are out of the picture. This is called "capitulation." A large spike in volume means that there are a large number of sellers, but remember that for every seller there is a buyer. This means that the stock is moving through a lot of hands. Weak sellers have gotten rid of the stock, and new owners have entered. These new owners bought at a low price. They have more patience and stamina. The greater the volume grows, the more weak sellers are being replaced by strong buyers. Remember: a stock traded at its lowest with large volumes is what we want to buy, not sell.

- **Rule 5: Bad news has no impact at bottom**
  When a stock is at its lowest, bad news and even more anticipated bad news is already embodied in the price. When all the weak sellers have left, the remaining buyers are not disturbed by bad news. This rule needs to be integrated with information on the financial state of the company and its sector. If the company is wiped out, or is in a sector that suffers from a very poor macro-economic situation, bad news may prevent it from redeeming debentures, and then control may be turned over to its shareholders.

- **Rule 6: Wait a bit longer…**

This is the final and most important rule. Have you decided that you want to buy? Stop! Hold out a bit longer. It might even be worth waiting for a further drop, proving to you that your assessment of the bottom was incorrect. One of the most common mistakes relates to our tendency to identify too many bottoms in too many instances. True, if you observe this rule, you may discover you've missed out on a good trade, but in most cases you will be happy to discover that the bottom is even further down. Even if you miss several trades, your overall success rate will still be improved from this last step. Remember: bottoms don't happen quickly. There is usually plenty of time.

Identifying the Market Bottom during the 2008 Financial Crisis: SPY

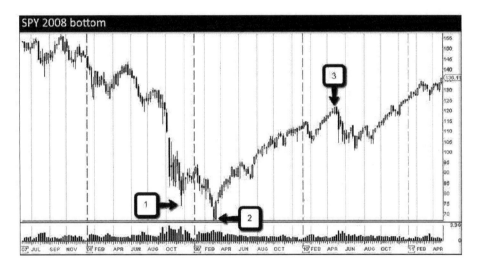

In October 2008, the markets crashed. The SPY (the S&P 500 ETF) dropped from a peak of $175.52 to a low of $67.1 [2]. Then it shot up by 82% in 14 months [3]. Notice that the first bottom [1] was not the real one. Could you have identified the bottom and profited from the highs that followed? That would have been very difficult. Even if you had identified it, most likely you, like many others, would still have been filled with fear that prevented you from thinking clearly. Like many others during that period, I also felt as though the sky had fallen and the world was about to come to an end, and that the entire financial system was about to sink. I had no idea whether the ATMs would still provide cash the following day.

As traders, we profited well from the continuing price drops, but were fearful that we were in a crisis of a scope the world had never experienced, and hence were afraid to buy. That does not mean we did not profit from some of the upward movement, especially once it became absolutely clear that the market trend was indeed upward. But we did not join in the uptrend festivities as investors who bought at the bottom and held out for the long term. On the other hand, how many investors really identified the bottom and bought? Very carefully, however, as short-term traders we profited from a long streak of days with upward trends.

When the market started trending up continuously and determinedly, as it has done since March 2009 [2], a rare situation occurred in which the long-term trader could profit more from the market than the short-term trader. The sadder aspect is that generally such investors also absorb all the lows. The overall outcome is that they tend to cover their losses, and no more. I have yet to meet a long-term investor who knew how to exit prior to the collapse, and buy exactly at the bottom.

Integrating Tools

On May 28, 2010, our trading room traded in a stock that, extraordinarily, integrated several of the tools we have learned about in this chapter. It was an excellent trade, which provided my colleagues and me with the best trade of that day. We traded the stock of 3Par Inc.

Trading with 3Par, PAR

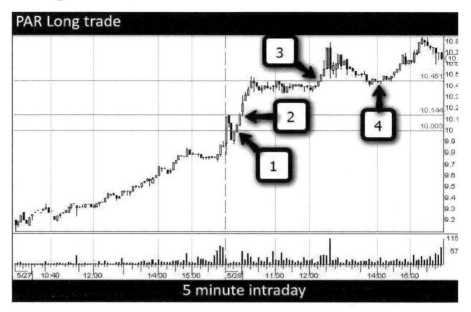

On the day before our entry, PAR rose almost 10% from around $9 to $9.89. We call stocks like these "momentum stock." They are strong stocks, which we like finding prior to the day's trading, assuming that the previous day's momentum will draw new buyers and will also continue into the next day.

PAR's momentum did not disappoint, and when trading opened, the stock jumped to $10.14, pulled back, and executed a classic reversal [1] followed by a move of over $10. At the reversal point [1], we bought. There was reason to doubt, since we did not know if the stock would go higher than its previous peak. When it did [2], we increased the quantity. The stock shot up to a new peak, where we realized good profits for most of our shares. We then noticed that the price was consolidating around the peak point with almost no pullback. The volume at the consolidation area was not too large: in other words, not many new buyers or "weak hands" were entering, and the stock was slowly developing a classic breakout formation above $10.45. We bought more at the breakout [3] and sold again close to the next peak.

Which tools learned so far were applied to this trade?

1. We learned that we love stocks rising above the $10 mark, since that is the point where funds show interest.

2. We learned that we need to buy above round numbers: therefore, above $10.

3. We learned that we need to buy at reversal [1], which is our first entry point.

4. We learned to buy at breakouts [2], where we add quantities.

5. We added a quantity at an additional breakout, since we learned that a long consolidation at the peak with low volume is a good recipe for continued highs [3].

6. We learned that when the stock breaks through the line of resistance, this line becomes the line of support, and the stock may execute a "reassessment" (known as "retest") [4] of the breakout point [3] before continuing to new highs.

How to Take Advantage of a Retest

We discussed the concept of a "retest" in the section explaining support and resistance, but because of its importance, I will now expand on the initial information.

Often, following a breakout of the line of resistance (and the reverse is true for a breakdown below the line of support), the stock will **retest** the line. It drops back down to the breakout point, is supported at the line of resistance which has been broken out, and thus becomes the line of support followed by continuing highs. In the PAR chart we saw the breakout [3] and the retest [4].

Retest is a common phenomenon, and therefore in most instances it can be anticipated that the stock will find support and continue to trend up. In order to understand the retest, we need to analyze the predictable behavior of buyers and sellers. Let us analyze the example presented by PAR:

- **The disappointed trader who missed a good chance**

Traders who missed the breakout [3] watch the trending up stock with disappointed eyes and regret to the depths of their souls that they did not buy it when it was still a good opportunity. Following breakout, they are no longer interested in buying at a high price and therefore wait for another opportunity to buy when it pulls back. When PAR executes a retest [4], they take advantage of the chance to buy, thereby helping to push the price back into highs.

- **The disappointed buyer**

These are the people buying PAR at the breakout [3], but even when they profit, they aren't happy. They feel stupid because they did correctly identify the breakout, but they didn't buy an even larger quantity of shares. Of course it's easy to be smart in retrospect, but when PAR drops back to the breakout price [4], they are happy to take advantage of the pullback and increase their position. They, too, are helping the stock price go up again.

- **The short trader**

Traders with shorts in PAR prior to the breakout hoped it would drop, but were disappointed when the price broke through the line of resistance [3]. Now they are losing, but are not interested in exiting with large losses. They therefore wait hopefully for PAR to drop. When to their great joy it does, they take advantage of the retest point [4] in order to close their shorts "before the catastrophe." In other words, they too are buying and helping the stock price rise.

The conclusion is simple: all the players in the market share the same goal of buying at the retest point [4]. No one is interested in selling there, so that in most cases, a stock which has broken out and pulled back to the breakout price will receive the support of buyers and return to highs.

The retest point can be used to our advantage in two ways: by placing a stop order below the retest area in case the stock should suddenly not receive the anticipated support; or to increase our position in a stock based on the assumption that it will return to highs.

SMART MONEY	*A stock breaking out will generally execute a retest of the breakout area, i.e. it returns to the line of resistance, which now turns into the line of support. The opposite is true for breakdowns.*

The Top Down Analysis Method

"Top down analysis" is an accepted method among careful traders. Before trading opens, traders review the strong industries and sectors and follow their movements. If the pharmaceutical sector excelled on the previous day relative to the market index and other industry indicators, these traders will check a list of stocks belonging to the pharmaceutical industry and seek out the notably dominant ones. Of these, the traders will choose several with attractive technical formations and follow them as potential candidates for the coming day's trading. During trading, these stocks will be bought at planned entry points, on the condition that all of the criteria we have studied are properly filled:

- The market is trending up
- The specific industry is trending up
- The stock is at the correct technical point

Top down analysis considerably reduces chances of failure, but requires no small amount of preparatory work and follow-up. It is recommended for traders with plenty of time, or who are particularly wary and cautious. Since you have the support of so many components of the market, the probability of winning is much higher.

Summary

This was one very heavy chapter! We studied breakouts and breakdowns, volume change, buy and sell points, reversals, gaps, trading strategies, scalps, pre- and post-market trading, VWAP, small caps, reciprocal ranges, how to use financial announcements, identifying the bottom, retesting, and more...So, where do we start?

It would not be normal to be fluent with all this information at this stage. As novice traders, you should choose one method and get to know it well before moving on to new methods.

A practical suggestion: focus on reversals. Look for stocks with a clear trend, very strong for buying or very weak for shorting, which display daily reversals (one-day candles) if you are interested in a swing of several days, or intraday reversals (five-minute candles) if you are interested in trading within the same day. Trading with reversals is simple, slower and clearer than trading at breakouts and breakdowns, or any other method. Once you have reversals pretty much under control, move on to the next method.

11

Risk Management

We have learned how to play offence, now we will learn to play defense.

Learning to Play Defense

Some months ago, an old friend called and recommended I buy a certain stock which "without any doubt" should be shooting up fairly soon. As a good friend, he tried to explain to me what a dreadful mistake I would be making if I didn't buy. Since such good ideas had already lost me no small amounts of money in the past, I politely promised to consider buying the stock, but of course I chose to forget the whole thing. Some days ago, I met my good friend again, but he did *not* forget to ask if I bought the stock. "Wow, I forgot…" I pretended, and asked if he had bought it. "What do you think!" he answered, and asked with some amazement,

"Why didn't you buy it? I'm telling you, you lost out on the deal of your life!"

"So in the end what happened to that stock?" I asked.

"Well, so far it's dropped about 20%," he said, "but just wait and see what's about to happen soon!"

I truly admire my friend's psychological stamina in holding a stock that drops over several months and even years, in the hope that it will make a comeback. I can't do that. I'm a coward. I need to know in advance precisely how much money I might lose in any transaction, not just in percentages, but especially in dollars! I also want to know that I am able to limit my losses to a predefined figure. Remember that in order to be successful in most sports, we first need to learn how to play defense: as they say, **defense wins championships**. If you know how to limit your losses, profits will be made.

There is no stock exchange in the world that approaches the volume of activity on Wall Street. On the London Stock Exchange, some 200 high-volume stocks are traded. On Wall Street, some 10,000 are traded, of which about 1500 show high volumes of more than one million shares per day. Large volumes allow you to buy a stock at the click of the mouse, and no less important, sell it in one click too. Low volume stocks usually have low supply and demand, and the spread between bid and ask prices is likely to be large. This means that you cannot enter and exit such low volume stocks at any price: for example, when you want to sell, you may discover that the closest lone buyer is several percentages below the last traded price. Selling at that price means you will need to absorb heavy losses. You can always try placing a limit order at a high price, but that means waiting patiently for a buyer who may never show! You will encounter the same problem in reverse if you want to buy a stock, or worse, if you want to cover a short (in other words, buy) only to discover that the closest seller is far above the stock's last traded price.

Large volume stocks usually have small spreads and high liquidity. This means you can use automatic orders to realize profits or losses and rely on the computer to provide you with fast, effective executions as close as possible to your chosen entry or exit point.

Several stop orders can be applied, the most familiar and important being a defensive order known as a **stop loss**, which we discussed in the section detailing trading platform orders. In this chapter, we will understand their significance and how to use them.

Fundamental Risks

Every occupation carries its inherent risks. The athlete's risk is a physical injury; the surgeon's risk is human error. Every profession is a world unto itself, which makes it difficult to comprehend the risks until we dive deep into that profession.

An athlete's risks or those of a surgeon can be estimated, and therefore they can be insured. Athletes insure themselves against injury, doctors are covered by medical malpractice insurance, but no company in the world will agree to insure a stock trader's accounts. Insurance companies employ professionals to calculate and manage risk. Since insurance companies will not insure us, it is up to us to manage our risks. We cannot do that unless we understand just what the risks are.

Risk Management and Loss Management

First, we need to define "risk management" by distinguishing between two areas that most traders mistakenly tend to lump together: **risk**

management and **loss management**. Correct loss management is a stand-alone theory having nothing to do with risk management.

Risks must be managed under the assumption that part of our trading activities will lead to losses. Correct risk management should limit us to absorbable losses, which we will need to manage separately according to a different set of rules.

Figuratively speaking, risk management is how a pilot plans to avoid an accident, whereas loss management is how the pilot must execute an emergency landing.

Fundamental Capital Risk

How much money did you deposit in your trading account?

What percentage of your trading capital are you willing to lose?

How much of that figure are you willing to lose in one trade?

Before you start trading, you must have clear answers to these questions. They will help you define your trading strategy. Each of us has different red lines based on our backgrounds, psychological capabilities, financial soundness, and monetary commitments.

Define the percentage of trading capital you are willing to lose. This figure is your first red line. Many of the traders I know have never defined a red line, and sometimes become aware of it only when they actually reach it. This is a big mistake: setting limits in advance will help you cope better with the psychological aspect of trading.

Psychological Risk

Willingness to absorb risk does not derive from our financial status, but rather from our psychological stamina. "Hating to lose" features strongly in research which unequivocally concludes: we hate to lose far more than we love to win, at a 2:1 ratio (Kahneman & Tversky, 1991). Research indicates that loss is perceived as a change in our financial wealth relative to a neutral status. Each of us has a different relative status, derived from both our actual financial status and our perception of the significance of loss. For example, when we buy stock at a higher than normal price but do not sell at a profit, we tend not to see the buying stage as an expensive error, but rather focus on our lack of profit when we sell.

By contrast, when we buy an item at a higher than usual price for personal usage, we tend to view the transaction as a loss.

What significance do you apply to losses derived from stock trading? A pro will absorb losses as an inseparable part of the profession. This does not meant the pro reaches a 1:1 psychological balance between love of profit and hate of loss, but it is reasonable to presume that his or her psychological stability will be greater than that of an amateur for whom loss holds greater weight, even if the amateur loses the same amount as the professional trader and their point of neutrality is identical. In short, we can conclude that the amateur trader's red line will be different to that of the professional, or simply put, each person's red line will be different.

This is why it is essential for you to define your own, private red lines in advance. Doing so will improve your chances of success. Your red line should be based on the amount of available money you are prepared to lose. Money intended for buying a new car or for the family's vacation is not available money and should not be used to fund your trading account. This is **scared money**, which you are scared to lose. Later we will discuss mental management more deeply.

SMART MONEY	*Trading with "scared money" causes improper psychological management, increases hatred of loss, and almost always leads to real losses.*

Leverage Risk

If you open a trading account with a US broker, you will be able to get margin of 4:1 by simply signing a margin agreement with the firm. If you are not a US resident and you open a trading account with a non-US broker, you will be able to get a margin of up to 20:1. A 4:1 margin means that if you deposit $10,000, you will receive leverage when you execute intraday trading of up to $40,000. This is called **intraday margin**. By contrast, if you hold stocks overnight, you will be able to receive margin of only 2:1, called **overnight margin.** A 2:1 margin will let you sleep on stocks valued at double the amount you deposited in your account. The reason for the broker reducing margin on overnight usage is due to the fear of financial announcements that may go public after trading hours, endangering your money as well as the leveraged funds, which are the broker's money.

A 2:1 margin held overnight will cost interest, but the 4:1 intraday margin or even 20:1 margin does not. Most traders use margin. If you also plan to do so, you need to be aware of the risks involved and manage them correctly.

Using leverage correctly brings successful traders much higher returns on their investment. Here, too, the correct way of coping with leverage risk is to define your red lines for leveraged trading. Avoiding any deviation beyond the red line will prevent you from suffering heavy losses in the future. If you are not cautious, one heavy loss can take you completely out of the game forever.

Are you familiar with the double-down roulette method? It's very simple: you place $10 on the red in the hope of winning. If you lose and black shows, you gamble on the red again, this time with $20, and so on. Each time you lose, you double the bet until eventually red comes around again, returning all your losses with the addition of a small profit. The problem is that if you do this for a long time, sooner or later you will get a sequence of the same color. I met someone who lost a huge amount of money when red came up 24 times in succession! That's definitely enough to put the kibosh on what could have been a pleasant evening.

Now, back to stocks. By way of example, let us assume you are using personal capital to the tune of $25,000. You set your loss red line for any single trade at no more than 2% of your trading account: in other words, you are not willing to risk more than $500 for any single trade. Strong self-discipline is one of the most important aspects of trading, and you will need to stick to this maximum loss factor which you yourself have defined.

Note that following a loss of $500, your trading account balance will be $24,500, so that now 2% of that new balance will be $490. If you adopt the 2% factor, you will always be able to calculate in advance the amount of money left in your account after a losing trade, however many sequential trades may end up as losses:

- Following 10 successive losses, there will be $20,486 left in your account
- 100 successive losses will leave just $3,315 in your trading account

The probability of losing 100 times in succession is extremely low, but nonetheless you need to be aware of your red line at all times from the angle of maximum loss as well as the single-trade loss figure.

Technical Risk

Correct entry and exit points must be determined, first and foremost, according to the stock chart's technical behavior. The exit point must be planned in advance and cannot be set according to a figure you are willing to lose, but rather based on volatility and the unique technical behavior of each of the stocks in which you are trading. As we have already learned, when you buy a stock, you must set your exit (stop) in advance. For example, let us say that your entry point is at $30 and your stop is planned for $29. If you buy 100 shares at $30 and the price drops by one dollar to $29, you have taken a loss of $100. But if the maximum loss you are willing to absorb is no more than $50, then you must limit yourself to buying only 50 shares and not allow yourself to buy 100 and "self-compensate" by setting a stop at $29.50, which was not the correct technical stop in the first place.

In addition to the calculation you have set in advance, you also need to understand that your actual exit point might be further than the planned exit. For example, if the price dropped to $29 but has not yet executed a five-minute reversal, you may have to absorb a greater loss than planned. Therefore, you need to take into account in advance an additional margin of error that allows you to operate correctly at the technical level and wait for the reversal, while still preserving your planned reasonable-loss framework.

Exposure-derived Risk

Part of the risk of trading in stocks derives from dependence on unknown factors. These include political news, financial and market announcements, company bulletins on the stocks you have bought, sector information, analyst recommendations, and any other rumors that may affect price. Since no one can anticipate the timing, content, or impact of any news, the best way to reduce risks is to reduce market exposure time. The less exposed you are, the more you reduce risk.

SMART MONEY | *The more you reduce exposure to the market, the more you reduce your risks.*

Since day traders operate with large quantities, they exit most of their transactions during the trading day. Holding stocks means taking risks. Swing traders buy smaller quantities and are therefore willing to take the risk, which can last several days until they close part of the transaction. But even swing traders will try to sell 75% of their quantity as early as possible to reduce the risk of exposure to market mood shifts. Medium and long-term investors who hold stocks for weeks, months, and years are even more exposed. Conclusion: the more you reduce exposure, the more you are reducing risks, allowing you to increase your trading quantity.

The "Stop Loss" Protective Order

This order does exactly what its name says: it limits losses. After entering a stock, I place a stop loss order into my trading platform and define the precise price at which I want to exit should its direction move against me. In some trading platforms, such as COLMEX Expert, the stop loss can be entered even before purchasing the stock. In this way, it is only activated when the stock is actually bought.

Generally, I do not trade for more than two successive hours per day, but I do hold some of those stocks while I am taking a break. This is when I use stop orders for positions that are still open.

Usually, when I am actively trading and following my screens, I don't tend to place automatic stop orders. I use what traders call the **mental stop**: in other words, I will exit the stock with a click of the mouse if it reaches my pre-set stop point. This will be described more fully later on. When I am holding more stocks than I am able to handle easily, I am careful to always place a stop order. As with most trading platforms, the stop orders I place are kept in the broker's computer, so that if for any reason my computer crashes midway through trading, or the Internet connection falters in any way, there is no need for concern: the stop orders will be executed as set.

Not All Stop Orders are Stop-loss Orders

First let's talk terminology. It is important to understand the difference between stop orders of various kinds, such as stop limit, stop market, and so on (see section on "trading orders") and the stop loss order.

- Stop limit, stop market and others are defined trading orders found in every decent trading platform.
- **Stop loss is not a defined order.** You will not find the words "stop loss" in any professional trading platform. Its meaning is simple: "cut my losses." With this order, you define the exit price if a stock you

bought starts to fall.

- In contrast to the word "stop" in stop loss, "stop" in stop limit, stop market, etc. means "put on hold." Thus, a stop limit means "wait until you can execute a limit order at the set price."
- Not all stop loss orders are orders meant to reduce losses. In many cases, it is simply a higher exit point for a stock that is rising. For example: you bought at $30 per share, and placed a stop loss into the system for $29.70. This indeed is a stop loss. But if the price had risen to $31 and your stop loss was set at $30.70, clearly you have not absorbed any loss, in which case the most appropriate term is simply what traders call a **stop**.

How to Set the Stop Point

The loss exit point should already be set at the trade planning stage, but as we will understand soon, we cannot always know in advance exactly where the exit will be. In any case, even if we cannot pinpoint the actual exit with certainty, we can plan it in advance. We do this for two reasons: it is correct professionally, and it is good psychologically.

- Professionally: Before each trade you need to check the risk/reward ratio. How can you figure the risk if you do not know where the stop is? Traders who do not set their stop point before entering the trade are operating very unprofessionally. A pro first calculates the risk, not the reward.
- Psychologically: Can you set a reliable stop after entering the stock? No. Once you've bought, you are no longer the same clear-thinking person.Greed taunts you, and fear of loss plays with your emotions, infringing on the ability to stay rational, and possibly causing you to realize profits too early or cut losses too late.

Some traders will set their stop before entering the trade, but then the demon gets to work: as the price approaches their stop, they cancel it and set a new one further off. What do they do as the price approaches their new stop? Correct, they reset it. The greater the loss, the harder it is for them to admit losing. Exiting at loss is a painful event. The human body has a psychological trait of protecting against pain. Is exiting the stock painful? Then let's not hit the button. When they need to choose between the hope that the stock will turn about and begin showing profits versus the pain of loss, they choose hope. As the scope of the loss increases, they turn from short-term traders to long-term investors. They ask themselves, "Why did this happen?" and then begin searching for reasons to explain the dramatic change in the stock's direction. They deny the truth and seek to justify the situation in which they are caught with any excuse possible: "The company has good products," or "It's got top management," and so on.

In my view, the stop can move only in one direction, and that is NOT towards increasing a loss. As explained in the section dealing with trade management, after realizing the first profit, the stop can be moved as close as possible to the entry point or above it, in order to prevent a profitable trade from becoming a failed one.

Repeat this in your mind until it becomes embedded: **We never give money back to the market.** This is one of the stock trader's most basic rules, although for most, it will take a great deal of time to learn and understand it.

The Importance of the Stop

Over time, I learned that the main error enacted by failed traders was the difficulty in cutting losses on time. Your main resource is the capital you deposited in your account. If you do not do everything possible to preserve it, you are doomed to a complete wipeout. "Everything possible" means ensuring losses are as minimal as possible. Always.Without any allowances or excuses. Without "just this once," and without, "I'm just testing..." Without "I trust myself, I know what I'm doing," or "I'm prepared to pay the market for my education." Small losses. First and foremost, play correctly from the defensive position. Always.

SMART MONEY	*A better trader is not necessarily one who chooses the right stocks, but one who knows how to cut losses faster than everyone else.*

Loss is an inseparable part of stock trading. In fact, many professional traders lose on about half the trades they execute. The significant difference between a failed trader and a pro is the ability to cut losses on time, but not exit a stock too quickly when it is moving in the right direction. When professional traders lose, they immediately admit their error, cut their losses and move onto the next trade. They do not comfort themselves with excuses or justify their loss with statements such as, "but the stock shows good earnings," or "the market is trending up, so the stock will no doubt reverse." All these actions start with loss and end with lamentations.

Time-based Stop

It may happen that you entered a stock and it has gotten stuck. It makes no difference if that occurs when you have made a small profit or loss. It is just not conducting itself in the way that you had anticipated.

First, you need to understand that there is a good reason the stock has stopped moving. Generally, you will not know the reason, but it is probable that something is happening. For example, when you buy an up-trending stock and it gets stonewalled by sellers, it is reasonable to assume that the buyers will soon despair and start looking for the exit door. You, like others, have noticed the perfect technical formation and bought, hoping for success, but it is best that you are among the first to exit.

How much time should pass between your entry and your exit? The answer depends on each trader's personal experience, but if you want a guideline I would say that if it has not "provided the goods" within ten minutes, then something not good is going on. When a stock stops moving, I exit! When stocks are not moving fast, they usually will not move at all.

I realize that sounds very simple: "Not moving, so exit." In reality, it is not simple at all. Our brains resist clicking the button. We believe we have made a good choice, and we are afraid that in the end it will be a success but without us if we exit. Yes, this is a tough psychological decision, but you need to persevere and click the button. If you stay with the stock, chances are high that first it will "visit" your stop point and then it will either succeed or fail. Remember that you entered the stock because you believed that it needs to move fast in the planned direction. If that did not happen, you have made a mistake. Now you are in casino territory. You leave nothing to luck. Take your money, even if you are in loss, or no more than a small profit, and invest it in a more successful stock. Keep in mind that discipline is the name of the game.

The Five-Minute Reversal Stop

This is the correct technical stop, but it is not necessarily the correct stop for every trade. This is the stop that requires the toughest nerves of steel, which are not usually in the arsenal of novice traders. When I enter a stock, I never know if I have chosen the precise entry point. I enter a strong stock trending up at a correct technical point or execute a short in a weak stock, but the stock or the market may not "agree" with my entry choice.

Example of Shorting in Moody's Corporation, MCO

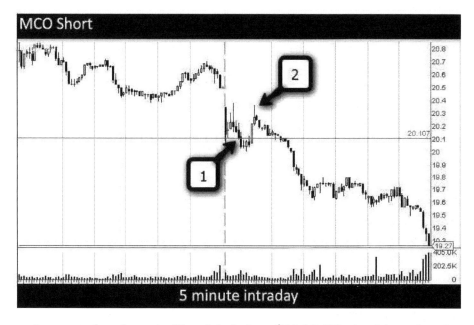

I executed a short in Moody's below $20.10 [1]. At this point, the stock was looking good for further lows. It started with a gap down of 2% and the path seemed paved all the way. The market also started with a gap down. Of course I was concerned about the gap closing (i.e. the market trending up), but the market had been weak for several days and I estimated that chances were good it would continue to drop. I was wrong. The stock dropped to $20, encountered round number support (which we have already discussed) and the market then moved against me. In other words, it trended up towards closing the gap. In just a few seconds, Moody's changed direction with the market, and rose to $20.37 [2]. Ouch!

What does one do in such cases? Where is the stop? As we have learned, a stop loss should have been determined at the outset, whether it is actually placed into the trading platform or kept in mind. When you expect a stock to break and crash quickly and powerfully, but in fact it moves ten cents against you, understand that something not good is happening. In such cases, the stop loss should get you out of the position at between ten to fifteen cents from the entry point.

Two scenarios now become possible. One is that you exited at the correct stop and this is precisely what should have happened. The other is that for various reasons you did not exit on time, and now, in contrast to your plan, you are absorbing a larger loss than anticipated. If you got swept up with the stock into territory where you should not be finding yourself in the first place, you need to handle it using the **five-minute reversal rule.** Unfortunately for me, this was my situation with Moody's. The stock literally shot up and I did not manage to exit at the planned stop.

While the stock was moving up, I had no clue where it might stop. It could have gone another dollar higher without looking back. I was short 3000 shares, with a loss of more than $800, so that every ten cents the share price rose increased my loss by $300.

What would you have done, fled or held on? Once upon a time, as a new trader, I would have run like a frightened rabbit, absorbing the loss, and been sorry afterwards when the stock pulled back. Not anymore. Now I simply realize that the stock "did nothing bad." There was no argument about the fact that the stock was weak. The chances are strong that it would reverse into lows, but during the process of falling, it might also trend up briefly even if I am in a short, or even if I am losing my pants. All I need to do is wait until commonsense and the weak stock's downtrend take over again. In most cases where a weak stock moves up with the market, as in this case, it stops and then reverses back down--which is what happened, happily for me, after the reversal [2]. What might have happened had it not reversed? I would have lost a good deal more, but that too would have been okay. I have no problem with losses as long as I know I am operating correctly, and then I do not get angry with myself. To start with, you should not reach this level of loss, but if it does happen to you, manage the situation correctly from the technical aspect. In this case, the correct technical management requires placing a stop above the reversal point [2] and hoping for success.

Quantity Test: Think about what you would do in my place, if you had bought 3000 shares. Would you exit, or wait for the reversal? Would you do the same if you had bought 1000 shares? 200? Only 50? If your answer relative to a quantity of 50 shares, which creates a $13.5 loss at the pullback peak, is different than your answer for 200 shares, then your problem is not the method but the quantity of shares you are trading in. **Conclusion**: reduce your size. The day will come when together with your cumulative knowledge, experience and confidence, you will start increasing size.

Moody's executed a reversal in five-minute candles [2], returning to a downtrend, and closed the day with a drop of 6%. A trade that started well continued in the possible-error zone but eventually ended brilliantly. The five-minute reversal principle states very simply that if you get caught in an awkward situation,wait for a change in direction in five-minute candles before you set your stop beyond the reversal point. In this case, that stop was above $20.37, but only after a clear reversal was identified by being comprised of at least three candles.

The stock was weak. It started low and continued dropping. The only reason that the price temporarily moved against me was the unfortunate fact that the market was moving in the direction of closing the gap and dragged Moody's, among others, along with it. Remember that Moody's had been weak at the open, and stayed weak until the close. It started with lows and therefore chances were good it would continue down. Generally speaking, a stock showing relative weakness compared to the market will continue down, even if the market trends up.

Market Behavior at those Particular Points: Five-Minute Candles for Two Days

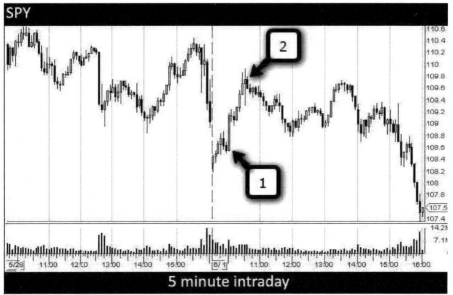

5 minute intraday

On the market's ETF (SPY), it is clear that [1] was the turning point for upward movement, which matches [1] on Moody's chart, the point at which it dropped and stopped at the round number. At [1] Moody's "wants to continue down," but gives in to the changed market direction and trends up. When the market executes a reversal [2], the same reversal point [2] shows on Moody's chart, where Moody's capitulates and returns to lows.

Summarizing, if I had not kept the five-minute reversal rule in mind, I would have panicked from the uptrend, exited with losses higher than planned, and missed out on the later lows. The five-minute reversal was my protection. It gave the stock time to cool off from the market's movement up, and allowed bears to keep in mind that it is basically a weak stock. The five-minute reversal rule let me realize the trade with a nice profit.

Extreme Situation: On rare occasions, the five-minute reversal will nonetheless cost you a searing loss. A stock might move very far against you before executing the hoped-for reversal. These are also the rare cases where, despite the pain, it is worth temporarily absorbing what appears to be a loss, since generally the stock will return to its initial trend and justify your confidence in its overall movement.

Under what conditions should you flee if the stock keeps moving against you? This is where you need to be level-headed. Sometimes, it becomes very clear that "something bad is happening there" even if the stock has executed a five-minute reversal. For example, if the stock goes higher than its intraday high [2], then that is a good reason to exit fast with a loss even if it did not yet make the five- minute reversal. This is the only point at which you might suspect a reasonable chance that the stock has changed its trend. Should you be angry with yourself over this misjudged trade? Absolutely not: you shorted a weak stock, you waited for the reversal which almost always brings the stock back to lows, and you operated in strict accordance to "the rule book."

In Moody's case, we concluded that going higher than the intraday high was the furthest level of tolerance. With other stocks, you may not always be able to identify the alternative exit points. What might happen if a stock moved against you without executing the five-minute reversal, and without your identifying a different, logical exit point at a reasonable distance? This is an extremely rare, but possible, situation. Sometimes you might find you have traded in a stock that intraday news has caused to spike against you, and the price may not pull back, causing a shocking loss. I remember this happening to me some two years ago, ruining profits I had accrued over an entire week. Even if you do encounter this very rare eventuality once every few years, you should still respect the five-minute reversal rule, since in the great majority of cases, statistics will be on your side.

What can happen, nonetheless, if the stock goes seriously against you? Imagine a situation in which Moody's would have risen to $20.70, and only there starts pulling back. It is probable to assume that from this high, it would not go back to lows. In such a case, you need to start thinking about an exit with as little damage as possible. The solution is to wait for a pullback just below the peak. I would set a buy order (in order to exit the short) at $20.40, hoping that a pullback from a $20.70 peak would reach $20.40 and allow me to exit with a more absorbable loss. This is a LIMIT order and will execute only if the stock price drops to my limit. On the other hand, I would also set a stop above $20.70 in case the price does not drop, and exit with a larger loss than planned. True, this is not a pleasant situation to be in, but by comparison to so many other successful trades providing good profits, a situation like this definitely conforms to the statistics.

Hard Stop or Mental Stop

- A **hard stop** is an order placed into the trading platform. If and when the stock price reaches the pre-set stop, the broker will execute the order automatically.
- A **mental stop** is one we decide on in our minds, but do not feed into the trading platform and therefore will not be executed automatically. We will execute it manually if and when the stock reaches the point which we have defined for ourselves.

Each of these stops holds advantages and disadvantages, and we will later learn how and when to use them.

SMART MONEY	*A hard stop can be serious trouble! Avoid it as much as possible and opt for the mental stop. Using it can save you no small number of unnecessary losses.*

What is best: setting a hard stop, or exiting the stock manually when it reaches the point we have chosen as our stop? The answer will differ from one trader to the next, and also depends on a trader's experience. For new traders, I recommend placing an automatic (hard) stop. It helps you cope more correctly with fear and will likely improve your achievements. For more advanced traders, I strongly recommend not using the hard stop and using the mental stop instead. The reason is chiefly technical and derives from the unpredictability of intraday volatility. With a hard stop, you may encounter a situation where a large-quantity seller might cause the price to momentarily plunge, showing a sharp, fast red candle, and shake you out at your stop. Then, the price might return within seconds to its original level. You do not want to be shaken out under this kind of volatility. In most cases, the price will return to its high and you will feel like the perfect idiot for having exited.

When is It Worth Placing a Hard Stop?

- When I am concurrently holding several (usually more than three) stocks and it becomes difficult to track each of them
- When my stop point is very far from the current price and I am not afraid that unexpected spikes might shake me out
- When I leave my desk for more than a few minutes

Different strokes for different folks: some traders are unwilling to lose more than a specific amount of money per trade, irrespective of the stock's technical formation, and will always place a hard stop in the trading platform. Sometimes it will be a timely rescue from loss, and at other times the traders will be shaken out sharply and suddenly without enjoying the highs that follow, since they have not given the price a reasonable breathing space. This is not my modus operandi during trading, but that does not mean using hard stops is an incorrect method. Both options have their good and bad points. Either method is correct if it contributes profitability over the long term and suits the trader's personality. Hard stops may be excellent for the novice trader, since they ease the psychological coping with market fluctuation, but may be harmful to the experienced trader who is less likely to react to sudden market movements.

Summarizing: The hard stop is usually worth avoiding. Use it only when you have no other choice. The mental stop, despite its disadvantages for the inexperienced, is the correct one to use. As you develop your trader skills and your self-discipline, try to become accustomed to it.

Risk Reward Ratio

Before trade opens, you have scanned the stocks in your follow-up list and chosen those that interest you as trades. Some are marked "to buy," but your buying power is limited, and by nature you will want to lessen financial risks as much as possible. How will you choose what to buy? Among the various parameters that must be checked is the **Risk Reward ratio.**

It is known simply as the **RR**.

- **Risk** refers to the sum of money you are willing to lose in a trade from the entry point to the predetermined stop point.
- **Reward** relates to the sum of money you wish to gain from the trade, from the entry point to the predetermined exit point.

In reality we calculate the risk to reward ratio in **points**. A typical sentence may sound like: "It looks to me like the stop is half a point and the target is one point." In other words, I am taking the risk that the price will move against me by half a dollar, in the hope that I will profit by one dollar.

If you ask professional traders, they will usually say that they expect an ideal RR of 1:3, but in practical terms, they are willing to accept a 1:2 ratio, and sometimes, even lower than that. What they mean is that during the process of choosing a stock, they will be looking for one that may jump by $3, but has a planned exit point (their stop) of only $1.

To determine the RR, traders will analyze the stock's daily chart and its intraday chart, watching for the closest support and resistance points and the intraday volatility.

Why would we look for a 1:3 or even a 1:2 RR? What is wrong with 1:1? Our goal, of course, is to earn money with as little risk as possible. Let us say you are experiencing a bad luck streak in a tough market, and you successfully beat the market in only half your trades. If you profit in only half the trades you execute, and are additionally paying commissions, you will be doomed. By contrast, if you succeed to maintain a 1:2 ratio, so that for every trade where you lose $1 you earn $2 in another trade, you will maintain a positive balance. In this way, even if you choose the right stocks in only half the instances, your status remains stable. Obviously, choosing stocks with a good RR means you need to accumulate no small amount of battle experience.

Calculating the Risk to Reward Ratio in Aon PLC, AON

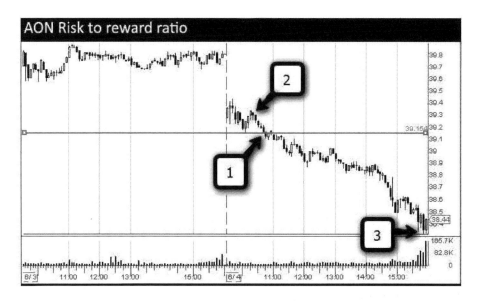

Aon gapped down at the open, then continued dropping, found support at $39.15, rose to $39.34 [2], executed a reversal to lows and broke support [1]. This was also the point where I entered a short. But before entering, I calculated the risk/reward ratio as follows:

- First, where is the stop? That's easy: it is without any doubt above the reversal point [2]; in other words, 20 cents above the line of support, the short entry. But this is just half the answer.
- To complete the calculation, I need to estimate where the target is. Glancing at the chart, we can see the outcome in retrospect. Aon dropped to $38.32 [3], which is 82 cents below my entry point. We can see that the RR was 1:4, in other words, I risked 20 cents and I could have profited 82 cents.

Of course there are none so wise as those with hindsight, but clearly I did choose a correct stock with an excellent RR. Could I have known where the target was, and what risk/reward ratio could be expected in the final outcome? To determine the answer, I need to examine the stock's intraday volatility over the last few days of trading: no better tool

for that than the daily chart.
Aon Daily Chart, AON

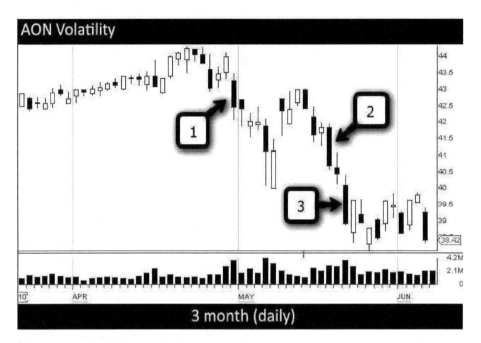

If we examine the stock over several days and concentrate on the black (down) candles by checking the height of the candle from end to end including tails, we see that the intraday trading range in Aon at the marked points [1,2,3] is around $1.50 between the highest and lowest prices. If you really want to, you can translate the outcomes from points to percentages: the daily volatility is some 3%. Looking at the last few trading days, I can see that Aon had some less volatile days, and I can therefore carefully estimate with reasonable expectation an intraday fluctuation of $1.

Now I return to the intraday chart and see that Aon's high is $39.44, which is a difference of some 30 cents between the intraday high and the planned entry point [1]. Conclusion: based on a check of past volatility, we can reasonably assume that Aon is able to move another 70 cents or so below the breakdown price. Since the risk is 20 cents and the profit target is 70 cents, the risk to reward ratio is 1:3.5. Very decent! In actuality, as you have seen, the stock moved 82 cents, a little more than the expected figure. I executed a careful short of 1000 shares, added another 1000 at the start of the fall, and locked in several pieces of profit on the way down. In short, I risked $300 but profited $752.05.

| **SMART MONEY** | *Planning the trade is usually the easy task. Sticking to the plan is where, psychologically, things get much harder! To stay with the plan, we need to maintain the rules for correct money management.* |

This is how the result looked in my trading account:

Symbol	Currency	Open Pos	Tickets	Buy Qty	Sell Qty
AON	USD	0	7	2,000	2,000

Blotter EXCEL

A word of warning: even though a high risk to reward ratio seems better, from my experience it tends to make successful trades more difficult. By contrast, a reasonable 1:2 ratio is usually more accessible. Additionally, despite the 1:2 ratio sounding much better than a 1:1, note that if you succeed in only one of every three trades, you will be losing money. However, if you go for a 1:1 ratio but succeed in two out of every three trades, you will be profiting. The only way to choose the ratio that suits you best is through experience. Over a long term, follow your results, examine the ratios and see which trading method suits you.

Money Management

You have chosen a stock correctly, and bought or shorted it at the correct point. What happens next? **Correct money management** is the difference between the professional trader who earns a living from trading, and the amateur who provides the pros with their earnings! Many new traders place too much weight on technical and financial aspects and view money management as extraneous, although it is an imperative tool.

Ask yourselves what you would do when a stock you bought at the correct point breaks out and trends up strongly. Amateurs will look at the stock's chart, rub their hand with glee, admit their good fortune, and perhaps even increase the amount. What does the pro do following a breakout? Certainly not shout out, "I've got a winner!" The pro shouts out, "Who's the sucker I can now push this stock onto?"

If you have ever bought stocks, try to remember and reconstruct the trades you executed in recent years. Let me describe the process. I am familiar with the stocks you bought and your methods of managing them. Is this what you did? You usually bought at the right time. I will also give you credit and say that shortly after buying, you almost always were in the money and were even quite pleased with your decision to buy: am I correct? The only problem was that you held on to them for a fraction too long, enough for the whole episode to end in a loss.

Correct money management allows you to profit even if your success rates are below 50%. One day recently, as I was writing this book, I closed a day's trading in profits even though I lost over eight trades and gained in just three. Correct money management lets me exit a failed trade with a small loss, and milk a successful trade to the maximum.

- **Rule 1: Lock In Profits**
  In trading jargon, a **partial** means realizing a partial profit. Once the stock has broken out, immediately when its first weak point shows, you need to sell at least 75% of the shares you bought at the breakout. This is called **selling into the power**. Then, continue trading with the remaining quarter amount alone. The smart thing, of course, is to identify the first weak point, but not to flee too early. One rule of thumb says that you

must try to ensure that the distance between the entry point and the first profit target is not shorter than the distance between the entry point and the stop. In other words, you must try to attain at least a 1:1 ratio for the quantity you sell.

When I worked as an entrepreneur in the world of hi-tech, I devoted a good deal of my time to recruiting investments for the company I established and managed. One of the most important facts I learned is that "money needs to be recruited when it is available and not when it becomes needed." In day trading, as in hi-tech, we need to sell when buyers' craving is at peak, and not at its decline. True, sometimes you might see a stock continue moving up and will regret selling too early, but generally the first target point will be the only profit you will see from the stock. Remember that after a strong upward movement, some traders will realize profits, others will short based on the assumption that the stock will pull back, and yet others are experts at shaking out. The function of this last group is to shake out weak buyers and force them to sell by causing the stock to drop below the entry point. I will generally sell 3/4 of the quantity I bought after a rise of some tens of cents. In cases where the stock rises quickly beyond my first target, I will wait for its first sign of weakness and then execute a partial.

A common mistake by new traders is to trade in quantities that are too small. If, for example, you bought 200 shares and your partial point is at 20 cents profit, how much will you sell? Since, as we have learned, you are supposed to sell round figures of hundreds, you have little choice but to sell 100 shares. This means that you will make just $20. For a stock successfully breaking out, this is not enough, since the other half of your quantity still puts you at risk. However, selling 300 shares from a total quantity of 400, or 800 of 1000, already promises you good profits at the partial point. Starting with a good profit early in the trade allows you to put doubts and tensions aside and continue trading in the technically correct way without having to suppress emotional reactions. I must say that I have not changed my earlier recommendation to accrue initial experience with small quantities of less than 400 shares per trade, but several weeks into trading, the quantities you trade in must start increasing.

SMART MONEY | *Novice traders, unlike experienced pros, tend to exit a successful stock too early, and a failing stock too late.*

As noted, you must take a partial at the first pullback beyond your first target. How will you know this is the correct partial point? At first you won't know: that comes with the "art of trading" as you gain experience and insight. Generally, I would say that a partial for a share priced between $20 to $60 should be between 20 to 40 cents from the breakout price. The problem with a generalization of this kind is that sometimes the price will break out without looking back for up to one dollar from the breakout point, so that realizing 20 cents is far less than the potential profit. To identify the correct partial point, you need to "feel" the stock, understand it and have tens if not hundreds of attempts at figuring that point until you come to understand naturally where to take the partial piece. Sometimes, the difference between the successful and the unsuccessful trader shows precisely at the first partial. New traders, unlike the experienced hands, exit too quickly from a stock running up and too slowly from a failing stock.

- **Rule 2: Buy More**

Has the price broken out, have you realized your initial profit, and is the stock proving to be strong? **Buy more!** Always give preference to a stock with which you have already booked gains over another that is about to break out but with which you have no experience, good or bad. No one can tell if that new breakout will succeed, and never will, but the one you are currently trading in has already proved itself. It has broken out, you have taken a reasonable partial, and now you are ready to join it for round two.

SMART MONEY	*Show faith in a strong stock: wait for the pullback and buy more. Buy it even if you do not see a perfect technical reversal.*

How and when should you buy more? Once you have taken the partial of 3/4 of the quantity you are holding, set a limit order at a lower price but which is just slightly above the original buy price, and wait for the pullback. For example: you bought 1000 shares at $29 and took a partial with 800 shares at $29.25. Set a buy order for 400 more at $29.05, using the limit order which waits in the BID column and will execute only if the stock reverses. In many cases, you will find that in a short time, the stock will execute a **retest** (described in earlier chapters) close to the initial breakout point.

Why is it necessary to enter a limit order rather than simply wait for the stock to pull back, and then click the button if and when it starts to trend up again? The answer is simple: when a stock retests, it usually drops, then shows rapid upward movement. Usually, you simply will not have a chance to wait for the clear technical reversal in five-minute candles, nor even in two-minute candles. The correct way to buy more and increase quantities at the retest point is to set a limit at a low price. The limit waits for the price to drop and will execute only when the preset conditions are fulfilled.

What is the correct price for adding shares? That depends on the breakout point. For example: if I took a partial of 20 cents per share for a stock that rose by 25 cents, I would be happy if the stock pulled back to just five cents above the breakout. If I took a partial of 50 cents out of a high of 60 cents, I would be happy to buy more even at 15 cents above breakout. In other words, I am willing buy more if the price pulls back by 70% to 80% of its post-breakout movement.

As with the partial point, the point at which we buy more is also part of the "art of trading." Until you reach that level of capability, think in these terms: "After realizing a profit of x cents per share, what is the highest price at which I am willing to buy this stock again?" This is a simple business management question which has nothing to do with stock trading.

- You sold "merchandise" for profit at a certain price. You are sorry you did not have a greater quantity of that same merchandise at the original price, and now someone is offering you the chance of buying at slightly above your original purchase price.
- You already know that this is good merchandise since the stock broke out and you booked a profit, and you believe that you are able to sell more of this merchandise at a profit. You see that the price is now a little higher, and do not wish to take too much risk by buying the same amount that you bought the first time around.
- How much should you be willing to pay? How much should you be willing to buy? Answer this question for yourself, and that is where you will place your buy limit order for the additional quantity you wish to buy.
- The quantity I buy at the retest will never endanger my profits from

the original partial. In other words, the maximum quantity I will buy is about half of the quantity I already locked in with the partial.

Here's how it works: I bought 1000 shares at the breakout, took a partial by selling 800 shares, and was left with 200. Now I buy another 400 at the retest, 400 being half the quantity of my partial. The total quantity I now hold is 600 shares.

Q: Do all stocks execute retests?

A: Of course not. Sometimes you may find that you've taken a partial and the price keeps moving up without returning to its breakout point. This is a happy occasion where the small quantity leftover after the partial will bring you greater income than the partial. Enjoy it!

Q: What happens if I bought more at the retest, but the price keeps dropping?

A: No one can guarantee that you bought at the right point. Statistically, stocks that begin with a trend up will continue to follow through unless the market changes direction. Wait patiently for a five-minute reversal, since it is reasonable to assume that the price will continue trending up. Since you have already locked in a partial profit, you are currently holding a smaller quantity of shares even though you have bought more. You can let the price drop slightly without ending up with a loss. Stay calm and relaxed. In eight out of ten instances, the price will begin to trend up again. You should be able to easily allow yourself to absorb two out of ten unsuccessful moves.

Q: How long should you wait for the retest with an open order?

A: Usually no more than five minutes. A quick retest may occur after several seconds, a slower one might take a few minutes. With a slow retest, wait with your finger on the mouse and execute your second purchase with the click of the button. With a slow retest which is taking more than five minutes, you will need to wait for a clear reversal, since the price may then drop even lower than the retest point. If the retest executes over more than a half hour, be very careful: it could be that the stock has decided to change direction.

- **Rule 3: Realize Profits Again!**
  Did you buy more at the retest? Let the price move up and look for another partial, which will generally be slightly below the previous peak's line of resistance. At this second partial point, you should sell half

of the quantity of shares you are now holding. The goal is to "put behind" you the risk that buying more shares brings with it as the price moves above its previous peak.

For example: you bought 1000 shares at $30.01, taking a first partial with 800 shares at $30.35. The stock retests and you buy 400 more shares, which is half the amount sold at the partial, for $30.05. Now you have 600 shares. The price goes back up and you take a second partial at $30.30 with 300 shares. You are now left with 300. Result: you have taken two partials and still hold a larger quantity than after the first partial. You use these shares to try to capture a bigger gain without any real risk.

Why is the second partial taken below the first peak? Sometimes, when a stock is strong, you may succeed in selling above the peak, but the fear is that the price will encounter resistance at the same level as the previous peak and then reverse. Taking a partial before the new peak will reduce your risk. Occasionally, when the stock is particularly strong, I keep my finger on the mouse and try to let it reach a higher high before taking the second partial. These are usually the "big winners" for that day's trading.

Over time you will learn which stocks are strong enough to let you buy more a third time, but generally the more a price trends up, the weaker its new breakouts will be. Buying additional amounts gets trickier, therefore the target for a third buy needs to be closer and the quantity smaller.

The opposite of a breakout is a breakdown. For breakdowns, the rules are identical, as we will see in the example below.

Short and Retest Adder with Illumina Inc., ILMN

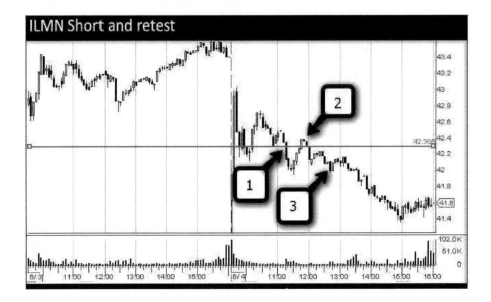

I shorted Illumina below $42.30 [1] for 1000 shares, and took a partial with 800 when the price dropped towards the round number support level of $42. I was left with 200 shares. Next, the price rose and executed a retest several cents above the entry point [2]. Imagine how you would have felt had you not taken a partial! Around the retest area [2], I increased my short position by 400 shares so that I was now short 600 shares. The price dropped and I took a second partial with 300 of those shares [3] just above the round number support line. I have now taken two partials and am holding 300 shares in short. The price continues to trend down, to 90 cents below the entry point. The psychological calm I was afforded by taking the first two partials gave me the focus needed to realize a full profit for these remaining 300 shares.

- **Rule 4: NEVER GIVE YOUR MONEY BACK TO THE MARKET!**
  Let us say you have taken a second partial with a stock in an uptrend. The price is sufficiently far from the entry point and you are left with a small quantity of shares which, with a bit of luck, may give you even greater profit than the two partials. Now you need to **raise your stop** to the entry price or slightly higher. In other words, don't lose on the

quantity you have left.

Remember the rule we have repeated: never return your money to the market! At the most, forego the profit and let the price slide back to the entry point.

This is a **golden rule** that every trading newbie must constantly keep in mind. If you are operating correctly, your entry point should also be the point at which the original line of resistance breaks, and as we know, a broken-out line of resistance now becomes a line of support.

When you raise your stop to the line of support, which is also the entry point, you simply cannot lose. In fact, you are trading with the market's money and removing all risk from the quantity you are still holding.

- **Rule 5: How to Manage the Balance**

At this stage, when you are holding only a small percentage of the original quantity of shares, you need to decide how to manage it. **First, check what the market is doing:** is it supporting the direction of your trade? Even a very strong stock can capitulate to a market that has changed direction. If you feel there are clear signs of a market directional change, move your stop closer. How is the stock behaving? Is it holding its trend? Is its sector showing and holding a matching trend? Now you need to decide if you are going to "sleep on the stock" or make do with the profit you have already made. Generally you need to take this decision during the final minutes of the day's trading, since that is when sought-after stocks tend to take off!

Sell all the quantity you are still holding towards the end of the day's trading or earlier, if the stock or the market has changed direction. By contrast, if the particular stock ends the day with a clear uptrend and is sufficiently far from your entry price, consider whether it is worth holding the entire remaining quantity or perhaps reducing it further.

Why would you want to reduce that quantity a little more? To avoid too great a risk. It is really dangerous to "go to sleep" with stock in hand, since you can never know the reality you will wake up to in the morning. I have already seen situations in which a stock shot up one morning and plummeted the next. Leaving yourself a small quantity, based on the fact that you have sufficiently profited from all the stock you have sold so far, greatly reduces risks. I tend to decrease quantities as a matter of course. If you have chosen to "sleep on" the stock, known in trader jargon as

Swing Trading, you will need to continue managing it correctly in the coming days. More on that later.

| **SMART MONEY** | *When you are in a multi-day **swing** trade, you need to disconnect from intraday trading rules. Your decisions must be based on the daily charts alone, and not on intraday volatility. This is a worthwhile guideline that pays off!* |

- **Rule 6: Raise Your Stop**

Are you staying for a swing? Excellent. The profit potential in a swing is higher, and you need to aim for a swing with a strong stock. Often, you will rake in more on the balance of your remaining stock than you did on the intraday trades. Now you need to understand that you are in multi-day territory, which is completely different from intraday conduct. You need to relate to the stock's volatility from now on only in terms of its daily chart.

Has the price changed direction? **Within** the trading day, that is no longer interesting information. But at the daily level, yes, it **is** interesting. Do not get angry over the price movement even if its trend changed at the intraday level, or the next day, or even if it opens on the next day with a gap down which wipes out half the profits you made the previous day. On the contrary: if it drops below your entry point, or below yesterday's low, that's another story.

Every day, raise your stop on the quantity left. Raise it to a point about 2 to 3 cents below the previous day's lowest price, on condition that the low is still higher than your entry point. In other words, you absolutely must not lose on the remaining quantity of shares you are holding if you can help it. On every additional day that passes, you need to raise your stop to the lowest point of the previous day. When that lowest point breaks, you will be out of the stock. The only risk is that the stock gaps down on news.

Swing with PAR

Do you remember PAR from the previous chapter?

Take note of the daily chart for several days after the entry [1] at $10. I left a small quantity of shares over for a swing. Three days after the original entry, the price had already reached $11 [2]. Notice that on the second day of trade the stock rested, not going down to the entry point, and not going up to any new high. This continued into the third day. As we have learned, in such situations, the stop order for the remaining quantity is a slightly lower than the previous day's low. On the third day, the price had not yet awoken, but to my joy nor did it drop below yesterday's low. The first three days formed the bull flag formation.

On the fourth day, the price broke out of the bull flag and provided a handsome yield for the rest of the swing. The stop can now be raised to the fourth day's low, and so on.

What are the chances of the trend continuing? High: but is there any risk? Of course there is. As I said above, the price can open with a gap down below the stop and wipe out all the profits accrued from the swing! Is the chance of continued uptrend greater than the probability of a drop? Absolutely. The stock is in an uptrend, and the smallest item of negative news can topple everything. But if you manage the situation in this way, out of 100 opportunities you will take home extra income

70% of the time. It not only pays, but it is correct to take strong stocks for the swing.

Notes: Every trader, every trading method, every market period, whether moving sideways or volatile, has a different money management mode. My trading method may not necessarily suit other traders, but every trader must develop a method that suits him or her. There is no single "correct" or "incorrect" method, but there does need to be a method of some kind. Traders who operate only on "gut instinct" rather than an organized method rarely see anything good come of their efforts in the long term. They are the people from whom I earn my living. You can, and should, use the rules in this book as your infrastructure for developing rules that suit your psychological and financial abilities. Occasionally you may also need to alter those rules to suit your own development or market conditions. In a market moving sideways, you should take a partial of less than 20 cents. In a strong market you should be able to take a partial of half the quantity and not three-quarters, and hold at least one-quarter over to the next day.

Some months ago, I experienced an extraordinary event. I lost for over three consecutive trading days! With my self-confidence now in the dirt, on the fourth day I was forced to change tactics. The solution best suited to me was to trade in much smaller quantities, with much closer partials. Some days later my successes once again became more regular, my self-confidence was boosted, and I resumed my original money management methods.

The 3x3 Method

I am aware of the fact that not all readers of this book can devote several hours each day, or even each week, to trading. If you do not have the ability to spend more than an hour or two per week in trading, buy stocks that from the outset you wish to hold for swing periods.

In other words, focus on stocks you want to hold for anything from several days to several weeks. Work with them according to the **3x3 method.** Even if you do have the time for daily trading, you need to understand that swings can contribute nicely to your profits, so there is no reason you cannot "spice up" your intraday trading with several stocks held for more than one day, or even bought in advance for this very purpose.

SMART MONEY | *The more you distance yourself from the computer, the better off you'll be. Use a set of automatic orders to manage your stock. This reduces the element of psycho-emotional involvement and stress.*

The 3x3 method of money management which I've developed and fine-tuned over the years is likely the simplest, important, and effective way I have of teaching you money management. It is so good that I'm prepared to vouch for it by saying:

If you keep its principles, you will find it very difficult to lose!

You can, and should, apply the method's principles using a set of automatic orders, especially if you are among those traders who are active daily. The method is valid for buyers and short sellers, but for the sake of convenience I will focus on long buys.

- Choose a stock according to the rules we have learned so far. After buying it, operate in the following manner:

1. Stop Point

Enter a stop order 3% below the entry point. Why 3%? When a stock you believed would trend up goes against you by 3%, it would seem you've made a mistake. You thought you bought at the right entry point, you thought it would break out strongly and put money in your pocket, and that's not what happened. Of course, with a little luck it will return to its uptrend, but usually you'll do better admitting the error, abandoning that stock and focusing on another stronger one. Should you ignore the support and resistance lines? No. If you identify a clear support line in a 2 to 4 percent range below the entry point, use it.

2. First Profit Target

You need to sell three-quarters of your quantity at a first profit target of 3%. Why three-quarters? Because of the demons! When you profit or lose, you need to cope with your deepest inner voices. Get to know the one perched on your right shoulder yelling into your right ear, "Remember the time you reached a profit of 3%, waited a bit too long and then the stock fell and you lost it all..." And then there's the demon that sits on your left shoulder, simultaneously yelling, "Remember the time when you profited 3%, locked in a gain, but if you'd only waited a bit longer, you'd have made a bigger profit..."

There's only one way to stave off these demons: sell three-quarters of the stock. This way, you appease both demons. "You on the right, saying the stock's about to fall: here's your three-quarters. Now leave me alone! And you on the left, telling me it will go up? Here's one-quarter and now go prove yourself!"

Only realizing a profit releases the stress. Once you've realized a yield, you'll be much calmer and will be able to manage the remaining 25% with almost no emotional involvement.

Why 3% rather than 5%, for example? Stock prices rise, but always pull back. The question is only one of when and how much. From my experience, the pullback generally occurs after a high of 3 to 4%. Why? Prices pull back once the public begins buying: the public never buys at the start of the uptrend. They only buy once the stock has "proven itself." Usually the public is persuaded that the stock has proven itself only after a 3-4% rise. At that point, why is the price not going up further? Because it is convenient for institutional traders to take advantage of the large quantity of buyers in order to unload large quantities of shares. Since the institutional traders comprise 80% of the money involved in all the stocks we trade in, when they sell, we can reasonably presume that the price will drop. In short: over the years, my records repeatedly show that **3% is the figure**.

3. **Rising Stop Order**

After selling three-quartersof the stock, you need to raise the stop order for the last quarter to the entry price. Since our law states "never return your money to the market," you want to be sure that the profits of that three-quarter quantity stayin your pocket. If the last quarter returns to the entry point, you've lost profit only on that quarter. But if you let the remaining quarter drop to below the entry point, then you'll be doling out money that you've earned to cover the loss, and that of course is against our rules!

4. **Second Target**

Lock in the remaining quarter at 6%, or manage it according to methods we have already learned. For example: raise the stop a little below the previous day's low each day that you remain in the trade.

Q & A

- **What should you do if you have bought stock, but it is moving sideways and deciding to go nowhere over several days?**

Sell it! Remember, when you bought it, you thought differently: that it would shoot up to your target. It didn't. What does that mean? Simple: you have made a bad choice. Admit it quickly, and sell. If the price has not chosen your direction, you are in a gambler's territory. Remember the rule: if the price does not reach its profit target by the end of the second week of trading from its purchase, sell three-quarters of the quantity, regardless of whether you have made a profit or loss. Continue managing the remaining quarter according to swing principles.

- **What should you do if the price approaches the target towards the end of the trading day?**

Give it some thought. Let us say the price has already reached 2.5%, but it is also clear to you that it will not reach the 3% target by the end of the day. Sell three-quarters before trading closes and reduce your risks of what the next day might bring.

- **Price gaps**

  When you are about to buy a stock for a swing at the start of the trading day and a gap shows of up to 1% above the trigger, you can still buy the stock. In this case, calculate your profit or loss point according to the **3x3** rule relative to the actual entry point. When a gap of more than 1% develops, cancel the buy order.

- **Earnings reports**

  Before publication of quarterly earnings reports, we will always sell our full quantity. As we learned in previous chapters, you need to carefully check which reports are expected and sell the day before anything major is to be released. It is common knowledge that the results of these reports are not known in advance, and the risk to the price is too great.

- **Time of purchase**

  I never enter a swing later than the middle of the week's last trading day. We are looking to buy stock with strong chances of reaching its target already within the first week of trading. If we buy stock at the end of the last day of the trading week, its chances of reaching the first target or even moving far from the entry point are far less. Going to sleep over the weekend with a full quantity of shares that still endanger my trading account is just not on my agenda.

- **Which Stocks are Suited to the 3x3 Method?**

  Most of the stocks we trade in, with a share price of between $10 to $80 and volume of over one million shares per day, suit 3x3 trading. Some do not. Before choosing a stock, you must check that you are not buying anything too volatile, or lacking volatility (such as MSFT and others that trade similarly). Volatile stocks will more naturally suit the **4x4** or even the **5x5** method.

Summary

The 3x3 method works well! Using automated buy and sell orders solves a good deal of the psycho-emotional aspects of money management, and therefore, coupled with good choices of stocks, should virtually guarantee success. If you have a limited time only for trading and cannot find suitable opportunities for active intraday trading, you can at least devote one hour each week to trading with this method.

The Tradenet investors club is very successful when it applies the 3x3 method. As these lines are being written, average monthly returns over the past six months have been 8.4%. Is there any good reason *not* to invest an hour each week in trading this way?

Noise Cancelling

With due respect to classic technical analysis, stocks do not need to behave "by the book." Most of the money in the market belongs to the long-term investors, to funds, and of course to a group of Warren Buffet-type folk. They do not always check the chart before they buy a stock. Did the stock breakdown in the perfect "head and shoulders" formation? Why on earth would that interest them!? They may be buying right when you sell, for entirely different reasons. Technical analysis does have its limitations. In fact, I can assure you that if you operate according to perfect technical rules, you will end up losing.

Technical analysis states that the uptrend is defined as a succession of higher highs and higher lows. Let's say you bought a stock currently trending up, and its price has now dropped to a new low. Would you sell it at precisely the point where it drops **under the last low**? Technically speaking, yes; but in reality, no.

It is most likely that everything you have experienced during the price's drop under the last low is nothing more than "noise". It could be that you are seeing the first signs of a direction change, but in many cases it is nothing more than a temporary pullback caused by someone selling thousands of shares without checking the chart. At the start of my trading career, I would set the stop order one cent under the last low. I would forget that the stock owes me nothing: neither behavior according to the technical analysis, nor according to the price I bought at. The reason it may drop several cents under the last low can be very simple: someone might have sold 1000 shares with a market order, which drops the price by several cents under the last low. Does every small change in price draw you out of the game? Sometimes, yes; generally, no.

Noise in stocks is also one of the reasons why I try to avoid, as far as possible, using hard stop orders. Stock prices constantly show spikes in either direction. To understand the stock's general direction, we need to relate to its overall framework of movement rather than chance price volatility, since the latter may cause you to imagine all kinds of unrealistic statuses. I am not saying that in such cases you should bury your heads in the sand. You do need to be cautious, and remain ready for a change of direction, while not fleeing or buying on the basis of any small price change.

How can sharp fluctuations be neutralized? Switch to displaying fifteen-minute candles and try to see the bigger picture. Jerky behavior seen in five-minute candles will look completely calm in fifteen-minute candles. That's one reason why we hardly use two-minute candles except when trading the first hour. The amount of noise after the bell is unbearable!

Points, Not Percentages – Quantity, Not Sums of Money

A math question for you:

Danny bought stock when its shares were $100. In the afternoon the price rose by 20%, but later dropped by 20%. What is the price of the share after it dropped?

If your answer was $100, think again.

After the price rose 20%, its value was $120. When it drops 20%, the drop is calculated on the new price of $120. Therefore, after it drops, the price per share is $96.

What is the conclusion? **Percentages manifest relative values and not absolute values.**

If I say that the stock of ABC yielded a profit of 10%, how much money did I actually make? There's no way of knowing. It could have been $10 per share if the share was bought at $100, but it could also have been 10 cents per share, if its buy price was $1.

Here is another example:

Danny bought stock at $100 per share. One fine morning the price dropped by 50% to $50. By what percentage does the price need to go up in order to make $100 per share again?

If you answered 50%, think again.

To return to the original price, we need to see an uptrend of 100% of its current price of $50.

By contrast, in **absolute values**, there is no confusion: the stock lost $50 and must add $50 (i.e. 50 points) to return to its start value. This example demonstrates exactly why percentage-based calculations can get so confusing.

- **Remember:** Traders do not calculate profits in percentages. They calculate in points, i.e. dollars, where each $1 = 1 point.

| **SMART MONEY** | *A fundamental principle of stock trading management is based on measuring gains and losses in points and not in percentages, and when buying, in quantities and not in sums of money.* |

When you ask traders what sums they trade in, they will find it hard to answer, since they operate in **quantities and not in sums of money.** A novice trader will start off trading in quantities of 100 shares per trade, and over a year of accruing experience will gradually increase towards the 1000 shares per trade mark. Old hands at trading with several years of experience up their sleeves buy stock by the thousands of shares per trade, and in even more advanced stages, may even reach single trades involving tens of thousands of shares.

I realize it sounds a bit odd to you: a trader may buy 1000 shares at $20 each, for a total of $20,000 and then on another occasion, without even blinking, he may buy 1000 shares at $50, operating with a figure of $50,000.

And that is how it really works.

Here are three main reasons for referring to trades in these terms:

Reason Number 1: Fast Calculation of Profit or Loss

Traders who tend to buy 1000 shares per trade can easily calculate their profit or loss: for example, if the stock you bought goes up 23 cents, you have profited $230 (23 cents x 1000 shares); if it rose by $2 you have profited $2000. This is not a calculation of yield on capital, but profit in dollars per trade.

If you were to ask the owner of a shoe store what his monthly yield is, you would likely be given a "what on earth...??" look. Ask what the earnings per month are: that can be answered instantly.

| **SMART MONEY** | *You never count your money when you're sittin' at the table. There'll be time enough for countin' when the dealing's done*
-Kenny Rogers: "The Gambler" lyrics |

When you are completely focused on a stock's breakout, analyzing the stock and its market direction, the number of bids and asks, its sector status, volume and so on, the last thing you need to be doing is figuring yield in percentages and multiplying by the amount of money in order to calculate profit or loss. This is where the **points system** comes to your aid: profit or loss of ten cents on 1000 shares will always be $100,regardless of the price of the share.

One of the mistakes I made in my early trading days was buying a quantity of shares according to a sum of money. For example, I would decide to allocate $5000 per stock. This is what I did: if I chose stock at $36.49 per share, I would divide $5000 by that figure and buy the result, 137 shares. Now let's say the price rose by 17 cents: how much have I made... See the problem? I would be spending more time on math than on market direction.

Now imagine yourselves trading in three different stocks simultaneously! But if I round off to "batches" of 100 shares, it gets a lot easier to calculate the effect of 17 cents profit: $17. I can assure you, it's better to focus on actual trading than to start reckoning complex monetary calculations.

Reason Number 2: Buy in Round Figures Based on 100

As we have already learned, executions of orders that are not round figures of one hundred get delayed. The great majority of bid and ask orders are set in round hundreds, known as "lots." The ECN systems give priority to round-lot orders. If I try to sell 137 shares, called an **odd lot**, and at the same time a buyer wants 200 shares, the buyer may receive a round 100 quantity from my stock. But it is highly probable the buyer will not be interested in the additional 37 shares, which is not a round figure, since it will be difficult for him to find another 63 to make up a round number of 200.

A simpler solution for the buyer is simply to execute the trade with a different seller who can provide the full round-figure quantity. Worse than the above is the **AON (all or nothing) order** which buyers use, and which translates simply into, "If I can't have the entire quantity I'm looking for, don't buy anything." This means that if I am holding 137 shares, that buyer will not receive 100 from me. Instead, the system will look for round-figure sellers.

Incidentally, **AON is not an effective order for traders. Please avoid it.**

So, to sell those 37 shares, I will need to wait for a buyer who specifically wants that amount. This could take a long time, and may even end up costing me an additional commission. The only instance where you might consider using non-round quantities of shares is while you are learning to use the swing method, where holding shares for several days makes you less sensitive to sudden changes in price.

Reason Number 3: Stocks Move in Points, Not in Percentages

When a price rises or falls, the average buyer does not think in terms of percentages but in price per share. For example: I want to buy a stock at $20 per share. I waiver a little and the price goes up by two cents. I buy at $20.02. Another example: I want to buy a stock selling at $2 per share. I wait a little and it goes up by two cents. I buy at $2.02.

Do you see what happened here? My decision to buy or not was based on the price moving up by one or two cents, rather than on percentages. My consideration in both cases was that the price is reasonable, and relatively close to the price I initially wanted to pay. But note the difference in percentages: for the $20.02 share, I bought at 1/10 of a percentage above the planned price, whereas for the $2.02 share, I bought at 1% of the planned price.

The principle is simple: people buy stocks according to their movement in cents, not in percentages. Because of this standard human behavior, a good breakout for a share at $20 will be approximately 20 cents, and a good breakout for a share costing $2 will also be around 20 cents. So how does this tie in to fixed quantities? Where does the problem lie?

If I were to insist on buying stocks according to a fixed sum of money, let's say $10,000 per stock, I would then be buying 500 of a $20 stock or 5000 of a $2 stock. If both break out at 20 cents, and breakouts can occur within seconds, then I have made $100 on the $20 stock, and $1000 on the $2 stock. Cool, right? No, not cool at all. Remember: the potential for profit equals the potential for loss. Within seconds, before you have time to say "there goes my account..." the $2 stock can just as easily move 20 cents against you and wipe $1000 out of your account.

SMART MONEY	*Traders naturally tend to buy stocks according to their movement in cents rather than percentages. A successful breakout for shares priced at $20 will be 20 cents, just as it will be for shares priced at $2.*

Summary

Be disciplined about buying according to quantity rather than sum of money. If you are comfortable with buying in multiples of 500 shares, then do that always, irrelevant of the share price. The exceptions to this norm are for shares at $70 and up, or small caps with clear, very low volatility. Remember that every stock has its own "personality." Therefore, a good rule of thumb is to always buy a fixed quantity. Before clicking the buy button, just check the stock's volatility thoroughly and take your decision on whether to increase or decrease the quantity.

Learn from Your Experiences...Keep a Diary

No infant learns to walk without falling. The infant keeps trying until the sequence of actions called walking becomes embedded in the brain and turns automatic. Every trader undergoes "infanthood" and "childhood" as he or she learns. Mistakes are part and parcel of a trader's learning curve and a very important aspect of shaping the new trader's capabilities and resilience.

Mistakes are a vital asset in learning how to succeed. Even old hands make mistakes, but to lesser degrees than new traders. When I started out, I made far more mistakes than I do now. I remember days filled with self-directed anger. There were days when I would lecture to students, teaching them what to avoid, then go and do exactly that action I had warned against! Of course I felt like a complete idiot. Now, years later, I still make mistakes, but far less frequently. The fascinating thing about trading mistakes is that they are known and familiar, but we make them anyway, even though we know we are crossing into forbidden territory. It's as though something stronger than us is pushing us against our will.

The first step in coping with mistakes is to know what you should and shouldn't do. This book is meant to help you a lot in that respect. The second step is your own determination to correct your mistakes and strengthen your psychological stamina towards eradicating them one by one. Traders need to know how to take best advantage of mistakes rather than waste them. Mistakes, by virtue of their unavoidability, are a valuable asset. As with any valuable asset, they need to be documented and conclusions reached. The only way to do that is to keep an activities diary.

Students in my courses are taught how to avoid typical trading mistakes. I go over, emphasize and demonstrate every typical mistake there is until I am certain the message is absorbed. At the end of every discussion, there is that moment I am so fond of when I tell them: "And I know that despite everything, you're going to make this mistake..." When I look at their faces, I see them all thinking, "Does he think I'm a complete idiot? I listened, I understood, I wrote it all down, and I have no intention of making that mistake!"

I know that's what they're thinking, but that's not how it works in real life. In real life, they'll make every mistake covered by this book. For each mistake, they'll pay with their hard-earned money. Nonetheless, the big advantage is that unlike others who did not study the rules of trading, they have learned what those common mistakes are. Most traders active in the market try to learn by themselves and from their own experience. That, too, is a mistake. Trying to learn trading by yourself means you cannot pinpoint the common mistakes and try to avoid them, thus prolonging the process of gaining experience and knowledge. So while even someone who has taken a course will still make mistakes, that person will be more aware of what to avoid, and will err less frequently. Identifying and acknowledging your mistakes is the first and most important step to eradicating them.

Keeping an ongoing diary is the perfect solution. It will help you understand when you have erred, and how to handle the situation in the future. When I started out trading, I read an article on keeping an activities diary. Truthfully, at first I could not understand how important this aspect was, just as it likely sounds to you now that I am filling your head with petty ideas. I was sure I remained aware of my mistakes and that I had no need of further documentation. In retrospect, I was sorry for not keeping a diary earlier. I discovered the need to manage an activities diary the hard, costly way. If you take my advice, you will save yourselves an unnecessarily long and expensive learning process.

SMART MONEY	*An amazing thing will happen to you when you start keeping your activities diary. You will find that the kinds of mistakes you make are within a relatively small range. If you see the same mistake showing up all the time, then it's time to make a change!*

My wife, without even realizing it, helped me realize the need for an activities diary. When I started my trading career, I would repeat one of the most common mistakes of new traders: I would buy at the right time but then sell at too small a profit or too great a loss. Every evening I would tell my wife more or less the same story, "If only I had done this... or not done that... I would have made a bigger profit..." Every day it was the same thing, until she got sick of hearing how I "almost" made money. What was abundantly clear to my wife, but not to me, was that I described the exact same mistake, over and over. It was time to look that mistake in the eye. It was time to make a change.

An interesting thing happened once I started keep a diary. I found that the range of mistakes I made was limited. I found that I consistently make the same classic mistakes of new traders. But I found these things out only after I started my activities diary. At the end of each day, I jotted down my trading activities, and once a week I would sit with the diary and review the outcomes recorded there. Most of my failures derived from a small range of repetitive common mistakes.

From this point on, the path to success was shorter and sweeter. All I needed to do was decide to kill off those mistakes, one by one. The biggest, toughest battle, obviously, is psychological. But by the end of the first week in which I declared war on my mistakes, armed with my trusty diary, I was amazed by the results. By the end of the second week, I was convinced that this was the best method, and the war got easier. All I needed to do was keep a diary. So simple, and so amazing.

What to Record in your Activities Diary
- Date, hour and minute of your trade. This lets you study the stock's chart later.
- Stock ticker symbol
- Quantity of shares you bought
- Trade direction (long, short)
- Planned entry price
- Actual entry price
- Reason for entry (e.g. technical formation, stock in the news)
- Price of first target; actual first target
- Price of final target; actual target
- Stop loss point
- Hour and minute of exit
- Actual exit price
- Reason for exit (e.g. price reached target, market changed direction)
- Monetary outcome (profit/loss, how much)
- Notes: mistakes, changed market direction, etc.

I know of traders who rely on a broker's activities printout. Don't rely on that alone. A broker's printout will never be enough. You need to manage your own lists in a handwritten booklet or Excel-type format, whichever manner you find easiest. But you must record every single trade you execute. I can assure you that as the conclusions become clear, you will be amazed to find that you make only a few types of mistakes. Once you've identified those that are typical for you, you're on your way to neutralizing them!

Putting It All Together

Now you need to set goals. Don't try to make that goal eradicating more than two mistakes simultaneously. If you discover that you tend to make the same five mistakes, choose two and declare that over the coming ten days of trading, which is two business weeks, you will make sure not to repeat them. For example: you see that you tend to exit a stock before it reaches your pre-set target. Decide that unequivocally and without compromise, you will not exit even one cent below your target. Enter a sell order at your target price, and avoid changing it. You need to hit the target with a bull's eye. You have to resolve that for the coming ten trading days, you are going to place a huge X over the two mistakes you've marked. Ignore all bothersome information, and mainly ignore the profit/loss concerns. Stop counting your money while you trade (one of THE most common mistakes!) and start focusing on trading correctly while remaining in control. I do not wish to imply this is easy work, but it is definitely achievable. I was there too. I applied these tactics, as did many of my students. Without exception, I've always been told later how great this method is.

Keeping an activities diary works. Fact.

12

Choosing a Winner Stock

From the thousands of stocks traded, how can we choose the best?

Around 10,000 stocks are traded on Wall Street. How can we choose the best ones for the current day's trading? A pro chooses stocks according to predefined rules, not according to whim.

Do Your Homework

Before each day of trading, do homework. Start the day with a list of candidates. Sometimes I get lazy and don't prepare in advance. On one such day, trading opened with a sharp gap up, and I had no candidates on my non-existent list. As trading progressed, I quickly reviewed my favorite stocks in search of a good opportunity, but to no avail. The feeling that everyone else is making easy money and you're the only one wasting time is one of the worst psychological states for a trader. It is fertile ground for stupid moves… and this mistake didn't take long to become apparent. I convinced myself that a certain stock was looking great, and with an impulsive click, placed the trade. For a very short time I did well, but in the long run I took a searing loss.

SMART MONEY	*Advance preparation for our day of trading contributes to our psychological resilience and helps us cope successfully with market conditions.*

Important moral to the story: when you really want to hit the button, you'll find that you possess awesome powers of self-persuasion. Every so-so stock looks great. Remember this: sometimes we profit more by not trading at all!

The conclusion is simple: for each day of trading you need to have a list ready with stocks you have analyzed, which will prepare you mentally for the market. These are the stocks which would offer the lowest risk of disappointment and the highest chances of success. Later on, we'll look at several ways of searching for stocks.

Using Analysts' Reports

A professional, experienced analyst who invests a good deal of time and energy in searching for stocks will succeed far better than a new trader with no experience. The success rate of Tradenet's trading room analysts is about 65%.

The disadvantage of relying only on the trading room analysts' picks is that it draws you into laziness and can create dependence. I know traders who have been operating for years with only analysts' reports. They are pleased with their outcomes, but are constantly dependent on someone else and will never learn to identify stocks themselves. It is an unhealthy status, since your ultimate objective is to be independent. If you allow someone else from now on to choose stocks for you, you will never progress as a trader and gain that vital self-confidence and experience.

SMART MONEY	*You must learn to identify stocks yourself. It contributes to your self-confidence, experience, and development as traders.*

I will waive my opposition to my recommendation only when you are starting out as traders. I believe that initially it is worth being assisted by the knowledge of a more experienced trader, but that would be for one purpose only: to learn and understand why your mentor chose the particular stock and how you can do that yourself. As long as you are earning income from someone else's recommendations, you need not give up being assisted. However, always check well that the stocks chosen by the analyst will not constitute more than half the trades you execute, and compare your rate of success on stocks you have chosen with those chosen by the expert. Your long-term goal is to improve your rate of success, to reach that of the expert.

How does a daily analyst's report look? Reports are adapted to the nature of your trading. Swing traders use a report that analyzes up to ten stocks each week, and intraday traders use a report that analyzes up to ten stocks daily. The report contains a list of "candidates" for the coming day's trading and their trigger points (entry, stop loss, targets), a technical and fundamental market review for the previous day, predictions for the coming day, charts and analysis referencing the main sectors and indicators, a list of specific stocks due to announce quarterly reports or important statements, lines of support and resistance closest to the main indices, a review of important upcoming market announcements and their publication times, and an updated follow-up table with targets and stop loss points of stocks in swing.

Sample of Stocks Table for Intraday Trading as Publicized in the Report

Symbol	Trigger	Company	Sector	1st Target	Stop Loss	Earnings
CPX	34.75	Complete Production Services, Inc.	Basic Materials | Oil & Gas Equipment & Services	$35.79	$33.71	-
ACI	34.75	Arch Coal Inc.	Basic Materials | Industrial Metals & Minerals	$35.79	$33.71	-
CVE	38.45	Cenovus Energy Inc.	Basic Materials | Oil & Gas Drilling & Exploration	$39.60	$37.30	-

Managing a Watch List

Many traders prepare a list of stocks for follow up. Generally, the list runs from dozens to hundreds of stocks, sometimes up to two hundred. Later I will explain how to prepare your own list. What characterizes these stocks as desirable is their high volume and volatility. The symbols are entered into the trading platform under the **Watch List** field. At one click on any symbol, that stock's chart opens.

Every day before trading begins, traders manually check the charts for those stocks they are following as they look for technical entry points. Stocks identified as having potential for trading will be divided into three sub-groups:

1. **Hot shares** – which are close to their trigger point (planned entry point) and seem likely to be traded that day
2. **Rising shares** – showing an uptrend and which could enter the "hot" list over the coming days
3. **Falling shares** – showing a downtrend and which might enter the "hot" list over the coming days for shorts

Every so often, the main list should be checked and updated according to the three follow-up divisions. List the stocks you plan to trade over the current day in a separate table, including organized columns for the trigger point (entry price), stop loss point, first profit target (the partial), and final profit target.

SMART MONEY	*Prepare a follow-up list of 100 stocks sorted into three categories: hot stocks, rising stocks and falling stocks. Frequently update the lists and mark stocks suitable for trading.*

How should you construct your follow-up list? I recommend beginning with a list of up to 100 stocks, and expanding it over time as you gain experience. You can choose leading stocks from two important lists: the NASDAQ 100 and the S&P 500. Note that some NASDAQ stocks will also appear on the S&P list. To find the symbols for stocks in each of these two lists, Google the words "NASDAQ 100 index" and "S&P 500 index" and copy the symbols from one of the financial sites.

Filters
- Remove from your follow-up list all stocks priced at over $100, as they will not only be too expensive but also too volatile for novice traders.
- Remove all stocks below $10. We have already discussed the fact that as beginners, it is best to avoid trading in small caps which institutional traders are generally prohibited from buying.
- Remove all stocks with intraday ranges of less than 30 cents per day, including the "heavy" stocks that show little volatility, such as Microsoft (MSFT).
- Remove all stocks with very low volumes, initially those showing less than 2 million shares per day, and later as you expand your list, to those showing less than 1 million shares per day.
- Compile your list from what is left.

Over time, once you get to know the stocks you like most, and even if they are not included in either of those indexes, you can add them to your list while removing others, as you see fit. Most likely, after some months of trading you will have developed your winner list.

Following Up on "Stocks in the News"

In addition to stocks you have identified through your watch list, you also need to keep an eye open for "hot" stocks from the previous day and add them to your daily list.

Don't make the mistake that the bulk of the public makes: don't think, even for a moment, that there's any simple way to profit from shares that trend up quickly because of some announcement, or that crash because of bad news. Usually, these are stocks that will start the day with a gap and the ability to move either way, sometimes completely against all logic. In principle, they are unpredictable, but sometimes a good technical entry point can be found and the resulting move can be strong because of the interest generated by news.

When a significant article appears on a specific stock in such prestigious media as the *Wall Street Journal*, and you make the mistake of buying the stock along with millions of others, you no longer have any advantage as far as price. Will a million readers all make good profits on the same stock? How will the market react to the news item? Will the price go up or down? One guess is as good as the other. In most cases, a stock in the news has already seen its uptrend prior to any public announcements, based on insider information or the grapevine. If you are on either of those radars, you have an advantage. If not, forego the urge to buy.

The well-known catchphrase "**buy the rumor, sell the news**" alludes to the principle where the herd buys on hearing the news and therefore the herd loses. The ones who profit are usually those who break the law. They have received information from a friend inside the company, or had access to the company quarterly report printed some few days before the official publication. If you thought the stock market does not operate like this – think again. Manipulation and corruption abound in such subtle ways that the regulatory bodies simply cannot catch the criminals.

In that case, should we buy a stock in the news because of an analyst's recommendation or removal of recommendation? Do analysts know how to choose good stocks better than you do? Every year, research is published that examines the outcomes of analyst recommendations. Can you guess what your situation would be if you based yourself on the analysts? It's a certain way to lose your money.

If so, why should you be scanning for stocks in the news? I read the news for a different purpose altogether: I want to know what the herd is up to. I want to understand the herd, but I would never operate automatically the way it would expect me to. I want to know which stocks are in the news so I can follow them and perhaps find good technical entry points during the day's trading, no matter which way prices are moving. Stocks in the news tend to be highly volatile. And high volatility is important to me. Every day, I prepare a list of some five to ten stocks in the spotlight and keep checking them for technical opportunities. Sometimes I get lucky, sometimes I don't.

An example of a stock in the news is British Petroleum, BP. The price crashed due to the leak from the company's drilling rig near America's shores in an event that came to be labeled "the worst ecological catastrophe in American history." Anticipated compensation claims reached the billions of dollars, and a potential total bankruptcy hovered over the company's head. For several days we monitored BP in the trading room, and finally, due to the alertness of an analyst, its day arrived!

Trading Room Trade in British Petroleum, BP

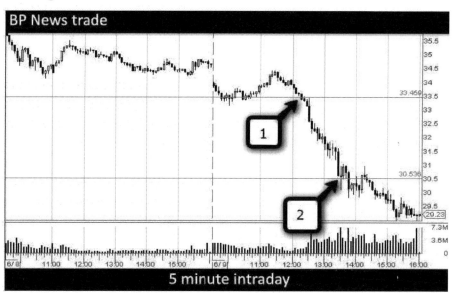

As is common during crises, BP opened with a gap down. Can we immediately short because of the news? Had you tried to enter a short at the start of trading, it is highly probable it would have shaken you out at a searing loss when it rose to close the gap. Later BP moved down again and provided us with an excellent technical breakdown point when it broke the intraday support line. Without doubt, this was an impressive short for a weak stock in the news. The short was executed at $33.45 [1] and the exit was executed when it first started to show signs of a bounce [2]. For a moment, I thought BP had run out of steam for further lows (notice the long tail indicating the intraday reversal). In retrospect, I was slightly in error concerning the exit point, but the earnings amounted to $2,920, as you can see from my trading account:

Trade Details

Account	T/D	Currency	Type	Side	Symbol	Qty	Price	Amount
COLM0001	06/09/2010	USD	2	S	BP	1,000	33.45	33,450.00
COLM0001	06/09/2010	USD	2	B	BP	1,000	30.53	(30,530.000000)
TOTAL (2)						2,000		2,920

Summary

Every day, dozens of stocks can be found in the news for a variety of reasons. It makes no difference if the news is good or bad, since there will always be strong volatility which provides interesting trading opportunities.

Mergers & Acquisitions

A company being bought or merging with a competing company is not a rare event. There are many reasons for mergers and acquisitions, and the reason most commonly tossed about is "synergy." Mergers and acquisitions create enticing trading opportunities.

SMART MONEY | *When one company buys another, usually the price of the buyer's shares will drop due to the risks involved in the transaction, and the purchased company's share prices rise due to the premium being paid for its shares.*

As traders, mergers and acquisitions interest us since the shares of both companies involved – the purchaser and the purchased – can usually be anticipated: the price of the buyer's shares will drop, whereas the price of the purchased company's shares will rise.

On one hand, investors are expressing their concern that the purchasing company has "bitten off more than it can chew" and that the new purchase will weigh heavily on its balance sheets. On the other hand, the purchasing company also takes control of the acquired company's shares at higher-than-market price and pays a premium to the shareholders. By doing so, the purchasing company takes a certain risk, but also displays its ability to absorb the purchased company as part of its own, creating a greater whole than its parts (hence the "synergy"). While no one can guarantee that the acquisition or merger will succeed and that the merged companies will be more successful, the simple fact is that the acquiring company will show a massive expense on its balance sheets. Nonetheless, the acquired companies were bought above market price, and will soon be traded in the market at this premium price. Simply put, this means profit opportunities for investors.

For example, the pharmaceutical megacorp Merck (MRK) announced its purchase of Schering-Plough (SGP) for $41 billion, a huge transaction by all reckonings. Schering investors would receive 0.57 shares per Schering share they held, plus $10.5 in cash. The outcome: on the day of the announcement, Merck's share price dropped by 8%, whereas Schering's rose by 15%. I wish to emphasize, however, that even though this is highly expected behavior on the part of both stocks, you should nonetheless carefully check your best entry point, and the risk to reward ratio.

Staying Loyal to a Stock

Traders will often become "familiar" with stocks they feel more confident in than with others. Each timeframe has its "stars," stocks with prices that are continuously trending up, drawing traders, investors and funds to buy in for varying periods of time. Should we get to know the more popular stocks and join the party?

First, I don't believe in marrying any stock. Realistically, during any timeframe, some will be defined as "wild kids" in the market. These are traded in gigantic volumes and with crazy volatility. As I write these lines, I can say that the two currently most popular ones are AIG and SEED. By the time this book reaches the printer, most certainly others will be the public's favorites.

AIG's story belongs to the financial crisis, that amazing crash and the swift recovery. At such times, emotions work overtime. Some will remember the company's good days as a leader in the international insurance market, and might buy AIG "for the children's future." Others, like us traders, take advantage of this outpour of emotion to trade the stock through days of fantastic volatility and high volumes.

Daily Behavior of AIG over Several Months

In August 2009, the share's price leapt from $12 to $55 [1] during crazy trading days and in volumes of hundreds of millions of shares per day. In fact, AIG's story began some time earlier, but without a doubt, August and September of that year showed the wildest moves in stock trading.

AIG, along with other "public favorites," can show highly volatile movement within a single trading day with high volumes and liquidity, which is why many day traders earn a great deal of money from them. Public interest causes price spikes, the company is usually assessed at far above its real value, and most often will not uphold market expectations. In most cases the share price will drop [2], volumes will fall sharply [3] and the price will cease showing its earlier volatility. If and when interest renews in the stock, it will likely "go crazy" once more.

Conclusion: if you really want to "marry" a stock, get married to the way it is traded within a specific timeframe rather than with the stock itself. It is far better to avoid becoming "big experts" on any stock, when we know that within several months the party will be over and we will want to move on to something else. Stock traders seek intraday entry points that allow them to trade in that stock once or twice during the same day for profits. This method works only if the stock maintains high volatility and volume, and these can calm down at any time or even eventually disappear.

The snowball usually gets rolling only once the institutional players start buying the stock, pushing its volume and price up, and bringing it to the attention of the investing public and traders. While investors and day traders "acclimate" to the stock, institutional traders who pushed the price higher are selling it to you in mega-volumes. Slowly, the price uptrend calms down, day traders stop playing, institutional buyers are generally out of the picture by now, volumes drop, and the price begins to plummet back to its natural position.

| **SMART MONEY** | *We never "marry" a stock for long periods. We trade in it during interesting timeframes and abandon it when volumes drop and its price ret urns to its natural and less interesting state.* |

How do investors behave? Let's take, for example, AIG, which began at $12, spiked to $55 and pulled back, at least for now. Most investors did not enter at $12. Very few of them held the stock before the price began to rise. The "lucky" ones discovered it at around $20 or even higher, and rode it up to $55. Were they pleased with their success and realized profits at that point? Mostly, no. Greed drew them in further. When the price dropped all the way to $35, did they realize profits? On the contrary: they started to "get smart." They convinced themselves that they "know" the stock, and are sure it will move back to its previous high. So now, they buy more shares at $35, planning on making easy money when the stock repeats its highs. Eventually they discover that the price is continuing to move down, below their original purchase price, and they end the trade at a loss.

It should come as no surprise to you that this scenario repeats itself several times throughout the year. It also happens to more experienced investors. Every year we will meet "the public's favorites" along with the investors and traders who "know" the stock, conclude they are experts on its behavior, and find themselves well on their way to losing money.

Intraday Search for Stocks

I find about one half or slightly more of the stocks I trade in during the trading day by staying tuned to several sources. The most important for

me is the online trading room where I trade together with h
other traders every day. Many of them present interesting stoc
their watch lists, or stocks they identified during trading hours
suggestions are inexhaustible! The hard thing is to know which ones
choose.

SMART **MONEY**	*One of the most useful tools is identifying strong and weak stocks during the trading day. Follow them and look for good technical entry points.*

I also make use of my trading platform. Each platform contains special tools for locating intraday stocks exhibiting uncommon behavior. For example, lists of the strong stocks in each stock exchange (New York, NASDAQ), the weak ones in each stock exchange, and those with particularly high volumes. The COLMEX Pro trading platform I use displays a "Top 20" scanner from which I gain a good deal of intraday ideas! The method for using it is simple: during trading hours I open each stock's chart, for example for the strongest stocks, and look for interesting technical entry points. Correct follow-up can produce several good trades on any given day.

Top 20" Scanner

	...Nasd	LossNasd	GainNYSE	LossNYSE
1	BDCO	RDCM	KV.A	LAQ
2	NEXM	LSCC	KV.B	CNAM
3	ICOP	EMMS	UTI	PCG
4	LULU	SCOK	ANX	APP
5	SIGA	SWHC	DIN	NSM
6	DMAN	TNDM	MNI	SKH
7	CBAK	CBEH	LNG	CMO
8	DSTI	HILL	RES	DYP
9	RDNT	RBCN	AIB	SOXL
10	RUE	SNTS	FVE	DTO
11	ALTH	CRUS	BORN	AZC
12	SONS	XPRT	LEI	SCO
13	GPRC	INTT	RIG	TRW
14	ACET	AVGO	WMG	WPI
15	VICL	EXTR	MCO	PMI
16	MDCO	POWI	SRZ	SNV
17	CMTL	ISIL	FR	ADI

As you see, the window is divided into columns, each of which shows a list of stocks with the relevant criteria:

(1) NASD Gain – 20 strongest NASDAQ stocks
(2) NASD Loss – 20 weakest NASDAQ stocks
(3) NYSE Gain – 20 strongest on the New York Stock Exchange
(4) NYSE Loss – 20 weakest on the New York Stock Exchange

Every few seconds, the scanner executes a data update, so that any particular stock may be replaced by any other. Displayed data can also be filtered to suit your individual requirements. If your trading platform does not display these details, you can find the information gratis on a number of financial sites constantly updated in real time, such as searching Google for *stock gainers and losers*, and choosing the site you find most comfortable to use.

Using Special Stock Screening Platf

Most traders who use special stock screening
programs geared to locating them at the end c
use them for intraday searches.

A wide range of stock screening platf(
are Internet freebies and others can be pu
hundreds to thousands of dollars along with a ...
are generally geared toward professional traders.

Two useful sites are www.stockfetcher.com and www.finviz.com, and
both provide free basic services and paid advanced services.

How Does the Scanner Work?

A stock scanner for the end of the trading day is based on an analysis
of trading data for the entire stock market. This data includes the opening
and closing prices of every stock, its low and high, and its volume.

To locate suitable stocks, you need to conduct a search. First, you must
define the program's scan parameters. For example: if you want to trade
only in stocks with high volumes, activate a filter that displays stocks
with average daily volumes over the past month of more than one million
shares. An additional filter may display stocks whose volumes increased
over the number of days that you specify. You can set the program to focus
only on stocks that on the previous day showed double their average
daily volume over the past month. An additional filter could be applied
for identifying stocks with prices above 20MA, i.e. stocks trending up. A
more advanced filter would require that the 50MA is below the 20MA,
and that the 200MA is below the 50MA. In this way, you not only assure
yourself that the stock is indeed showing an uptrend, but is trending up
for a period of no less than 200 periods.

The more filters you define, the more you limit the search results,
until at some point a click of the button will return "zero results." The
ideal result will be around several dozen stocks, which you will then
check manually, one by one, to find those with your required formations.

Over time, you will learn how to define filters that best suit your
trading method, and access the appropriate results with just one click,
displaying a daily list of likely candidates.

The Fundamentals of Using the Scanner

• The objective: identifying stocks suited to your trading method

uld not be wise to reach a "perfect" set of filters since
ss out on many stocks that do not look ready for immediate
t may nonetheless prove worthy of continued follow-up and
ly being included in your watch list.

at Are We Looking For?
Classic breakout and breakdown formations
- Reversals
- Patterns, such as "cup and handles," "head and shoulders," etc.
- Stocks showing up or down trends
- Gaps
- Volatile stocks
- High volume stocks (above 700,000 shares per day)
- Increasing volumes

Setting Up the Filters
Every program has its own method for setting up filters, but they are all fairly similar. The examples shown here are taken from the **Stock Fetcher** program.

Example: Let's say I want to find stocks at no more than $1 from their year high (i.e. towards a breakout), priced between $10 to $70, with daily average volume over the past 30 days above 750,000 per day, and trended up on the previous trading day.

This is the filter:
1. Show stock where close is between 10 and 70
2. and Average Volume (30) is above 750000
3. and 52-week high is less than 1 point above high
4. and close is above open

Once this filter is entered into the scanner program, one click on "search" will display stocks fulfilling the above criteria. Were too many stocks on the list? Increase the volume to 1 million.

Filters that search for formation will look like this:
1. Show stocks where pattern is a head and shoulders
2. Show stocks where pattern is a cup and handle
3. Show stocks where pattern is a double-bottom

To all these filters, we add the definitions for price range, volatility, and average daily volume.

Example: a filter searching for bull doji formation with reversal (we are looking for reversals formed by candles rising after the doji) will look like this:

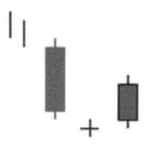

1. close is above open
2. and close 1 day ago equals open 1 day ago
3. and close 2 days ago is below open 2 days ago
4. and open 1 day ago is below close 2 days ago
5. and open is above open 1 day ago
6. and close is above close 2 days ago
7. and close is below open 2 days ago
8. and close 2 days ago was decreasing for 2 days
9. and average volume (3) is above 750,000

Example: searching for a gap up of more than 2% over 2 trading days:
1. show stocks where low is above close 1 day ago
2. and open is more than 2% above close 1 day ago
3. and open 1 day ago is above close 1 day ago

Summary

My recommendation to you, the novice trader, is not to get involved in intraday stock searches. Just do the end-of-day search, prepare interesting stocks for the coming day of trading, learn from your mistakes, and improve your formulas until you attain reasonably good control over the search results. The majority of traders do not activate intraday searches at all.

13

17.12

42.15

27.09

22.47

23.37

91.66

95.61

25.22

24.82

How to Get Ready

for Your First Day

of Trading

Important tips before you click the button for the first time ever

Starting Slowly

You've read books, learned the principles of trading, bought a powerful computer, connected to a trading room, and now at last you've opened a trading account and deposited money in it.

That's it. The much-awaited day is here. It's your first day of work as a stock trader. Understandably, you could be feeling euphoric, but equally understandably, there's tension and uncertainty. Did you sleep well last night? Did you eat breakfast? Please – start your day slowly. Be calm. Begin small. Operate carefully. After all, before you test your swimming skills in the stormy ocean of the stock exchange alongside sharks and whales, practice first in a quiet lagoon alongside the shore. Go for just one trade a day throughout your first week. Learn from each trade by examining it from every possible angle.

Why did you buy that stock?

What was the market doing when you were buying – trending up or down?

What did the sector do?

Was the technical formation correct?

Did you operate professionally, or from an uncontrollable urge to hit that button?

Learn to sit on your hands and do absolutely nothing but watch, listen, and learn. There's a long road ahead of you.If you feel that for every moment you're not trading, you're actually losing money, then you first need to learn how to stay very calm. Thinking about money causes losses. Instead, think about the methods and the goal (money).

By the way, if you're human, I don't expect perfection from you. Consistently careful, measured behavior is not human, in fact. I'd be surprised to hear you withstood all temptations in the trading world. I know that right now you're thinking something along the lines of "he doesn't know me at all, I have incredible self-confidence, and I *can* withstand temptations!" Mark this page with a yellow highlighter and come back to it two weeks after you've begun trading, and let's see who's right. If I'm wrong, let me know and I'll be thrilled to send you my best wishes and honest admiration. If only I could always operate according to the rule book!

The good news, though, is that as time passes, you will experience an ongoing mental transformation as you become a professional trader. Now, as you start out, you are much more exposed to errors than you will be in future. Over time, you will discover your weaknesses and learn how to control them. Over even more time, your control over your emotions will also improve simultaneous to the full assimilation of your trading method.Correct trading behavior will become second nature, and impulsive, irresponsible behaviors will become the rare deviation. Yes, there is light at the end of the tunnel... it just takes a while to get there.

Making Millions...with a Demo

When I was a young kid, I loved to play Monopoly. I bought buildings, land, jumped turns, waited two, profited lots, and sometimes lost a lot, too (and don't I ever hate to lose!). It was all with small bits of paper having no true value. It's fun to play Monopoly. You always walk away with your real life accounts intact. And that is exactly why it never readied me for the real world of business. Back then, I could lose a million in one go and still sleep as well at night as if I'd made two million!

Demo trading is a demonstration program, also known as **paper trading**. It is technically very similar to real stock trading, but it all operates on "pretending," just like Monopoly. You get to use a real, professional trading program working with real time data, known as **streaming live data.** The program operates on "play money," allows buying and selling of stocks, and displays profit and loss balances that look as though they're derived from real money. Mostly, there's **no risk, and no pressure.** It's the ultimate adult computer game. Sounds great? Well, not always, and now I will explain why.

SMART MONEY | *Demo trading is important for practicing how to use the trading platform, but using it for too long may cause the novice trader to become overly confident.*

After several classes in Tradenet's course, and after studying and practicing the principles of trading, 95% of my students were earning big money on the demo! Profits of thousands of dollars on a single trading day by students carefully keeping to the rules is not an unusual phenomenon. It made them feel like richly-experienced old hands at trading. But naturally, these profits made many of them dream of the "big money" they would surely make upon completing the course, and that's when phone calls started from students who lack patience. They felt that time was slipping by when they could be earning thousands of dollars, based on their paper trading. They wanted to start playing the real market. They wanted **instant gratification with real money**.

A student profiting at demo trading may think real time trading is the same; the student may think trading with real stocks is easy. Let me warn you: trading with real money is **NOT** like trading on the demo program. They are two completely different worlds. Demo trading is Monopoly.

Now the arguments start: most of the students are certain I'm wrong and that seriously bad situations will never happen to them. They have strong self-discipline, they are sure they will stick to the rules even when trading with real money. The more polite students smile and keep silent. That smile indicates that they are right and they are sure I'm wrong, but they are too well- mannered to say so. The brasher ones are not shy at insisting I've made a mistake. The more I try to cool their enthusiasm, the greater it becomes. It's a battle with precisely foreseeable outcomes.

SMART MONEY | *Even if you're a champion sharpshooter, it will be hard to aim precisely when the enemy's weapon is aimed at your temples!*

Why is demo trading unlike real life trading? After all, it's the same program, the same market, and the same trader using it. So where does the difference lie? One of my students, a pro basketball player, described it in these words, "I know players who get the most amazing hoops all through training. The big question is what happens when they're on the playing field. Pressure, the shouting crowd, whether your salary check is going to go through this month... all these influence the game. How many of them can shoot incredibly during a real time game? Very few!" Here too, it's the same basket, the same player, and the same game... but the outcome in competition is very different. There's a well-known story about a dueling champion who was invited to a pistol duel. Beforehand, he warned his foe that he was able to hit the stem of a champagne glass from a distance of ten strides. The foe, more experienced with real battles, answered, "Let's see if you can hit the stem of the champagne glass when the glass is aiming a loaded pistol at you..."

One vital component is absent in demo trading: emotion. When you play with real money, a loaded pistol is being aimed at your brain. Basic weaknesses such as fear and greed make it much harder for you to remain cool and rational. You simply will not be the same person in real time as you were in demo time, and even though right now you are certain I'm wrong, you will quickly discover how profits on the demo easily turn into losses in real time trading with real money.

Don't be mistaken: I'm not saying you shouldn't use the demo. If you keep its disadvantages in mind, you will benefit well from its advantages. A trader profiting "on paper" during the study period will always remember that in an environment without pressures, it is easy to beat the market. If and when that trader loses money in real time trading, he or she will smartly seek the differences between demo training time and real money trading, analyze them, internalize them, and correct what needs correcting. Sometimes the new trader may even stop trading in real money and go back to the demo for a very short period, to better understand the differences now that some real experience has been gained. Demo trading trains the trader to execute technical actions quickly, and more importantly, teaches that it is possible to make money if you maintain the rules and do not involve emotion.

Avoid internalizing bad habits when you practice with the demo. Use the demo to improve your reaction speed, practice trade orders, and learn the trading program inside out. Even when using the demo program, trade in small quantities and small numbers of trades, as though you were dealing in real money. Analyze each trade well, as though it was executed with real money. Stay tuned to experienced traders in the online trading room. Don't trade alone. And don't bite off more than you can chew.

Preparing for the Day of Trading, Step by Step

The work of day traders begins a while before trading opens. Readying yourself from the technical and fundamental aspects is important for both choosing advance stocks suited to trading, and preparing yourself emotionally, which improves your degree of success.

How Much Time Should You Devote to Preparation?

In theory, you can spend hours preparing, without any real benefit from so much time invested. If you want to read financial news, you will find its scope on a daily basis can fill entire libraries, and in the long run, most of it is meaningless. By contrast, if you want to execute technical analysis on hundreds of stocks, you will be spending unnecessarily long hours at your computer screens. To focus on the core requirements and not waste time on activities that at best will not assist and at worst cause damage, I recommend you follow these outlines, adapting them to suit your own personality.

Currently, as an experienced trader, thirty minutes is enough for me to ready myself. It may be that if I devote more time, my results will improve, but that is true for everything in life. If you roll out of bed one hour earlier in the mornings for any business activity, you will almost certainly earn more. But thirty minutes is the balance I set for myself between work and play. Golfers (my real occupation...) tend to say "a bad day at golf is better than a good day at the office." As you start out, I recommend devoting more time, perhaps a full hour, to preparing for your day of trading. A good one hour of preparation should greatly assist in shortening your learning curve. Spending a great deal longer than that on preparing will not contribute to your success.

SMART MONEY	*Devote no more than one hour to preparing for your day of trading. More than one hour contributes nothing and may even prove harmful.*

If you are a member of an online trading room, a good part of the preparatory work will already be done for you and presented on a virtual silver platter. This is the "daily report," produced several hours before trading opens. Later on, the same report is scanned and analyzed in the trading room by the analysts about fifteen minutes before trading opens. Traders who consider themselves professionals will not rely only on this report, but will also personally analyze the market and the leading indexes, while additionally searching for relevant trade ideas. Traders might present these ideas in the trading room, so that all traders can benefit from their work and increase their chances of success.

Here is What You Should Look For:

Will the Market Go Up or Down?

We learned that 60% of a stock's movement will be dictated by market direction. Therefore, the first thought I start with every trading day relates to expected market direction. I will buy a larger quantity of shares with an uptrend if I presume the market is trending up, and vice versa. We discover the real market direction, unfortunately, only when trading hours have ended, but as detailed below, there are several tools to help us predict the direction in advance:

- Market behavior over previous days

Market trend is an important component of anticipating the direction. What is the general market direction? If the market is trending up, there is a feasible chance it will continue to do so. If it has trended up over three consecutive days, it is reasonable to assume that on the fourth it may rest or pullback. If it pulled back on the fourth and fifth days, it is reasonable to assume it will resume its uptrend on the sixth day, and so on.

- Futures and the pre-market

About an hour before trading opens, we begin trying to anticipate market direction via pre-market activity for futures, which unlike stocks are traded 24/7. We can check the pre-market ES activity, or if you do not have access to charts of futures, check the SPY pre-market chart which is also traded during pre-market hours.

Several times each month, about one hour before trading, various financial data are publicized such as the previous month's inflation rates, the status of unemployment, and so on. These data influence early trading on futures, and you can see pre-market direction very clearly. Good news will often influence the market open with a gap up. Even if there is no news, you will be able to see the market trending one way or another. For example, after a very strong day of highs closing with peaks, there is a good chance the market will open lower than the highest high and pull back for part of that high at least at the opening of trade. By contrast, after a day of sharp lows, buyer hysteria and pressure may dictate an even lower opening. As we learned, opening above or below the previous day's close is called a gap, and we know that gaps generally close on the same day they occur, helping us evaluate market direction during trading.

Market Direction and the Psychological Component

Market direction is determined by an encompassing range of psychological aspects reflecting the views of all market components. My recommendation, therefore, is not to belittle your gut feelings. Stock trading is far from being a precise science, and in fact is much more of an art than a science. Even if your "artistic" sensibilities are not at all developed when you start trading, I recommend trying to assess market direction and you will be surprised how often you are right. When I was young, before I had a sight corrective operation, I needed distance glasses. Every year I would go to a well-known ophthalmologist who would trouble himself to point out that he is not an optometrist. At the stage of the annual test where I needed to identify the row of smallest letters, he would say, "You're also allowed to guess." The interesting thing was that although I knew I couldn't see a thing, my guesses were very often right! The conclusion is simple: we know a lot more than we are consciously willing to admit. Multiple and often concealed components help us consolidate our views. Even if you do not have easy use of all the tools, take a guess! You'll be surprised at your higher-than-expected success rate.

Read the Financial Headlines

Surf over to your favorite financial website, read the headlines and perhaps the first few lines of key articles. Remember that the authors may be excellent at analyzing the past, but generally have no clue about the future. The reason for reading headlines is to absorb the financial atmosphere and look for events that may impact trading. The financial atmosphere will help you understand market direction. Special events may help you examine entry points for stocks with extreme behaviors. If, for example, headlines report that at the after hours, IBM is intending to publicize its quarterly report, I can assume that speculations prior to publication may cause the stock to be more volatile than usual. This would allow you entry opportunities that do not appear on a regular day, as we've discussed in detail in earlier chapters.

Announcements Calendar

Choose your favorite financial site, search for the "Announcements Calendar" link, and jot down topics of interest and important announcements for the coming week of trading. Remind yourself every day when the announcement will be appearing. We will deal with announcements and publication behavior separately.

Take a Rest: the Quiet before the Storm

Intraday trading is a process requiring a great deal of mental energy. After the first two hours of trading, I tend to feel very tired. To ready myself for another two hours of rigorous activity, I freshen up, equip myself with strong coffee, and get back to work.

The Workday Components

The trading day comprises three main sections. We need to understand how professional traders behave in each of them.

1. Opening

Between 9:30 to 11:30AM, New York time, are the most significant hours of the trading day. These two hours can be further subdivided into two parts: the first thirty minutes, and the remaining ninety minutes up until the lunch break.

The first half hour is typified by high volatility, particularly high volumes and noticeable difficulty in determining market direction. Our goal during this timeframe is to establish the trade that should accompany us throughout most of the trading day.

After this half hour, and for the remaining hour- and-a-half until the lunch break, market trend is more clarified and traders seek winning trades which will yield their daily earnings. In these trades, both the quantity of shares and the target will be relatively high.

2. Lunch Break

Between 11:30 AM to 1:30 PM, New York time, we usually see light volume since many of the big players,the institutional traders, are out to lunch.The market is calmer and generally consolidates.

This is a good time to rest, take care of existing trades, realize profits, set new stops and targets, and prepare trades for the last part of the trading day. Meanwhile we can trade in **small caps.** Since they are not traded by the institutional traders who are on lunch hour, but by the public, these stocks are not affected by the decreased volumes.

3. Close

The close is from 1:30 to 4:00 PM, New York time. It can also be divided into two parts:

The first is the trading session following the lunch break, between 1:30 to 3:30 PM. It is typified by increasing volumes and sometimes a strengthening of the trend from the day's opening. This stage is very suited to expanding existing trades or for scalping (trades with narrow defined goals of 20 to 30 cents).

During the second timeframe, between 3:30 to 4 PM, we avoid starting new trades, close the ones we do not intend to take for a swing into the next day, and take advantage of this time to check trades for the following day, based on interesting patterns identified as the trading day closes.

Each timeframe has its own particular characteristics as far as trading potential, specific methods, opportunities and risks. Professional traders will adapt themselves to the timeframe in order to take maximum advantage of the inherent potential offered by the different parts of the trading day. Other traders may specialize at trading during a particular timeframe and invest all their effort there.

Summary

Just as an attorney must prepare for a court hearing, you must also prepare for the day of trading, your "hour of judgment." Practice trading techniques with the demo program, prepare lists of stocks as suitable candidates for trades, get into the atmosphere of the trading day ready and confident in your preparations. Self-confidence improves your mental state and increases your success rate.

14

The Demons are Coming!

The logic of the market is the illogic of the individuals trading in the market.

Examine the Basic Premises

At a university, students of economics are taught two important basic premises:

1. Financial markets are effective.
2. The individuals active in the market operate logically.

Most economists claim that people trading in the market have all the relevant information, and they use it to achieve their personal goals with the highest level of efficiency.

I ask you: true or false?

Market Psychology

As a disciplined student, I must accept the conclusion of the academic consensus, read and understand the logic inherent in company profit and loss reports, and invest my money according to these premises.

For years, the approach of economists has consistently been the above. But informally, we all know that something here is not quite right. We found that the market has a life of its own, and in many instances, we saw market behavior completely contradict these economic premises. After all, if life were so simple, we would be able to read the economists' recommendations, buy shares of various companies at lower than their real value, and always make money.

But not anymore! Formally, we now acknowledge the fact that alongside the fundamental economic approach, there is also the safe and secure psychological approach. We have moved into the era of the reign of psychology. Since the Israeli psychologist Dan Kahneman, 2002

Nobel Laureate for Economic Sciences, has taken the lead in the field of economics, we can openly state that something is definitely going on! Now, in contrast to the basic premises of "universal logic" and "market efficiency," we understand that the market is driven by flesh and blood people, regular folk, with emotions, fears and wishes. And their behavior can be anticipated. Since their psychological conduct can be anticipated, correct analysis will help us anticipate market behavior. This is the road to success.

In an efficient market where knowledge is accessible to all, the phenomenon of price trends and basic laws of trading cannot exist. An efficient market conducts itself randomly. In an efficient market, there is no meaning to past, present, or future. In an efficient market, there is no technical analysis, only economic analysis based on fundamental principles.

Multiple studies clearly show that technical analysis, at least to some degree, really works. One research study examined the effectiveness of the technical formation of "head and shoulders." It was found that the trading volume on the day the formation broke out was greater by an average of 60% than on the previous day. Many traders make their living by buying and selling stocks based on technical formations appearing on the charts. Since an increasing number of traders rely primarily on these charts, even if we are sworn believers in the efficiency and logic of markets, we cannot just stand on the sidelines, thrust our heads into the sand, and ignore the psychology of the masses.

Behavioral Models

Since we are dealing with flesh and blood humans, we need to check the basic psychological models according to which these humans conduct themselves. Let me name a few:

- Opportunity assessment: in many cases we tend to ignore information we hold, and judge events only according to our assessment of our ability to succeed or fail
- Conservatism: despite new information and events, we change our views too slowly
- Distortion of truth: we tend to credit ourselves with successes, but blame failures on events or external factors
- Excessive self-confidence: we tend to overestimate our abilities. Understanding our shortcomings will help us comprehend why the illogic can be perfectly logical, or as they say, "When the sun shines on

Wall Street, open your umbrella."

In *The General Theory of Employment*, Interest and Money written in 1936, John Maynard Keynes stated: "There is nothing as disastrous as a rational investment policy in an irrational world." Translating that into the language of stock traders, it means that if others invest unsuccessfully based on logic, hoping to achieve a correlation between share prices which they perceive as illogical and fundamental data which they perceive as logical, then the more they fail, the greater are my opportunities for success.

SMART MONEY	*What would you prefer: a certain profit of $1,000 or an 80% chance of earning $1,500… which carries a 20% chance of earning nothing?*

By way of explaining my claim, let me present for example a company that reports on better-than-expected earnings. The fundamental prediction is that the share price will rise, but as happens so often, it actually falls.

The reason might be very simple: a large investment fund may have decided that it has earned enough on the stock, decided to sell, and used the high volume of buyers to its advantage. The fundamental investor will relate to the dropping price as "illogical" and will buy it "on the cheap," while the professional trader perceives the drop in price as very logical (the will of the market) and tries to profit from the lows with a short trade.

Anyone who does not know that the dropping price is the outcome of a fund selling will perceive the process as illogical. But can we say that the market behaves illogically? Conclusion: if you hold an economics degree, your chances of losing have just gone up a lot.

How do fundamental investors cope with loss? Generally by doubling the investment, based on the premises that they are right and that eventually the logical process will lead to success. As with the casino, so with the stock market: a losing gambler doubles the gamble, hoping (usually in vain) to beat the casino. The more the gambler loses, the higher the gamble rises. At some point the gambler will reach the maximum capital limit (or the limit at the table). And the casino? The casino wins, of course. Fundamental investors will claim it is worth taking the risk, since in the long term prices adapt themselves to logical values. Concerning that, Keynes had a killer response: "In the long run, we are all dead."

Let me demonstrate the illogic of the individuals comprising the market by presenting the results of research conducted by Nobel laureate psychologists Dan Kahneman and Amos Tversky, who examined the willingness of individuals to take risks.

A group of people being studied were asked to choose from the following two options:

(a) Gambling on an 80% risk of earning $4,000 with a 20% risk of not earning anything

(b) An assured income of $3,000

What would you choose? Kahneman and Tversky's research unequivocally found that despite the financial logic of choosing option (a), when faced with a choice of assured income, four out of five participants in the research group chose option (b) as best suited to them.

Now let's look at the results when the research group faces the following options:

(a) Gambling on an 80% risk of losing $4,000 and a 20% risk of not losing at all

(b) Losing a known sum of $3,000

Here, the overwhelming majority in the research group, being nine of every ten research participants, preferred option (a) to take the risk rather than absorbing an assured loss.

The parallel behavior of investors in the stock market has been familiar to me for a long time now. One of the greatest mistakes made by beginning traders is their cognitive inability to exit a losing trade at their predetermined stop point. They prefer to gamble on the stock price recovering to the purchase price rather than take the loss. They even tend to double their investment when they see a larger than expected loss. In professional jargon, they **"average down."** When the market is moving in the opposite direction, trending up, they tend to realize profits earlier than necessary and make do with a safe profit rather than wait for the larger profit.

Summary

The question each of us must ask ourselves as a trader or investor is: "Can I adapt myself, my behavior and my thoughts to those of the market?" The majority of people answer "yes," but unsurprisingly the majority, as usual, is wrong.

Are You Psychologically Suited to Trading?

I'm going to ask some questions, and you need to answer them with complete honesty. Don't try to bluff yourself. Many people are not able to examine themselves objectively. For them, this is a useless test.

"Scared Money" Test

When Tradenet was still very young, a man in his late twenties phoned and introduced himself as David. He was married, had a young child and had prepared all his homework, gone through the Tradenet site inside out and backwards, read all the study material, watched the video clips, and concluded that his future lay in stock trading. In our conversation, David sounded very decisive and determined to succeed.

He had managed to save some $15,000, which he was designating as his initial trading capital. David requested to join the next course of studies. But he failed the "Scared Money" test. David was fundamentally unsuited to intraday trading.

The "Scared Money" test states that you must solidly believe that even if you lose all the funds you designated for trading, the loss will not significantly impact your economic and mental state. The term "significant impact" is, of course, subjective, but in general I can say that if the loss means you must forego your annual vacation or will be unable to take your car to the garage for urgent repairs, then you have not passed the test.

David was about to trade with "scared money." He would absolutely have to profit in order to pay his rent and support his wife and child, and therefore his chances of success were small. If David would have had an additional source of income, or far more significant savings to cover his expenses while he learned how to trade, I would have evaluated his chances of success as high.

When you trade with "scared money," you are not psychologically free to function well. Success as a trader derives chiefly from your psychological capabilities. If you are about to risk all your savings, or worse, borrow money from the bank for trading, your fate is sealed in advance. True, I have met a rare few who started out with small sums that just grew and grew, but they are the extremely exceptional Cinderella cases and not the majority of us who are fated to live in the world of reality. And in reality, there are no shortcuts. Stock trading can be an enjoyable, challenging activity, and I fully recommend as you start out that you relate to it like learning a hobby. As with any hobby, invest only money that you can afford to lose and do not expect returns other than the pleasure of learning how to trade.

My hobby is the most popular sport in the world: golf. The cost of golf lessons, equipment and an annual membership to the golf club is far higher than what I expect you to invest for intraday trading. By contrast, your chances of profiting from intraday trading are higher by far than my chances of ever being a pro golfer!

The Self-Discipline Test

Ask any veteran intraday trader the secret of success, and you'll get this answer: strong self-discipline. Intraday trading is a technical profession based on statistics and fixed, known rules. The rules are simple, but the mental exertion needed to uphold them is tough and requires a high level of self-discipline. The psychological conduct of the novice trader runs against market behavior. The novice trader finds it difficult to play "by the book" when it looks as though the market is behaving differently to expectations, when it looks like the profit accrued is becoming an impending loss, or when it looks as though staying with the stock, even though it is moving against the trader, seems like a good idea in the hope that it will still make a comeback. These are just a few of the many examples of mental states that cause the novice trader to deviate from the straight and narrow path and betray the rules of trading.

I already know what your answer will be if I ask, "Do you have self-discipline?" In all honesty, I have a problem with your answer. I have never met a person yet who thinks he or she lacks self-discipline. It seems that we all truly believe we are disciplined, just as alcoholics are certain they can stop drinking whenever they want and smokers reckon they can put cigarettes aside at the drop of a hat. This is also why there is no need to test you on this question. Your answer is predictable, but I accept it with a good deal of skepticism. I sincerely hope you're right and I'm wrong.

Was I strongly self-disciplined when I started out? In my dreams! Even if you discover, as I did, that you lack discipline, don't worry. Most pro traders build their self-discipline as they develop their trading skills. It may cost you a lot of money, but every slap on the face you get from the market when you shift away from the rules will reinforce your self-discipline.

The "Hate to Lose" Test

Hating to lose has no connection whatsoever with our financial situation. Even some of the very rich are not psychologically built to cope with risks that cause them monetary loss. It's just that some people hate losing money more than others.

How does the test work? It's based on a visit to the casino. For many, the casino is an enjoyable outing. Beforehand, most of us define our maximum gambling loss, enjoy the atmosphere, lose a little more than we planned, and call it quits. Later we will dress for dinner, return exhausted, and fall asleep immediately. The day will be remembered as a fun outing.

But not all of us will enjoy this experience. Some people will hate having lost. They will be angry with themselves for losing two days' pay in just two hours, and may even punish themselves by foregoing other pleasures for several days to compensate for the gambling loss which they perceive as a really stupid activity. It is almost too obvious to say that they will never set foot in a casino again, not because they lack money but because they just loathe the idea of being a loser. Losing is a phenomenon that causes pain, but most of us take a casino loss in stride with a smile. Which description best fits you?

SMART MONEY	*A loss resulting from correct behavior is not painful. It is simply a lack of luck. And lack of luck is also an inseparable part of intraday trading.*

How do we cope with the pain of losing? If we know that despite a casino loss we would enjoy the evening out, then we cope well with loss. The same is true of trading. Every trader, no matter how successful, must cope with the pain of loss. Traders who understand that this pain is an inseparable aspect of the trading process are able to cope, and pass the test.

Keep in mind that as you start out, you will need to cope with days of multiple losses based on mistakes generally derived from a lack of self-discipline. Coping with the mistakes is painful, but remember that every loss contains a learning curve. Over time, the pain dissipates and you will mainly enjoy your successes. The reason that the pain dissipates is simply because over time you will learn to avoid the silly mistakes of novices. With a bit of bad luck, even a correctly executed trade can lead to a loss, but loss caused despite correct behavior is not painful. It is reasonable, and part of the game. As long as you keep operating correctly and the overall outcomes are positive, there is no reason to feel pain.

A little about me: when I started out, I didn't pass any of these tests... not the scared money, not the self-discipline, and not the hating to lose. I hate to lose more than almost everyone else I know. Novice traders who find themselves in my state would usually opt out during their first year of trading. Not me. I succeeded because I am stubborn to the extreme. I had set myself a goal and knew I had to reach that level of other successful traders. My stubborn character made up for my other deficiencies, and over the years, I learned to uphold the criteria for two of the three tests. As my finances improved, I passed the scared money test; as my trading capabilities improved, I learned to take losses with a smile. As for self-discipline...I'm still working on that.

Take Maximum Advantage of Your Tuition Fees

Losses are part and parcel of the market's "tuition fees." Few traders are able to sustain themselves within just months of starting to trade. Most lose money as novices. Keep this in mind before you start trading. Why do I expect you to lose? Because trading with real money is unlike anything you are familiar with, and because despite all my warnings, you will make every mistake possible on your way to success. Reading the book, taking the course, and participating in the online trading room are all important, useful elements that reduce the period of losses and the amounts you will lose. Never trade without knowledge or practice, but these are not enough for success. To earn real money consistently, you must accrue real life "screen time," invest effort, and be determined. There is no profession in the world that can be learned and attained within just a few months.

Losses are not the aftereffect of trading, but an inseparable part of trading. Becoming a winning trader rather than a losing trader, you need to learn from every loss. Wring every bit of advantage possible from the "tuition fees" you "pay" to the market. Analyze every failed trade: its entry and exit points, the reason for entering, the reason for the loss and so on, as explained in the section on **keeping a trading diary**. I highly recommend printing out the stock's chart and analyzing it. Once a week, go over the data you have accumulated and try to understand the reasons for your mistakes. Very quickly you will learn enough to avoid repeating them. Leverage each loss and turn that knowledge into a gain.

Succeeding...the Wrong Way

One of the worst things that can happen to a trader is to succeed... the wrong way. For example, executing a trade against the trend which produces a handsome profit. The sweet taste of profit leaves a strong memory in the trader's mind, who then continues trading against the trend. But the outcome will too quickly "straighten out" and the trader's account will end up "crooked," since trading against the trend does not pay off in the long term. The trader who has learned to execute bad trades will repeat that error in the future. Then, believe me, this sure recipe for a gradual wipeout will become apparent soon enough.

SMART MONEY	*The stock exchange has a shameful habit: it gives loans to anyone asking, but wants them back with shameless interest rates!*

Sitting on Your Hands

Sometimes the best thing to do to avoid losses is simply not to trade. Every employee has days off from work. Stocks traders need them too. Some may be predetermined, such as when Wall Street closes for the Fourth of July, but there are also days when the market moves in too narrow a range to make trading worthwhile. On those days, just don't trade. The surfer needs the right waves to surf. The trader needs market volatility. This is the trader's daily bread. If, after an hour of trading, you see the market is flat, take a day off. Who are you working for? Believe me, the only ones who have earnings on flat days are the brokers.

Handling Loss

Our success depends on our mental conduct. The psychological baggage we carry with us strongly impacts our decision-making processes, and therefore our chances of success. Before making important decisions, we must examine our psychological preparedness. On days when we are too deep into negative moods that could affect our decisions, it is far better to keep a distance from the market and find other things to do. These are days when we may be fatigued, have argued with our spouse or someone else, when there are problems at work, and so on. A well-known axiom states that "knowing when not to make decisions is just as important as knowing when to make them!" Deciding *not* to do anything is far harder than deciding to do something.

How often has it happened that after making a bad decision, you berated yourself with "why did I do that??!" Most frequently, bad decisions derive from an unconscious negative frame of mind or mood. We need to be far more wary of the unconscious than the conscious. The problem is that we usually identify such states in retrospect, and usually when it is already too late.

A familiar problem is our psychological state after absorbing a loss. Every trader, even the most successful, experiences periods of losses. They affect us mentally and emotionally, and impact our decisions. They are the first and foremost reason for additional financial damage. Get to know the scope of impact that loss has on you and how to best cope with it.

Don't We Just Hate to Lose!

Research proves that the effect of loss is double that of the effect of profit (Kahneman & Tversky, 1991). One of my favorite examples from Kahneman's book is the coin gamble. In conferences where I lecture, I often conduct that experiment: I flip a coin and ask a volunteer if he or she is willing to participate in the gamble. If the volunteer guesses the answer correctly, I will pay $120, but if the volunteer gets it wrong, then he or she will have to pay me only $100. Despite the clear profit in the gain, 95% of lecture attendees refuse to take on the risk. Why? Because losing $100 is far more loathsome to us than gaining $120. Research has further proven that only if I up the ante to $200 for a correct guess compared to $100 paid to me if the volunteer guesses wrong, a 2:1 ratio, the majority of the audience will be willing to take the chance.

Losing Hurts

The human body is built to resist pain. It is therefore natural that we deny loss and hope for the best. When hoping for good is illogical, it is reasonable to presume that we will experience further damage. If you check the investment portfolio of the average investor, you will almost always find at least one stock showing a loss of 50% or more.

In my view, there is no logical reason to let any stock cause a loss of this scope. Denying loss at the outset and moving to inexplicable, somewhat euphoric optimism are the reasons for losses of this scope.

Another interesting phenomenon is that the stocks that have lost the most are those that the investor ceases following. The psychological handling of loss by most inexperienced traders is to ignore that stock. This is when self-justification steps in, and the investor spouts such phrases as, "it will make a comeback," or "the company has good products," "the organization's management is strong," or "it's no more than a paper loss." How about: "the prices always go up in the long run" or even pleading with the price itself: "please, just go up 10% and I swear I'll stop smoking!" Occasionally self-justification turns out to be a self-fulfilling prophecy. Generally, though, it doesn't.

A few weeks ago, a golfer friend told me about his 92-year-old father-in-law who recently lost $150,000 in the stock market. That was half his capital. He lost it on a failed investment in several stocks showing price drops over the past few months of trading. Concerned for his father-in-law's psychological state, my friend invited him to dinner, and was surprised to discover he was in an excellent mood. Asking how that was possible, the old man said, "I'm not worried. In the long term, the prices will go back up..."

Here's a possible scenario: you bought a stock and discover you've made a mistake. The price drops and comes very close to your planned exit (stop loss). When you bought the stock, the exit point seemed very far off and perhaps unreasonable, but now it is threatening you with a searing loss. The stock continues to new lows, and you think: "I didn't make a mistake, I chose a good stock. It will change direction for sure. I'll just give it a bit more time..." The greater the loss is shaping up to be, the stronger your powers of self-persuasion become. You're certain that this is *not* the time to sell, and move the stop down a bit, then a bit more... and the stock keeps dropping till you're losing so much that if you exit, the loss will be almost lethal. Realizing the loss at this point translates into strong pain. Keeping the stock translates into hope. And hope suppresses pain.

| **SMART MONEY** | *Loss causes us to drop our guard and switch to crazy buys and sells, hoping to recover the loss, which will generally lead to even greater losses.* |

Continuing to hold a losing stock is much like holding a lottery ticket before the winners are announced. In both cases, the chances of succeeding are very poor. The principle of "as long as I haven't sold, I haven't lost" is simply wrong. That's a fact. Nor has the chamber of horrors ended: the stock has reached an all-time low, and institutional traders won't touch it. But you have reached the amazing conclusion that since it is already so cheap, instead of reducing the quantity you are holding and closing out on the losing trade, you double the quantity of shares in the hope that the price will recover even half of its drop, returning your account to a state of balance.

Sound unbelievable? You cannot believe how many such cases I have come across. If you're smiling now, that means you've already been there, done that. If you're still doubtful, wait until you do just that yourself. This phenomenon, already mentioned in previous sections of the book, is called **averaging down**. In some cases, the method will save you from loss, but only one instance of a stock on which you have averaged down which does not recover and that will be the last trade you ever execute.

Identifying Loss-derived Behaviors

As noted, our psychological state has a determining impact on our chances of success. Intraday traders must be functioning at their best when they sit down to trade. A bad mood, a stormy argument, a headache or stomach pain, a baby that kept you up all night... all these will increase the probability of mistakes, which obviously reduce the probability of success. In these or similar situations, keep away from the screens. If you open the day with a loss or two, your ability for reasonable decisions will almost certainly be detrimentally affected.

We hate to lose. Losing causes pain. Our bodies resist pain. We are naturally not built to voluntarily exit at a loss, since that translates into pain and failure. But when failure leads us to denial, which affects the results of our activities, the result can be catastrophic.

When I had to absorb losses as a novice trader, I suffered. I love the sweet taste of success and winning. Losing several times in succession left me with weighty psychological baggage, and I did not learn quickly enough how to cope with it.

SMART MONEY	*Learn to turn your hatred of loss into acceptance, and use it to successfully avoid additional losses. You must remain conscious of the fact that your psychological state alters as a result of loss.*

Loss causes two contradictory reactions. On the day of trading itself, we seek to cover the loss with fast profits. The outcome: we tend to drop our guard and trade on everything that moves. We exchange good, healthy logic for embattled hope and convince ourselves "everything will be all right." You must surely have heard about casino gamblers who lost everything they own by trying to recoup their losses. Only in retrospect, they understand what actually happened, that their mood spiraled down to the point where they denied the dangers involved. Experienced traders will acknowledge this phenomenon as it is developing. The warning bells and red lights will go off in their minds and they will take steps to halt the downward spiral immediately. Do you know what happens on the trading floor on "black" days when stock exchange prices are falling too fast? The main computer is programmed to stop trading, and an announcer sends the traders home. Not a bad idea! You should adopt it, too.

Here is a possible scenario. You open the day with a loss. It can happen and it's not a big deal. Another loss makes your head spin uncontrollably. You quickly discover you've executed an extraordinary number of trades. Then you go ashen when you see you have doubled or tripled your loss. By the end of the day, you realize only too well what happened, and you promise yourself not to repeat this set of behaviors. Surprisingly, the next time it happens, you discover you've learned nothing at all! (Hey, are you keeping that trading diary?) This is usually the stage where you acknowledge and begin to understand the process, realize that the urge is stronger than you are, and that you need to build a prevention plan.

The day after the loss you wake to a new day of trading and discover new problems. Now you have become hesitant about clicking the buy button. You avoid trading, miss out on good trades, and quickly discover that yet another day has passed and you've earned nothing. You remember the pain of yesterday's loss and naturally try to protect yourself from re-experiencing it. The psychological effect is petrifying you. What is the solution? Avoid empowering the loss on the first day by identifying the problem early and taking preventative steps, understand that losses happen even to the best of traders, and learn to put yesterday's troubles behind you.

Using your hatred of losing productively can turn into significant profit, which is why I think we need to love our hatred. We need to leverage it, take advantage of it to learn how to cut losses before they balloon, and distance ourselves from a psychological state that leads us into further losses which, like a magic wand, will quickly make our trading account disappear!

Know Thy External Foe

Who is your enemy? Remember that it takes two to tango in every trade. Naturally, both buyers and sellers think they are making good trades, but only one side is right in the end. If sellers profit (i.e.buying at a low and selling at a high), then in their minds the stock "has done what it needs to do." On the other hand, even if sellers lose on the trade (buying at a high and selling at a low), they feel they have done good business by getting out of the stock which was causing losses and may continue doing so. In both cases, each side is convinced it is smart and the other side is stupid. So which side is smarter? Traders sometimes think they are buying stocks from a machine that does nothing but fulfill their requirements. Perhaps they think that if the word "wall" is part of the name Wall Street, they're playing squash against themselves. And this is their big mistake. On Wall Street, traders play "tennis." On the other side of the trade is an investor, an intraday trader, a market maker and a specialist, all of whom want to take as much of your money as they can lay their hands on. These are not colleagues but bitter, cruel foes, and they are not interested in captives.

Keeping in mind that on both sides of the trade are flesh and blood humans like yourself, driven by fear and greed, will help you keep the upper hand and attain successful trades. Look at the chart of a stock that is crashing. Can you hear the pain?

And Know, Too, Thy Home-Grown Foe!

A common question at job interviews is, "What are your drawbacks?" The typical response is usually one that evades presenting a negative character trait, and instead takes a positive one to an extreme: "I am a bit too thorough."

Intraday trading is a business just like any other. You are your own CEO. Interview yourself for the job and ask yourself, "What is my drawback?" Answer honestly, without evasion, without prettying anything up, because your answer will have tremendously important influence on your trading ability. Are you impulsive? Do you handle pressure well? Can you take loss? Are you covetous?

| **SMART MONEY** | *The trader's biggest enemy is… him- or herself!* |

The Rules of Psychological Conduct

Most of the time we live in denial. When we make severe errors we need to admit it, and when we are in a tight psychological place, it's very hard to admit any error. Denying our state causes greater losses or makes us realize profits too early. One of the ways to cope with denial is to identify the existence of the denial mechanism and process which bring us to problematic places - before there's a chance to spiral down. We must let go of those actions that undermine our capability, and stop them as they are happening. I doubt most of us would be willing to admit we are incapable, but if we admit to the existence of the process and set suitable rules of behavior, we will overcome our unwillingness to admit we are in a bad state. So, let's set some rules.

- **Three Straight Losses**

  Consecutive losses are known to lead to psychological incapacity. You've started your day of trading. The first trade is a loss. Not so terrible. The next one… is also a loss. Not so nice. If the third is a loss, you are not in a suitable psychological state to trade capably and responsibly. You may not want or like to admit it, but turn the computer off and do other things. *Note* that I did not say "go away" from the computer, but actually turn it off. If you don't, you will be tempted to "just take a look" which leads to "just recouping the losses" and we are back at square one, still with a compromised psychological state.

- **Set a Daily Loss Limit**

  Set a daily maximum loss figure and stick to it. If you have reached it, turn off the computer. You really want to keep on trading in order to recover the loss, but in 70% of such cases, you will only make things worse. When you go over that maximum, you are no longer capable of trading responsibly and are in a compromised psychological state.

- **Never Return to a Losing Stock**
  Did you exit a losing stock? Then forget about it. Reentering will usually only lead to another loss. Once you've lost money on a stock, it is natural to want to recoup the loss. Our tendency is to deny the fact that we have made a mistake, and we look for a second chance with that stock to make good. Sometimes, we even take a third chance! This is the outcome of the human reaction known as "I'll show it!" When you exit a losing stock, do not return to it that same day. Keep your distance from it as you would from wildfire, otherwise you will get badly burned.

- **Exit a Stock That's Going Nowhere**
  You bought a stock, and nothing is happening. Is the price is moving sideways, wavering between profit and loss, for ten minutes? Exit immediately. Perhaps it will work, perhaps not, but the only reason you're still holding onto it is... ego. You're not ready to admit that buying it was a mistake. So own up, and tell yourself that the stock is not doing what you thought it would. Within ten minutes, you should have been seeing one or the other, profit or loss, but not continued sideways movement. If the stock hasn't decided which way it is going, both options are still open. That means there is a 50% chance of profiting. But also a 50% chance of losing! Give up on the trade and devote your attention to another stock. Free up important screen space, free up your buying power, and don't look at that stock again. In fact, perhaps more importantly, free up your mind to concentrate on something that isn't stuck in place. To do so would be no more than an irrational gamble rather than a considered, careful decision.

The Top Ten: 10 Things Failing Traders Say

1. **I don't want to realize a loss.**
   Every huge loss started out as a small loss. Your exit plan must be clear. Be disciplined and stay with it. Most traders encounter their psychological issues when they need to stick to a stop loss which seemed very logical before it started moving in a losing direction, but

now looks eminently movable "just a little bit..."

2. **I'll wait until the losing stock recovers to my entry price.**
   Duh... as though the market cares if "your" stock is ever going to recover! You know what? For the sake of the argument, let's say it does recover. Presuming your investment is limited, you are tying up good money to a bad stock and losing out on other opportunities. Get out, forget about it, and focus your attention on more beneficial options. Losses happen.

3. **If I don't sell now... it'll go down!**
   It's well known that inexperienced traders sell winning stocks too quickly and exit losing stocks too late. Instead of selling a good stock fast, take a partial and raise your stop loss on the quantity that's left. Stay with a stock showing a winning trend.

4. **I lost $100 on ABC, so I realized a profit of $100 on XYZ.**
   Since when does a loss on one stock have any connection with success on another? Manage your winning stock and forget the loss on the other (despite the psychological difficulty), no matter how fresh that loss. Statistically, if you're operating correctly, you should succeed in more than 50% of your trades. Every trade is an independent entity having no relationship to the outcomes of any earlier trade.

5. **I'm not taking partials. I buy and sell one stock, once.**
   Maintaining correct money management will help you succeed. If you take a partial on a winning stock, you will build up a good "profit cushion" which will allow you to take better care of the remaining quantity of shares. Yes, this is no more than a psychological solution meant to assist in overcoming the need to sell when the stock is still doing well, but remember: correct money management will avoid arousing those dormant demons buried deep within us all.

6. **I'm bored. I've got to buy something!**
   No day is like any other. Some days, the market is "heavy." Bored? Go out and enjoy the day away from your trading rig. The disease known as "overtrading" is a tough one, and sometimes it's hard to prescribe medication for it. Some of the best traders around felt desperately ill with this disease when they were novices, and some traders fall so ill

that they end up losing their trading account. The psychological urge and need to click that button, no matter what, brings many a good trader down. By the way, the disease has a unique name: "Clickitis."

7. **I should have done that differently.**
Easy to be smart in hindsight. Everything looks simple. Trust your instincts, trust your knowledge, and take the right actions in real time. Then have no regrets. Every loss is a learning curve. The way to success is paved with learning curves.

8. **I'll average down just this once!**
Let me remind you that a trader who thinks this way is already in a losing streak and has increased the quantity of shares to "average down" the loss. The trader hopes that the price will correct to trending up, allowing an exit with no gain but at least no loss. The only thing I can say about this method is "ha, ha, ha." To anyone who tells me it worked once and therefore it's worth repeating, let me add one more "ha."

9. **I invest only for the long term.**
Long-term investment proved its effectiveness over the years, but is becoming increasingly difficult to maintain. In our parents' time, one could buy IBM, for example, put it beneath the pillow (yes, once upon a time real, thick paper certificates would be given to the buyer!), go to sleep, wake the next day and know everything was still just fine. Those times have passed from our world. I do not oppose long-term investment, especially if the method works for you, but at least diversify your investment portfolio with some short-term activity.

10. **It's the market's fault.**
It's so easy to blame the market: I wasn't taught well, I was promised millions, the floor's slippery, the stock market is known to be an ungrateful place... and more. Not everyone is suited to intraday trading and the market is not suited to everyone. In closing this chapter, let me quote John Burroughs:
"A man can fail many times, but he isn't a failure until he begins to blame somebody else."

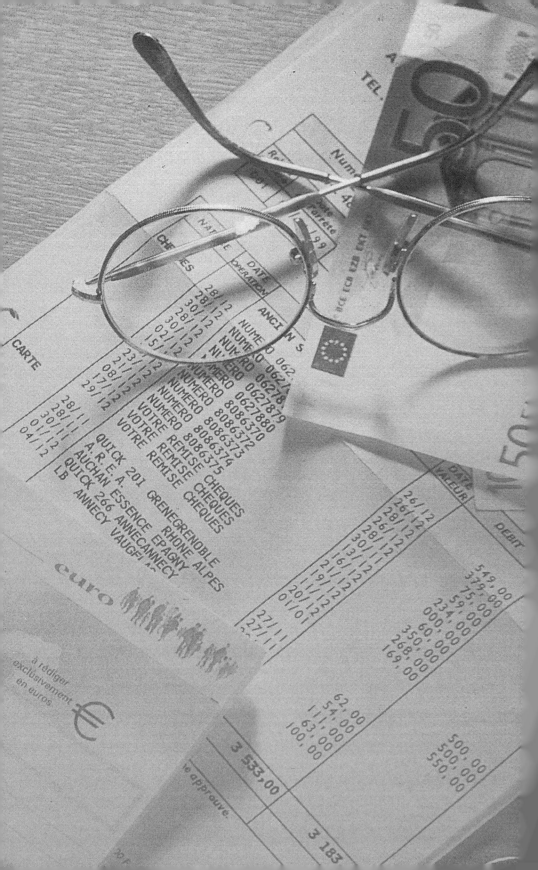

15

Special Occasions,

Special Rules

The market, like humans, needs its own special days.

Prepare for the Expectable

On certain days, at certain times known in advance, the market will behave in special ways. This requires us to prepare specially for such occasions. Sometimes the meaning of "prepare" is simply not to trade on that day, and sometimes it will mean that those are precisely the times when amazingly interesting opportunities will fall in our laps. Each occasion has its own particular character.

The Last Day of the Week

The last day of the trading week is Friday. A drop in tension is felt by stock traders on this day, and the volume of activity usually plummets during the second half of Friday's work hours. As activity thins on the stock exchange floor, it signals the time for us, the traders, to close our week as well. Without volume and other traders, there is no volatility or direction, and the market is open to the manipulations of the big players and the market makers who go to work in the "vacuums."

On Fridays, most of the trading opportunities occur during the first two hours of trading. Trading throughout the rest of the day depends on market behavior, which can be very shallow though occasionally does surprise for the better. My wife used to say that if I never traded on Fridays, my trading account would show a higher balance... Well, it's not exactly like that, but I do admit that the quantity of successes on Fridays is very low.

Note Market Behavior on a Typical Friday

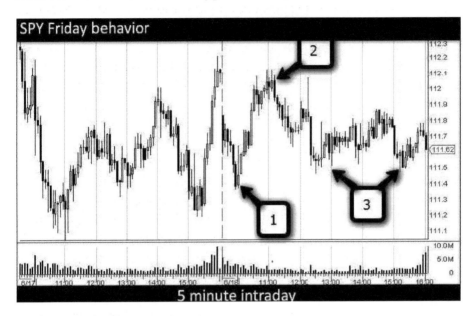

A classic Friday. The whole day was an "inside day," meaning a day on which trading occurred within the boundaries of the previous day's trading (to the left of the perforated line). In short, a disappointing, directionless day. The day starts with a gap down and drops to a low [1], changes direction, kills all my shorts, and closes the gap [2]. When I finally convince myself to take some longs, it kills them, too, by moving sideways the entire day [3].

On Fridays I tend to close, or at least greatly reduce the quantity of open swing trades I am holding. If you are thinking of sleeping on some stocks over the weekend, be aware that you are taking a risk, since you can never know if some crisis will erupt during those two long weekend days. This is even more applicable if you're taking a day off, making this a longer weekend. The more time you hold those stocks, the more risk you take. I tend to keep stocks over the weekend only if I have taken a partial of three-quarters the original quantity bought for a handsome profit.

Options Expiration Days

These are very significant days. Every third Friday of the month, on the Chicago Stock Exchange, stock options expire. This book does not describe trading options, which is an entire profession in itself, but we do need to understand the meaning of these expirations. This is when the big options players, professional organizations, can dictate market direction. Of course you may ask what connection exists between options expiration and intraday trading. Well, there is a connection. Options trading is highly varied, and much of the trading is impacted by the activities in the options market. Therefore, as I will explain later, options expiration noticeably influences intraday trading, especially on the actual day of expiration.

What is an Option?

To understand the influence of options on stock prices, I will try to give a definition at the most superficial level for options. An option is a contract between the writer (seller) and the buyer, according to which the seller allows the buyer, in return for a set price (the option price), to buy or sell a stock for a predetermined quantity and price (the strike price). Instead of trying to understand the previous sentence, let's focus on the following example: Assume that you believe that Apple's stocks will drop in price. You can profit in two ways from this drop: by shorting it (which we learned) or by buying options called **put options.** By contrast, if you believe the stock price will rise, you can either buy the shares or buy the options, known as **call options.** Let's say you bought a put option and the price did indeed fall. When the option expires (the third Friday of the month), you can realize a nice profit. But if the price did not fall, or even if it fell slightly less than what you expected, you may lose the entire cost of the option purchase, and the seller of the option will profit. Of course the total process is somewhat more complex and includes various expiration dates and strike prices, but the above is sufficient to grasp the concept.

Pros Always Profit

Options writers are experienced pros who earn their living from trading in options. They know better than most investors how to evaluate the probability of Apple's stock falling, for example, and can price the option accordingly so that their risk of loss is extremely small. Statistics show that most options expire worthless, and the pros, as can be expected, make their profit.

SMART MONEY | *On the week that options are due to expire, expect volatility in the stock market on Tuesday and/or Wednesday, though more often on Wednesday, and sideways movement on Thursday and Friday.*

What happens when the majority of the public believes Apple will fall, buys large quantities of put options, and towards expiration date Apple does indeed drop? Does this mean the pros have taken a loss? Occasionally, yes, but not always. The pros who write the options have deep pockets and are capable of shifting almost any stock back to the price where most options expire worthless. Moreover, their way of protecting themselves from any fall in the price of Apple stock is to short the stock. When they short Apple, they profit from the drop in the share price and can pay you your profit on the put option. When do they close (i.e. buy) their short? On expiration day itself. When they close shorts, which means they are buying stocks, they help the stock price rise, and often cause the price to return to exactly that point where most put options expire as worthless.

An exercise in logic: Let's say that the public buys a large quantity of put options on the market index. In other words, most of the public thinks the market is going to go down. What do you think will happen in the market towards expiration of the options? You're right: the market will go up! Since the options writers could lose from a drop in market prices, they will bring the market to the price level where the options expire as worthless. Remember that the options writers are serious pros, and pros *never* lose.

When will we feel the professionals' activities? Usually, they start shifting market direction towards the required price over Tuesday and Wednesday of the expiration week. After reaching the required price during the first half of the week, Thursday and Friday will generally be "flat" days.

Conclusion: expect a very volatile market on Tuesday and/or Wednesday of options expiration week.

The period is the week ending on July 18, 2010. It is a fairly erratic time, towards the end of the financial crisis, and several weak European countries are on the verge of bankruptcy. There is real concern over a sharp fall in the stock market. Many funds and investors fear market plunges, and by way of protection buy SPY put options to hedge their long-term investments.

These heavy investors presume that if the market drops, they will lose on their stocks, but will cover these losses through the profits on options. It's a bit like buying insurance meant primarily to cover your own back rather than to actually help your clients. Who is selling options to the heavy investors? The pros! With the period above being a highly agitated one, the quantity of put options is far greater than call options. All that is left for the pros to do is bring the market price up on Tuesday [1] to where most of the put options expire as worthless, and maintain that target until Friday [2]. It doesn't take a genius to predict the likely outcome. One only needs to be familiar with the rules of the market.

Note the Behavior of the SPY ETF during Expiration Week (daily chart)

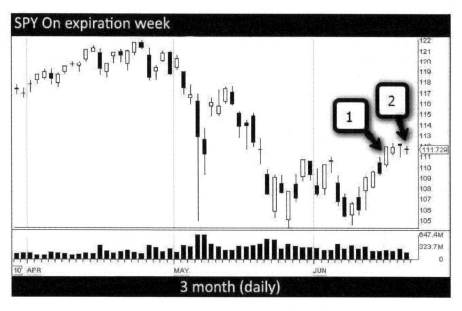

On the third Friday of every third month, meaning March, June, September and December, three types of options expire: stocks, futures and commodities, and indexes. This is also why the day is known as **"triple witching day."** What that means for us as traders is that market activity will be even more extreme than on a regular options expiration Friday. Volatility will be higher, and the lack of clear market direction will be more strongly felt. These are the days when you need to be extremely careful.

Another very interesting phenomenon is that of options expiration for stocks at round numbers. Options are issued in round numbers: for example, you can buy put or call options for XYZ priced, let's say, at fifty dollars. This means that if you bought a "fifty dollar put"and the stock falls below that price on the expiration day, you have profited. If you bought a "fifty dollar call" and the price is above that on expiration date, you have profited. As with the white numbers in roulette where only the house is a winner, here too there is only one price, where the options writer is the only one who can profit from it. What is that price?

Yes, you're right. Fifty dollars! In other words, towards the expiration date which is the end of Friday's trading, the options writer will try to shift the stock price to the exact round figure. To see which round figure the stock will aim for on expiration day, check your trading platform's "Options" window (if your broker provides this information on your trading platform), and look at the price at which the options were bought. If on expiration day the share price is close to the round number at which the bulk of options were bought, in most cases you can presume that the stock will end exactly at that round number at which most trades were made. In other words, most of the options will expire as worthless to their buyers and with profits to their writers. It's such a rigged game that it makes me laugh each time.

Now let's take a look at the quantity of options on Legg Mason Inc., the capital management company:

Options on Legg Mason Stock, LM

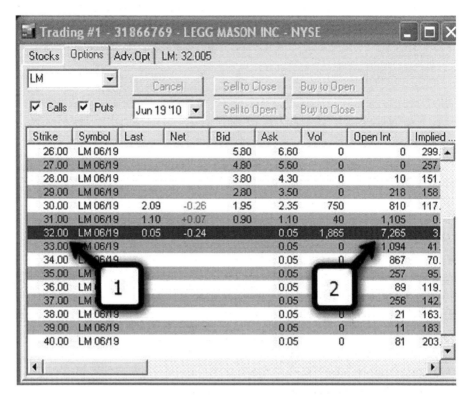

Notice that at the round figure of thirty-two dollars [1], we find the largest volume totaling 7,265 options [2] (known as open interest) on the stock. Where do you think the price will be at the end of trading on expiration day? As we have discussed earlier, there is only one price at which the pros, who write the options, are the only ones who profit.

Now let's look a little further:

Expiration Day Five-Minute Candles for Legg Mason, LM

As you see, the last trade on expiration day was executed at thirty-two dollars. [1]. Now, pay attention to the thirty-two dollar line running across the chart. LM is drawn to this price already at the start of the day, and all it has to do once it reaches thirty-two dollars is to consolidate above or below this figure until the day ends at thirty-two dollars [1]. The pros know exactly where they need to bring the price, and that's where you will find it.

SMART MONEY | *Because the options writers want to profit on expiration day, they will try to shift the stock price on that day close to the strike price of the largest open position of options.*

In summary, if you insist on trading in stocks on expiration day, first check the price their options were sold at. If you wanted to short LM based on your conclusion that it would drop to below thirty-two dollars, you need to understand that your chance of success is almost nil. A more reasonable conclusion is that the stock will close at precisely the price for which the greatest number of options were written, and that is the price at which... yes, only the pros profit.

Interest Rate Day

The announcement of the periodic interest rate is the most important of decisions and has immediate, strong impact not only on the US markets, but worldwide. Interest rate decisions are known for determining impact on stock market behavior for both the short and long terms. The decision is announced on fixed dates eight times throughout the year, when the Federal Open Market Committee (FOMC) meets. The FOMC sets the short-term interest and thereby influences the price of credit, and thus the entire market.

Interest, as we know, is the **price of money**. The higher the interest, the more expensive money is. The lower the interest, the cheaper money is. When money is cheap, it pays to "buy" money. We do this by taking loans. When money is expensive, it pays to "sell" money, by giving loans. A savings account is a way of you lending money to the bank. Simple, right?

So how is all this connected to the market? That, too, is simple. When money is cheap, the return or yield on money loans (savings) is low. People with money who fear its value will be undermined (known as inflation) turn to other investment channels such as real estate and the stock market, in the hope that they will gain better returns. Cheap money means more money available to the stock market, which translates as more buyers, which means rates go up. In fact, it is even worth borrowing money from the bank to invest in other channels such as stocks and real estate. In addition, when money is cheap, the amount of money available is greater and is therefore worthwhile putting to use, which drives the economy and increases the profits of companies traded on the stock exchange.

SMART MONEY	*On interest rate decision day, we prefer trading only in the first two hours. After that, the market waits for the decision. In limbo, it shows very low volatility. Immediately following the announcement, volatility will often be too high for trading.*

So if everything looks so good, why is interest not kept constantly low? Cheap money can cause two eventualities. First, it can lead to inflation: that is, raised prices deriving from the undermined value of money which is cheap. The second is the formation of a bubble, a situation where the prices of real estate and securities swell disproportionately to their real value.

When the Federal Reserve Bank raises interest, it increases savings and restrains other economic activities such as investment and consumerism. By contrast, when it drops interest rates, it decreases saving and encourages economic activities in the marketplace. The Federal Reserve's interest policy determines the medium and long-term value of investments and savings, and is therefore very important to all participants involved in the stock market.

A week of trading in which an interest rate decision is announced is usually a week in which the market shows agitation, since many professional traders choose to "sit on their hands" rather than trade close to announcement time. Once the announcement is publicized, the market goes mad! Immediately following the announcement, the market will usually move in three sharp waves of completely unpredictable directions. Those who care about their money do not usually try to ride these waves.

Unlike market direction, which is unforeseeable immediately following the interest decision, the interest rate set by the FOMC is generally very predictable. So what causes such erratic behavior in the market if the interest rate can be fairly well predicted? The announcement's formulation: how it is worded is no less important than the actual decision on the interest rate. Reading the announcement enables an understanding of probable future interest rate changes and the economic mood as expected by the committee members. We can conclude that the wording of the announcement, rather than the interest rate itself, is what causes market agitation.

What should we do on interest rate decision day? Generally, we trade only during the first two hours. After that we can expect the market to remain static until the announcement, always given at 2:15 PM, New York time. The high volatility thereafter is usually "too much too late." Before the announcement, exit all trades currently showing prices close to your stop loss. The probability is high that the volatility caused by the announcement will send your stocks up and down so wildly that your stop orders will be executed even if those stocks eventually do move in the right direction.

End of Quarter Window Dressing

Reliable fund and money managers handling the public's finances must announce the results of their investment actions at the end of each quarter.

Among a variety of data are two items of particular importance: the list of stocks in which the fund invests, and yields of those investments. But the managers want to present a rosy picture to investors, so they tend to do some "window dressing" in the form of prettying up investment portfolios with a few improvements. One of these improvements is dumping weak stocks that caused losses, and buying up strong stocks. This is how they show their shareholders a different list at the end of the quarter from the actual list they traded with during most of the quarter. This improved list leads clients to feel that the fund managers know how to choose the right stocks. Additionally, on the last day of the quarter, they tend to prop up the price of stocks they are holding and prevent them from falling. Since most of the money in the market belongs to funds, the outcome is that at the end of the quarter, the market usually does not drop and sometimes even trends up. Of course, poor monetary outcomes eventually float to the surface, but the window dressing phenomenon is known and will likely continue.

What does this mean for you? Simply this: do not expect the markets to push lower during the last days of the quarter. If the market needs to drop, it will do so at the start of the next quarter. You can also expect that weak stocks from the previous quarter will continue falling, since the funds exit them to swap for stronger stocks. On the other hand, strong stocks being bought up by the funds will continue climbing.

The Market at Year's End

What happens at the end of the year to a stock that showed strength throughout the year? Will it pull back? Will buyers realize profits?

Indeed, for reasons generally tied to taxation, the pullback will generally not come at year's end. In the US, taxes are paid only on profits from stocks sold at a profit during the calendar year from January 1 to December 31. An investor postponing the sale of stocks showing a profit to the start of the next tax year can delay paying the tax by a full tax year, and perhaps end up not paying it at all, depending on the overall status of the next tax year.

Conclusion: strong stocks which rose during the year are expected to continue rising in the final weeks of the year, since investors avoid selling due to tax laws. By contrast, weak stocks are expected to sell in order to "lock the loss." In other words, a strong year will generally end with continuing new highs and a weak year will typically see continued lows until the end of the tax year.

It is commonly believed that investors who avoided "locking profits" at the end of the year will realize their profits at the start of January. This is not necessarily true. Strong stocks do not sell easily. The more their price rises, the more the interest in selling them decreases. The greater probability is that investors will continue holding winning stocks well into the new tax year.

For how long will they hold these stocks? Until there is no choice but to sell. April 15th is the date by which tax returns must be filed, together with any payment due. Deposits to the IRS account can also be made only until April 15th. As a result, many investors sell their stocks only towards the end of March or early April to raise money to pay their taxes.

An investor who needs the cash will execute sales generally up until the first week of April, since brokers take three days to release cash to their clients. The third day is known as **settlement day**. It takes another two days until the settlement actually shows in the client's bank account.

Holidays

The stock exchanges are open most days of the year, other than certain holidays. About a week before any of these, your broker will send you a "short trading week" reminder with details.

Pay attention to the fact that sometimes trades will be executed only during the first half of the day. You should receive information from the broker on that as well. Shortened trading days are usually "bridges" between vacations and are known to have low volumes, making it best to avoid trading altogether.

Naturally, the risk of holding stocks for a swing over several consecutive days of holidays is greater than for a regular weekend. More days off means a greater risk that something bad could happen. Towards vacations and long weekends, I tend to reduce the quantities of stock I hold for a swing.

Summary

Below is a summary of non-trading days you should keep updated and mark in advance on your personal calendar (highly recommended!)

Special Occasions	What You Need to Remember
Last day of the trading week (Friday)	Volumes are likely to be low. The market is generally not volatile after the first two trading hours. It is wise to reduce quantities of stocks held for a swing.
Options expiration days: the third Friday of every month	The market is not expected to be volatile. Stock prices tend to hover near round numbers.
Options expiration week	High volatility is expected on Tuesday and/or Wednesday. Low volatility expected on Thursday and Friday.
Triple options expiration, "triple witching day": the third Friday of every quarter	As above, but even more extreme
Interest rate decision day	Do not trade beyond the first two hours. Reduce quantities prior to the announcement. Trading immediately afterwards tends to extreme volatility and can be highly risky.
Interest rate decision week	The week in which the announcement is due is typified by highly agitated trading in advance of the public announcement.
End of quarter "window dressing"	Institutional traders can be expected to guard the market from lows, equip themselves with strong stocks and exit weak ones.
End of year	Expect sales of weak stocks, while strong stocks can be expected to maintain uptrends. At the end of a weak year, the market tends to continue falling. At the end of a strong year, the market tends to keep rising.

Income tax payment day: April 15th	7-10 days in advance, expect investors to sell stocks in order to finance their tax payment.
Holidays	No trading, or shortened trading hours with low volatility and poor volumes. Avoid trading.

16

Preparedness and Empowerment

Be ready, take the opportunity by the horns, and succeed.

The Fear of Taking Risks

Willpower drives humans. It drives us to reaching our goals. The very fact that you have read this book means you have a dream, a goal, and the will to succeed.

Willpower drives people to succeed financially, but the simple fact is that most don't. Their failure can be put down to two main reasons: they lack the knowledge of how to operate in order to become wealthy, or they know what should be done but take no action for fear of the dangers involved. Humans are driven by fear. The dangers that drive fear, in 90% of the cases, do not ever turn into the nightmare scenarios that people might imagine.

The path to success is paved with risks. People who opt for "safe" their entire lives will never go anywhere. The mental fear of risk comes from our upbringing. From early on, we were programmed to avoid risks, to go and learn a solid profession, to raise a family, to get a job and achieve financial security. Yes, financial security – and not financial independence!

The education we received instills fear in our hearts to step outside the box and take a chance on change. Fear of risk paralyzes us and returns us to the structured template which we incorrectly perceive as secure. The way to break free from the chains of fear is to recognize our ability to overcome obstacles, or in other words, boost our own self-confidence.

Self-confidence

On the way to success in stock trading, as with life and business, we must cope with obstacles. Most people avoid that, since they believe from the outset that their chances of success are poor. Lack of belief in oneself indicates a poor level of self-confidence and deficient self-esteem. People who are born with a strong sense of self-confidence are very few and far between. The rest of us need to learn methods for improving our self-confidence.

Self-esteem is built while we are young. Initially, we develop insights such as "I'm good at..." or "I have a problem with..." At this point, we switch our brains onto autopilot and adopt positive or negative programs as though they are decrees from heaven. One random unsuccessful coping episode can create the feeling of failure that causes us to quietly accept that the situation is due to our own negative traits. The feelings we experience during failure are, in fact, the way we choose to translate reality. We may translate failure into disappointment, depression, lack of appetite, oversleeping. But we can choose differently: we can translate failure into challenge, the urge to improve, to feel adrenalin flowing strongly. Only you can choose how to translate your reality. What differentiates between the behavior of an outstanding athlete and a failed one? Their perception of reality. Being confident of winning lets the outstanding athlete translate reality positively. The way sports champions translate their reality is identical to the way successful stock traders translate theirs. When Thomas Edison was asked if he felt he had failed after 700 attempts at developing the ideal electric light bulb, he answered that he had discovered 700 ways that do not work.

If you were not born with Edison's self-confidence, don't throw up your hands helplessly. Self-confidence can be improved through diverse techniques known as "internal communication."

Boosting Self-esteem through Internal Communication

Internal communication includes those 1000 words that pass through our minds each minute. When we think, we use our own unique vocabulary, telling ourselves what is allowed and what is not, who we are and what we think about our abilities and limitations. The key to self-confidence depends on the words we choose. To improve self-esteem and self-confidence, we need to examine our vocabulary of words and phrases, and if necessary to change our internal dictionary.

We need to peel away all words that do not offer a positive contribution, such as "perhaps," "I'll try," "I can't," and more. Do these strengthen or weaken you? Change them to "I can" and "I will succeed." Talk about yourself to yourself in the first person: I'm successful, I'm a money-making machine, I'm a magnet for other people, I'm sure of myself, I'm happy, I'm pleased. The more we use constructive phraseology, the better our perception of self becomes. Believe in yourself and your abilities, since the views of others are negligible. As long as you maintain your self-confidence and belief in yourself, you will succeed and your financial success will improve in direct correlation to your self-esteem. Good internal communication improves your quality of life, your self-confidence, and no less valuable, your external communication.

External Communication

This is the way you express yourself, the words you say, your body language, your facial expressions. External communication is power. It is your power to impact others and the way they perceive you. Everything you wish to achieve, everything you lack, you can reach through those very same people. First, you need to find them and connect to them. If you mingle with people who have money, sooner or later something of it will cling to you too. If you mingle only with the people you grew up with, you won't get far. During the most challenging financial timeframe of my life (see what I mean? I swap "difficult" for "challenging") when I had not a penny to my name, I joined an exclusive golf club. That was my way of mingling with the haves rather than the have-nots.

Despite my dreadful financial state, how did I manage suitable external communication with millionaires as an equal among equals? When you come from a lower economic class, it's not so easy to communicate naturally with someone who is leagues above you. Try imagining how you'd behave if invited to lunch, one-on-one, with Donald Trump. Would your external communication be natural? Now try to imagine the lines of communication between Trump and Warren Buffet. Would they be more natural? Of course they would.

How does one millionaire approach another? Does he look him straight in the eye when speaking, or look down? My way of structuring good external communication was to structure constructive internal communication. I constantly repeated to myself, "I'm a millionaire. A check for one million dollars is on its way to my account, but hasn't been deposited yet." Once I convinced myself I was a millionaire and that the check was merely delayed in the mail, being a millionaire was a given. With that problem behind me, my external communication altered. The expensive membership fees quickly paid off and were dwarfed by the scope of deals in millions of dollars I closed on the golf course.

External communication puts amazing power into the hands of those who know how to use it. Look how far external communication led people like Barack Obama, or at the other extreme entirely, Mussolini and Hitler. Strong external communication is the outcome of correctly applying internal communication, which is the source of power in individuals who succeed.

Aspiring to Be Powerful

The aspiration for power has impacted human history more than all the forces of nature put together. For those doing the controlling, their power is positive; for those being controlled, that power is generally negative. It makes no difference how you feel about power. You need to accept the fact that in the world we live in, the powerful control and the powerless are controlled. So what is it that you prefer: to set your own agenda, or live your life according to an agenda set by someone else? Simply put: are you the sheep or the wolf?

Power itself can be controlled. Power does not necessarily mean controlling the fate of other people. We can accumulate great power, but use it only to the degree where we have absolute control over our own fates. Power does not have to carry negative connotations, but can be used positively by assisting others. I tend to lecture free of charge to high school students, college students, and soldiers. The demand for my knowledge gives me a great feeling of being powerful in a different way.

The significance of power altered as civilization developed. In prehistoric human history, the powerful individual was the physically strongest. Over time, as the world developed into an economic organization, the focus of power shifted to those with capital. The wealthiest was the most powerful. At some point, an interesting shift became apparent when the socially-accepted norm determined that power would be passed down by inheritance from the nobleman to his son. If you were not born into nobility, your chances of succeeding, influencing, and accumulating power and assets were zero. The only way that might happen was if you were close to the nobleman in some way. These dark times, in which nobility was richly remunerated and the commoner found no positive incentive, typified the Middle Ages, a time in which the world almost stopped progressing. The Industrial

Revolution, when the holders of capital and therefore power were those who owned machines, put an end to the power of nobility.

In our own times, power once again changed hands, moving from those who held capital and assets to those who also held knowledge. Up until some decades ago, it would have been impossible to compete with heavily-invested companies such as General Motors or IBM. To compete with a giant like IBM, a dreamy capital in the billions of dollars would have been needed. All this was true until a "geek" in jeans named Bill Gates overthrew IBM from the top by the use of initiative and knowledge. So too for Apple, Facebook, Google and tens of other companies that now control our lives, but were established not by holders of capital but by holders of knowledge. The beauty of our current times is that the chances of success are open to every single person, even if you have no physical power, capital, or title of nobility. Knowledge is power. Knowledge is the key to success. And knowledge can be bought.

Knowledge and Action

Knowledge moves the world. Until the end of the nineteenth century, if you had neither capital nor title, you could never break out from the class into which you were born. In those times, knowledge was for the privileged few, and banks funded the upper classes rather than those with knowledge. Our world is completely different: we live in an era where knowledge is readily accessible, and capital seeks good ideas even if the person presenting them is a youngster with a ponytail who never even finished college. Billionaires like Bill Gates and Steve Jobs were not born into the nobility--they were simply born into the right time. And they didn't have a college degree.

Knowledge and ideas are available to anyone seeking them. If knowledge is available to all, how is it that there are not more people who are successful, happy, driving Ferraris and living in Beverly Hills villas? Because knowledge in itself is not enough. Knowledge is the potential for power, but to realize it, actions are needed. Success begins with knowledge and ends in actions.

Knowledge in stock trading is also available to anyone seeking it, so why isn't everyone rich? Because operating in the stock market also requires integrating knowledge with action. The world is full of people with broad knowledge but who are inactive. What is unique about the successful individuals is that they, unlike the bulk of the public, take action. Their success, their power to control their own futures, derives from accrued knowledge and cumulative actions.

If you want to succeed, use other people's knowledge and emulate the successful. You don't even need to come up with an original idea. Did Steve Jobs invent Apple's graphic interface, the mouse or the iPad? No. He took existing ideas and upgraded them to such a state of perfection that he created an entirely new market. He fine-tuned solutions and took action. Nor did Bill Gates invent the DOS system which turned him into such a wealthy individual. He bought it from an inventor who did not realize its inherent potential.

A Role Model

Success does not require you to reinvent the wheel. Find a working model and copy it. I am not suggesting you give up on being the next inventor of a dot-com enterprise. I am just trying to stay practical. From the experience of decades of business activity, I've learned that the chances of success are higher when emulating and improving upon existing products, knowledge and methods. During the dot-com bubble era, I failed in my attempts at inventing products and services which I was sure would change the world. But I did succeed in improving on existing ideas and products. Nor did I invent day trading, but I was the first to turn it into a model for schools and brokerage companies operating in various countries outside the United States. This was a successful model I initiated, which did not require my own capital. I brought knowledge and entrepreneurial initiative to the table, and recruited investor funds. My life was not one of successes only. I experienced some tough failures, but I always kept one thing in mind: if I don't try, I won't succeed.

Success does not need to follow a model of worldwide scope such as Facebook. If a business is doing incredibly well in Los Angeles, there's no reason it should not do well in San Diego. I suggest you keep your eyes wide open, find a worthy role model, copy and upgrade. If a stock trader is a role model for success, there is no good reason why you shouldn't contact that person, learn from him or her, and try to emulate his or her success. You have to believe that if someone succeeds, you can too! If you don't believe that, then first work on improving your self-esteem.

It is difficult to hide success. Successful people leave clear footprints. Go after those footprints and try to copy the steps, one after the other. You can do more than just copy: you can improve to such a degree that one day you may be the role model for someone else. Never forget that for every action you take, there is a price tag. The price is measured in resources such as money and time, where money is the cheaper of the two. Time is your most costly resource which, if wasted, can never be recovered.

For success, you must have true, burning faith in your ability. You must infuse yourself with this faith every day. Talk to yourself, tell yourself how strong, smart and successful you are. Convince yourself, believe in yourself, and simultaneously gain knowledge, knowhow, and take a risk...take action.

Believing in Success

Believing in your ability is the key to success.

If you limit your belief, you limit the results in kind. If you convey belief in your ability to your brain, there is no limit to what you can achieve. We are not born with this kind of belief. We gain such beliefs and develop them throughout our lives. Current negative beliefs can be exchanged for new, positive ones. If you lack faith in your capabilities, try to look back and find the source, perhaps in childhood, religious belief, or politics. From our earliest childhood, we develop in the shadow of our parents. In my childhood I was not taught to initiate, take risks, or reach financial independence. I was taught to choose the safest options because my parents felt that was correct, either because that is how they were raised or because certain life circumstances shaped these views. Most people do not develop opinions and beliefs independently, but inherit them from parents and the media.

As a condition for breaking out beyond the framework in which you currently exist, develop independent beliefs of your own, adopt them warmly, and take command over your future. If you're ready to formulate a new belief, then choose a task, preferably a tough one, perhaps even one in which you failed in the past such as losing weight or quitting smoking. If your gut reaction to this task is, "Wow, that's too tough, it doesn't sound doable..." then you've chosen the perfect option!

A Five-Step Plan

Here are five steps to formulating, internalizing and realizing a new belief:

FIRST, repeatedly embed your new belief into your mind. Like every belief you've developed over your lifetime, a new belief must be meticulously implanted within your mindset. Repeat your goal over and over to yourself until you firmly believe in your ability to achieve it.

Your parents may have said umpteen times, "You need to learn a profession." The media relentlessly penetrates the political messages you adopt, day after day, year after year. Even your religious beliefs were not absorbed in just one day. Now your job is to choose a goal and hammer that ability to achieve it deep within yourself. No one can do this for you.

When I was twelve years old, I decided to become a millionaire. In the economic environment of my reality, I had never met such a person, but the target was marked and repeated in my mind daily. Every time a momentous event occurred, I repeated my mantra, "I want to be a millionaire." Over the years, this belief became so much a part of me that I never doubted my ability to succeed. With success now a given in my mindset, the only thing left was to choose how to achieve it.

One of the most effective ways to embed a belief is to write it down every day in a notebook dedicated for this purpose. Doing this reinforces your belief at the subconscious level. I would even suggest writing it down on sticky notes and attaching them to all kinds of objects in the house, but then your friends might arrange to have you hospitalized before you've reached your goal.

SECOND, try to imagine success. How would you look if you were a whole lot lighter? What sort of clothes would you buy? How proud would you be when you join friends who knew you as a smoker and they see you no longer disappear every twenty minutes to grab a smoke? Imagining helps reinforce determination and helps cope with the process of reaching your goal.

My golf coach, Ricardo, actually trained as a psychiatrist before becoming a pro golfer. During one lesson, Ricardo taught me that a successful golf shot requires me to imagine the outcome. "Before hitting, imagine the flight of the ball and your target," he would repeat. And it works! The body amazingly moves according to what we imagine.

THIRD, spread your belief. Tell everyone you can about your goal and your determination to achieve it. Start with people close to you and then expand the circle. The more people you tell, the more committed you will feel to upholding your stated goal. At age twelve when I decided to be a millionaire, I told all my friends, and kept reminding them over the years. I joked with them that they would end up working for me, which is indeed what happened to some. The more I shared my goal with others, the more obligated I felt to overcome the obstacles encountered on my way to realizing it.

FOURTH is application. With the belief now an integral part of you, you're ready for action. The stronger your belief, the easier it will be to cope with the obstacles in the application process. One of the most common mistakes is trying to take action before your belief is fully established. Did you decide on the spur of the moment to stop smoking? Your chances of success are poor. But once you have fully internalized the belief that you can, the process will be simple and natural. To apply your belief, you need to write up an organized program comprised of targets and timetables.

FIFTH, we come to evaluation. Set intermediary targets, measure your progress, and give yourself a small reward each time you reach a new target. The process may be long, but there is no reason why it should not be enjoyable. Training a puppy takes time and is reinforced with treats. Retraining an adult human is no simple matter and definitely deserves rewards for sub-targets reached: dinner in a good restaurant, an electronic gadget, or whatever it is that makes you happy. As you move forward successfully, your belief in yourself and your ability to realize your goal will also improve. Write down the results, track your progress, and don't rely on memory alone.

Coping with Obstacles

Will you be able to overcome all the obstacles along your path to realizing success, and realize your belief?

The answer is YES, YES, YES!

Sounds crazy? But that's the truth. It is a historically and scientifically proven truth. Nothing stands in the way of our will.

Handling Obstacles the Easy Way

On your way to realizing your belief, you will encounter obstacles. Acknowledge in advance the simple fact that obstacles do not signal the end of the process. An obstacle is no more than a temporary detour route. If I could change the dictionary entry for "failure," I would insert "obstacle" instead, in its sense of challenge. Challenges arouse our creativity and draw us into seeking solutions. Would you prefer an easy crossword puzzle or a challenging one? Obstacles and overcoming them teach us to look for alternatives, gain experience, and learn so that success becomes easier to achieve at the next obstacle. Experience is one of your most important assets on the road to success. There is no obstacle in the world that was not overcome by someone, somewhere: if someone else could, so can you.

Success, like obstacles, is not finite. What happens once you've reached your goal? Most likely at this stage you'll set a new one, backed up by a new belief in your ability to achieve it. In my development as a trader, I set a target of attaining $200 profit each day. Once I reached that, moving the target to $500 no longer seemed impossible. And so on. This is what makes humans competitive, and so very different from animals.

Failure, or challenge, is perceived very differently by successful individuals than by the general public. For successful people, failure is an opportunity to start again, from a new angle and with improved methods. Never for a moment even give a thought to the idea that you might fail. As infants and children, we naturally seek ways to overcome challenges. As adults, we need to recover that innate sense of being able to achieve. If you leave even the narrowest chink open to the concept of failure, that concept will swell, become empowered, and swallow up you and your hopes for a better life. If you fear failure, fear will handcuff you. People fear failing at studies, sports, in relationships, parenting and at work. Fear weakens our willingness to cope with challenges that life places in our paths. Yes, some of the blame can be placed on how we were raised and educated, generally with methods that punished our failures rather than encouraging our resilience. Successful athletes are known as being target-oriented, strongly self-disciplined, and intensely determined. Research the histories of famous athletes and you will often find at least one parent who imbued the child with the spirit of winning, neutralizing fear and failure. Earl Woods, father of Tiger Woods, golfer and the richest sportsman in history, prepared his son for the game from the age of two. Earl himself was a commando combatant in a Special Forces unit in Vietnam: facing challenges was not a new concept for him. Earl stuck with the goal he set for himself and his son. Despite the challenges, he created one of the greatest achievers in sports history.

Obstacles are those frightful things you see when you take your eyes off your goal. - Henry Ford

Commitment to Success

We've all heard Cinderella stories of people who made it rich overnight due to some brilliant idea.

Don't let these stories blind you. Success is achieved through hard work and boundless determination and commitment. Extraordinary commitment is what marks unique success stories.

That is also the story of Lionel Messi, the current Number One soccer player in the world. At age eleven, Messi was diagnosed with a growth hormone deficiency, or in simple language, dwarfism. When the family was required to pay some $900 a month for growth hormone treatment, far above what it could afford, Lionel was forced to find a sponsor. He was forced to play soccer like no one of his size had ever yet succeeded in playing, anywhere in the world. His commitment produced results. At twelve, he was chosen to join Barcelona's children's team and earned the much-needed funding. At seventeen, he made history by being the youngest player to ever join Barcelona's all-star adult team. Messi joins the pantheon of other famed, physically short success stories such as the basketball player Tyron Bogues (159 cm/5'2), who played fourteen NBA seasons and was the shortest league player in the history of the NBA.

Control Your Mood

Our moods change from day to day and even from hour to hour. When we need to apply high levels of attention and concentration, such as when trading, we must be at our best. Some days we wake up full of energy and creativity, the world smiles at us, and it seems as though anything we do works fantastically. Other days, nothing seems to go well, we feel as though the whole world is against us, and everything we do is doomed.

Have you ever wondered how amazing it could be to just press a button and turn a bad day into a good one? Well, you can do just that.

First, we must understand where changes in moods originate. Moods are determined by chemical balances in our brains. The balance is so delicate that the smallest deviation can change our mood from happy to blue. Mental balance is impacted, among other things, by such environmental conditions as weather, strong winds, scents and smells, sounds, taste--all the information that our five senses can absorb.

Since the dawn of human history, humans have tried to find ways of controlling moods. These include hypnosis, yoga, religious rites, sports, drugs: all are among the options we use to alter moods. We are all sensitive to situations that cause us to shift from one mood to its opposite in almost no time. Just try and play rap anywhere near me... and see what happens to me! So, what makes your mood change? And what helps you stay in a good mood? Music, color, lighting and warmth all affect us. Coffee and chocolate are quick pick-me-ups, but usually have short-term influence and can leave you feeling a lot worse. The heightened blood flow after a workout can help improve mood. Find out the things that affect you positively, and then use that information to your benefit.

Controlling Frustration

Since we know that the path to success is paved with challenges, frustration is a natural outcome of coping. But we need to remember: beyond the frustration is success, which is why we must find the right way to first cope with frustration.

Frustration is our personal translation of the reality we find ourselves in. Therefore frustration, too, can be successfully coped with by applying a different interpretation to that same reality, such as by exchanging the frustration for a challenge.

Obstacles are temporary setbacks on the way to success. Frustration results from not having the knowledge needed to cope with the setback, whether the setback is a matter of bad luck, another person's stupidity, rejection, or anything else. Rejection is, in fact, one of the main factors in frustration. We live in constant fear of rejection: by our partners, boss, a client, or society. The champions at dealing with rejection are sales staff. Ideal salespersons never let the word "no" get the better of them, but instead it encourages them to look for an alternative, creative way of solving the situation.

Why does one person handle frustration easily and another fumes until sparks fly? The answer is buried deep within the human mind. People who believe they can cope well will cope well. Understand the reason behind your frustration, define it, and choose a method for handling it which allows you to recover your calm. Have you ever thought about the way movie producers use music to control your mood? The same clip set to one type of music will arouse your fear, but set to light-hearted music might even get you to laugh! Be your own movie producer, jot down phrases on sticky notes that help keep you positive and hang the notes on your mirror.Do whatever helps you control your frustration. Only you know what's best.

Accepting Responsibility

Did you make a mistake? Blow it? Don't look for those responsible for your failure. Take responsibility for your actions. We naturally tend to blame our parents, teachers, employers, and the government. The starting point for many who achieved success was much tougher than for the average person. Many experienced extremely tough times in their lives, and nonetheless succeeded. Did the obstacles they encounter diminish their commitment to their goals, or reinforce them? For most successful people, the obstacles are what drive them to greater strength. The desire to succeed is greater than the need for a warm meal at the end of the day. Successful people hold their own ability to succeed in high regard, which is often viewed by others as arrogance. Successful people can rightly be proud of their success, but they are equally prepared to assume responsibility for their mistakes. This willingness to accept responsibility derives from power; evading responsibility derives from weakness.

Eric Schmidt, former CEO of Google, said, "I screwed up" when he and other Google top-level staff did not handle the fledgling Facebook startup and fight back at a company that dared take on the biggest possible competitor in the Internet. By contrast, Bill Clinton with his famous statement, "I did not have sexual relations with that woman" evaded responsibility and paid by almost losing the presidency. The public relates to acceptance of responsibility with understanding and respect, and to evasion as a sign of failure. Accepting responsibility is a sign of power and maturity. It also reinforces your faith in your ability to overcome obstacles, and understand that they are an inseparable part of the path to success. What do author Mark Twain, ketchup king Henry Heinz, and automobile giant Henry Ford share in common? At some point on their way to success, they all went broke, took responsibility, recovered and came back bigger and better than ever.

Do You Like Your Job?

To succeed, you need a good reason to get out of bed in the morning. You need to love your work. If salary is the only thing keeping you in the workplace, you will not get far. Having worked for years in the high-tech industry, I can tell you that the greatest aspiration held by most high-tech employees is "not to work anymore in high-tech." In other words, even high salaries and great benefits are not enough to make an employee love the job, let alone excel at it.

To succeed, you don't need to be brilliant. You just need to be a little better than average, and to do that, your work needs to interest you. Your work needs to more closely resemble a game than a chore. Find the job that pleases you so much that you never look at the clock. If salary is what guides you, you could likely end up finding you've devoted most of your life to a reality that has not led you to a greatly-improved financial situation. At some point when you reach the end of your tether with your job, you will discover that you're too scared to try and change your field or place of employment.

I'm very aware of the fact that changing your place of employment is not easy. We acclimate easily to a particular routine and environment, and any change rocks us. If, on one hand, you're dying to leave your job but find that hard to do, how should you overcome the dilemma? Very simple: plan the future, define the goals, and create the belief that you can achieve those goals. Remember the five steps to formulating your belief? Establishing, imagining, spreading, applying, evaluating. The process is slow and requires a lot of patience, but you have no choice: you must start somewhere, and if not now, when?

Choose work that you love, and you will never need to work another day in your life. – Confucius

Preparedness and Opportunity

I began trading in stocks in 2000, at the height of the Dot-com crash. The market burst and short sellers enjoyed a lot of success. As we have learned, a plunging market is a wonderland of profits, but unfortunately for me I could not join the festivities since I lacked knowledge at the time. I was just starting out, inexperienced, lacking self-discipline, and bereft of knowledge. A chance to make big money was just lying there on a silver platter, but I was a novice, poorly-prepared trader.

Luck has little to do with the path to success. *Luck is when preparation meets opportunity.* Every day, hundreds of opportunities pass right beneath our noses, but our unpreparedness prevents us from realizing them. Develop your state of readiness and await the opportunity. Knowledge and experience in stock trading during a bubble or crisis poses readiness against opportunity. In 2008, during the sub-prime crisis, that same opportunity resurfaced, and my readiness was at its peak.

Give me six hours to chop down the tree and I will spend the first four sharpening the axe. - Abraham Lincoln

Success is an Avalanche

How will you measure success? Every small change is significant. If you managed to make $100 and not $1000, never mind. The main thing is that you're learning how to profit. Success is like an avalanche: it starts as a snowball and grows and grows. Success starts slowly and gets easier all the time, until one day you wake up, look to the heavens and say, "Thank you, thank you, thank you. I am so grateful for getting to this place!"

It makes little difference how successful you are. Bottom line, your life can be better if you just decide to change it. Everyone has the power to change his or her life. It's not necessary to hold three university degrees or be extremely intelligent; it's not even necessary to work hard physically. All you need to do to change your life lies right there in your subconscious.

So, Make a Decision!

You need to make a decision, right now, a decision that will change your life. You know that doubting moment of "dive into the deep end, or don't dive into the deep end..." After you jump, you discover that the water is fine, even if it was a tad cold at first. My advice to you? Take the plunge! Now! Change your life. If not now, when? I've helped you up to this point, and want to help you further. But now... it's all up to you!

To your success!

Special offers for readers:

Tradenet Trading Room –
A pivotal tool for trading success

My online trading room is a pivotal tool in any trader's professional development. Join me and hundreds of other traders from across the globe who connect daily, creating one of the world's largest trading communities. You will be able to hear me trading live, join my trades and learn from the overall experience.

Try the FREE 14 day trial in:

http://www.tradenet.co.uk/trading-room-0

The Self-study Course

My online self-study course includes dozens of individual study units which can be accessed and referred to at your leisure. During this invaluable course you will learn the foundations and principles of trading, technical analysis, trading strategies, and much more.

You can find more information about the self-study course in:

http://www.tradenet.co.uk/market-trader-pro-online

Open a live trading account

My favorite broker is Colmex, where I have been a happy user since 2008. I currently use the "Colmex Pro CFD" platform, which is the most suitable and reliable platform for my trading style. I have an exclusive agreement with Colmex; when you open a live trading account and you would like to join the Tradenet trading room and/or take my self-study Course, Colmex may cover the costs of the trading room and course fees on your behalf.

Get Colmex special offer in:

http://www.tradenet.co.uk/colmex-pro

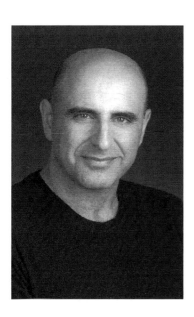

Visit Tradenet

Visit Tradenet's website where you will find a vast array of useful free resources, tutorials and updated information on interesting new products.
Visit Tradenet website:
http://www.tradenet.co.uk

Contact me

If you would like to know more about these offers, or have any other question for me, feel free to email me at any time:
meir@tradenet.co.uk

Made in the USA
San Bernardino, CA
15 August 2016